CHRIST-CENTERED

SPIRITUALITY

CHRIST-CENTERED

SPIRITUALITY

A HANDBOOK OF *CATECHESIS*
for
the training of novices
in
THE WAY OF CHRIST

JOEL ELIES

Acknowledgements

Diagram of the "Architecture of the Soul" adapted from *Renovation of the Heart* by Dallas Willard. Copyright © 2002. Used by permission of NavPress, All Rights Reserved. www.navpress.com (1-800-366-7788)

Scriptures taken from the *Holy Bible: New International Version* ®, NIV ®. Copyright © 1973, 1978, 1984 by Biblica, Inc. ™ Used by permission of Zondervan. All rights reserved worldwide. www.zondervan.com
Also used: The King James Version, KJV.

Library of Congress Cataloging-in-Publication Data
Elies, Joel
Christ-centered spirituality: a handbook of catechesis / Joel Elies
p.cm.
ISBN- 0615461018
1. Christian Life.   2. Spirituality—Christian.   I. Title

Cover Design by Cedric Ranchez
Cover Art: Celtic Wall Cross by Roman, Inc. All rights reserved. Used by permission.
www.roman.com

Printed in the United States of America

To Larry and Diana Elies—

You led me to Christ with your lives.

Table of Contents

PART I. Meditations on the Mysteries of CHRIST

PART II. Meditations on the Mysteries of GOD and the SOUL

PART III. SPIRITUAL EXERCISES for
the Elevation of the Soul

PART IV. The Practice of INTERIOR CHRIST-LIKENESS

PART V. *Your KINGDOM MISSION of Sacrificial Love*

APPENDIX:

Preface

"There is nothing new under the sun." ~ Ecclesiastes 1:9

"Every age has its own outlook.... We all therefore need the books that will correct the characteristic mistakes of our own period.... The only [medicine] is to keep the clean sea breeze of the centuries blowing through our minds, and this can only be done by reading old books." ~ C. S. Lewis, *Introduction to "On the Incarnation" by St. Athanasius*

n these pages is nothing original. It is simply a recycling of what has already been stated over and over again by other Christ-captivated souls in tattered scrolls scattered through the vaulted halls of history. I have only waded thru the shallows; others have gone much deeper. Browse the aged pages of the Desert Fathers and Mothers, the Doctors of the Catholic Church, the Celtic Mission, the Medieval Mystics, the Eastern Orthodox Hesychasts, the Reformers, the Puritans, Richard Baxter, Thomas a Kempis, Ignatius of Loyola, Francis de Sales, Brother Lawrence, Jeanne Guyon, Jeremy Taylor, John Wesley, C.S. Lewis, A.W. Tozer, Dallas Willard and countless other masters of the spiritual life. You will find the genesis springs from which I have been drinking.

I wanted to gather up a tiny taste of the vast wisdom of the ancients into a little handbook of instruction that is digestible by the novice learner. This *catechesis,* or training process, not only reflects much of the content of the classical spiritual writers but also a bit of the feel of them-- simple, earthy, and sharp as a knife. So, fighting off the urge to impress and embellish (with exciting, explosive, sensational stories!) and embracing the sometimes awkward tempo of an older, simpler age, here is my meager offering, a little rule for beginners, my *summa* of the spiritual life.

For the reluctant majority of the reborn race (I do think the followers of Christ are becoming a different species of creature;) who hesitate to tread through the rich treasure troves of the spiritual classics, I have arranged a sample, a cheat sheet, a simple map for the pilgrim just beginning the journey. My hope is that after you have handled and seen and sampled the scent of a little bouquet from the garden, you will be emboldened to venture yourself into this foreboding territory— the writings of wisdom so named above. I am deeply indebted to these towering souls whose works I have absorbed. While I quote a few directly, almost everything else is only my paraphrase of their ideas that have subconsciously slipped into my bloodstream. How old is Christ-centered spirituality? It is as old as the hills and as new as the morning— having been practiced by saintly men and women for thousands of years... yet you must discover how to live it out today— on today's earth, under today's sun, in the life you call your own.

Indulge me for a moment as I acknowledge the friends and teachers who have played instrumental parts in God's orchestration of grace in the composition of my life. First and foremost, I owe my life, both biological and spiritual, to Larry and Diana Elies who first taught me the Way of Jesus. A parent's wisdom is not often apparent to us: "No discipline seems pleasant at the time but painful. Later on, however, it produces a harvest of righteousness and peace for those who have been trained by it." I can now fully appreciate the two modern-day saints I had the privilege of calling Mom and Dad.

I would also like to thank the following mentors I met along the way: Kelly and Angie Hilderbrand, Richard and Debbi Ross, Paul Edwards, Steve Peich, Jordan Seng, Dan Chun, Kelii Akina, Ralph Moore, John Honold, Mel Isara, Klayton Ko, Brady Bobbinck, Gene Breitenbach, J. P. Moreland, Dallas Willard, Richard Foster, Ron Youngblood, Robert Coleman, Archibald Hart, and Tony Campolo, all of whose feet I have sat at. I also thank and apologize to all my brothers and sisters at Hope968, who have found themselves as guinea pigs in my mad scientist experiments. Also, I want to thank Jennie Hirata, who helped re-type the manuscript when it was lost, Cedric Ranchez, who helped with the cover and proof-reading, John Rush, a constant companion and conversation partner, and David Sanford, who pointed me in the right direction for publishing. And, lastly, I thank Amy, my long-suffering and beautiful bride, and my three wonder-full boys, Jordan, Evan, and Jonathan. I love you more than words convey.

2

CHRIST-CENTERED

SPIRITUALITY

A HANDBOOK OF *CATECHESIS*
for
the training of novices
in
THE WAY OF CHRIST

PART I. Meditations on the Mysteries of CHRIST

1. Introduction to Christ-Centered Spirituality

s your soul thirsty? The book you now hold is a *meditation guide* for all those world-weary wanderers who thirst for that spiritual reality that satisfies the human soul. It is an *instructional manual* for all those who know they have a soul and want to know how to bring it to life! It is a *guidebook* for finding that ancient and reliable path which has led saints and sinners alike into a deeper spiritual life for many centuries, the Way of Christ. Plunge into the rushing torrents of living water! Bathe in the Presence of the Living God! Christ beckons you: "If anyone is thirsty, let him come to me and drink. Whoever believes in me..., streams of living water will flow from within him."

What is "Christ-Centered Spirituality"? It is *an orientation toward life that centers upon the person of Jesus Christ as the entry point into flowing connection with that infinite, creative Spirit of Spirits that fills our universe and beyond, most commonly called "God."* According to the New Testament documents, *this is life to its fullest!* It is in Christ that we experience *the good life*— the most *natural* and *ideal* state of existence for humanity! It is what you were made for—a life aligned with eternity, a cooperative friendship with the Creator. It will shape your interior world and color your exterior world to form a self without selfishness, an animated soul without animosity or hatred, a heart calmly beating with quiet confidence, brimming over with love and joy— passionate, authentic, fearless and free! Build a life of substance on solid bedrock, tested through the ages, tried across the globe. Apprenticeship to Jesus stands in sharp contrast to the do-it-yourself, "designer spiritualities" of today, founded on the shifting sands of modern opinion and preference.

A Christ-centered spiritual life is open to ordinary people of all walks of life: business people and the unemployed, children and adults, students and teachers, customer service representatives, computer technicians, and fast-food workers. All across the glorious spectrum of human diversity, from every tribe and nation, everyone is invited! This is not an unattainable realm reserved only for a special class of esoteric, religious types with lots of time on their hands. Nothing can disqualify you from this world-transcending life—not your past, your mistakes, your hurts, your weaknesses, your failures, your doubts, even your sins! Nothing can separate the seeking soul from the furious love of Christ!

Christ-centered spirituality is a journey of discovery: a seeking and a finding, yet seeking still! It is not so much doctrines and dogmas as it is a real life conversation with the Absolute, "Our Father who art in heaven." It is experience-able and practice-able, more difficult than training for the Olympics and easier than breathing. This *catechesis* will not make you into some kind of "expert." If you are using it for that purpose, it may even prove harmful. These pages provide only a scaffolding to construct and cultivate your own familiar friendship with God. Apart from his ethereal Presence, it will not do much for you. You must hear the soundless voice calling! You must sense the intangible touch deep within! This book is only a supplement to the Scriptures, relationships, experiences, sufferings and other divinely-decided designs that truly transform your sojourning soul.

Don't read with the cold detachment of a scientist in a laboratory, objectively trying to dissect and explain. Instead, approach God with the curious wonder of a child. Come as a mystic, a pilgrim, a learner, an artist. Read slowly, meditate, participate, reflect upon and reason through, question and express your thoughts. Explore the obscure landscape of your own subterranean soul. Every question mark you see in this book is an *icon*, an invitation to pause and activate your intelligence and imagination, your memory and your desires. Look beyond these black-and-white letters on a page. Reach out with child-like fascination to touch the fiery, invisible Presence behind them!

Ask yourself: "*What think ye of Christ?*" Your answer to that question will determine all else. Can I assume that you truly *want* to follow Christ? Are you convinced (or willing to be convinced) that Jesus Christ knew the true ways of the spiritual life, or more accurately, *is the Way, the Truth, and the Life?* Most misgivings about Jesus are really reactions to the appalling abuses, the horrific deformities and glaring imperfections of those who wear his name. So let's clear away the underbrush, the dead bark that has often overgrown and choked the flowing life out of the historic Christian church. Can't we avoid these excesses?

This is what Christ-centered spirituality is not: it is not a justification for judgmental, condemning attitudes towards "those dirty sinners" nor is it a divinely-sanctioned excuse for careless disregard of our own sin since "we are forgiven". It is not a competitive endeavor for showing off our Bible knowledge, how long or beautifully we can pray, how convincingly we talk "theology", or any other of the amusing contests that religious people often play. Neither is it a narrow-minded attempt to explain away all of life's mysteries with shallow answers, nor is it an evasion of our God-given responsibility to think for ourselves. It is not a naive, cult-like  conformity to a subculture of plastic smiles and bland "niceness"— or of offensive and hateful hostility! It is not pressure tactics to coerce converts into manufacturing ecstatic experiences or perfect profession of approved doctrines. Nor is it a method of controlling the world to ensure a prosperous and successful life of individualistic health, happiness and comfort. Whenever Christ encountered such self-serving, ego-driven religion, he opposed it vehemently! All of these unhealthy extremes are distortions, deviations from the perfect center, which is Christ himself. And when you live from this Center, you will find it is a *way of life* perfectly suited to your own unique, God-woven personality.

So embark with me on a voyage of discovery. First, find a seaworthy vessel: if you have not already enlisted with a Christ-centered *community of faith*, find a crew to sail with on the shoreless sea of mystery. Then, find a *mentor*—a seasoned sea captain who can show you the ropes, help you chart your course and navigate the inevitable twists and turns of your own inward odyssey. You will also need a clear translation of *the Holy Bible*, which is your compass, your map, your ultimate source-book. Lastly, pick up a *journal* (any cheap notebook will do) to record your reflections and conversations with God. This is the travel log of your soul's journey into the soundless depths of God. For the next few months, I recommend you set aside at least half an hour a day to cover each chapter and meditation exercise.

But first, it is only fair to warn you from the start that while this adventure holds many indescribable joys, it also holds many difficulties, dangers, desolations and dark nights. It is not for the faint of heart! There is no victory except through battle; no glory but through testing. *Christ-centered spirituality is not something you can "dabble" in-- it is a life-consuming, total immersion experience!* You cannot simply add Christ on to a "me-centered" life. This is not a self-indulgent ego-massage to help you to *feel better*—our aim is to help you to *become better*. Jesus intends to replace your natural life with a supernatural life of a very different substance (although it may resemble the old life in many superficial ways). If a life-altering encounter with your Creator is *not* what you desire, *please go no further!* This book is not for you at this time.

Exercise

1. Open your journal (if you don't have one yet, use a blank sheet of paper) and begin to describe some individuals or groups that made a negative impression of what Christ was supposed to be all about.

2. Next, describe some of the people whose lives provided a positive picture for you of Jesus Christ. Do you need to contact them and thank them for their extraordinary example?

3. What are the characteristics of Christ that most draw you to him?

4. End with a prayer, telling Jesus what you love about him. Tell him of your soul's thirst. Ask him to remove the scales from the eyelids of your soul that you might see him more clearly. Then wait and listen. See if he replies...

2. On the Mysteries of Jesus

"Do not suppose that I have come to bring peace on earth. I did not come to bring peace, but a sword..." ~ Jesus of Nazareth

"...Christianity got over the difficulty of combining furious opposites, by keeping them both, and keeping them both furious."
~ G. K. Chesterton, *Orthodoxy*

L et me show you the door. The gateway through which we will enter into this Christ-centered spirituality is through *meditation upon the life of Jesus Christ.* Immerse yourself in the sacred mysteries of Christ. Step into the ancient world laid out line-by-line in the pages of the gospels. Explore its timeworn terrain. Enlist your intelligence and your imagination. Allow yourself to feel with your feelings and reason with your reasoning. Use every faculty at your disposal to search out and learn from the Master of Life. But beware! When you wander the trackless wasteland with the wandering Teacher, you run the risk of transformation. Prepare to have your preconceptions pummeled, your cherished ideas challenged and stretched, and your lifestyle questioned and changed. Try not to resist the sweeping force of this enigmatic Stranger as he woos and whispers and draws you to himself. Unless your soul falls so madly in love with the person of Jesus Christ that nothing else holds the same fascination to your mind and affections, the practice of spirituality will be dull and lifeless religion rather than the raging love affair it was intended to be. Let the following pages kindle the spark of fleeting hope into a roaring flame of soul-intoxication with the consuming reality of Christ.

Who was Jesus, really? What kind of person was he? What images are summoned to mind when you hear his name? Can we *love* whom we do not *know*? Crucial to the practice of Christ-centered spirituality is a first-hand rediscovery of the forgotten figure of

Jesus recorded in the eyewitness accounts of Matthew, Mark, Luke, and John. As we become familiar with that old, old story of stories, we watch in wonder as he treads upon all our cherished assumptions. This is your initiation into Mystery. (Why do I use the term "mystery" more than "truth"? A *truth* is *a successful attempt to know and describe actual reality. A mystery is a reality about which what-we-don't-know far outweighs what-we-do-know.* So while we are discussing "truth", I think "mystery" is also appropriate.)

By all credible accounts, Jesus of Nazareth was and is a radical paradox, a wondrous contradiction of such rich texture and beauty that he is impossible to ignore. Like a finely-cut crystal, he has many facets, some of which seem diametrically opposed to one another. To use Nicholas of Cusa's suggestive phrase, he is the ultimate "*coincidence of opposites*": He is a lion... and a lamb. He is a holy man, a rebel against society, a simple carpenter, an apocalyptic prophet, a critic of religion, a faithful friend, a miracle worker, a failure who changed the world. He is a teacher, a learner, a servant, a master, a soul physician, a martyr, a revolutionary, a peacemaker with a sword-- dangerous, compassionate, wild, gentle, tenacious, unpredictable, burdened with sorrows, soaring with joy, and utterly without fear.

Let his life speak for itself without trying to fit him neatly into a box. Most attempts to explain Jesus have ended with a domesticated caricature that strangely resembles the author's own biases, ideals, and culture (a danger to which this book also is not exempt!). The marginalized of his day were drawn magnetically towards him while self-righteous religious leaders were repelled by this same dynamic force. He touched lepers, overturned temple furniture, angered the religious establishment, frightened military and government leaders, and chatted with children. He was down-to-earth and larger-than-life, immanent and transcendent— the ideal picture of both strength and submission, of peace and passion, of confidence and humility, of man... and God.

One thing cannot be denied: *he had an unbridled intensity for the liberation of the human race.* He was arrested, scourged and crucified because he posed a significant threat to the existing power brokers of the world-system. The notion that he was just "a nice, decent man" who told others to become "nice, decent men" is simply an uninformed fiction. Burning within his chest was a revolutionary agenda for global transformation. He had a plan to undermine and overturn society by freeing individual hearts... a plan still going strong to this day. Jesus alone brings a realistic hope for confronting head-on the core complications of our desperate human condition.

Like the Greek legend of Prometheus, Christ descended from the heavens bearing within himself the torch of living flame that gives light to all humankind. Yet this is a revolution born in the very heart of God himself! *Imagine*-- the Creator inciting an uprising among his own creatures! He offers illumination to all who do not love darkness more than light. I invite you now: lift the eyes of your heart and look upon the blinding brilliance of Jesus. Through tracing out the luminous lines of his birth, life, teachings, death and resurrection, you will sketch the schematic drawings for the original prototype of humanity. You will also catch a fleeting glimpse of the unseen face of God. Gaze upon the illumined face of Christ as a *mirror* and a *window*: through which you can truly "know thyself"... and also find enfleshed in him the invisible visage of God. *The ultimate truth about God and man is revealed in the person of Jesus Christ.*

Meditation Exercise

One of the best ways of connecting with God is through the free flight of the imagination guided and anchored by the sacred Scriptures— subjective experience grounded upon objective revelation. Try the following meditation exercise. (Note: In all the meditations in this book, take your time! If any point particularly resonates within you, just remain quietly reflecting upon it until your soul feels satisfied that you have received all that you were seeking. You are in no hurry.)

Preparation: Sit up straight, close your eyes and spend a minute in silence...

Scripture: Now slowly read Jesus' statement from **John 8:12**:
"I am / the light / of the world. / Whoever / follows me / will never / walk in darkness, / but will have / the light / of life."

1. Re-read it, pausing for at least 5 seconds at every slash mark. During each pause, try to savor its meaning as fully as you can. Exercise your mind using pictures, definitions, synonyms, questions, associations, feelings, prayers... or just breathe. What comes to mind?

2. Imagine Jesus' dusty, sandaled feet walking, walking, walking along the windswept landscape of the Judean hillside... Don't try to imagine his face or body, just his feet and ankles, up to the hem of his garment. Close your eyes and spend a minute watching his dirt-stained, rugged feet making their way along the rocky path...

3. What is his pace-- fast or slow? Where are his feet taking him? Who or what does he encounter along the way?

Response: Now imagine carrying on a face-to-face conversation with Jesus. (In doing this, your imagination may be more true to reality than your eyes...)
Ask him if you can follow him. What do you think he would say to you? Conclude by asking to see him *as he truly is*. Ask him to clear up any confusion you may have about him. Spend a minute quietly resting in his Presence...
Write in your journal any insights, reactions, questions, observations or prayers from this exercise.

3. His Annunciation
Promised Messiah of Ancient Prophecy

he whole of creation has been groaning in anticipation. We have been waiting for a *Messiah* since Adam and Eve, when God declared in the crisp air of Eden that the seed of the woman would strike the head of the serpent. However, this cryptic message was always shrouded in the mists of mystery. Like an intricate riddle embedded in the ancient scrolls of the sacred *Torah*, foreshadows of this "Anointed One" began to echo faintly through the holy writ. The rumblings began, almost hidden, as the underlying theme continued to build throughout the history of the nation of Israel: an almost inaudible whisper in the psalms of the poets, a deafening thunderclap in the shouts of the prophets. God's people waited-- indeed, *the earth itself* waited in eager expectation for the unveiling of the Chosen One.

What exactly would this Messiah do? The message was unclear, the signals mixed. Both "Christ" and "Messiah" are the words in Greek and Hebrew, respectively, to designate the *anointing of a person*— being smeared with oil upon the forehead as the symbol of the Holy Spirit's power and authority to carry out a specific calling before God. This oil was used to "fuel the fire." But what exactly was he called to do? Would he suffer or would he  conquer? The contradicting images formed a perplexing puzzle-- like this ambiguous account from Isaiah 42:1-2: "Here is my servant, whom I uphold, my chosen one in whom I delight. I will put my Spirit on him and he will bring justice to the nations. He will not shout or cry out, or raise his voice in the streets." We wonder: *which is it?* Would he conquer the nations or remain quietly anonymous?

Whose child was he? Born in the City of David, but raised as a refugee in Egypt and the backwoods town of Nazareth. Descended from the royal line of kings, yet not even biologically related to his own "father". Concerns of his *illegitimacy* trailed him through life as everyone wondered who he really belonged to. This son of mystery must grow into a man for all nations, a universal savior, yet he must remain a child of the Jewish community. *Jesus was and is thoroughly Jewish*, steeped in the traditions of Torah, bathed in Hebrew culture from infancy to adulthood. We dare not imagine him a tanned European westerner or a sophisticated Greek sophist. This child of wonder was of Abraham's seed; yet his wonderful message must escape his ethnicity to encompass the whole world.

The questions multiply: Would he set up a triumphant new regime or suffer utter rejection? Was he the Deliverer of Israel or the Savior of all nations? Was he a *Priest*— a *Son of Adam*, who would make atonement for sin, representing humanity before God? Or was he a *King*— a *Son of David*, who would sit on the throne forever, representing God before humanity? Or perhaps a *Prophet* in the tradition of Moses, the Lawgiver—a *Son of Man* who would call the people back into covenant relationship with their Creator? Some even had the audacity to hint at a cosmic origin before the created order— wishful whispers of the ageless *Son of God*. With the clock of prophecy counting down and all of these conflicting, confusing conclusions at fever pitch, the Messiah was the focal point upon which all the hopes of the oppressed nation of Israel rested. They were sure he was to be their Hero, their Conqueror, their Liberator. It was in this swirling whirlpool of apocalyptic expectancy that the young virgin Mary has the following visitation:

Meditation Exercise
Preparation: Calm your mind. Close your eyes, breathe normally and spend a minute or two quietly repeating the phrase in your mind:

"Christ in me, the hope of glory..."

Note: In each meditation exercise, whenever you see a three-dot ellipse (...), that is your cue to stop reading, pause and reflect, actually taking that time to *do the exercise*. When you see a question mark (?), ask yourself how you would answer the question.

Scripture: Now slowly read through **Luke 1:26-56**, pausing momentarily upon any word or phrase that stirs you...
Open your journal and write down any observations, questions or other notes...
Now read through it once more, imagining yourself in the role of Mary. Try to experience it from her first-person perspective...

1. Imagine the immediate reaction of this gentle and innocent young woman in full flower of youth when she first sees the glorious angelic being appear... What do you think was going through her mind? What fears, what questions, what doubts, what wonder? Was she afraid? Was she excited? Was she confused? Was she calm? Was her heart racing in her chest?

2. Ponder each of the jarring declarations of this divine messenger:
"Greetings, you who are highly favored! The Lord is with you..."
"Do not be afraid, Mary, for you have found favor with God..."
"And now you will conceive in your womb and bear a son, and you will name him Jesus..."
"He will be great, and will be called the Son of the Most High, and the Lord God will give to him the throne of his ancestor David..."
Could this have possibly made sense to her understanding-- that the Son of the Most High would be conceived within her mortal flesh?

16

3. Listen to her response of child-like trust: *"Here am I, the servant of the Lord; let it be unto me according to your word..."* How could she so readily embrace this unexpected future of uncertainty, chaos, disgrace, and turmoil? What was her experience of her Celestial Father that she could abandon herself so completely to his divine will?

4. Gaze upon the face of Mary as she opens her glorious song of *Magnificat*: *"My soul magnifies the Lord, and my spirit rejoices in God my Savior, for he has been mindful of the humble state of his servant..."* What emotions are seen in her eyes? Could you sing these words from the depths of your heart?

Response: In your journal, talk to God about any thoughts that surfaced in your heart during this meditation. Are you trying to control everything in your life or will you *let it be done unto you according to his will?* What are the travails of soul before you now in your own life? What are some of the unexpected or difficult things that have been done unto you recently? Could you recognize this place of chaos and confusion as a possible birthplace of Christ in your life? Does God have your permission (like he really needs it!) to lead you along strange paths, uncomfortable paths, dangerous paths to bring forth his will in your life?

4. His Virgin Birth
Newborn Child of Heavenly Origin

The Creator became created. It was quite possibly the greatest miracle ever performed. The Divine Essence of Triune Deity was fused permanently into quivering human flesh, *"neither confounding the persons nor dividing the substance."* The Only-Begotten Son of the Eternal Father becomes *one of us.* The blessed Henry Suso describes the incarnation as if God had said, *"When I, supernatural and unchanging Good, give myself to a creature according to its capacity to receive me, I wrap up the brightness of the sun in a cloth."* What kind of unfathomable mystery took place in a tiny corner of a great, great world? The heavens themselves announced his birth with a celestial spectacle that drew the stargazers, the wise men, *magi* from the east.

Jesus' nativity was the convergence of a wide spectrum of messianic prophecies from the Scriptures: *"But you, Bethlehem, in the Land of Judah, are by no means least among the rulers of Judah; for out of you will come a ruler who will be the shepherd of my people Israel."* *"For unto us a child is born, unto us a Son is given, and the government will be upon his shoulders. And he will be called Wonderful, Counselor, Mighty God, Everlasting Father, Prince of Peace."* But it was not just by his words that Christ was declared the Son of God, but by his works. Through deeds of power and valor, the king earned the kingdom that belonged to him by birthright.

Throughout the writings of the Hebrew prophets, the Most High God continually warned of that dreadful day when he would roll up his sleeves and personally intervene into human affairs, when the Ancient of Days would come down from his throne to clean up our mess. It was the fated moment of Kingdom Come— a consummation long-awaited, long-delayed. Yet when heaven finally pierces through to the rebel planet, we find not a destroying army of flaming warriors on fiery steeds, but a frail, defenseless child. Maybe God doesn't want to "conquer" us after all, except in the way that a helpless newborn conquers his mother's indefensible heart.

This is the glory of the incarnation in one stark, shockingly mismatched image: *a baby lying in a manger.* This most precious gift to all the world, the hope of humanity contained in a tiny, fragile body lying amidst the putrid, grimy realism of our messy world. That's the God who rules the universe! He doesn't sit aloof in his lofty tower far above the fray, barking down orders from on high. He dives into the stinking cesspool of human existence to rescue a drowning race from the vicious vortex of sin and suffering. Behold your God! He has become just like us— skin for skin! To say that "Jesus was God in the flesh" does not lower our estimation of God; instead it exalts it beyond all imagination. *This is Immanuel-- God with us!* Not God at a distance but up close, with his cheek pressed to the rubble and dust. This is a God with dirt under his fingernails, a God with scars, a God with dirty diapers.

Meditation Exercise

Preparation: To begin this meditation exercise, spend a minute or so quieting your mind, recognizing God's penetrating Presence all around you. Close your eyes, breathe normally, and quietly repeat in your mind this humble request:

"Jesus Christ, Son of God, reveal yourself to me."

Scripture: Now, slowly read over **Luke 2:1 – 20** in your Holy Bible. Don't rush through looking for bits of information, for as St. Ignatius of Loyola says, *"it is not much knowledge that fills and satisfies the soul, but the intimate understanding and relish of truth."*

Pay attention to any words or phrases that lodge in your mind. Turn each phrase over in your heart, savoring their flavor and digesting them. Open your journal and jot them down, as well as any questions or observations...

1. Now use your imagination to recreate the scene before you in your mind, complete with sounds, sensations, and all the details you would notice if you were actually there...Observe how the cave or stable is arranged...Run your fingers over the rough-hewn texture the wooden manger, filled with bits of hay, shreds of half-eaten vegetables, dirt, grime and filth...Smell the nauseating odor of donkey droppings mixed into the dust... Hear the buzzing of the flies...

2. Now look upon this precious baby... Do you dare to touch the soft, smooth skin of the baby's rosy cheeks? Would you venture to lift this fragile, squirming child in your arms, holding him tight to your chest? Listen to the thin cry of the newborn, echoes of his future cries of agony and pain... Reflect on the life that lay ahead of this tiny child as "a man of sorrows, acquainted with grief"...
Now look upon the face of his mother... What emotion does it show? Is it joy? Pain? Love? Peace? Confusion? Trust?

3. Listen to the prophet's predictions: "The virgin will be with child, and will give birth to a son, and they will call him *'Immanuel'* -- which means, *'God with us!'*" Contemplate the meaning of this pregnant phrase...
Now reflect on the words, "For unto us a child is born, unto us a Son is given, and the government will be upon his shoulders. And he will

be called Wonderful, Counselor, Mighty God, the Everlasting Father, Prince of Peace..." Ponder the meaning of each word...
Feel the weight of destiny pressing down on this frail newborn's chest...

4. Imagine the unbounded, infinite, Almighty God who "fills the heavens and the earth" confined to the tiny torso and flimsy limbs of a helpless infant! How did God "fit" his glorious eternal essence into this weak little body?
Why did God do this? What does this mean to us?

Response: Stir your heart within you to worship and adore this Child-King...
Join the host of angels, singing the resounding refrain from deep within your heart, *"Glory to God in the highest!"*
Ask whatever questions are on your heart... "Almighty God, why did you do this?"
Imagine yourself simply holding this tiny child in your arms...
Write in your journal anything God spoke to you, anything you spoke to God, or any impressions or observations from this meditation exercise.
End by spending a few moments in soul-cleansing silence...

5. His Baptism

Blood Brother of Sinful Humanity

 esus never takes shortcuts. He never requires of us what he is not willing to do himself. Baptism has become the initiation rite of the apprentice of Christ: a simple physical act with a profound spiritual significance. It signifies immersion into a *new reality*— being soaked in the surrounding Presence of God's pervading Spirit. It is a *washing*— a purification of sin's stain upon the soul. It enacts *rebirth*— a newborn emerging from the womb into a larger world than its placental darkness. It expresses humble submission to the authority of a *new community*. It designates *death and resurrection*— letting go of an old life and being reawakened to a new kind of existence.

Jesus, the sinless Son of God, was completely covered in our muddy world and our muddy race. He even submitted himself to the baptism of another, the baptism of John, the barbarian prophet. He identified completely with the weakness of our species, embracing us, *homo sapiens*, as brothers and sisters. In the shocking words of Irenaeus of Lyons, Christ *"became what we are, so that he might bring us to be what he himself is."* Jesus humbly subjected himself to the same humiliations, limitations, and traditions to which we are subject. He doesn't claim any special exemption from starting at the bottom where everyone else starts. He entered fully into the human experience, lugging the burdensome baggage of an imperfect world with a dreary history of contention and conflict. Jesus was a hated Jew before he ever became a Light to the Gentiles. He knew the stinging scourge of racism, discrimination and oppression.

And like everyone else, Jesus gains spiritual authority by submitting to spiritual authority— even one who was admittedly inferior to him! And in this simplest of rituals, a window to heaven was opened. The resounding voice of God the Father Almighty thundered with joyous approval, like a proud Jewish Father, proclaiming his Beloved Son's debut into the world. And the Holy Spirit, flaming into visible form, alights upon him as a dove.

Meditation Exercise

Preparation: Begin by quieting your mind for a couple of minutes. Breathe normally. With every breath, breathe the request, *"Spirit of God, surround me."* Recognize God's Presence engulfing you.

Scripture: Now slowly read through **Matthew 3:1-17** paying attention to any word or phrase that jumps out at you. Chew upon this word or phrase, extracting any savor and meaning that it brings to your soul...

1. Picture in your mind this stream in the desert, the river Jordan snaking through the wind-washed wilderness of Judea. Is it narrow or wide? What does the water look like? Is it clear or muddy? How fast does it flow?

2. John the Baptist was forerunner to the Messiah, the way-maker. He is the herald who walks before the coming King, the standard-bearer who announces the conquering Savior. And what a character he was! Intense and primal, he was a desert hermit— ascetic, extreme, a social outsider and prophet, painfully out-of-step with the rest of the world.

Now try to see John the Baptist... What does he look like? See his savage and severe appearance; Touch the course, hairy clothing made from the hide of a camel, the rough-cut leather belt...

Consider his unusual diet: Taste the tangy crunch of locusts and the unrefined, raw pleasantness of the wild honeycomb...

What would cause someone to live with such wild austerity?

Hear his voice carried on the hot desert wind, crying out for social reform, personal integrity, and a radical return to God and his rulership...

Why did God choose such a manic madman as his precursor?
In fact, why choose the wild and often brutal Old Testament as the
foundational context of the Messiah? Why such blood and fire?
Could not God find a more inoffensive and refined representative?
Look into the fiery eyes of John the Baptist— what do you see
there?

3. Now experience being washed in the cleansing waters. Imagine
you are one of those people being baptized there by John the
Baptist.
In your imagination, begin to walk out into the water... Your bare
feet stumble on the submerged rocks but you continue to wade out
into the middle of the stream... You shiver a little as the flowing
water washes over your ankles...to your knees... to your waist...
As you turn and face the shore, who is standing there watching you?
Look at the faces you see there...Are there any familiar faces there?
As you stand there shivering in front of this crowd of witnesses, you
confess your sins silently to God...What particular sins should you
be confessing?
Take a deep breath as you prepare to plunge beneath the surface...
Feel the icy fingers of water on your skin as you are enveloped into a
watery grave...
What goes through your mind in those liminal moments underwater?
You are without breath, without sight, without sound or smell, in the
utter darkness at the threshold of a new world...
Feel the water of God's Spirit saturating the inner fibers of your soul,
carrying away all of the filth and grime that has accumulated through
the years...
As you emerge, gasping for breath, what do you feel?
Is anything different? Do you sense anything has changed?

4. Now watch Jesus arrive...What is being said about him? What do
you notice about him?

Gaze upon his face as he makes his way out into the stream... What fire do you see dancing in his eyes?

What is your first impression of him? Does he match up to your expectations?

Now watch as he is submerged beneath the rippling surface of the river and then resurfaces with a silvery splash... Does he need to be baptized? Why is Jesus doing this?

5. Watch the clouds of the sky torn apart for an instant as the sun pierces down like a spotlight upon this glistening figure, water dripping from his hair and face...

Hear the gentle flapping of a white dove descending like fire upon him...

Then you hear what sounds like the rumble of distant thunder... or is it a voice?

Let the thundering words echo in your mind: *"This is my Son, my Beloved! With him I am well-pleased."* What do these words say to you? Do you also long to hear such words of fatherly delight and approval spoken over you? Pause and see what God is whispering to you right now...

Response: Now watch as Christ emerges from the river... He walks towards you until he is standing there dripping before you. Stare into his eyes... Begin to speak to him, revealing your innermost thoughts to him as you would to a trusted friend...

What does he say to you?

Record these interactions in your journal.

6. His Temptation

Courageous Conqueror of Human Nature

e are our own worst enemies. We sabotage our best intentions, carrying around with us the weapons of our own destruction. We set out upon a high road of generosity and unselfishness, yet we are dragged down by our foe... and the hand grasping our heel is our own. When we look deep into the dark pool of our own human nature, we see golden images of celestial beauty and pale phantasms of ghastly horror. We are enslaved to our own traitorous desires, ruled by the triple scourge of pleasures, power and possessions. If only we could be liberated from these merciless inner slave drivers! *"O wretched man that I am! Who can save me from this body of death?"* Is there any escape from the unruly inclinations of our flesh? Jesus shows us the way of conquest.

Jesus was an ascetic holy man, skilled in the art of self-denial-- disciplined to the point of complete mastery over his own person. For Jesus, *self-denial was never an end in itself, but a means to complete self-control.* As any master musician or athlete knows, there is a freedom that comes only through discipline-- when the instrument of the body responds flawlessly to the slightest whisper of the spirit. *He who has mastered himself has mastered the world.* Jesus won a decisive victory over the tyrannical temptations common to all flesh.

The setting for his historic duel is "the waste howling wilderness" of the Judean desert. Immediately after the crowning, transcendent moment of divine approval at his baptism, Jesus is "cast out" by the Holy Spirit, beyond civilization into the untamed barren wastelands. Every spiritual journey eventually leads into the wilds. The desert is the anvil of the soul, revealing what we are made of. It is a place of extremes: dryness, heat, loneliness, thirst, emptiness. It is the place of dis-illusionment, where our masks are torn aside and our cardboard cut-outs come crashing down, forcing us to confront the naked reality of terrors incarcerated within our own breast. It is in the flaming furnace of temptation where we confront our true selves... and where we meet our Maker.

Meditation Exercise

Preparation: Close your eyes and spend a minute in utter silence before moving on... Quietly whisper this prayer, *"Holy Spirit, lead me."* Then pause for a moment to try to focus your attention upon God's Spirit dwelling deep within your heart.

Scripture: Slowly and meditatively read **Matthew 4:1-11.**

1. First imagine the setting. Place yourself in the mountainous deserts of Judea...What sensations would Jesus have experienced in this desert? See and touch the sun-baked rocks and sand... Look at the sparse, rugged vegetation, bleached and wind-swept...Feel the extreme dry heat on your skin... Listen to the forlorn whistling of the wind...Feel the inner isolation, the loneliness, the lostness... What happens to your soul when you feel alone? What do you do when you are deserted and have no one to turn to? What do you lean on when you have no external props or distractions? Why would the Holy Spirit lead someone to a place of such desolation and emptiness? Has God lead you into the desert recently?
Are you there now? Is God also there?

2. Imagine skipping a meal or two— then imagine skipping every meal for forty days straight...Taste the thirst upon your parched tongue in this arid place of dryness... Feel the churning hunger in your stomach... Feel the weakness of limb... Jesus carried no bread for the journey, no wallet, no extra sandals...
What was Jesus seeking? What deeper hunger drove him to this?

27

What is your soul hungering for? What are the strongest appetites of your soul, the most unrelenting desires? How do you deal with feelings of emptiness inside? How do you usually satisfy your soul's thirst? Does sin become more seductive when you feel empty and alone? Does awareness of God also become more acute?

3. In this solitude, Jesus confronts the voice of Satan, full of accusation and deception. Imagine hearing the repetition of ridicule: *"If you are the Son of God..."*
Satan's scornful scrutiny questions Jesus' very identity, calling into doubt whether he is truly beloved of his Father... It pressures him to perform, to prove himself through proofs of power... It implies he will be a floundering failure, a nobody...
Now ask yourself: have I heard this voice of the Accuser before?
What does it say to you? Write down some of the lies it speaks to you...

4. Consider Jesus' first temptation, *"tell these stones to become bread"*... Have you experienced the temptation to meet your physical appetites, even at the expense of your spiritual desires? To place God on hold while you satisfy your own hungers and get what you want? Have you heard that whisper to use God's instruments for self-serving purposes rather than for the service of God and others? Feel the temptation clawing at your skin...Feel the anxiety of missing out on pleasure...Ask yourself: am I willing to deny myself temporary pleasures to fulfill God's eternal will?

5. Consider the Tempter leading Jesus to the pinnacle of the temple. Feel the stomach-churning feeling as Jesus looks over the steep 150-foot drop at his feet... Hear the Scripture-twisting invitation, *"throw yourself down..."* What is going through Jesus' mind as he stares over the edge? The Devil tells him to seize the attention of the crowds with a sensational spectacle. Do you think God would prove himself by a miracle to stop this suicide mission? How do you face

the temptation to impress the world, to show the world that you matter?

6. In his final temptation, the Deceiver literally promises Jesus the world: *"All of this I will give to you..."*
What if you were offered the world with all of its pomp and pleasures, power beyond imagining, just to step outside God's will? Would you trade your trust and loyalty to God for all the world? Could you ever compromise the very thing closest to your heart?
Do you ever feel like, perhaps, God does not have your best interests in mind? Do you ever wonder if, perhaps, he is withholding the greatest blessings from you? Do you ever think that maybe you are really *on your own*?

7. Now picture Jesus' confident and triumphant return from the wilderness... His rawhide sandals are dusty and worn but his step is sure and steadfast...
Jesus endured the most rigorous testing and responded with unflinching courage. He has battled and won. Feel the sense of excitement, the exhilaration, the satisfaction of victory...
What would it feel like to face down your demons, your most seductive sinful desires, and actually subdue them? Imagine it!
Imagine the overflowing power of the Holy Spirit surging like electricity through Jesus' sinewy body... Feel the effervescent energy cascading off of his clothing, spilling unseen onto hopeful hands in swirling cataracts, ready to work wonders...

Response: Can you enter the wilderness of your heart to confront the lies of the devil? Which of these temptations feels the most familiar to you? Record these in your journal.
Ask God which temptations he wants to help you to beat...
How would it feel to stride confidently away from them victorious?
Now spend some time conversing with Jesus. Write out this conversation in your journal.

7. His Disciples
Wise Mentor of an Apprentice Community

et ready for school. One of Jesus' first tasks was to build a little community of followers, a sacred brotherhood. These were his apprentices, the chosen few who answered his call. They eagerly abandoned everything, jettisoning all the cargo of their old way of life, all in response to two words of a mysterious and mystical stranger, thrown down like a gauntlet before them: *"follow me."* What reckless, uncalculated commitment! What fierce loyalty!

Theirs was a tribal bond stronger than blood, a camaraderie tested in the fires of living experience. This rag-tag bunch of misfits shared a depth of friendship, not based on the superficialities of social compatibility, but woven from the very fibers of the heart, a sense of divine duty. Despite different personalities, interests, social standings and political views, they were bound together by the unbreakable cords of a higher calling and purpose. How could these outstandingly ordinary, rude and crude, often idiotic men be transformed into the elite band of heroic spiritual warriors that they eventually became? Jesus produces community without conformity, unity without uniformity, diversity without division. All were unified on one unyielding conviction: *Jesus is Lord—Master of All!* He alone has the words of eternal life! Are you also mastered by this one foundational fact?

Jesus spent the majority of his time with a handful of faithful friends, not a crowd. While Jesus occasionally spoke to the thronging masses, he consistently poured his life into a select few. His was a life soaked in solitude and steeped in community. He intentionally carved out blocks of time alone and blocks of time in the company of his companions. Jesus was a stern critic of hypocritical religious institutions, but a staunch advocate of genuine spiritual community. This was his school of spiritual instruction:

twelve men together— walking, talking, serving, questioning, arguing, healing, living in community. As these run-of-the-mill sinners entered into a student-rabbi relationship with Christ, they were initiated into a life-long mission. He carefully and prayerfully selected a small band of brothers in whom he would replicate his own life-force, breathing his own Spirit upon them. It was a learning community of spiritual formation, a training camp for soldiers in supernatural combat. Class was always in session. And unlike the other rabbis of his day, Jesus also welcomed many women into his circle of friendship as well!

Jesus was a saint-maker. He forged indestructible lives of steel out of the raw material of plain, ordinary lives. Look not only at the examples in the Bible, but at others throughout history who chose to make Jesus their Lord and Master, patterning their lives after his. Read a biography of St. Antony of the Desert, St. Augustine of Hippo, St. Francis of Assisi, George Fox, David Brainerd, John Wesley, George Mueller, Hudson Taylor, Sadhu Sundar Singh or Mother Teresa of Calcutta, to see Christ's template, his image recreated in different shades and hues.

Would he be willing to forge that same living likeness in your life? Could he take your mind, your personality, your unique past as his raw material to sculpt a *masterpiece*— a Piece of the Master? Are you willing to undergo the hammering, the heat, as he smiths you into a sword of tempered steel, an instrument of striking beauty? What more proficient teacher has appeared in all the pages of antiquity? Is there anyone at all you would rather learn *"the art of living"* from than Jesus of Nazareth? Will you enroll in the Master's class? Ponder the following words of Albert Schweitzer from his book, *The Quest of the Historical Jesus*: *"He comes to us as One unknown, without a name, as of old, by the lakeside, He came to those men who knew Him not. He speaks to us the same word: "Follow thou me!" and sets us to the tasks which He has to fulfill for our time. He commands. And to those who obey Him, whether they be wise or simple, He will reveal Himself in the toils, the conflicts, the sufferings*

31

which they shall pass through in His fellowship, and, as an ineffable mystery, they shall learn in their own experience Who He is."

Meditation Exercise

Preparation: Spend a minute quieting your heart, slowly repeating the phrase: *"O Lord, you have searched me and you know me."*

Scripture: Now slowly read **Luke 5:1-11**, pausing at any phrase that stirs you.

1. Now set your imagination to work. Galilee (i.e., Geneseret) is a very large lake, many miles across. Now imagine the shoreline of a small coastal fishing village... What color is the surface of the lake? Is it calm or rough? What sounds do you hear (water, waves, boats, birds, etc.)?

2. Imagine the day-to-day existence of these unschooled, ordinary fishermen before their fateful encounter with Jesus. Watch them as they go through the familiar routines of an average day: Listen to the playful banter among friends as they go about preparing nets and loading supplies as they set off for a night of work... Hear the lap of the water as they push their boats out to sea... Smell the fishy smell of the nets and boat... Touch the sea-worn ropes of the net...

3. How do you think these expert fishermen felt as they toiled all night long without success? Imagine their tired limbs and sore muscles, exhausted from hours of fruitless labor... Feel the weariness, the anger, the frustration at having failed.... What words were exchanged? How do you react when the methods that usually work for you stop working? When was the last time you poured your heart into a project or task and failed completely? What have been your biggest failures in life? How do you feel when you fail? Don't just name it, try to feel it...

4. What thoughts must have run through Simon's mind when Jesus (who was not a fisherman) told him to "put out into the deep water and let down your nets for a catch"? How would you react to Jesus telling you how to do your job? How do you respond to Jesus' correction? What if he told you to go back to something you failed at and try again? Would you do it? Would you go deeper?

5. Go with the disciples as they set out into the deep and let down their nets... Watch as they begin to feel and see the tug of the fish in their nets... Hear the sounds of a net bursting with wriggling fish... What emotions must have filled their hearts? Excitement? Humility? Exhilaration? Fear? Awe? Hope?
How would you respond?

6. Mull over Simon's words, "Go away from me, Lord, for I am a sinful man..." What could have caused such a reaction? What do you think he meant by that? Have you ever felt like this in the Presence of God? How would you describe it?

7. Ponder Jesus' cryptic invitation: "Follow me and I will make you fishers of men..." In response to this simple command, they left their old lives behind to become *what he was*. What did it cost them? What did they leave behind when they decided to follow him? Ten years, twenty years, forty years later, do you think they regretted this choice? If you were in Simon's sin-worn sandals, would you have done the same? Would you leave everything behind?

Response: Close your eyes and imagine that Jesus is standing before you. Allow him to extend his invitation to you personally... Is he calling you to follow him? How will you respond? What are the things you must leave behind to pursue Jesus? What will it cost you? Do you need to place anything in his hands right now? What else does he say? Talk to him about all of this...
Record anything significant from your conversation in your journal.

8. His Proclamation

Apocalyptic Prophet of Kingdom Come

esus was driven by one simple sentence-- a sentence that would turn the world upside-down. It was always on his lips, embodied in all his actions, written on everything he touched. His life *was* his message; his message *was* his life. And what was this astonishing vision, this wonderful news, this revolutionary cause he gave his life for? *What was Jesus' singular obsession?* That you will go to heaven when you die? That you should stop sinning? That you should go to church and read the Bible? That you can be forgiven? Certainly these may prove to be pieces of the puzzle, but none of these is the central burning core of Jesus' gospel. Here is the constant, throbbing drumbeat of Jesus' essential proclamation in his own words:

Repent-- for the kingdom of God is at hand!

The kingdom has come! It is here— available to you right now! The reign of the Heavenly King has arrived! It's time to reconsider your life's direction in light of this glorious in-breaking reality! Jesus offers us the chance of a lifetime—we can be integrated into God's strategic plan for setting the world to right. It is our invitation to switch loyalties in the cosmic conflict, to align ourselves with the Absolute, to participate in what God is doing! We were never meant to be completely independent beings; we were created to find our highest freedom and purpose in joyful submission to the highest Goodness, to God's eternal kingdom.

What is a *kingdom*? It is a *community arranged around and governed by a ruler*, a social order derived from a *relationship of rulership* between king and his citizens. It is a *realm*, an allegiance, a nation one belongs to, lives for, fights for, and dies for. Jesus announces the arrival of *theocracy—where God's will is done* (*not* to be confused with the will of an imperfect church!). Wherever God is, God rules—He can do no other! And where God's rule is embraced, his goodness tears down evil, his righteousness tramples injustice, his power heals the sick, his freedom releases the oppressed! Do you want to be a part of such a radiant reality? *The Kingdom of Heaven is accessible to you today!* It is not relegated to some distant afterlife in a cloudy pseudo-existence. Eternity has already begun! It includes the immediate present! We can right now turn our lives into outposts, colonies of God's eternal reign! Catherine of Siena says, *"It is heaven all the way to heaven."* But, be forewarned: You are joining an uprising which is at odds with every other political allegiance.

Jesus was the only true "radical" to cross the canvas of recorded history. All other so-called revolutionaries are mere children in comparison, proposing shallow and short-sighted solutions to narrow and ill-defined problems—a revolving door where today's heroes becoming tomorrow's oppressors. Jesus alone leads a revolt that overthrows the true obstacles to the liberation of humanity. He instigated an insurrection that is still going on today, *a civil disobedience led by God himself!* It is a God-inspired rebellion against the powers of oppression in this world. And the seeds of revolution have already been planted in human hearts.

The quest for an ideal society pursued by such perceptive thinkers as Plato, Aristotle, Guan Zhong, al-Farabi, More, Bacon, Hobbes, Locke, and Marx will finally find its fulfillment in a Perfect Ruler with infinite power and wisdom who delights in the freedom of his beloved subjects! He lashes out with blood-red passion at anything that enslaves the heart of humanity. Jesus flatly refuses the sickening hatred of religious fundamentalism enforced with the sword. He proposes something far more dangerous than violence: The bloodshed required would *not* be the blood of his enemies, but *his own!* His was the subversive way of crucified love. Are you willing to participate in an underground movement so radical, so self-giving that it could require your own blood?

If so, Jesus challenges you to voluntarily bring your little kingdom into alignment with his all-colossal kingdom. You already have a kingdom: it is *wherever your will is done.* Each of us are rulers over a tiny corner of the universe, perhaps our home, our room, our body, and at the very least, our own thoughts, our own hearts-- *where what we say goes.* Only by surrendering our micro-kingdoms to him are we enabled to reign with him in his macro-cosmic realm. Will you cast your crown before him? Will you allow God to establish his will, his desire within you? His invitation is open to you. Could you forever leave behind "normal" and aim for "glorious"? Never again be content with the comforting mediocrity of following the wide path everyone else is on. Awaken, O Sleeper! Rise from your grave! Heed the call of the coming King. Gain the world by surrendering it.

Meditation Exercise
Preparation: Close your eyes for a minute and imagine yourself kneeling face down before heaven's throne... What feelings flood your soul?
Repeat the phrase: *"Thy kingdom come, Thy will be done..."*
Allow it to sink slowly into your sub-conscious thoughts...

Scripture: Now slowly read **Matthew 4:12 - 5:16.** Imagine hearing these words, like the first hearers, not in a religious context, but in the midst of ordinary life.

1. Ponder the words, *"The Kingdom of God has come to you..."* What images come to mind when you hear this phrase? Consider how this statement sounded to those who originally heard it. Would they have seen him as a rival to Caesar's empire?

2. Jesus proclamation was demonstrated by his "healing every disease and sickness among the people." Imagine seeing Jesus surrounded by a sea of pain: the poor, the sick, the deranged, the demon-possessed. Watch as he heals the hurts of humanity... What would you think of a man who was able to do these things? What do Jesus' actions say about the essential nature of God's rule and reign?

3. Reflect for a moment on the meaning of each blessing:

"Blessed are the poor in spirit..." How are the spiritually-bankrupt blessed?

"Blessed are those who mourn..." How do the broken find bliss?

"Blessed are the meek..." How are the humble endowed with glory?

"Blessed are those who hunger and thirst for righteousness..." What benefit is there for those not yet satisfied with their own goodness?

"Blessed are the merciful...the pure in heart...the peacemakers...
Blessed are those who are persecuted...." What do we make of this?

4. To whom is God's kingdom available? Who may become vice-regents with God?

Jesus extends this extraordinary invitation to anyone who will respond... and he gives special advantage to the disadvantaged! This is truly an upside-down kingdom-- where prostitutes and beggars are beckoned to sit upon thrones! Where drug addicts and the mentally ill receive gold-embossed invitations! How glorious! How beautifully incongruous! Is anyone unacceptable? Is anyone disqualified? *Perhaps the only outsiders are those who choose to be!* Can you picture such a beautiful rabble—this royal riffraff?

5. Ponder the rewards of the kingdom: *"they shall be comforted..."* *"They shall inherit the earth..." "They shall be filled..." "They shall be shown mercy..." "They shall see God..."* What do these blessings look like? Are these the kinds of rewards you are seeking? Jesus never says that following him will make your life *easier.* In fact, it may become more difficult for the time being... Would you embrace that kind of life? Would you stand under the reign of heaven?

Response: Consider whether you would want to be part of such a society. Count the cost. Write down in your journal the pluses and minuses of enlisting with the kingdom of God. Spend some time speaking to Jesus about his summons.

9. His Teachings

Sage Instructor in Spiritual Reality

 ow do we achieve spiritual integration? How can we properly align ourselves with reality-- with God, with ourselves, with others, with the world? When we want to learn, we go to an expert. When we want to know arithmetic, the French language, martial arts, or painting, we sit as a student under someone whom we trust has knowledge and experience in the field we wish to learn. Jesus comes to us as an expert teacher of the human experience, as one who knows the spiritual side of existence like no one else. Therefore, if we trust Jesus, we must take his word as our guide when we descend into the living chambers of the human heart.

We are amphibious beings. We straddle two worlds: *physical* and the *spiritual*, inextricably linked in practice but inescapably distinct in property. Physical existence is fairly simple at its foundational level: All matter (including your body) is made up of subatomic particles, combining and interacting in various ways to produce all you see, taste and touch. It helps to know the natural laws, the predictable cause-and-effect processes governing the material world. It is even more useful to know how the spiritual sphere works, for this is the domain of wisdom. *"What is seen is temporary, what is unseen is eternal."* Yet how often we hear the self-contradictory (and un-prove-able) sentiment: "Only physical matter exists. Only what we can see and touch is real."

When I say "spiritual", I am referring to *that mysterious "something more"* than the material world. *"Spirit"* is *non-physical substance, undetermined by the mechanics of matter. Spirit is a form of energy with personal freedom.* It includes all of the very human ideas you cannot set down in a Petri dish, dissect and explain empirically. Into this very broad category, I would put all the invisible "stuff" of which our lives are made: love and hate...will and intention... meaning and purpose... morality, creativity, beauty... relationships, responsibility, conflicts, courage and justice...the human spirit... and, ultimately, God. And while many claim that all human behavior can be reduced to the bubbling of chemicals in our brains, few are foolhardy enough to try to live that way in real life! We know intuitively that deep inside, we have this independent ability (and responsibility!) to choose our course. We have an unseen *agency*, capable of generating self-caused movement. Often we can answer the *how* just by looking at our physical world, but in order to answer the *why,* we must look beyond matter to the mind, the principle motive behind it.

As our ultimate spiritual guide, Jesus is the specialist on all things spiritual, the non-physical part of the human equation. He is obviously the authority on *God,* but he is also the expert on *life.* Jesus shows us how to live in a world sparkling with the living Presence of God. Jesus didn't come to organize a religion-- he knows we already have enough of that! He came to show us reality at its depths. He invites us into his school of spirituality, where we begin to understand the unseen framework of our souls. He trains our thought-life to cooperate with the current of the cosmos. He provides a paradigm of primordial existence within which we can work out our greatest questions and difficulties. He directs us in a diet of the senses for the nourishing of our amphibious nature. He regulates our relationships with God and others so that they may flourish into their fullest potential. He clarifies with razor-sharpness which habits are healthful and which are harmful for the human soul. If only we would live this way!

In Jesus' pivotal teaching, usually called "the Sermon on the Mount", the greatest rabbi and teacher of Israel outlines *the essentials of human living.* This sage of the soul tackles the basic issues debated and discussed throughout history: in philosophy, literature, poetry, art, psychology, daytime talk shows, and soap operas. What is the good? The true? The beautiful? What do I do with my anger, my desires, my broken relationships, my worries, my insecurities? How do I achieve a worthwhile life? If you truly trust Jesus, won't you learn to do everything he says is good for you? If you really want to be his student in the spiritual life, won't you eat, drink, and breathe his teachings as if they were your oxygen?

Meditation Exercise

Preparation: Quiet your heart. Consider how the unseen Presence of God saturates the air all around your body right now. Ask God to speak to you.

Scripture: As you slowly read **Matthew 5:17-48**, let the force of these masterful teachings knock the wind out of you. Spend some time chewing on any phrase or sentence that strikes a chord in you. Each time you read something that somehow sounds right to you, ask yourself what it is about this that resonates with your heart strings.

1. Consider Jesus' teachings on law and morality. "I have not come to abolish them but to fulfill them..." Jesus, at the same time both upholds the law (the rules of do's and don'ts) and yet points out their inadequacy. His was never morality for morality's sake. Instead, he sought to develop the kind of love and goodness of heart that would render the law unnecessary. Why are laws unable to change the human heart? What role do laws have? What would a city with no laws look like? What kind of person could live lawfully without laws?

2. In your journal, try to restate each basic teaching in your own words. Give examples of what they would look like in specific situations in your life.

3. What would it look like to actually begin living this way?
Imagine a life in which anger never leads to even verbal assaults...
Imagine a life in which conflicts and misunderstandings are dealt with respectfully instead of turning into opposition and accusation...

Imagine a life in which red-blooded sexual desire is never out of control...
Imagine a life in which marriage is a place of passionate faithfulness...
Imagine a life in which words are consistently followed by action...
Imagine a life in which insults are met blessing instead of retaliation...
Imagine a life in which revenge is never even an option...
Imagine a life in which hate-filled enemies are loved and prayed for...
Imagine a life in which we always do what we know is best because of an indelible law of love written deep in our hearts...

4. No one is born this way, but anyone can be re-born this way-- including you. Do you believe this? Can you picture yourself living this kind of life? Is it even possible?
Consider the mindset of a person who could effortlessly "turn the other cheek": What kind of thoughts would fill their mind? What kind of attitudes would they have towards people? How would they feel about their life? Can you imagine the inner experience of freedom for someone who automatically lived this way out of the depths of their being? What keeps you from living this out right now? Would you like to be the kind of person who lives like this?

5. Jesus ends his training session with a warning not to just hear but to do. Make a decision right now to learn from Jesus how to live according to his teachings! Try to put these instructions into practice today. What are some specific ways you could act upon his teachings this very week? As you attempt to do so, you will find much more about the brokenness and ugliness within your own heart... You will also find that it will take a miracle... Ask God to do this miracle each and every day-- imprinting his face upon your desires daily.

Response: Imagine you were sitting in the crowd and just heard these teachings. What questions would you want to ask him? Spend some time now asking him these questions. Talk to Jesus about anything else that surfaced during your reading. Write it in your journal.

10. His Miracles
Mysterious Master of the Natural Order

ot only is Jesus master of *the spiritual side of reality*, he is also perfectly capable of achieving anything he wishes in *the natural side of reality*! He is the designer and sculptor, the engineer and manufacturer of every speck of matter scattered throughout the millions of galaxies of our created order. *"All things were created by him and for him... In him all things hold together."* He crafted the cosmos from chaos, forming existence from emptiness. He brought order to that ancient anarchy, the abysmal void. He is the legislator of natural law. He is the *Logos*—the cosmic Principle, the Reason behind all that is. From walking the waves of Galilee to guiding the gaze of Galileo, Christ is Master of the Elements! No part of reality is beyond his reach. His Spirit undergirds and upholds all, interpenetrating matter more easily than neutrinos. His Spirit binds together and integrates both the seen and the unseen. His Spirit sets the swirling strings of the cosmos singing.

He rules it all. He commands the sun, the stars, and the seas. It is all at his beck and call! As the disciples asked, breathless upon a calm lake, *"Who is this? Even the wind and the waves obey him!"* He not only knows all the *why's*, he also knows all the *how's*. Jesus can manipulate the very building blocks of our physical universe to accomplish his purposes. He can effortlessly set aside the natural course of events in ways that even the most brilliant scientists and the most advanced technology cannot do!

Through his miracles, Jesus restores the supernatural sparkle to the natural order. May he open our blind eyes to see our iconic cosmos brimming with an overflowing Presence! Have you lost your ability to wonder? If so, stop and retrace your steps. Where did you lose it? Go back as far as you need to recover the *"wow"*, the involuntary gasp of a child, the ability to be astonished at the glory of creation. As we grow into adults, we often forget what children know instinctively: This is not a stark wasteland of bare facts without meaning. It is an enchanted world, an almost magical place, a living universe of *matter* responding to *spirit*. This is my Father's world! What is possible? What is impossible here?

This in no way negates the normal, scientific notions of nature. It only says there is Something glowing beyond it, like the sun behind stained glass! Nature is not eliminated but illuminated! Do you limit yourself to what you can explain empirically? Imagine if someone took a microscope and looked at all the individual cells of your body. What if they could then see the molecular structures, atomic and sub-atomic particles, electrons, protons, quarks, strings, down to its elemental simplicity. Would they then, after studying every cell of your body so carefully, now truly understand *you*?

Look carefully at your hand before your face. See the living tissue, each crease and wrinkle. Move each finger, deciding which you will move next. See how *your mind moves matter!* Change your mind and change the world! But where did this will, this decision originate? Could your brain, the brilliant super-computer that it is, be the primary interface between your body and that wondrous and free undetermined thing we call "spirit"? Thus the simple desire and command of your creative, independent will activates the physical matter of your brain and nervous system and muscles to achieve this physical action (perhaps a "miracle" of sorts?).

Could God perhaps have the same control over the rest of the physical universe that you have over your body? What if through a word, a thought, a command, he could move, change, rearrange or even create matter according to his own decision? What if he could, with no effort at all, set aside the normal way things happen, the laws of gravity or the conservation of mass, and just do things differently when he wanted to? This we would call a miracle-- yet God would only say, *"My ways are higher than your ways."* Every miracle is intensely personal.

Take off your sandals for you are standing on holy ground! It is physical reality responding to Spirit. And yet we think it is only dirt, and because we can explain dirt, it cannot be holy. We humans have a strange relationship with the miraculous. We crave miracles, yet we disbelieve them. We demand that God show himself by miraculous feats and when he does, we explain it away.

Meditation Exercise
Preparation: Quiet your heart, acknowledging God's surrounding Spirit. Repeat in your heart the earnest request:
> *"Give us this day our daily bread."*

Scripture: Slowly, meditatively read **Matthew 14:13-33**.

1. Imagine the thousands of people gathering in this desolate, unpopulated place... Consider the many miles they walked along the lakeside to arrive here... See the crowds sitting, listening intently to every word from the lips of Jesus... Why did they walk so far and sit all day in the hot sun? Now listen as the children start to squirm and whine... Feel your stomach's churning complaints for food...

2. As the sun begins to approach the western horizon, Jesus takes a break from teaching. Listen in as you notice a heated discussion that develops between Jesus and his disciples. What is written on their faces? What is the tone of voice? What does Jesus' expression say? What do you think went through their minds when Jesus said, "You give them something to eat"?

3. Now watch as a little boy is brought before Jesus with his meager offering... What do the disciples think when they see him? How do Jesus' followers feel as they begin to seat people for a meal that did not yet exist? Watch carefully as Jesus takes the hard loaf of crusty bread in his hands... At what instant do you think the miracle began to occur-- when he took the loaves and fishes, when he gave thanks, when he broke it, when he began passing it out, or when the disciples passed it out? Do you think they actually participated in the miracle?

44

4. Watch as the crowd finishes their food... Hear the sighs of satisfaction... Now imagine the conversations of those disciples as they collect the leftovers... Why do you think there were twelve baskets left? As the sky darkens, set out with the disciples in the boat across the lake... Why does Jesus stay behind?

5. Now imagine being in the boat as the storm-surge engulfs you... Taste the salt spray of turbulent waves as they wash over the boat... Feel the freezing chill of the wind, the stinging slap of the water on shivering skin, the violent tossing of the boat beneath your feet... Hear the roaring crash of the waves and the tempestuous whistling of the wind... What would be going through your mind?

6. Now watch in astonishment, as the shadowed silhouette of Jesus approaches you, walking dreamlike upon the face of the waters... Watch your Master's sandaled feet up close, as he lifts each step dripping from Galilee's trembling surface... What would be your reaction? Now, hear Jesus authoritative words spoken to you, *"Take courage... It is I... Do not be afraid."*

7. Place yourself in the soaking sandals of Peter... Would you have dared to imagine that "follow me" could apply even *here*, in the deepest impossibility? Hear Jesus say to you, "Come." How do you think Peter feels *before* he steps out of the boat? How does he feel *after* his first step? Now imagine sinking down as your mind struggles for answers... Feel the strong hand of Christ gripping your own... How would you answer your Savior's gentle rebuke, "Why did you doubt?" Years later, do you think Peter ever regretted stepping out of the boat?

Response: Why does Jesus seem to wait until the worst possible moment before unleashing a miracle? What is the purpose of these miracles? Would you attempt the impossible if Jesus called you? What doubts or fears might stop you? Talk with Jesus about all this.

45

11. His Healings
Caring Physician for Body and Soul

 here do we put our pain? Where can we find solace for our suffering souls and broken bodies? Who can mend our minds and cure our diseases? Who cares for our weeping, wounded world? One of the most striking features of Jesus' life was the miracles of healing that followed him wherever he went. He sought out the sick and the sick sought him out. Illnesses as minor as a common fever or as serious as death itself bowed their backs to the command of this supernatural physician, the master mechanic of the human machine. Surely the Maker of the human body is able to remake it when it is broken! Surely the fractured mind can be renewed! Surely the damaged and abused soul can find restoration! Just one touch from Jesus, one word from his lips can bring wholeness to the diseased tissue of body and soul.

Jesus radiated the effects of God's kingdom wherever he went, and this included physical healing. Contained in the Greek word for "Savior", *sozo*, is also implied the idea of "Healer". He was the restorer of health to the sick. The coming of God's reign brings a restoration of divine intent, a renewal of the original health of humanity. Jesus was able to repair the sickness of body, mind or spirit. His physical healings were both proof and picture of his ability to heal the soul. He knew the mysterious give-and-take between bodily well-being and spiritual well-being. Often a cure in one sphere affects a cure in the other.

He was most notorious for touching the *leper*, the lowest caste of the outcast and unclean. Leprosy was an incurable skin disease that attacked the nerve endings, rendering them useless. The one afflicted with this festering fate could no longer *feel*, becoming numb to pleasure and pain alike. Because of this, lepers would slowly destroy themselves, unaware of the damage they inflicted on their own bodies unwittingly, an agonizing death by inches. They would risk passing on this contagious condition to anyone with whom they came into contact. How is this similar to the effects of lust, hatred and selfishness upon our souls?

Every leper began life as a healthy baby boy or girl, full of life, innocence, and dreams of the future. Then came that tragic day when they caught the disease— whether through their own carelessness or compassion, through another's deception or malice, or just being in the wrong place at the wrong time. From that moment on, they wore the dreaded label of "unclean": untouchables, the scum of the earth, the rejects of society, unable to draw near to anyone. Their twisted frames would gradually deteriorate until they finally died a lonely death, saying farewell to a cruel world that couldn't wait to be rid of them. Was this their fault?

Meditation Exercise
Preparation: Begin by quieting your heart. Breathe normally. Whisper John the Baptist's prayer in your mind. As you inhale, say, *"You must increase..."* As you exhale, whisper, *"I must decrease..."* After doing this for a minute, ask God to speak to you.

Scripture: Slowly read **Matthew 8:1-17**, listening to what God may be saying to you specifically.

1. First, look upon the body of this poor, disfigured leper. Observe the ravaging effects of this wasting disease... Notice the grossly discolored skin of the leper with its oozing, putrid ulcers. See the infected, gangrene-covered limbs, dashed against stones never seen or felt... What do his hands look like? His feet? Smell the sickening stench of infection and rotting flesh still clinging to the bone...
Imagine what his daily existence must have been like... What were his first thoughts upon waking? Where did he go, what did he do each day? What were his last thoughts before he rest his head on his tattered, tear-stained pillow? Look into the leper's eyes, once

brimming with life and laughter, sparkling with joy and beauty...
What do you see there now?

Imagine the rejection of never being touched, the irritated stares as people walked hurriedly past, the mothers' sharp whispers to their staring children... Hear the questions of his broken heart... Was this all life had to offer? Where was God? Does God even care? What did I do to deserve this?

2. Can you relate to this picture? Do you ever feel a brokenness in your soul that needs healing? When have you felt isolated, lonely, alienated? Do you feel a secret shame, an unspoken unworthiness? Do you feel unclean or dirty inside, like there's a stain in your soul that cannot be washed away? Do you feel there is something deeply wrong with you that makes you unacceptable? Or have you felt like you just don't fit it—like no matter where you go, you don't belong? If so, when did you first feel this way? Why?

3. Imagine you were in the crowd around Jesus the day the leper came near...
What is the reaction of the people next to you?
What is your reaction?
Hear the staccato whispers of the people-- whispers of rejection, hatred, revulsion, contempt, and pity... See the soul-wounding stares of horror... What is the leper thinking as he draws near to Jesus?

Reflect on his words, *"If you are willing, you can make me clean"*...
If you will, if you want to, if you desire, if you choose to, you are able to cleanse me...*but do you want to?*
What sorrows, what hopes, what fears, what longings are contained in this plea?

4. Reflect on Jesus' reply, *"I am willing... Be clean..."*
What is Jesus really saying?

Hear the crowd gasp as Jesus reaches out his bare hand and touches the leper's skin... How does it feel to this leper? Was this the first human touch he has felt since he was a little boy? Does Jesus look him in the eye? Does Jesus embrace the leper, pulling him close to his chest? See the tears well up in the leper's eyes... What thoughts flood his mind in this moment? What is he *feeling*?
Spend a minute in silence, listening...

5. Now imagine the Roman centurion's creased face as he looks at the ceaseless suffering of his beloved servant... Ponder this high-ranking military officer's statement, *"Just say the word, and my servant will be healed."* What does this conversation teach us about Jesus' authority? Is there someone you love who is in desperate need of physical, emotional or spiritual healing? Will you come to Jesus, full of faith that he has the authority to "just say the word" and bring healing?

6. Imagine walking into Peter's house. What does it look like? Now look upon Peter's exhausted mother-in-law lying sick in bed...
Feel the heat of her forehead...
Now see Jesus arrive at her bedside... Watch as Jesus heals her with a touch of his hand... See the glow of health return to her pale face...
Feel the strength return to her limbs as she stands up and immediately begins serving her houseguests!
Now listen to the chatter as the word spreads from house to house...
Watch the neighbor's begin to drag their sick and needy children to the house where Jesus is staying...
See the love in Jesus' eyes as he heals each one...

Response: Talk to Jesus. Where are your places of brokenness and pain? Tell him where you need healing: "Lord, if you want to, you can make me clean." Repeat these words silently in your heart, allowing him to bring healing to you, body and soul.
Write the high points of this conversation in your journal.

12. His Exorcisms

Fierce Warrior in Supernatural Combat

od has placed a warrior spirit in every human being. We were born for warfare, designed for combat. Beating deep within every heart is a heroic instinct, a fierce courage that rises up to fight, to defend, to defeat. We know on some subconscious level that cowardice is loathsome, that fleeing in fear instead of facing our opponents is not honorable. But then how do we reconcile our violent tendencies with Jesus' direction to turn the other cheek? Why would God create soldiers if we are called to love our enemies? Why are Bible stories so full of bloody inter-tribal wars? Did God make our species too dangerous and war-like for its own good?

God made us warriors because we were born on a battlefield. This is a world at war, where the cosmic battle between good and evil is being waged every day. According to the Hebrew writings of antiquity, Adam and Eve were born with an ancient evil already lurking in the garden and a historic decision before them. Humankind was destined from Eden to crush this serpentine foe, and yet it was not to happen in the opening pages of the story. We were born to conquer an antagonist far greater than ourselves. Although the decisive blow has already been struck, the fate of the cosmos is being contested everyday and we are the ground troops in this epic struggle. Most of us find ourselves wounded and scarred from earliest childhood. A spiritual warfare rages around us: unseen arrows fly, missiles explode, and the casualties have been many. True spirituality is a dangerous thing.

Evil has a name and a face, but it is not a human face. Jesus called him *Satan*, the accuser, slanderer, tempter, deceiver and the father of lies. We have an invisible enemy who delights in evil, who wants to see you destroyed. There is a will that is set against you-- in fact, they are legion. Our world is inhabited by a host of non-human spiritual entities of exquisite cruelty who seek to attack, oppress, even completely control and devour human souls. Feeding on anger, fear, and hatred, their whisperings are behind much of the horrific cruelty we see in the world. Does this seem far-fetched to you? We may write off demons as medieval superstitions. Unfortunately, we cannot write off the horrific evils and senseless atrocities that fill our world. Every child has imagined the darkness filled with hideous monsters; every culture has its "ghost stories". Perhaps they are not so misguided after all. Many believe these diabolical creatures were once angels, heavenly messengers who fell from God's Presence in a misguided rebellion of cosmic proportions. Humanity has borne the hatred of demons through simply being born. The crowning of Adam's race, these holy innocents, incites their deepest envy—a fury and a madness to watch the world burn. Their sole purpose now is to do to the individual soul what they could not do to the universe-- to wrest it from the loving hands of its Creator.

Unfortunately, throughout history we have constantly mistaken who the real enemy is. We have directed our God-given fighting instinct in the wrong direction, turning our gunfire against human beings instead of the demonic oppressors that hold them captive. In the Scriptures, Paul warns us explicitly, "We battle not against flesh and blood!" If they are a member of the human race, they are not our enemy! All of the bloodshed of every war is the blood of our own comrades. When we raise our fist against another, it is a sibling rivalry between brothers and sisters, following in the footsteps of Cain before us. Even when our foes are driven by the force of hell itself, they are only puppets, prisoners-of-war whom we should seek to free, not to attack. Throughout his public ministry, Jesus has many face-to-face confrontations with people possessed and controlled by powerful, supernatural beings. Jesus comes as a mystic warrior of the kingdom of heaven to liberate the prisoners, leading captives back to their true home. He frees us from the throes of these scavengers of death.

Meditation Exercise

Preparation: Take up the prayer of the psalmist:

"He is my refuge and my fortress, my God in whom I trust."

Recognize God's powerful Presence all around you, like an impenetrable fortress. Ask God to speak.

Scripture: Slowly read through **Luke 8:26-39**.

1. Imagine you are one of the disciples with Jesus as the boat draws near to shore in the darkening twilight...Hear the lapping of the water against the side of the boat...

Now imagine hearing a blood-curdling scream pierce through the cold night air... Does it sound like a tormented beast skewered on a serrated spike? Or like an other-worldly creature from a nightmare, fangs dripping red from a fresh kill?

Feel the icy chill, the hairs on the back of your neck stand up as you recall the stories the other fishermen tell of the Gerasenes Demoniac... A foe beyond any worldly strength with inhuman abilities... A self-mutilated man who feasts on the fear of his victims, slaking his thirst for blood at his own wrists... A man dwelling in the tombs, breathing the sickening stench of death...

When have you ever felt such sheer, naked, raw terror? Try to recall a couple of your most terrifying nightmares... Feel the sharp stab of adrenaline, the shiver down your spine, the freezing in your bones...

2. As your boat touches the shore, hear the scampering of feet and see the pale gray flesh of a ghastly naked form running towards you... See his body infested with a demonic swarm, writhing as if a hive of unseen insects were crawling across his skin...

Feel your heart racing in your chest as you see the frenzied look of an animal in his frozen black eyes...

You are not looking at a man, but at the face of a ghoulish, demonic presence wearing damned human skin...

3. Now see Jesus standing there, unflinching and unshaken in the face of stark, wild-eyed insanity... Why is Jesus unafraid? Hear his calm, confident voice as he commands without trembling: *"Come out of him!"*... Watch as the demonic man falls at Jesus' feet, cringing in fear at his Presence... Where does Jesus get that authority? Hear his cryptic question, *"What is your name?"* Who exactly is Jesus talking to? Why does he ask this? Now, hear the demonic horde within the man reply through tortured vocal chords, *"Legion, for we are many."*

4. Now look across the hillside at the filthy herd of swine swilling their slop... Why do you think this legion of unclean spirits asks for Jesus' permission to infest the mob of pigs? Why do they so fear the embryonic abyss from whence the cosmos was called? Why do you think Jesus allows it? Now watch as the squealing swine rush in a frenzied, headlong swarm towards the water's edge... Hear their last garbled gasps and cries as they charge into the murky waters...And after the last snout disappears underwater, a quiet swirling stillness...

5. Now watch as the prisoner of hate stands to his feet, stepping out of the shadows of the decaying dungeon of his own delusions... Watch him lift his eyes slowly to the horizon as the fire of dawn breaks across his face—a new man in a new world... His chest swells with deep draughts of delicious oxygen, pure and clear...
Now listen to the complaints of the townspeople who begin to gather... Why do they ask Jesus to leave? When Jesus' newly-freed friend asks to go with him, why do you think Jesus tells him not to?

Response: Talk to Jesus about this story. What stood out to you? Take up the prayer: *"Deliver us from evil."* Are there any areas in your life where you have allowed Satan a foothold, where you have given him an inch and he has taken a mile? Are there any deeply ingrained compulsions or addictions that you feel powerless to break? What are the bondages that control you? Record in your journal. Spend a quiet minute resting your soul before God.

13. His Parables
Enchanting Storyteller of an Invisible World

ll of life is a story. What is yours? What is your quest or journey? What are the challenges you must face? How will your character change? Will you end up a hero or a villain? What unexpected plot twists heighten the action? And how will the tale end? Unless we see the days of our lives as a story, we see them incompletely. Stories make meaning of seemingly random events. Stories give purpose to pain. Stories have a living logic that can only be unlocked by surrendering to them and watching them unfold. There is a wisdom that is gathered from the dramatic arc of plot and character that penetrates the heart even while it perplexes the head.

Only within the structure of story will your life make sense. Seen from this context, all the tensions and conflicts are good, even *necessary* parts of this dynamic order. You cannot savor the sweetness of victory unless you have tasted the bitterness of struggle. You can never say a scene was meaningless until you've seen the end of the movie! If the curtain has not yet fallen on your life, then the climactic conclusion is yet to come!

Our Maker is a storyteller, or more accurately, *The* Storyteller. The Holy Scriptures presents all of history as His Story, from Genesis to Apocalypse. This overarching macrocosm lends meaning to each microcosm. Linear elements of beginnings and endings mesh with cyclical repetitions and patterns as the wagon wheel of history moves forward on its predestined path. Within this mysterious meta-narrative are countless subplots and individual episodes, all of which find their place in the great Epic of Existence.

It comes as no surprise, then, that the Christ would come telling stories as well. The parables of Jesus are legendary-- giving intuitive moral measurement to actions without moralistic assertion. With stories of seeds and weeds and trees and sheep, he gives tangible shape to the map of the invisible world, tracing the frontiers of the unknown. Like the age-old fables and folklore, they take static statements of truth and breathe into them life and motion and vitality. Jesus made the most profound mysteries of the spiritual life into images even a child could understand.

These parables were used as a subversive sorting mechanism for testing priorities. Jesus did not seem eager to talk to the uninterested. Many of his parables were followed by the puzzling refrain: "He who has ears to hear, let him hear." It was an invitation to inquiry which only a few responded to. The rest of the stampeding mob was left in their smug and self-satisfied ignorance.

Jesus was an ingenious educator. Making generous use of questions and puzzles, examples and exaggerations, humor and irony, he aimed to provoke wisdom more than to impart knowledge. He did not seek to speak information but to spark insight. And, amazingly, if you "didn't get it," he was genuinely excited to explain it to all who really wanted to know! All who asked received. All who sought found. All who knocked had the door opened to them. Let confusion speak to you! Perplexity is part of the learning process! Confusion is the recognition of an area of ignorance. It is *knowing what you do not know*. Until we realize that there is a gap in our knowledge, we have no reason to try to fill it. We cannot search for what we do not know we do not possess!

Whenever you can't quite figure out what Jesus is saying, would you be one of those few students who sticks around and asks questions afterwards? Such persistent questioners were the only ones who became his disciples. Jesus' followers were not the brightest minds in the land, only the thirstiest. In all other respects, they were uncommonly common-- vulgar, rude, uncouth and lacking in social graces or status. Yet because they treasured the wisdom of Christ like a pearl of great price, these insatiable seekers became co-founders of a movement that conquered an empire.

Meditation Exercise

Preparation: Close your eyes. Ask Jesus, *"Teach me your ways..."*

Scripture: Slowly read **Matthew 13:1-52.**

1. Consider the constant theme: *"The kingdom of heaven is like..."* If you were to describe how God desires to restore his rule and reign to this broken world, what images would come to mind? How would your description compare to Jesus' answers? Most of his parables describe either relational realities or organic processes instead of militaristic or mechanical means... What does this tell you about God's way of working?

2. Reflect on the story of the sower of seed... How is God's message like a seed? How receptive are you to God's voice when he speaks to you? Is your heart hardened against anything he is trying to tell you? Is your relationship with him shallow? What are the weeds that are growing in your life: distractions, worries, secondary desires, and other priorities that crowd out God?

3. Consider the parable of the weeds sown by the enemy... As you look at the world, reflect on all of the horrific evil that exists in the world: abuse, genocide, rape, murder, oppression, injustice, greed... Have you ever wondered if God was responsible for these awful atrocities? Yet even as Christ assures us that these are the work of an enemy, do you find yourself puzzled at why God doesn't stop sin immediately? If God loves us, then why doesn't he eradicate the weeds of wickedness right now?!? And yet, when we're really honest with ourselves, we must admit that *we are responsible* for some of the hurt in the world... Our hands are also stained with blood! And God, in his amazing grace, refrains from punishing evil because *we ourselves are often part of the problem*! Have you ever considered that God's boundless mercy for the workers of wickedness is mercy for *you*? *He who has ears to hear, let him hear...*

4. Consider the parables of the treasure in the field and the pearl of great price... Jesus is essentially saying that the opportunity to participate in the purpose and power and Presence of God is the greatest privilege on earth! Is that how you see it? Does it pound like a fist on the door of your heart, demanding a response? Would you gladly give all your temporal possessions for this once-in-eternity invitation? If this doesn't sound anything like your experience, then consider whether you really grasp the world-defying Way of Jesus!

5. Now imagine Jesus' thick-headed disciples wondering what each parable means... Watch them exchange exasperated expressions as they try to figure out among themselves what he means... Imagine how they must have felt as they sheepishly approach their master to admit their ignorance...

As you read his stories, are you confused about anything? Are you desperate enough for answers to come and pester Jesus? Would you have the audacity to ask him to explain himself? Yap at his heels, chasing him around like a little puppy! He loves hungry hearts! Write out some of your biggest questions and ask him for help...Often our deepest questions can only be properly understood as part of our story. So don't be surprised if they slowly take shape over a lifetime of trusting conversation with the Alpha and Omega, the Author and Finisher of your faith.

Response: Look over your life so far and summarize it as a story. Between the bookends of birth and death, what is being written? Ask your Maker what he thinks of it so far... Ask him where the story is headed...

He may not spoil the ending by giving away the details of it, but perhaps he will give you some previews of the coming attractions for which he is preparing you... How could your story end well?

14. His Forgiveness
Merciful Friend of Sinners

veryone experiences guilt-- but not everyone knows why. We have all felt the discomfort, we have heard the alarm bell, we have seen the warning lights that tell us we are off course. *Guilt is the natural response to sin in a properly-functioning soul.* But it quickly swells into a bloated monster when we don't know how to properly dispose of it. One thing is for sure: we must find a way to deal with the weight of guilt or *it will crush us.* Self-awareness is a hazardous pastime. When you examine the details of your own pride and selfishness, honest self-reflection can drive you to depression. We have received the gifts of Adam: being and brokenness. Let us rejoice... and despair. How sensitive are your ears to the voice of your conscience (or is it the Holy Spirit?) that convicts you of right and wrong and the fact that it really does matter? How do you silence this inner witness when it speaks against you? We gladly listen when it speaks against others, pointing out the sins of others. We love to nail others for their wrongs but when the nails begin to press against our own flesh, we frantically grope for something to ease the pain.

How do you deal with the incessant throbbing of your conscience? The world offers many *pain-killers* to dull the ache. Do you justify yourself by finding someone else to blame? Do you blame it upon your circumstances, thereby transferring the blame to chance... or even to God? Do you look for someone whose sins are greater than yours and focus your attention on condemning them (a favorite tactic of religious types)? Do you excuse yourself by saying that "everyone does it"? Do you try to redeem yourself by doing many good deeds to try to outweigh the bad? Do you cover it up and hide it so that no one else will know? Do you convince yourself that it is not really wrong? Or do you simply ignore it, thinking that it will go away if you pretend it doesn't exist? Through constant practice of wrongdoing, it is possible to harden your heart, to sear your sensitive conscience with a hot iron, to numb your senses so that it no longer disturbs you. But in doing so, you lose part of your humanity. Every coping mechanism will short-circuit your soul. So what are we to do?!?

There is only one road back to innocence. *Only divine forgiveness can remove the burden of guilt forever,* leaving you as pure and spotless as a newborn child. Only the grace of God can wash us clean for all eternity in the waters of forgiveness. Do you want to experience rebirth, renewal, restoration? Guilt can be the first step on the road to ruin or the first step on the road to reconciliation. It all depends on which direction you take it. Will you turn toward God or away? *We can only receive mercy from the One who could rightfully condemn us.* So we must go before the Judge of the Universe, who calls all humankind to account for the deeds we have done. We admit before him that we deserve any punishment that he sees fit. And when we stand humbly before him, casting aside our cloak of excuses, our self-justifications, our blames, and our cover-ups, what do we find? We find compassion instead of condemnation! *"A broken and contrite heart, O God, You will not despise."* Instead of finding ourselves clasped in the handcuffs of justice, we find ourselves wrapped in the warm embrace of friendship, acceptance, and hope. Mercy triumphs over judgment!

We find that the Judge is our friend. He longs to show us compassion! He knows that the Law can only define sin; it cannot defeat sin! He wants desperately to show mercy to you! *He would rather die than to condemn you!* And that is precisely what he did. He was willing to do whatever it might take to extend grace to the farthest reaches of the globe! *But God can only forgive sins-- he does not forgive excuses.* Is it difficult to admit that you are undeniably guilty and in need of mercy? Until you have known the brokenness of being an unworthy sinner, you can never know the joy of being a blood-bought saint. He will pay the ultimate price for you—but only if you recognize your need for redemption.

59

Let me tell you a secret: Jesus absolutely loves ungodly, dirty, rotten sinners! *While we were still sinners, Christ died for us.* When the Pharisees set out to slander Jesus, they could think of no more outrageous insult than to call him a "friend of sinners." And Jesus wore the description proudly! The Majestic Lord is also the Friend of Sinners! He was a friend of whores, lowlifes, criminals— surely he will be your friend too! He attended their parties, he enjoyed eating and drinking with them, he defended them. He actually *liked* being with them. If you will come to Jesus as a sinner, you will find an ally. But if we come in smug self-righteousness, our Judge will have no choice but to confront our lies. He must set the record straight—He will not abide unacknowledged sin.

Meditation Exercise

Preparation: Close your eyes and imagine Jesus before you. Repeat this prayer for a few minutes:

"Lord Jesus Christ, Son of God, have mercy on me, a sinner."

Scripture: Slowly and meditatively read through **John 8:1-11**.

1. Imagine the crowded streets and marketplaces of the middle-eastern city of Jerusalem on this festive morning... See Jesus entering the city early in the morning from Mount of Olives just outside of the city walls... Hear the bustle of morning activity as Jesus walks through the busy streets of Jerusalem on his way to the temple courts... Now watch as a crowd gathers around Jesus in anticipation of his teachings... Listen as Jesus sits down in his usual spot and begins to spin a humorous story of a man with a log stuck in his eye trying to remove a speck of dust from someone else's eye...

2. Now in the midst of Jesus teaching, there is a commotion from the back of the crowd...Watch as a group of Pharisees and religious leaders drag a woman caught in adultery before Jesus, interrupting his discourse... How are the Pharisees dressed? What is etched in

their expressions? What is going through their minds? What are they hoping to see? How do they look upon this woman? Why is no man accused? Hear their voices calling out for her to be stoned...

3. Look into the eyes of this woman caught in the act of adultery. What do you see there? Do you think she was a prostitute or an unfaithful wife? Which do you think is worse? Does it really matter to Jesus? Now imagine you are this woman, standing stripped of all your defenses before your accusers... Look at the crowd... Feel her shame and sadness... How does it feel to stand disgraced before Jesus? What does she need more than anything else right now?

4. Now watch Jesus' response to their question: Watch him slowly squat down and begin to plow his finger through the dust... What do you think he was writing? Why does Jesus ignore them and write in the dust? What is written on his face? Now listen to his words, "Let he who is without sin cast the first stone." What truth is contained within this short reply? Now watch as each of these Pharisees drop their stones and slowly walk away... What is going through their minds? Why do you think the older Pharisees leave first?

5. Finally, Jesus is left alone with her... What does this woman see when she looks into Jesus' eyes? Why doesn't Jesus condemn her? Does he not care about sin? Why is Jesus' response to her sin different from the Pharisee's response?

Response: Spend a minute repeating the prayer, *"Forgive us of our trespasses... as we forgive those who trespass against us..."* Do any incidents in your past still plague you even now? Do you ever wonder, "Can anyone love me—the *real* me? With all my selfishness, bitterness, and brokenness?" Talk to Jesus about it... Ask him if he would ever forgive you for these sins... In your imagination, bundle all of your sins, all your anger, your mistakes, your filth and garbage into a bag... Lay it all down at his feet...What does he say to you?

15. His Transfiguration
Heavenly Lord Revealed in Glory

hy doesn't God show more of himself? Why not peel back the skies for all to see and shout like thunder, "Here I am! Everyone turn to me or be turned to stone!" Wouldn't that be more spectacular than coming to earth as a simple carpenter? Why the hiddenness of the incarnation? Wouldn't he recruit more to his ranks with a flashy "in-your-face" approach? Why the geographical and chronological specificity? Why the lack of publicity? Why so inefficient a strategy? Couldn't he easily remove all doubt if he wanted to? Are you *disappointed* that God has not shown up when and how you wish he had? Has he failed to meet your expectations?

We find, in the sacred archives of divine interaction, a strange reticence on God's part to reveal himself with the certainty we crave. His appearances on the stage of history seem so few and far between. And even as he reveals, he conceals— never quite dispelling the mystery. Isn't it ironic that God's greatest manifestations have been to those gaping few who didn't *need* to see anything to believe? For the most part, God revealed his glory to those closest to him—to Moses, Elijah, Peter, James and John. And even on those rare occasions when he shows up with fireworks and miracles to the multitudes, it only seems to convince those who were already prepared to believe. We might almost say that God seems *shy,* preferring to hide in the shadows. Why is this?

Let us consider for a moment the very personality and purposes of God himself. Perhaps God is not boastful or forceful when it comes to relationships. Perhaps he is an Artist and a Storyteller who prefers subtlety to formulaic predictability. Perhaps he is a humble King who prefers to rule by inspiring loyalty through love, rather than subjugating slaves through servile fear. Perhaps he is a wise and strong Father who wants to raise us as sons and daughters, free to learn responsibility rather than to "just shut up and do what you're told...or else!" Perhaps he is a Lover who prefers to woo us with fascinating conversation rather than dazzle us with his riches. So he gives us breathing room. He leaves us space to think, to learn, to try, to fail, to doubt, to trust, to question, to pursue, to seek, to love. Perhaps the liquid laws of relationship apply even with God. Maybe a friendship with the Almighty must be built like all others: step by voluntary step.

God knows the fragile nature of love. He knows love cannot be coerced or it is not love. He knows our odd fascination with the mysterious, the unknown. He knows there is no trust where there is no possibility of doubt. He knows the damage done to the soul when one attempts to force what should be done freely. If God wanted robots, he could have, he *would have* created robots! But instead, God created *us*—spiritual beings with will, creativity, choice, intelligence, emotion. What does that tell you about the kind of communion God seeks? At the very least, it tells us that God does not need unquestioning slaves cringing before him as before a volatile volcano.

If God wants children, friends, and lovers who thrill at the wonder of his Presence, then he must go about relating to us in certain ways. If he captures us with his power, he cannot captivate us with his love. If he overwhelms our senses with fear or pleasure, we will not develop the kind of selfless, sacrificial love that makes us more like Christ. Perhaps what he is looking for is *trust.* The question must then be answered, "Will we trust the humble tradesman of Galilee, even while there is room for doubt?"

We look now at the moment when Christ momentarily removes the veil, giving us a tiny glimpse of his true nature: the radiant Lord of Heaven in all of his splendor. Like a ray of eternity's flame slicing through a crack in time and space, Jesus is revealed as *"the King of Kings and Lord of Lords, who alone is immortal and who lives in unapproachable light, whom no one has seen or can see."* Up till this point, Jesus has been trying to convince his disciples

63

of his divinity without overwhelming them. And finally, in response to Jesus' probing, Peter makes his earth-shaking confession: *"You are the Christ, the Son of the Living God!"* Only *after* this discovery, does he manifest more of the dread mystery of who he is.

There will be a day when faith becomes unending sight. But it is reserved for those who pursued him in the darkness. Those who finally see will be those who have sought the unseen. Follow him further into the heights, through the cloud of unknowing. He wants us to trust him *before* he rewards us. The invisible Bridegroom waits until after we have bound ourselves to him in covenant love before he unveils himself as he truly is. Perhaps the ongoing discovery of God's infinitely-faceted glory is our eternal adventure— the one thing that will continue to thrill our ever-growing capacity for wonder. This is the expedition that will last for endless ages, where each awe-striking vista is even more amazing than the one before— so that for all eternity, the best is always *yet to come!*

However, we still dwell in a dark vale filled with disappointment, scarcity and sadness— an incubator of faith. And no matter how powerful and vivid our experience of divine glory and beauty, it never lasts. The raw thrill of touching God soon fades. The mystical vision recedes into the background of life as usual. The most powerful moments of our lives become profound but distant memories. Inevitably, we must descend from the resplendent mountaintops and re-engage with the mundane routines of these gray flatlands beneath the veil.

Meditation Exercise

Preparation: Ready your heart for a steep climb. Meditate upon these words from Psalm 24, *"Who may ascend the hill of the LORD? Who may stand in his holy place? He who has clean hands and a pure heart..."* How may you prepare your soul for this sacred ascent?

Scripture: Slowly read **Matthew 17:1-9.**

1. Place yourself in the role of Jesus' bewildered disciples... Why do you think Jesus only asked those in his "inner circle" to follow him to the mountaintop? Do you think they knew what lay in store for them at journey's end?

2. Imagine this mystical journey to the mountain of holy encounter, where transfiguration awaits... Imagine the path they must have travelled... What obstacles would they have overcome? What sights would they have seen? Now imagine standing at the foot of the holy mountain... what might it have looked like? Was it steep and jagged or gently sloped? What color do you imagine the rocks to be?

3. Imagine their climb into the heights... sweat upon skin, burning muscles, weary legs... See the clouds rolling in around them like mist, enveloping them in a pale white shroud...

4. Upon reaching the summit, they watch in wonderment as Jesus is transformed before their eyes, a momentary glimpse behind the veil... See his skin begin to glow softly, gradually increasing in radiance until it is a blinding luminosity, his face shining like the sun...What do you imagine his disciples were thinking?

Response: How has your own journey been thus far? What have been the high points and low points? How has Christ revealed his glory to you? Have you had any mountaintop moments when the curtain of eternity was lifted and for one timeless second everything made perfect sense? Do you yearn for more?

Have there also been disappointments? Have there been those moments when *he should have shown up... but he didn't?* Have you been grasping for the mirage of absolute certainty? Will you pursue Christ even when you see no sign of him?

Has your longing and aspiration become almost unbearably painful? Might there be a purpose for the experience of acute dissatisfaction and piercing desire? Talk to him about all of this...

16. His Last Supper
Exemplar of Loving Servanthood

he call to Christ is a call to greatness. God loves to see his children thrive! However, the only path to true greatness is the path of servanthood. We may be able to achieve a temporary, self-serving kind of greatness through other means. But if you want selfless, heroic, costly greatness—the kind that lasts for eternity—then you will have to follow the footsteps of the Servant of All. He commands submission and servanthood, not to put us down but to lift us up.

Jesus sets the definitive example of leadership, influence and personal gravity. It is in precisely the opposite direction of the rest of the world. How do we make our mark upon this spinning globe? Not through accumulating status symbols, property and prestige, fame and fortune, nor through control and manipulation. Jesus shows us that the path to lasting and eternal impact is through humbling ourselves and serving others. In the eyes of Jesus, *a leader is a servant.* He tells us in word and deed *that "whoever wants to become great among you must be your servant...For even the Son of*

Man did not come to be served, but to serve, and to give his life as a ransom for many." In a world full of corrupting power and self-exalting ambition, Jesus sets a priceless example of the self-sacrificing quality of divine love. He was the greatest man who ever lived because he gave the most.

Jesus is our Great Exemplar. We all need a *template for living*, a model to pattern our lives after. Most of us initially imitate our parents, who for better or for worse, launched us on a life trajectory that is largely subconscious. It is this process of *watching* and *learning* that children do so well. And if we have been reborn from above, we need someone to show us *how to live* from above! Our Savior not only provides us with new capacities, but shows us how to use them. What good is having wings if we know not how to use them? Jesus not only commands us to lay down our lives for our brothers, he shows us, in shockingly gory detail, how to do it. Jesus' earthly life etches out a blueprint of the kind of life his death has purchased for us.

Jesus' teachings would be incomplete without Jesus himself—the Word made flesh. The *principles* of Christ minus the *person* of Christ are pointless. This would only rehash the same powerless platitudes of the past, telling us what to do without equipping us to do it. It was his living example that lifted his simple commands to new heights. He produced a new vocabulary, not with words but with flesh. He not only tells us to love our enemies, but he himself kisses his betrayer. He not only tells us to pray for our persecutors, but demonstrates it with his own panting lips while his flayed flesh is draped upon splintered wood: *"Father, forgive them, for they know not what they do."* He not only tells us to humbly serve one another, but at his last supper, he vividly illustrates this teaching in mud and water.

Meditation Exercise
Preparation: Quiet your mind and heart for a minute and recognize that the Presence of God is here. Ask God to speak to you through your reading.

Scripture: Slowly and meditatively read through **John 13:1-17**.

1. Imagine you are one of the disciples gathered here for the Passover meal... Look around this upper room in which the last supper was eaten... How is it furnished and arranged? There is no servant here to do the menial task of washing the feet of the guests... Look at Jesus' face, eyes darker than wine... What emotions are written there? Does he look serious? Sad? Peaceful? Focused?

2. Now watch as Jesus strips off his cloak with all of its outer trappings of importance... Look how skinny, how pale and vulnerable he looks. He looks more like a slave boy in his undergarments than the Master of Worlds.... Where is his majesty, his glory? Now watch as Jesus takes up the towel and the dirt-smeared earthen washbasin... See Jesus kneel silently before the first disciple in the posture of the lowliest of servants... Does this seem inappropriate? Uncomfortable? What do you think as you see him there? Without a word, Jesus places his disciple's foot in the basin and begins to tenderly scrub the dirt into the swirling water... Hear the gentle swishing of the water...Feel the touch of Jesus' wet hands and the water on your feet...What temperature is the water? Does this touch feel awkward or does it feel like perfect bliss?

3. Why do you think Peter objects? Would you, like Peter, try to get out of it? Why do you feel uncomfortable? Is it too intimate for you? Too dirty? Too confusing?
Why does Jesus do this? Why does Jesus insist on showing his love in this way?
What is the dirt that you need to be cleansed of? In your heart? In your thoughts? In your words? In your past?

4. What do your feet look like when he finishes washing them and begins to dry them with the towel? Wiggle your toes.... How does it feel now? What do you want to say to Jesus now? Are you overjoyed over this outpouring of love or do you have questions? Now listen as he speaks gravely to all the disciples: "Now that I,

your Lord and Teacher have washed your feet, you also should wash one another's feet." How would you react? Are you excited? Scared? You don't want to get your hands dirty? Whose feet do you think Jesus wants you to wash, either figuratively or actually?

5. Now join Jesus at the table for supper. Watch each disciple eating... What are their conversations about?
Now look at Jesus' face... On this tragic night, what is written there? Jesus takes the Passover meal and assigns new meaning to each element. Watch as Jesus takes the flatbread and breaks it... Take a piece in your hands... How does it feel? Now taste the dry bread in your mouth as you chew and swallow it... Listen as Jesus speaks, "Take and eat; this is my body..." What does he mean by this? How does the bread remind you of Jesus?

6. (If you are struggling with alcoholism, you may want to omit or modify the following exercise.) Now watch as Jesus takes the cup of wine and says, "Drink from it, all of you. This is my blood of the covenant, which is poured out for many." Swish the wine in the cup... Take a deep breath, breathing in the aroma of the wine... Taste the tang of the wine, savoring it on your tongue... What does it taste like? What is the aftertaste? Sweet? Bitter? Why do you think Jesus calls it his blood? How is Jesus blood shed for you like the wine? Do you think the disciples yet realize that Jesus is going to die tomorrow?

Response: Imagine Jesus is standing beside you. Talk to him about what you have just experienced. How do you feel about serving others? Is there an area of need that he is calling you to serve? Are you afraid to do things that are "beneath your dignity?" How would you react to being treated as a servant? Record your conversation in your journal.

17. His Betrayal

Forsaken Soul in Gethsemane's Darkness

hich is more unbearable— physical pain or emotional pain? Some would say that no amount of relational turmoil adds up to the raw, burning, stinging, stabbing sensations transmitted by the nerve endings under the skin. For others, the throbbing inner ache of abandonment and rejection or the betrayal of a loved one hurts a hundred times more than any bodily affliction. The gnawing anxiety and agony of fast-approaching failure is far more devastating for many than bodily disease. Either way, we cannot always rely on our feelings to gauge the temperature of our spirit. Sometimes when we feel the weakest is when we are the strongest, at our moment of triumph. Before enduring the teeth of the whips, the razor-cruel thorns, the rusted iron stakes of the cross, Christ suffered the bitter loss of every friendship he cherished. On that fated night, one man felt the full weight of our sin pressing down upon his frail frame, the absolute low point of human experience. As Julian of Norwich wrote, *"he sorrowed for every man's sorrow."* Your hurts, my hurts,

and the soundless sobs of the untold unmourned victims of human hatred— all accumulated like boulders upon his burdened shoulders.

Before Jesus began his death march to Calvary, he had been deserted and denied by his closest friends, misunderstood and mocked by his own family, slandered and despised by his enemies, and subjected to the shame of public ridicule. He couldn't seem to do anything right. Everywhere he looked, he saw the hateful, haughty eyes of the mocking mob— filled with jeers, insults, and treachery. In this dark night of the soul, no ally was on his side. Every shred of emotional support and encouragement was ruthlessly ripped from his fingers until he stood completely, utterly, helplessly *alone*.

Even his desperate plea for simple companionship during his hour of grief was met with yawns. As he begged his closest friends to watch with him in the darkness, they could not tarry with him even  one hour. All his life's work seemed to be crashing down around him. And worst of all, it didn't even seem like God himself cared. In the consuming sorrow of this night, it *felt* like God had abandoned him. Have you ever felt this soul-crushing sensation? While Jesus knew his Father had not truly forsaken him, every ounce of his flesh contradicted this. Every prayer for deliverance was denied. Perhaps those familiar dark thoughts crept into his mind: "How could a loving Father subject his child to such cruel torment?" "Why doesn't God stop the pain?" "How could such a senseless tragedy be God's will?"

This is the pain that runs the deepest: the asphyxiated cry of Christ upon the cross, *"My God, my God, why have you forsaken me?"* Have you ever found yourself calling to God for help... and receiving a resounding silence instead of an answer? It steals the breath from your lungs. It is the forlorn feeling of a child lost in a department store, surrounded by a sea of strangers. You look for the one who can make everything better-- yet finding yourself all on your own. You find yourself wondering if no one cares who you are, no one cares where you are, no one cares *that* you are. Not even God.

Meditation Exercise

Preparation: Meditate for a moment upon a line from Psalm 116— part of the Egyptian Hallel, which Jesus would have sung that night before departing to the garden: *"The cords of death entangled me, the anguish of the grave came upon me; I was overcome by trouble and sorrow."*

71

Scripture: Slowly and reverently read through **Matthew 26:30-56.**

1. Now imagine the suffocating darkness outside the city gates under the hanging trees of Gethsemane... Feel the black veil of shadows closing in around him... What burdens were pressing upon Jesus' slumped shoulders as he trudged slowly up the Mount of Olives? What sorrows weighed upon his mind? Was he choking with a lump in his throat he could not swallow? Was he fighting back tears?

2. When he arrives at the appointed place of his betrayal, Jesus takes Peter, James and John apart from the others. Imagine hearing Jesus' choked whispers, *"My soul is overwhelmed with sorrow to the point of death. Stay here and keep watch with me..."* How would Jesus have felt when he returned to find them fast asleep in his hour of greatest need? Did he feel frustrated? Rejected? Deserted? Compassionate? Angry? Confused? Exasperated? These were men whom Jesus had poured his life into! Yet *the spirit was willing, but the flesh was weak.*
Imagine how miserably alone Jesus must have felt in that moment...

3. Gethsemane means "olive press." It was probably the place where the olives were crushed until the valuable virgin oil seeped out like tears of blood. Imagine the soul of Christ crushed like the tender olive... Ponder the words of the prophet Isaiah: *"We considered him stricken by God, smitten by him and afflicted. But he was pierced for our transgressions, he was crushed for our iniquities..."* How could God put his beloved Son, in whom he was so well-pleased, through such severe suffering and torment? Both his mind and his body were mercilessly assaulted and bludgeoned to the point of dissolution...

4. Watch Jesus as he casts himself upon the ground with loud cries and tears, *"My Father, if it is possible, may this cup be taken from me. Yet not as I will, but as you will."* Feel the knot in his stomach, the breathless sobbing, as he heaves out groans from deep within...

Feel his emotional exhaustion and physical fatigue... Listen to his tearful prayer as he wrestles with the impenetrable will of his Father...Why must he take this bitter cup and drink it to the dregs? Why must he go through such injustice and abuse? Why doesn't God stop it? Why?!? What other questions do you imagine may have gone through Jesus' mind in this moment?

5. Now, watch as Judas arrives, acting as if all was right between them, greeting him with a forced smile and a plastic kiss...What did the kiss of the betrayer feel like? Judas was one of Jesus' closest friends whom he had shared meals, laughter, and tears... When their eyes met, what was seen in one another's eyes? Listen to Jesus' simple reply, *"Friend, do what you came for"*... What was said in that short exchange? Why does it seem that the deepest hurts always come from those you love the most?

6. Finally, watch as all of his closest friends flee into the woods... How do you think Jesus must have felt seeing these men desert him, who only hours earlier had promised to lay down their lives for him? How could his own disciples have so easily abandoned him?

Response: Now imagine yourself on your face in the garden of Gethsemane as Jesus was. Pour out the hurts of your soul to your Father... Is there some betrayal, some rejection, some pain in your past that you cannot fathom how God could have allowed? Is there a cup of suffering set before you even now that you have begged God to take from you? Have an honest talk with your Father. Are you still able to say with Jesus, *"If it is not possible for this cup to be taken away unless I drink it, may your will be done"*? If you are ready to do so, imagine yourself receiving this chalice of sufferings from God's hand and drinking its bitter wine...

18. His Crucifixion
Sacrificial Lamb for Sinful Humanity

he cross of Christ is the central event of our world. The bloody murder of the Holy One and his willing acceptance of it *for us*—this is at once the low point and the high point of all human history. It is the essential moment of historical reality, transcending time and space, simultaneously affecting all times and places. Every person lives under the shadow of the cross, whether they know it or not. And by our lives we declare whether we bow in worship before it or turn our back on it.

The cross was stamped upon the cosmos before our fated race first breathed the untainted oxygen of Eden. In God's sovereign intelligence, he foreknew the restoration of humankind would demand the blood of his Firstborn before he set the universe in motion. The crucifixion is the chiastic center of God's story, anticipated through the brutal sacrifices of the Old Testament and breathing meaning into each word of New Testament instruction. It is the Tree of Life standing over the garden in the beginning, and standing still in the post-apocalyptic city of New Jerusalem at worlds end. The blood of Christ runs like a scarlet thread through the Bible staining every page red. The cross reveals the wickedness of our wicked hearts. God has granted us a terrifying freedom: the freedom to spit in the face of God. Like Nietzsche, we have tried to kill the God who loves us, who did us no wrong. It hasn't worked. He returns from the grave to tell us he loves us still!

Do not be intimidated if you cannot quite wrap your mind around this greatest of all mysteries. Anyone with the audacity to claim that they have completely figured out exactly how the atonement "works" is dangerously ignorant of their ignorance. Yet our hearts feel the gravity of the cross even while our minds cannot quite say why. The word, "mystery" is not a "KEEP OUT" sign; it is

74

an invitation to endless exploration! For twenty centuries, theologians have used a thousand metaphors to try to tell the significance of what took place upon Golgotha's hill long ago, yet we have only scratched the surface. We grasp at words of straw. Yet its most precise articulation is simply the groan of our hearts—eloquent emotion beyond expression.

Let me try to clarify two of the most important terms associated with the death of Christ: *substitution* and *atonement.* In some frightening and fascinating way, Jesus was our *substitute.* He died *for* us, in*stead* of us, in our stead. As he did for Isaac many centuries before, the Lamb of God took our place before the knife fell. That was *our* cross, *our* debt that he paid, *our* sins that he bore. In a horribly hobbled analogy, the blood of Christ *ransomed* and *redeemed* sinful humanity, condemned criminals doomed to die. He paid the price for our freedom with his tendered life. The perfect justice of God fully satisfied, yet swallowed up in perfect mercy.

The results are described as *atonement:* the bringing together of Holy God and sinful man, reconciling the separation between the two, God *with* us... at-*one*-ment. The cross stands as the connection point between imperfect man and perfect God—with its base planted in the blood-soaked mud of the earth and its crown stretched into the clear empyreal atmosphere of the heavens. In the Hebrew Scriptures, the slaughtering of bulls and goats  impressed upon people that *no sin is without grave consequences.* Every sin required blood—and an innocent victim would pay with his life to make peace with God. Yet here is the most stunning reversal of the primitive instinct of humans to appease the gods with a blood sacrifice: *it is God himself who provides the lamb!* On the splintered beams of the cross, God himself bears the horrific consequence of sin instead of us! God pays the price of expiation instead of us! On that day, a new definition of "love" was written in our Savior's own blood.

75

Upon the outstretched arms of the crucified Christ, all of the contradictions of life are for one timeless moment brought together in one supreme act of sacrifice. Every loose end of this tangled mess is grasped firmly in right and left hand—the tragic ugliness of human depravity and the sublime beauty of divine grace—all things reconciled in one eternal instant! In those pierced and bloodied hands, the furious opposites of the justice of God and the mercy of God are furiously united in one body, each poured out to the last drop. *The punishment that brought us peace was upon him.* The exacting payment of human sin is paid in full by the one human who could afford it— the only human who did not *need* to pay it. God's fierce hatred toward sin and his even fiercer love of humanity, his flaming wrath and his flagrant grace, both expressed without reserve— terribly, tragically, beautifully intertwined on that old, rugged cross. This was the tree of the knowledge of good and evil: where Christ felt the full force of evil from a viciously evil world and the world saw the spectacular goodness of a ferociously good God!

Strangely, the cross was not only the greatest suffering of Christ, it was also his greatest joy. The redemption of humanity was his consuming passion, his life's calling, his moment of glory. *The zeal of God has accomplished all this!* Like a champion rejoicing to run his race, he fixed his eyes on the joy waiting at the finish line. And what was this extenuating joy he fought through excruciating pain for? It was *you!* In his infinite divinity, *your liberation* was in his mind's eye when he proclaimed triumphantly, *"it is finished!"* This was a freely-chosen death, gladly embraced by the Savior-- *that he might set you free!* Can you believe it? Could you ever again wonder if you are loved after so staggering a display of sacrifice?

Meditation Exercise

Preparation: Close your eyes. Fix your mind for a moment upon this crystalline truth: *"While we were yet sinners, Christ died for us."*

Scripture: Slowly and meditatively read through **Matthew 27:32-50.**

1. Watch Jesus, brutally butchered to within an inch of his life, stumbling along the road to Golgotha, with Simon of Cyrene, under the heavy burden of the cross... His naked skin had been scourged and slashed with jagged shards and serrated spikes affixed to whips made of malice... Look at the lacerations raked across Jesus' maimed and mutilated muscles, human rage unleashed... Feel the unbearable weight of the thick, wooden crossbeams pressing down on his stinging shoulder... Ask the Father, "Why must it be so heavy?"

2. Watch the soldiers nail Jesus' hands onto the cross... Hear the stroke of the hammer fall, ringing out like a bell... Watch him wince in agony as the thick iron nails plunge into his quivering flesh...Hear his labored breathing, wheezing like an animal choking in a trap... See the steel-tipped javelin thirsting to split the side of the Savior and rip open his lifeless heart... Ask God, "Why so much pain?"

3. Hear the galling taunts and acidic insults... Look into the haughty eyes of his tormentors. See the stabbing stares of disdain and derision...Why do they hate him so cruelly? Does he deserve this? As you gaze upon the crucified Lord, fall at the foot of the cross, embrace the splintered beam tightly with both arms. Press your face against the rough texture of the wood...Feel the warm, red blood trickling down onto your head, your shoulders, your arms, staining crimson your clothes and skin... What does his blood mean to you?

4. Recall to mind with horror the many sins that you have committed... When have you hated another? What hurtful words have you spoken? What hateful thoughts entertained? Do you realize it is Christ himself who bore each of these sins? Now recall to mind those who hurt you...Can you leave those hurts at the cross, too?

Response: Kneel at the foot of the cross and pour out your heart... Ask: Was this only for humanity in general? Or was it truly for *me*?

19. His Resurrection
Triumphant Victor over Death

his was the day death died. On that bright Easter morning, as the first rays of sunshine began to sweep the darkness from the sky, mortality itself was dealt a death blow. *Imagine that moment*— an infusion of energy from beyond the world flows suddenly into a dead corpse that had lain pale and unmoving three days upon a cold slab of stone! A sudden gasp of breath, heart roaring to life—beating vigorously to the rhythm of new life! Cells suddenly re-animating, blood vessels pulsating, synapses firing—fully and gloriously alive! The eclipse of the Son cannot last forever. The stone will be rolled away and the Light of the World will shine again! This was his defining miracle—declaring Jesus' final undisputed victory over the created order.

He is *Christus Victor*, Christ the Conqueror, the defiant hero who stands alone against the forces of hell itself. And when the smoke clears, *he is still standing*. On the cross, we see Christ's humility. But on the third day, we see him "flexing his muscle." He has the ability to lay down his life—and to take it up again! And that unstoppable power that raised the Victorious Victim from the grave will also give life to our mortal bodies. The resurrection marks his decisive triumph over all the world. Sin and sickness, Satan and evil, even *death itself*, the Universal Marauder, was slain. Rich or poor, good or bad, all pass over the threshold of death into the darkness, never to return. This unknowable yet unavoidable fate haunts our dreams, hiding around dark corners, snatching its victims suddenly away-- our greatest fear and our greatest certainty. The grave has closed its icy fingers around the throats of every creature since the world began.

Yet Jesus tasted the bitter cup of death—and lived to tell of it! He draws out its poison so that the sting of death is no longer fatal. Look into the hollow eyes of death! Stare and don't blink or turn away! You may welcome death without fear, for you will not stay long in his keeping. Embrace him as an old friend, here to lead you to your true home. We need no longer fear death. The grave is only a doorway to a new and infinitely more glorious reality! Through the chrysalis of death, your perishable, earth-bound body will be transfigured into a celestial body whose glory will never fade. Your present life, like the nine months of gestation, is only a dim preparation for that day when you will open your eyes, blinking in the sunlight of a far greater world.

When Christ stepped out of the garden tomb, completely and colorfully alive, it signaled the inevitable defeat of all evil. In the universal struggle between good and evil, *good will have the final word.* If the dead are not raised, the teachings of Christ would be only empty philosophy, recommending ethical living with no guarantee that good will win. But Christ's resurrection is proof of the power of good to overcome evil. It is no longer wishful thinking when we say, *"everything is going to be all right."* It is an immovable statement of solid fact. The daunting problem of evil, with all of its insurmountable difficulties, is, at least, only a temporary problem. On that dreadful day of death, justice died, human decency died, true religion died, wisdom died. The world died at its own hand. But three days later, by God's own hand, a new and greater world was born. And a mysterious gardener walked unknown in the dawn of a new Eden.

This is also the foretaste, the first-fruits of Jesus' final supremacy over this rebel planet. If the tomb could not hold him, nothing can stop his return as promised, clothed in purple and riding upon a white horse. This is wonderful news for his allies and terrible news for his self-selected foes. The sky will be rolled back like a scroll and the risen King will return to claim his own. Sin, sickness, selfishness— all that is wrong under the sun, will be swept away with cleansing fire, the elements dissolving in blazing conflagration. And if we will not let go of our own sin, what will become of us?

His first coming was that of a Suffering Servant. His second coming will be that of a Mighty Warrior. When he first walked among us, he did not raise his voice. When he returns, it will be with a shout and a terrifying trumpet blast. He will come with a sword and will trample the winepress of his fury. If we will not respond to the ultimate expression of God's mercy, then we will face the dire consequences of divine judgment. On that day, there will be no excuse, no dispute. Even now, he is still trying to win us over with his gentleness and love, but if through stubborn defiance, we persist in rejecting him, we will see the fearsome side of Christ. The consequences of opposing the very embodiment of Goodness will be terrifying. You will eventually face your Doomsday, before the risen Christ. He is more persistent than death. And when you finally stand before him, it will be the greatest moment of your life or the very worst. Which will it be?

Meditation Exercise
Preparation: Jesus is with you right now. Repeat in your mind this ruthless request:

> *"I want to know Christ and the power of his resurrection."*

Scripture: Slowly and meditatively read **John 20:1-31**.

1. First, imagine the path leading to the tomb. Is it narrow or wide? Is it only dirt or paved with stones? See the garden, green and flowering with growing life... Now, imagine the tomb itself, with the stone rolled away from the entrance... Run your fingers over its cold surface...

2. Try to experience this story through the eyes of Mary Magdalene. Imagine preparing the spices with the other women early Sunday morning... Smell the sweet aroma of myrrh, a spice brought from the

Far East, given to the Christ child in preparation for this day... Walk along the path in solemn silence with the other women, feet shuffling along the path in the dark...Feel the shock and bewilderment as you arrive at the gaping mouth of the empty tomb...

3. Now imagine you are Mary crying in the garden alone...Taste the tears, feel the sorrow welling up within her... Hear the voice of Mystery asking, "woman, why are you crying?" How would you answer this question? What keeps you from recognizing your Lord? How did she feel when she finally recognized *who* it was...

4. Now run with Peter and John to the tomb... Are they sprinting or jogging? Are they sweating in the cold morning air? Feel the burning in their lungs as they draw in deep, panting breaths... What thoughts are racing through their scattered minds? Confusion? Excitement? Hope? Doubt? What did they expect to see? Peer into the darkness of the tomb... What do you see? Pick up the empty burial shroud and unraveled cloths that, just a few hours earlier, covered the lifeless corpse of Jesus... Touch the course fibers... See the red streaks and smears of Christ's own blood...

5. Now join the cringing disciples in the locked room... What is going through the minds of these deserters, who fled in panic when Jesus was arrested? Why are they afraid? What kind of conversations would you hear among them? Now imagine Jesus stepping out of the shadows into their midst... What would be their first reactions? What would you say or do if you saw this miraculous appearing?

Response: This is the pattern of a resurrection life: *"Weeping endures for the night. But joy comes in the morning."* Are you yet confident that all your tears, all your doubts, all your fears, all your confusion and sadness will eventually turn to joy?
Christ *has* risen... and he is truly right here with you! Talk with him... Ask him to make his resurrection real within you...

81

20. His Ascension
Cosmic Presence throughout the World

o you ever wish that Jesus was still walking around on earth in bodily form? Think very carefully about your answer to this question. Where would he live? Wouldn't he be almost 2000 years old at this point? Wouldn't he be more popular than the pope? How many millions of people would want to have a ten-minute conversation with him? Would ten minutes be enough for you? Is there any chance that you would be able to have a close relationship with this one man? Even when he walked the streets of Jerusalem, he left many listeners disappointed. He left many sick people unhealed. He left whole villages begging for more as he moved on to other places. Jesus knew the limits of the human frame. The human body has a finite amount of time, space, and energy it can expend. It needs to eat, sleep, and wash. It cannot be everywhere at once.

Jesus told his twelve followers it would be to their advantage that he go away. He would give up the narrow confines of flesh and bone so that his Presence might return to them in a more fluid, easily-reproducible form. This he called the Holy Spirit. Just as Jesus had been their constant teacher, encourager, counselor and helper walking beside them each day, they would now have that same divine Voice *within* them. This would make their Messiah and Friend *more* accessible, not less. The Acts of the Apostles tells the story of this momentous transition. When the Holy Spirit of Jesus came upon them, these unschooled, ordinary men would receive that same mysterious power wielded by Jesus! They would learn to recognize him speaking through the Holy Spirit, just as he used to speak to them face to face. *He was still with them,* still leading, still healing, still comforting, still convicting. They learned to cooperate with him just as they had done before. This same mystical communion with the risen Christ is available to *you* as well!

We may lament that we cannot see and follow Jesus in the same manner as the twelve did. Yet this was his promise to them and also to us: *"And surely I am with you always, to the very end of the age."* He can be your teacher too, just as he was to the twelve. We still have access to everything his apprentices had while Jesus still walked the surface of earth. The fact that he is no longer available to us in a human body does not mean he is no longer with us. The results of his present nearness through the Holy Spirit will be effectively the same as it was then. But now it is multiplied.

Christ still lives in human flesh. He still speaks his message through human lips. He still performs his works through human hands. But it is no longer just one pair of hands. Now they are millions. Jesus declares that *we are his body*, the *ecclesia*, the called-

out ones who follow him. This strange band of wanderers and pilgrims now *embody* the physical Presence of Christ to the world. We, the Spirit-sustained students of Christ, have become the Second Phase of the Incarnation! We are to walk in the Way of Christ. *"For those God foreknew, he also predestined to be conformed to the likeness of his Son, that he might be the firstborn among many brethren."* This was the original calling of the assembly which has come to be known as the church. But how we have lost our way!

If you have answered the call of Christ, you have been entrusted with this sacred responsibility: to continue the work of Christ through his very real Presence within you. He seeks to replicate himself in you. This is the meaning of the ascension: the disciples no longer needed God-in-the-flesh walking among them because they were now living it! Now they were to walk in his footsteps, to *be* Christ to the people around them, a new human race patterned after their Master. They were to be the healers, the teachers, the bringers of peace, the representatives of Heaven's Kingdom to this fallen world.

Now, obviously, we are not children of God in the exact same way as Christ was, the unique Son of God. We acquire *by grace* what he had *by nature*. We grow towards the ideal that Christ already had completely attained. We do not have the same degree of perfection that Christ had in this life. His origin was from above and ours is on this earth. And we do not independently participate in the divine nature, but only through the work of Christ. We are able to walk in the footsteps of Christ only because he has already and continues to do it for us. But this does not negate the fact that God expects us to do even greater works than Christ, even in all of our imperfection.

Although the community of his followers is his primary bodily expression in this world, Christ is not absent from everything and everyone else. For he is also the Cosmic Christ, upholding the universe by his word, for "in him, all things hold together." He is not silent to the rest of the global community. He is actively at work revealing himself to anyone who earnestly seeks him. He ignores no one, showing forth the invisible qualities of God's eternal power and divine nature by the things he has made. He is still and has always been the Eternal Word of God: that Creative Force and Wisdom and Rationality behind the created order. This did not change even while he had clothed himself in a particular human life. However, at the end of his brief sojourn upon this earth, Jesus visibly shows his reintegration into the fabric of the heavens with this most appropriate act: He ascends bodily into the soaring skies from whence he came.

Meditation Exercise

Preparation: Quiet your heart and recognize the Presence of Christ within. Take a minute to establish your heart upon three bedrock truths: *"Christ has died; Christ is risen; Christ will come again."*

Scripture: Slowly read **Acts 1:1-14**, pausing at any word that arrests your attention.

1. Imagine yourself as one of the disciples during the 40 days of post-resurrection appearances... Imagine seeing his many convincing proofs that he was alive... Imagine these encounters with the risen Lord...

He also instructed them invisibly through the Holy Spirit. Imagine their surprise upon hearing that Voice, the all-familiar voice of the Master, but now it was *within* them...

2. Why did he warn them not to go on their mission without first being soaked in the empowering Presence of the Spirit? Why was this mysterious anointing so important? What might have happened without it?

3. Now imagine standing with the disciples, upon the hillside as he said his goodbye's... Watch as Jesus body is slowly lifted up into the air, seeing his feet actually leave the ground... Imagine seeing his body float higher and higher, like a balloon disappearing into the clouds... And yet you could still feel that he was *there*, though now unseen... Finally, imagine seeing yourself sitting here looking at this page, *this same invisible Presence surrounding you now!*

Response: Talk to Jesus, for he is truly here by his Spirit, even though you cannot see him! Now listen to see if his voice is speaking to you from within.

Note: Before moving on, you may want to linger in such meditations on the life of Christ. You may take a gospel (Matthew, Mark, Luke or John) and slowly make your way through it, following the same pattern already set forth: vividly applying your senses, placing yourself into the story as if experiencing it first-hand, and allowing Jesus to address you directly about your own soul. Every story, every sentence of the holy writings can provide for you a feast of untold sweetness!

CHRIST-CENTERED

SPIRITUALITY

A HANDBOOK OF *CATECHESIS*
f or
the training of novices
in
THE WAY OF CHRIST

PART II. Meditations on the Mysteries of GOD and the SOUL

21. On the Mysteries of God

ow let us attempt to express the Inexpressible. We turn our attention to the glorious mysteries of that Incomprehensible Essence *behind* who Jesus was. Our next task in practicing a Christ-centered spirituality is *meditation upon the infinite perfections of the invisible God.* I hope, in these next few pages, to increase exponentially your appreciation for the breath-defying magnitude of God. We awaken our hearts to love God by gazing in amazement upon his loveliness. Contemplate the magnificent attributes and majestic images of the Godhead inscribed in our Holy Scriptures. As you dwell upon the descriptions of the Deity, *stir up your heart's desire for the Divine One*!

Who or *what* is God? What does this little three-letter-word mean? What images come to your mind when you hear this word? An old white-bearded man hiding in the clouds? A native bowed to the ground before a grotesque idol? A giant puppeteer pulling strings above the world? Impersonal forces of nature controlling our fate? Surely these pictures are unworthy of the Almighty!

We have been assigned an impossible challenge: *to know the unknowable God.* But can anyone truly know God? Can we really understand him? And yet, how can we love what we do not know? The Infinite God is so far beyond the comprehension of our little walnut-like brains. How can I find words large enough to contain this Mysterious Creative Beyond who spoke the heavens into existence? How can I find pictures beautiful enough to represent this Simple Unity of Being, the Source of all things seen and unseen? To try to fit the inconceivable, limitless Divine Abyss of Unapproachable Light into finite images and concepts is like trying to scoop the ocean into your hands-- you can only really capture an infinitesimally small fraction of the truth about his Absolute Goodness, his Transcendent Beauty, his Glorious Pure Essence in any statement. A.W. Tozer reminds us that, *"God is always greater* than *anything that can be said about him.*" As we try in vain to describe this Indescribable Reality, our words turn to straw and fall lifelessly to the ground. We can only use inadequate "creature words" (the language of created beings for created things) which strain under the weight of a burden they were never meant to carry.

And yet try we must. We must seek acquaintance with this Luminous Being whose searing glory blinds the intellect. The deepest hunger of our souls drives us upon a search for this Primal Entity. If we cannot know him exhaustively, perhaps we can yet know him truly? Perhaps we can scoop up a thimble-full of this vast ocean and in studying it, learn a tiny bit about the unseen depths of the infinite sea? Perhaps the best response is for all the earth to simply stand silent before him. Perhaps we can "know" him only as we "know" a friend, through interaction, not information. Perhaps we can at least affirm that he is incomprehensible, indescribable, ineffable, inexpressible... Can we speak accurately of God's Nature even if we cannot speak adequately? Obviously, we must hold the articles of God with profound humility and care. And when our flimsy assertions about God disappear beyond the horizons of the intellect, let us bow our heads in awe and whisper, *"Holy! Holy! Holy!"* Let us stand in reverence before the *Mysterium Tremendum*-- the Great and Terrible Mystery.

The only hope that we have in knowing this Unknown God is if he reveals himself to us. He must initiate communication. But why would the Everlasting King of Kings stoop to show himself to us? What if God *wants* to be known, person-to-Person? What if the Earth-Maker has intentionally left his fingerprints embedded into the patterns of creation? What if he has left clues in the writings of ancient peoples, using simplified concepts to draw "stick figures" of himself, as we would in teaching a three-year-old about electricity? Much of the Old Testament Scriptures sound like someone educating a child in the dangers, the potential, and the privilege of having a powerful, nuclear-force Entity in their midst! According to the Holy Bible, he *has revealed himself.* Like a father playing hide-and-seek with his child, he *wants to be found!*

What is God like? *He is like Jesus!* There is probably no better answer to that question. When Philip asked Jesus to show him the Father, Jesus said, *"Anyone who has seen me has seen the Father."* Jesus is the exact representation, the definitive picture of the Unseen Being that spoke our universe into being. Jesus is the personality of God in miniature, animated by the very Essence of God himself. As we cannot look directly at the sun lest we go blind, we cannot directly "see" God. And yet, by the illuminating rays of the Sky-Dweller, we can see all else. If we would stare into the brightness of this blinding, shimmering Reality, we must shield our naked eye with the covering of human flesh. As we look through the keyhole of Jesus' physical life in our world, we catch a fleeting glimpse of the Unapproachable Light from the world beyond.

Jesus is the essential first step of our soul's journey into God. Without Jesus firmly fixed in mind, we cannot help but misunderstand God. Without the cross of Christ embedded deeply into our psyche, we cannot know the depths of God's holiness and love. Now that you have spent some time meditating upon the mysteries of Christ, you are already familiar with that certain profound Presence, that intuitive recognition of God's personality. How does Jesus' life illuminate the character of God to you? If *God is like Jesus*, in attitude and disposition, wouldn't this be the most astonishing, exhilarating kind of Deity you could possibly imagine? In fact, if God is *not* like Jesus, I'm not interested! In the face of Christ we see a Creator that cares, that loves, that sacrifices, that lays down his life for you! In all the world's literature, I have never heard of such a thrilling and compelling idea of God! Beauty beyond compare! Goodness extrapolated far beyond imagining! I could not conceive of a God I'd rather believe in than the blindingly sublime Lavisher of Love and Life emblazoned across the pages of Bible! He is truly *wonderful--* full of wonder! Let this riveting vision of God captivate and fascinate your heart till you are *"seized with the power of a great affection!"*

Meditation Exercise
Preparation: Spend a minute now in silent, wordless adoration. Let your heart wander in worship where your mind cannot follow...

1. What are some pictures, synonyms or definitions that come to mind when you hear this word, "God"? In your journal, write out all the words you would use to describe God. Write as many words as you possibly can... Are any words completely accurate or adequate?

Scripture: Slowly and meditatively read through **Colossians 1:15-23.**

2. Reflect on the statement: *"He is the image of the invisible God."* What does this mean? What do we learn about "God's personality" from the stories of Jesus? What does God like? What does God dislike? How does God feel about you? In what ways is this man Jesus like God? How is his humanity unlike God?

3. Now think upon this statement, *"For in him all things were created, in heaven and on earth, things visible and invisible"*... What does "all things" encompass? For a few minutes, meditate upon the all the heavenly bodies in outer space... Now reflect upon the diversity of creatures on earth... Think also of the invisible spiritual realities he has created... Consider the statement, *"He is before all things"*... Think of all of the many historical events you could say he was before... Also think about what it means, *"In him all things hold together"*... What is this galactic glue we call gravity that effortlessly coheres one object to another? What immense power keeps such explosive energy safely encapsulated in the tiniest atom?

Response: Now in your journal, write out a prayer of thanks and worship to this wondrous Wellspring of Worlds.

22. God's Existence
The Ultimate Reality of the Absolute

 od simply *is*. Most people intuitively sense that there exists some kind of Living Entity behind the universe, holding it all together. When Moses, standing barefoot before a flaming bush, dared to ask this Nameless Reality for a name, the answer came, "I AM THAT I AM." What kind of name is that? This Ageless Uncreated One exists in actual reality-- in fact, *reality exists in him!* He is the *Source of reality!* God is *real*-- more real than anything else in all of creation. He *is* existence, the archaic Ground of all Being. Nothing else is as real as he is. He is the eternal "I AM", the Ultimate Reality—uncontingent, underived, uncreated, unlimited. God has always existed and always will. He is *not* an existential crutch constructed by our feeble minds to bring meaning to a harsh world. We do not bring him into existence by our faith; he brought us into existence by his love. Our job is discovery, not invention. We ignore him to our own peril, but he gains nothing by our faith. We do him no favors with our worship. He doesn't *need* us, but thankfully, he loves us. God is truly there, whether we know it or not, whether we acknowledge it or not.

What is God? The Westminster Shorter Catechism is a good starting point: *"God is a Spirit, infinite, eternal, and unchangeable in his being, wisdom, power, holiness, justice, goodness, and truth."* In the next few chapters, as we explore the attributes of God, we will learn *how to think about God*. However, we must not forget the advice of Fenelon: *"The attributes of God are not God himself, nor is the wisdom of God identical with the God of Wisdom."*

God is a *Spirit*. This signifies several things: first, that he is not made up of matter but of some other substance entirely—a non-physical, invisible substance. We cannot see or touch him physically, which means we must become accustomed to sensing him and interacting with him through our own spirit. Secondly, he is *alive*-- gloriously and truly alive! We worship a Living God-- in fact, he is the Source of Life itself. Thirdly, he is a Person-- a Mind, an Intelligence who thinks and feels, wills and desires, creates and communicates, likes and dislikes. Although, he may be "beyond personality", he most certainly is not *im*personal, a mindless force like gravity or magnetism. As E. Stanley Jones observes, *"you cannot talk to a Principle."* Lastly, he has energy, activity, power. He is dynamic, he moves, he acts, he does things. He does not just sit there like a stone.

God is *infinite* in every way. He is unbound, absolute, limitless perfection in every direction-- in time, in space, in attribute, in character. Whatever God is, he is absolutely. If we say God is good, we mean he is absolutely good— in fact, "goodness" is only a description of "the way God is." When we say God is powerful, we mean he has limitless power. We distort God beyond recognition when we imagine him as confined to some religious sphere of life or worse yet to our subjective feelings and imagination. We only begin to see him truly when we see him containing all things, within all things, before all things. When you are seeking to know God, *"you're on a journey into infinity,"* says Tozer. If we had all eternity to explore the absolute attributes of his character, our journey would never come to the end. The odd thing about Actual Infinity is that, no matter how much ground you cover, there is always infinitely more. Let his immeasurable Infinitude shock your reeling imagination to the ground in worship! As the majestic hymn declares, *"When we've been there ten thousand years, bright shining as the sun, We've no less days to sing God's praise than when we'd first begun."*

God is *eternal*—Alpha and Omega, Beginning and End, Source and Destiny of all things. From eternity past to eternity future, from everlasting to everlasting, he *is God*—the Uncaused Cause, the Uncreated Creator of all else. Unlike the universe, which is by nature contingent, God exists of necessity. He is *by nature* Self-Existent, the Unbeginning and Unbegotten One, who did not need to be created... because he already was. He is dependent upon nothing, and upon him, all else depends. He is the Rock, the solid foundation upon which the created order was built. His was the invisible hand that set up and pushed over the first domino. Nothing existed before him because *there was never a time when God wasn't there* (wherever "there" is!). No matter how far back into the past you go, before the cosmos crackled into being, he *is there*. And if you were to go eons into the future, world without end, still he *is there!*

God is *unchanging and unchangeable*—immutable, meaning he does not mutate from one thing to another. He will never alter his essential nature-- there is no need to. Yet the Unchanging One is perfectly at home in the ever-changing flux of our wind-whipped world. The Unmoved Maker becomes the anchor of our souls as time and motion toss us to and fro. He is still the same God who spoke with Adam in the garden, who appeared to Moses upon the Sacred Mountain, who raised Jesus from a cold gray tomb. And he seeks to interact with you today! You can count on him to remain the same. For an imperfect being, change can be good, often signaling a move in a better direction. But for a Perfect Being, a substantial change could only diminish his perfection. Ironically, *God is the simplest Being in the universe*-- he simply is what he is, without pretense, without hesitancy, without change. He is in complete unity within himself, indivisible, always knowing exactly what he needs to do. He cannot help but be exactly and absolutely all that he is. He cannot *not* be what he is. *Behold your God!*

Meditation Exercise

Preparation: Spend a few minutes reflecting on how God dwells in his creation: *"in the elements giving them existence, in the plants giving them life, in the animals conferring on them sensation, in humanity bestowing understanding. So he dwells in me and gives me being, life, sensation, intelligence, and makes a temple of me, since I am created in the likeness and image of the Divine Majesty,"* in the searching words of St. Ignatius of Loyola

93

Scripture: Slowly and meditatively read **Acts 17:16-34**.

1. Look at Paul standing amidst the pillars crowning Mars Hill... Imagine every detail of the Areopagus, that fabled site of disputing deities... Picture his Greek hearers gathered around... Look at the expressions on their faces... Listen to the sound of Paul's voice... Look at their most honest shrine: *"To an unknown God"*...Why do you think they have this anonymous altar?

2. Consider this strange species of Deity Paul is describing: Who is not *"served by human hands, as though he needed anything, since he himself gives to all mortals life and breath and all things."* What kind of self-sufficient God is this? Why would a God who doesn't need us still want us? Restate the verse in your own words...

3. Consider that Almighty God could instantly withdraw life from you whenever he wished, leaving you as a wisp of dust... Pour out your thanks to God for not only creating you but for giving you a new portion of life each morning for these many years... Do you *deserve* the breath of life each day? Have you done anything to earn the right to be created from nothing?

4. The Invisible God intends for you to reach out to him, to search and find him. Why does he want this? How enthusiastically are you searching?

5. Spend a couple of minutes slowly repeating the following phrase: *"In him we live, and move and have our being."* Ask yourself what it means... Write out some of the implications of this statement...

Response: Sit in silent wonder before the unseen face of God... Raise your hands as a physical expression of spirit reaching toward Spirit... End with a brief conversation with the Eternal Cause of the Cosmos.

23. God's Holiness
Transcendent Perfection of the Most High

ere is a truth you must never forget: God is *absolutely perfect* in every way. *If any thought of God is imperfect in any way, it is not God!* This must be our filter as we think of God Most High. If he were anything less than the highest conceivable perfection, he would not be worthy of the name "God". In the words of Anselm, *God is "something than which nothing greater can be thought."* Think about the infinite implications of that statement. This is the sacred assumption beneath every word uttered in Scripture. He is *morally perfect* in his intentions and *functionally perfect* in his ability to carry them out. All that God is, he is perfectly, absolutely, purely. He is already the highest degree of perfection achievable. He cannot get any better because he already is, and always has been, the very apex of anything that could possibly exist.

While I cannot scientifically prove or disprove such a Being, perhaps I can at least assign any other type of "god" to the junk pile of irrelevancy. Can I at least say that any "god" who is not 100% absolutely perfect is not worth discussing, so that we can move on to more pressing matters? After all, I am not interested in wasting my time talking about, worshiping or following a god who—like Zeus on Mt. Olympus—may be higher than all others but not the highest possible. Such an imperfect god, I boldly defy! But before the perfect, unassailably Holy and Sovereign Lord described in the Sacred Scriptures, I humbly bow in breathless reverence. If you want to prattle on about a "god" who is often good but occasionally mean-spirited, powerful but occasionally impotent, wise but possibly mistaken in some cases, then take your discussion elsewhere. This is not the God of Christ, or of the Bible, or of any interest. Christ-centered spirituality rises or falls with its conception of God: he *is either perfect or it all falls apart!* Nothing less than a perfect God will do. That is why questioning his goodness or his ability is actually questioning his very existence. For if he is not perfect, he is a very different kind of Being than we assume him to be. So while I may not understand all his actions, I trust all his intentions. I am as an earthworm before an Einstein. I know his ways are higher than our ways. I know that I am dust.

Our God is *holy*. The God of the Bible inspires the monstrous, fiery seraphim to hide themselves in humble reverence, crying, *"Holy, Holy, Holy, is the LORD Almighty! The whole earth is filled with his Glory!"* This is the God we worship! His Unparalleled Perfection is the very definition of the word "holy". It means he *stands alone, set apart, altogether separate, far above and beyond all other things. He is absolutely pure, undefiled, free from any blemish or imperfection. He is whole, complete, perfect.* He is worthy, deserving of devotion, honor, and consecration. He is special, exclusive, one-of-a-kind, un-common, different from all else. *He is transcendent, wholly other.* There is an infinite, uncrossable chasm between Creator and created things-- one will never gradually evolve into the other. When we pray, *"Hallowed be thy name"* we are proclaiming all of this. Our God is like nothing else!

The closer we get to the Holy One's transcendent perfection, the more we realize our own imperfections. As we become acquainted with his absolute righteousness, the more we feel our own sinfulness-- and the more grateful we are for his audacious grace! Before the glorious Giver of all good gifts, your good works are as filthy rags! If he did not love you of his own grace and goodness, nothing you could do would cause him to love you! And yet love you he does. The closer we are to his immeasurable immensity, the smaller we feel in comparison. God is, in the words of Rudolf Otto, the *mysterium tremendum*, the Awful Mystery that fills us with wonder and dread beyond description. Drop to your knees in hushed silence and whisper, *"Holy, Holy, Holy, is the Lord God Almighty, who was and is and is to come."* We stand at the margins of mystery. For many centuries, the descendents of Abraham would never even ventured to speak the revealed name of God, *"Yahweh"*, which simply means *"I AM!"* Do you dare take his Sacred Name upon your lips in whispered wonder?

Have you yet felt the holy dread, *the fear of God?* How small and microscopic you are when compared to our universe... yet how small and microscopic is our universe when compared to her Maker! Do you dare to stand before such majestic Grandeur with arrogance and self-righteousness? What can we, creatures of clay and water, say when we come face to face with his infinitely-faceted, iridescent perfection, the white-hot glory of his holiness? And yet the closer we come to him, the less we fear punishment and the more we fear to be separated from him, our Supreme Good. The fear of the Lord is not the sniveling, servile fear of a cowering dog cringing before a cruel master. Instead it is the filial fear of a humble child honoring a noble father. When we realize the respect God commands by right, we automatically accord him the utmost reverence.

Come glorify the Lord with me! What is the appropriate response to God's absolute perfection? To give him glory. *"Glory"* is the *recognition and expression of greatness.* As the moon receives and reflects the light of the sun in one reflex action, the human soul is a mirror of God's greatness. Do you see and feel God's blinding perfection? Then show and tell of his beauty and grandeur! Worship is born of wonder. God is glorious whether anyone sees it or not, but the cycle of glory is completed when we ascribe greatness to the Lord with our lips and with our lives. The heavens tell of the glory of the Lord. But as great as the heavens are, the greatness of humanity is greater...when it is reflecting the radiance of the Thrice-Holy King of Glory. Our whole lives can be a theater for the projection of God's splendor! *Humankind was created to reflect the glory of God.*

Meditation Exercise
Preparation: Take a couple of minutes to recognize how this Holy God is present with you... Do you sense him? Bow before him in fascination and wonder...

Ask that he might show his glory to you and through you.

1. Think of any thoughts you may have entertained about God that assumed he was less than perfect... Have there been incidents in your life that made you doubt God's love, his fairness, his ability, his intelligence, his being there? Talk to God about any such incidents. In your journal, confess any unworthy thoughts you have had of God...Ask for his promised forgiveness...

Scripture: Slowly and meditatively read **Revelation 4**.

2. When describing indescribable mysteries, the Biblical writers often resort to a language of symbols and imagery. Ask yourself what each of these symbols could mean. Try to write down several possible reasons for each symbol: the rainbow around the throne, various precious gemstones, the 24 elders on 24 thrones around the central throne, the crystalline sea, the crowns cast down, etc.

3. Place yourself into the celebration around the glittering throne of God's majesty... See in your mind each detail of this dazzling scene... Hear the deafening roar of the worship of millions of people and angels around the throne... Look at the angelic creatures, like mythic monsters, each reflecting a portion of God's matchless splendor...Feel the fear and trembling you would have if you saw such winged behemoths... Let their song fill your soul: *"Holy! Holy! Holy!"*

Response: Write your own hymn of worship declaring the glory of the King of Kings. Do not be ashamed if it does not sound poetic or beautiful. Even the most soaring strains of poetic brilliance could never come close to capturing the consummate perfection of God's transcendent holiness! The most important thing is that it echoes your own heart.

24. God's Goodness
Elemental Source of Love and Justice

hat does God want? What are his intentions and desires? We are often unsure of the motives of others. Often they are a mercurial mixture of good and bad. Even the best of people may sometimes have selfish agendas smuggled in with the selfless. With God, there is no doubt. *He is absolutely, unquestionably good.* There is not a trace of evil in God. He does not have a "mean streak". You never have to wonder if the Life-Giver is only using you or if he will harm you in the end. He unswervingly wants the very best for every one of his creatures. God choreographs all things in a harmonious dance that works out for the good of all! His desires for you are exactly what best suits you for reality-- in fact, they are far better than your own wavering wishes.

God always has your best interests in mind. His will for you is always good! This is the very definition of *love*: a *"will-to-good."* Human love is fickle and fragile. God's lavished love is limitless, powerful, and pure, beyond your wildest imagination! No matter what you have done, the Maker of Worlds cares more for you than you will ever know! It is his essential nature to love-- he *can't help but love you! That's just who he is!* God's love for you is ferocious! It's unrelenting! You cannot dodge it, you cannot exhaust it, and you cannot lose it! But you *can* reject it... and to do so is to separate yourself from the only Force that can guarantee that good will prevail in this dissipating universe.

God is the Essence of *moral goodness*. He does only what is right and never what is wrong. We live in a world of inescapable morality, of good and bad, of right and wrong, no matter how we try to deny it. We cannot flee from one set of morals except into the clutches of another one. We cannot even criticize morality except by borrowing its vocabulary of "better" or "worse"! Morality may sometimes be difficult, confusing, and uncertain, but it is undeniable that there are some ways to live that are better than others. And God himself is the yardstick, the definitive standard of right and wrong. Isn't it glorious that the Law of Living is a Living Person of infinite knowledge and trustworthy character rather than a written code? There is never a loophole to be exploited or an exception that is not considered. God is the Perfect Judge, whose Law is written most deeply in his own Unchanging Being. Yet he is also perfectly compassionate towards the one being judged, wanting their highest good! His judgments are a great deep, unfathomable and vast! If ever we imperfect creatures criticize God's actions (or inactions) or call his decisions into question, we only reveal the limits of our own understanding and the failures of our own flawed moral compass. We can be sure that whenever our finite idea of goodness conflicts with the infinite ways of God, it is we who are lacking, not him.

What is *justice* but *enforced goodness in society*? If God did not care about goodness in his universe, would he be truly good? Can a loving God stand by unaffected when we wrong one another? Perfect Justice knows good from bad. It divides with razor's edge the motives of every action. It sees through deceptions and denials and identifies truth without taint of error. The Great Judge of the Universe, unlike our imperfect human judges, cannot be fooled, swayed, biased, or mistaken. We search in vain for perfect justice among the swaggering sons of Adam. But God is just! He knows evil... and hates it with an everlasting hatred! Injustice is despicable— evil is detestable to the Holy One! He is not apathetic to our cries for justice. With complete fairness and equity, God will judge the living and the dead, all flesh and angels, this divided universe. Where will you stand upon that day--when all books are opened, when all tales are told, when all facts are laid bare? Will you stand innocent-- unblemished, untainted by selfishness, dishonesty, and hostility? Will you be able to watch your life displayed on the big screen and not flinch at certain parts which you wish could be erased? When your secret thoughts are broadcast from the rooftops, will you have any lapses to worry about?

How thankful I am for God's *mercy* and *grace*! For this also is an essential ingredient in God's perfect goodness! If God does not love us, who can stand? Without God's mercy, what would become of our imperfect kind? *Grace* is defined as *unmerited favor*. It simply means that *God really likes us*! God is a God of gratuitous goodness! No matter what we have or haven't done, the Ruler of Earth and Sky wants to bless us. How dreadful it would be if the Supreme Being didn't like you or if he was not morally good! How frightening if the all-powerful ruler of all was a selfish, capricious, spiteful, and mean monster! But then, he wouldn't be perfect, would he?

And because God is perfectly good, his life is filled with *joy*. The God we serve is not dismal and glum. He is joy-filled, happy, and perhaps even playful! God goes about his "life" with child-like delight, bursting with perpetual pleasure and passion. Look at this hilarious world he has made: flowers, rainbows, taste buds, sexual pleasures, and platypuses! Every morning he paints a thousand spectacular sunrises and every evening a thousand brilliant sunsets. And he obviously enjoys his work! With each new creation, he can hardly contain his enthusiasm as he exults with excitement, *"It is very good!"* What kind of Deity celebrates his work with such giddy delight? What a riotous, rollicking Fountain of Life!

So, then...what about God's *wrath*— the smoldering anger we hear spoken of in the Scriptures? Isn't this incompatible with love and goodness? Not at all! His wrath is intense precisely because his love is intense! *His anger is a function of his love, the only sane response to the harm of his beloved children, even when it is self-inflicted.* Our Father cares so deeply about the well-being of humanity that *anything* which jeopardizes it— namely, "sin"— is the object of his intense anger. Sin is the one threat that can ultimately destroy our immortal souls. And sin is the only thing that God cannot protect us from against our will. Our *will* is precisely the problem-- it is where sin dwells. But because God *loves* us, he refuses to override our will. Do you see the difficulty? To the degree that we are un*will*ing to part with our self-destructive habits, our loving Father is angry with us. It is *because he is absolutely good,* that he hates all that halts the flow of good in our lives.

It makes sense, doesn't it? That a perfect Father would be deeply saddened and angry when he sees his beloved children persisting in actions which will ultimately annihilate them? *God's wrath is never an uncontrolled outburst of rage* as we see amongst humans. It is *never a desire to hurt,* to get back at us in retaliation for being hurt. God doesn't hate or harm sinners; he hates the fact that we are sinning, that we are harming ourselves! He hates the possibility that we may miss out on the blessed life he has prepared for us, that we may waste our potential, and that we may degrade ourselves and destroy others in the process.

Meditation Exercise

Preparation: Take a minute to sense God's surrounding goodness.

Scripture: Slowly and meditatively read **Psalm 34.** Spot the different ways God's goodness is expressed to us. Write these in your journal.

1.Reflect on the phrase: *"Taste and see that the LORD is good."* Have you yet tasted, seen, felt, or sensed God's goodness? Or is it something you believe through second-hand knowledge? See if you can right now experience this inner perception of the goodness of the LORD on the taste buds of your soul...

2. Have you seen the jubilant, joy-rousing smile of God? Or have you always imagined a sullen and gloomy frown forever furrowing his brow? Why picture the Perfect Being as moody and miserable?

Response: Talk to God about the many good things you want for your life. Write these in your journal. Why does it sometimes seem like good is not happening in your life? Could the Father of Light ever curse you with something worse than what you want for yourself? Do we always recognize the blessings he bestows?

25. God's Omnipotence
The Raw Power of the Almighty

ll power finds its ultimate Source in God Almighty. Even evil, like a parasite, must borrow its energy from God. Yet even as God supplies power to the cosmos, he loses none. He remains absolutely strong. God is perfectly able to do anything he wants to do, ruling over heaven and earth with effortless expertise. He is supremely competent at running a universe. Nothing can stop God from accomplishing his eternal purposes. The entire natural order of the universe runs on God's energy. Picture in your mind the most powerful things you have ever seen: churning ocean waves swelling to a 30-foot wall of water, the explosive fury of volcanic lava erupting in fiery fountains, the deafening, shrieking winds of a massive hurricane, crashing waterfalls in cascade over a cliff's edge, the ear-splitting thunder and blinding lightning of an electrical storm—that's a glimpse of the raw energy of the Almighty in action! How does it feel to be at the mercy of such colossal forces of Nature?

The encounter with such staggering power may find us trembling. There is such a thing as healthy fear. The fear of the Lord is the gravity that grips us when we realize, *everything depends on God!* He could so easily dissolve the universe with a snap of his fingers! It makes sense to be very concerned about where we stand in relation to him. We must take him seriously—like the reasonable respect of an electrician for electricity. Such immense strength should inspire a reverence, an awe, and a sense of utter humility in the face of a force capable of destroying you in a fraction of a second. Standing before such all-pervasive strength, we may quake! Being misaligned with God is truly a dangerous place to be. In fact, there is nothing in the universe more dangerous than God! Could he not shake the earth like a baby's rattle? Could he not flatten Everest with his thumb? Could he not stop the spinning of the universe in its tracks if he chose to? And yet his perfect goodness guarantees our perfect safety... *if* we are listening to him.

The *fear of God* is not quite like being terrorized by something scary. Somewhere between fear and fascination is the *holy reverence* that falls upon those who have seen the Lord. There is an exhilaration that is only possible when you deeply fear what you greatly enjoy. The risk, the rush of imminent danger is pure adrenaline excitement when combined with a sense of ultimate safety and security. Have you ever looked over a cliff and felt a sensation of surging joy and paralyzing terror all at once? This is what it is like to gaze in wonder over the edge of the Divine Abyss of Holiness! If you find God boring and unexciting, I must conclude that you have never experienced the fierce, unstoppable power of God. The fear of the LORD is the beginning of wisdom. Perhaps you have tried to lock God up in a safe place, to keep him manicured and well-behaved. Perhaps you have never let him loose and experienced the wildness, the unpredictable force of God! You do not yet know the passionate intensity with which your Creator moves!

It is in the turbulent tempest of God's fearsome strength that we find his smile so thrilling! It is only in the midst of life-threatening danger that "being saved" has any real meaning. The followers of Christ must get used to walking into the lion's den. Until you face an impossibility, you will never see a miracle. As we walk in the footsteps of the crucified Lord, we must be prepared to live dangerous lives, filled with risk and uncertainty. But when you align yourself with the all-powerful Commander of the Starry Hosts, there is nothing else to fear. When you stand with the Sovereign God, he will stand with you.

God is *sovereign*—His authority is absolute. Not only does God have the *ability* to do whatever he wants, he also has the *authority*. No one can stop God. He is never overruled. The Supremely Sovereign Lord of the Skies has the power and the right to do whatever he wills in this sparkling universe of his. And while he may choose not to exercise his authority in certain situations, it is

104

always his choice. We have no rights except those freely bestowed upon us by our Creator. Is power inherently bad? Does it corrupt its bearer? Perhaps power only amplifies what is already there. Perhaps even a "small" character flaw becomes a catastrophic corruption when we have the power to get away with it. Perhaps God wants to delegate to us as much power as we can safely handle. And yet, when he grants us more money, we spend it more frivolously and wastefully. When he gives us a higher position, we begin to use it to our own selfish advantage. Why is it that every resource he gives us, we end up using towards self-glorifying ends?

Is anything impossible for God? Well, technically, *God's absolute power does not mean that he can do things that are logically self-contradictory*. No matter how powerful he is, God cannot create a round square-- this would not require ability, but insanity! God cannot lie; God cannot sin-- but it is not for lack of power. It is only because to do so would violate his perfect nature. It would require the Perfect Being to become less than perfect-- which obviously he cannot do! Why would he even want to do that? To do so would not be a sign of strength but of weakness. The Eternal Logos cannot be illogical, for he cannot deny himself. Sometimes our prayers contain hidden contradictions. Can God force a person to love? Is love that is coerced truly love? Can God make us grow character instantly? Can he give you fifty years of experience instantly? Can God teach you patience by making things easy? Perhaps even God himself cannot make you a champion unless you participate in the challenge. A trophy without a trial is a lie.

On the other hand, is there anything that God wants to do that he cannot do? If God is perfectly wise and perfectly good, then all that he wants to do is wise and good. Is there anything wise and good that God cannot do in your life? Is it possible for God to start a stalled vehicle? Does he have the ability to provide money where there is none? Can he restore the atrophied tissue of sickness into perfect health? Can he temporarily suspend the law of gravity over a

Galilean lake? Can he bend time and space to avert a disaster? Can he destroy anything that needs to be destroyed and create anything that needs to be created? Of course he is able! And yet, he rarely does for us what we could do ourselves. He won't do our homework for us. Trust him but don't test him. Beware of asking God why he does not intervene in specific situations-- he often wants to use human hands as channels of his power and he may ask if yours are available. And it doesn't matter how inadequate you are. His power is made perfect in your weakness.

Meditation Exercise

Preparation: Spend a minute in silence recognizing God's powerful Presence pulsating around you...and in you... Can you feel him?

Scripture: Slowly and meditatively read **Job 40-41:11**. Pause if any word or phrase arrests your attention; try to determine its meaning.

1. In this passage, God points out the scariest things that Job knows of and assures him that he is more than able to control these fearsome creatures. Try to describe how Job must be feeling...

2. Name your fears, one by one... What causes you stress, worry, insecurity or anxiety? What are your worst case scenarios, your "what if" situations? Think about all of the life situations that cause you anxiety. These are always driven by fear. Ask yourself, "what am I really afraid of here?" Write down a "fear list" of all of your fears in your journal. Go down the list and compare the power of each fear to the power of God. Which is greater?

Response: Talk to God about each of your fears... Do you ever feel like your Father is unable to do something about the things which you fear? Do you ever feel like God does not have control over a particular situation? Be honest. Have you ever felt like God let you down? If so, talk to God frankly about these experiences.

26. God's Omniscience
Infallible Wisdom of Eternal Truth

od knows all things-- and he knows what to do about what he knows. That is because he has infinite *knowledge* and infinite *wisdom*. We puny earthlings see only one tiny slice of reality, caged by our own limited perspective. Even when we get some of the facts right, we usually don't know what to do with them. *God alone sees reality objectively,* from every angle. With unsearchable wisdom, he sees every possible action and he sees every possible consequence. He knows all contingencies, all potentialities, and all forks in the road ahead. There is no "what if" scenario that God has not already carefully considered. All of this, he sees in an instant! In fact, he has seen it from all eternity, before the first star began to shine.

God sees all things, past, present and future. His understanding is limitless. What were you doing yesterday? Do you realize that before our galaxy was kindled, God already knew exactly what you would be doing yesterday? Before Tyrannosaurus Rex left its imposing footprints, God already knew how your life was going to be marked and scarred. When Columbus sailed the ocean blue, Eternal God already knew exactly where your life's pilgrimage would take you today. He knows the specific history of every atomic particle in the universe, without exception. And he knows history future as well as history past.

Before he painted the first golden sunset, God knew precisely where you will be 12 hours from now, 12 months from now, or even 12 years from right now, to the very second. He knows what food will fill your stomach, what worries will weigh on your mind, how your face will have changed. And even though his *foreknowledge does not cause your decisions and choices* (He didn't force you to do what you did yesterday, did he?), there is no decision that you have made or will make that will catch him by surprise. Yet with all of his

107

foreknowledge, God rarely plays fortune-teller. Most of his prophecies are forth-tellings, not fore-tellings-- less concerned with what will happen tomorrow but with what you should do today. God is always thinking long-term-- if you listen to him, he will prepare and position you for precisely what the future has in store. *Oh, the depths of the riches of the wisdom and knowledge of God!*

Can you trust an Omniscient Being like that? Don't you think that when he says "no", even when you can't understand why, you're better off listening to him? Nothing catches God unprepared. Our ignorance is astounding... when seen in context of the cosmos. Would we be impressed with the scientific observations of the most wise and learned sea slugs? (Rocks hard. Water salty.) Yet, in cosmic comparison, our understanding is closer to the slug than to God's limitless reservoir of knowledge. In all of your prayers, you have never given God new information. When he asks a question, it is not so that we can inform him of something he does not know. It is an invitation for us to think, to respond, to relate. Prayer is not a rational exchange of information-- it is a relational exchange of transformation. If any facts are to be exchanged, it is only when you are listening.

When God Almighty asked Ezekiel, "Can these dry bones live?" the prophet replied with one of the most sensible answers ever uttered. "Lord, *you know.*" No question will ever be asked to which I cannot say with complete confidence, "God knows." He has the answers to our every inquiry. But he doesn't always share them with us. Thankfully, he has given us two stepping stones of wisdom: *reason* and *revelation.* Some who seem sophisticated frown on divine revelation as if it was a replacement for reason. It is not a substitute but a foundation. Reason alone gives only relative knowledge. It needs yet a place to stand, a starting point. The Bible is that fixed point. But remember: *we are not the all-knowing ones-- we would do well not to act like it.* Even when we handle the perfect truths revealed by God, it still must pass through our imperfect hands. So let us give answers only with the utmost humility. And always direct others beyond ourselves to the One who is the Truth.

Look at the beauty and order of creation—not quite predictable, but bearing the unmistakable *logic of art.* Consider the creativity of our solar system. What skillful design and balance! Consider the computing capacity of the mind: could human intelligence have been created by anything less than intelligence? We have a God who knows exactly what he is doing! In light of God's creative artistry, listen to what the inspired writings say about our destiny: *"No eye has seen, no ear has heard, nor has it entered into the mind of men, what God has prepared for those who love him."* There is an immense intelligence behind the universe working day and night to orchestrate a world finale so majestic, so mysterious, so breath-taking that no human brain could ever have imagine it!

Are you in the dark, confused, or unsure? If ever you lack wisdom, ask God. He generously distributes it to desperately seeking souls! Sometimes it is clear direction, sometimes just a gentle nudge, sometimes God wants you to make your own decision, and sometimes he will bring up things which seem totally unrelated to your questions. Even when he leads us along paths of deepest darkness which confound our understanding, be assured. Our Shepherd knows precisely where he is taking us... and the path will ultimately lead to green pastures and still waters.

It's time to settle the issue in your heart: *Who are you going to trust with your life?* Where are you going to place your faith? Here are the three truths that form the foundational pillars of an unshakeable faith: *That God is infinitely good...That God is infinitely powerful... That God is infinitely wise...* To the degree that you are convinced of these three realities, *your faith will be indestructible.* Your life takes on a whole different hue when you are persuaded that the Creator of all things is intelligently working full-time to secure the best possible outcomes for your life and your world. Are you going to trust God's wisdom or your own? When God is leading you in one direction and you think you should be going another, who

109

will win out? Will you rely upon your own limited intelligence or God's limitless supply?

Meditation Exercise
Preparation: Quiet your heart. Ask God to speak to you through his word.

Scripture: Meditatively read through **Job 38:1-33**.

1. In this passage, God asks Job a litany of questions to show how tinny and tiny Job's knowledge sounds in comparison with the vast volume of the knowledge of God. How do you think Job is feeling in this situation?

2. Consider for a few minutes all of the inquiries to which you do not know the answer. Present to him all of your unanswered questions and confusions, doubts and difficulties, perplexities and puzzlements, each unexplained tragedy and inexplicable glory. Write them down in your tablet... How many there are! To do this exercise properly, we would need a LOT of paper! Now joyfully acknowledge that God knows the complete answer to all of our questions. He knows which parts of the answer are beyond our comprehension.

3. Consider all of the things God knows about you. He knows your name.... your history.... your secrets... your excuses... your lies.... your strengths.... your weaknesses.... He knows exactly what experiences will best develop your strengths... He knows the exact day and hour when you will draw your last breath... He knows how to make the most of your life between now and then....

Response: How much do you trust God? Where are your difficulties? Talk to the Heart-Knower about your faith in him... Tell him about the obstacles to trusting him... Ask for his help in overcoming these obstacles...

27. God's Omnipresence
The All-Encompassing Presence

here is God? In what vicinity is his Divinity? God is *everywhere*. He is all around you. As God rhetorically asked the prophet Jeremiah, *"Do not I fill heaven and earth?"* A.W. Tozer comments, *"That sounds as if God were contained in heaven and earth. But actually God fills heaven and earth just as the ocean fills a bucket which has been submerged in it a mile down."* Like a mist filling the room, occupying the very space displaced by your physical body, God's Spirit *overflows* our world, our tiny galaxy, extending beyond the farthest borders of time and space. God *contains* the whole of the physical universe which is a tiny speck of dust compared to the endless immensity of God's Presence. *"For in him we live and move and have our being."* The ancients used to say that the Eternal Lord of All is like a circle whose center is everywhere and whose circumference is nowhere.

Lift your eyes from this page at your "ordinary" surroundings and exclaim with Jacob at this stunning revelation, *"Surely the Lord is here and I knew it not! This is none other than the gate of heaven!"* Oh, that we could envision the cosmos as alive with his energy! God is *here*! Feed your fascination with this fiery Presence! Would you ever be scared again? Would you ever be alone again? Would you ever feel lost again? This is no empty, hollow universe echoing with the faintest sounds of activity from a dying planet orbiting a dying star. The universe is God's playground!

The created order pulsates with life, animated by the infinite God who fills and overflows the natural world. The very air, the oxygen you breathe, is charged with God's Presence. However, we must remember that while we may say that "everywhere" is his location, "everything" is *not* his identity. God is *present* in all things but he is not *equal to* all things. God is *not* a tree— although every tree is penetrated by his Presence, enlivened by his power, and exists only because it participates in his reality. A.W. Tozer quotes an old archbishop who once said, *"God is over all things, under all things, outside all things; within but not enclosed, without but not excluded... wholly above presiding; wholly beneath sustaining; wholly without embracing; and wholly within filling."*

God is *with* you. All day long, you swim through his golden Presence, like a fish through water. If only we could drink in this soul-saturating reality as we go about our lives of traffic, bills, mind-numbing work, and frustrating people. The great blue sky under which you have lived your entire life is brimming over with his vast and endless Spirit! Until you begin to see every location as a potential access point of interaction with the Divine Presence, you will not see the world correctly. When your eyes are trained with an expectancy of seeing God's vibrant goodness everywhere you look, you will begin to notice his smile playing across the surface of the ocean; you will start to discern the music of his laughter in the children's voices at play. Even in his "absence" when you cannot sense him, you will know that he is still *there*, like a friend standing unseen, beside you in the darkness, hearing your every breath.

At any point on this tiny blue globe, whatever else you may find, you may find God there. You are never out of range. No matter where you are, you can lose yourself in his glorious Presence, hide yourself beneath his wings, soak yourself under the ever-flowing waterfall of his grace. He is never far from us when we need him, even if he is hidden behind a veil of invisibility. His *awareness* and *activity* is at least coextensive with the universe. While he may not show himself equally at all places, he is always accessible. We cannot escape his face and do run and hide in vain. When we have done wrong, he has seen us-- even if no one else has. And when we have done right, he also has seen us-- even if no one else has. Do you ever feel excluded by those around you? You can always find a wide-open embrace, a place of belonging right here in the warm heart of God. When you are in stressful straits, whisper into the air, "Where are you, Lord? Are you here?" And know his unfailing reply, "I am."

God will never leave you or forsake you! He is with you always, to the very end of the age.

Why do we sometimes feel distant from God? Why do we feel remote, like he is a million miles away? Distance from God is never a matter of physical location but of relational connection. Closeness with physical objects is only a matter of inches, feet and miles; closeness with persons is more complicated. In a crowded room, we may be physically close to a person and yet relationally completely unconnected. Or we may be thousands of miles away from someone with whom we are connected so deeply and closely, they almost seem to be part of us. Think for a moment of a person who is one of your closest friends... Think of the unseen bond you share with them. What is it made of? Now compare that sensation of closeness to a person who is closest to you in actual distance.

Although God is always close to you, the relationship may not feel close for a variety of reasons. Maybe the distance is due to sin on your part-- or maybe it's not. Perhaps you are hiding from him for some reason. Or perhaps your Father is hiding from you, waiting for you to seek him. Perhaps he is just seeing if you notice his absence, seeing how much you want him. Or perhaps it is due to a lack of communication— you just haven't been making time to talk to him. If you are feeling far from God, ask yourself why this may be... And then decide what you should do about it...

Meditation Exercise
Preparation: Quiet your heart and recognize God's Presence. Ask for God to speak to you through this exercise.

Scripture: Slowly and meditatively read **Psalm 139**.

1. Look back over your life. Can you recognize that God has always been there? Are there points in your past you feel like asking him, "Where were you when this happened?" Listen and see if he answers you... Now look forward into your future... Are there any

doubts in your mind that God will be there every step of the way? If so, talk to him about it...

2. Have you ever tried to escape from your Maker? Why? How have you tried to hide from the Ever-Present, All-knowing One?

3. Now think of your body in the womb of your mother... Imagine your little limbs being formed, the tissues being shaped... Now imagine God looking at this little baby with joy-filled eyes and a proud smile on his face... See if you can feel the outpouring of your Heavenly Father's love upon his child right now...
Consider how God already knew how every day of your life would turn out... Consider how God knows all the bad you have done....
And he still loves you with an undying love! Bathe your soul in the overwhelming overflow of God's love... Pour out your thanks to your Loving Creator....

4. Picture a sandy seashore or desert.... Imagine picking up a handful of sand and allowing the individual grains to run out between your fingers... How many grains of sand do you think were contained in that one handful? Now take up one individual speck of sand. Imagine, upon inspection under a microscope, you find a tiny love note from God etched upon each tiny grain... Reflect on each of the unique thoughts God has directed towards you... Is there anyone else who thinks about you this much? Take a guess at some of the thoughts that God may have thought about you...Think back through your life. Has there ever been a time you felt like God did not see you? Have you ever felt like God was not there for you?

Response: Turn the last two verses of the Psalm to a prayer... Ask God to shine his spotlight through your heart. Ask him what parts of your life he likes... Ask him what areas of your life he doesn't like... Then ask him to lead you... Does he have any specific steps or changes he wants you to make?

114

28. God's Triunity
Eternally-Existent Divine Community

et us examine the paradox. There is *only One God*. There is no other. The ancient Hebrew *shema* proclaims confidently, *"Hear O Israel, the LORD our God, the LORD is One."* The Divine Unity is a welcome departure from a polytheistic pantheon of humanoid deities warring and cheating one another in a cosmic "soap opera" existence. To such a multiplicity of conflicted and confused gods and goddesses, we bid a fond farewell. Instead, there is but One Almighty God who rules river, sky, sun and ocean. Embracing a bracing monotheism simplifies reality. One Supreme Being controls everything, perfect in unity and indivisible in essence. Followers of Christ gladly proclaim the simple One-ness of God.

And yet, there is also a complexity of personhood in God, expressing itself in a Three-ness, that is unlike anything in the human race. There is within the Godhead itself a communal relationship, an interaction of Persons who are yet one and the same Substance. *God is Father, Son and Spirit*-- all three co-eternal, co-equal, and yet One God. In trying to make sense of the strange and exhilarating truth of God's existence as Father, Son and Spirit, the early community of Christ resorted to a short-hand expression to encapsulate this inexpressible mystery: they called it *Trinity*. They declared the revealed truth as boldly as the Scriptures did... without squeezing the confusion out of it. This is the God described in the Divinely-inspired Writings. And even if we cannot fully understand or explain it, we accept it, in all of its glorious paradox. We do not need to change or twist what the Bible says to make it fit better. We recognize that describing the Trinity is like drawing a three-dimensional object on a two-dimensional sheet of paper. Our flat formulations only superficially capture God's full-bodied Mysterious

Reality. Perhaps it is not $3 = 1$, but $3x = 1y$, when we do not quite know what x or y are.

The Father, the Son, the Spirit are all the One God and yet they are in some ineffable way distinct from one another, a Thrice-woven Unity. The God of Holy Scripture is *Father-- God far above us.* God stands transcendently beyond us, as an imposing but loving authority. But he is also the *Son-- God with us.* God himself stands next to us in this world, like an older Brother we can relate to and look up to, and emulate as he teaches us how to live. And he is also the *Spirit-- God in us.* God himself lives in our very souls, guiding us into a life that takes on a Divine texture. Through this indwelling Spirit, we participate in the Divine Nature! We are in some mysterious way drawn into the circle of the Godhead, where we experience the bubbling up of God's Spirit in our spirit!

The Trinity is the complete picture of a God of grace. This is not just a Father God telling you to shape up, as the Muslims have. This is not just a mythical avatar of God that lives a heroic life (for the most part), as the Hindus have. This is not just a divine force within doing whatever it is you want to do, as the Buddhists have. This is a holistic Tri-unity who, while infinitely great beyond comprehension, comes down to live out a life of outrageous love before our eyes, and then he comes rushing into us and lives it in us! *He commands, then he demonstrates, then he empowers!* If you take away any of these Personas from the equation, we are left with an incomplete God who doesn't quite provide all that we need for him to be. There is no room for egotistic narcissism or nervous striving when it is God-in-you that forms godliness in you! From first to last, it is all of God... and all of grace!

God is *essentially relational.* The Ultimate Reality is a *relational* Entity! Within his own Divine Essence, he is love, community, friendship, relationship. The Ground of all Being is Love— by nature! It is part of who he is/they are. Everything that flows between the Members of the Godhead is motivated by love, unity, and mutual respect. Acting always as one, never in strife, these

116

radiant Persons demonstrate intimacy at its primal level, providing the archetype for human community. The Eastern Orthodox Fathers describe the Trinitarian existence as *perichoresis,* an *eternal dance of love* of dynamic movement and co-operation— a mutual rotation around one another. It means that behind this universe, undergirding our existence, a party is going on of three magnificent Persons enjoying each other from all eternity. In many respects, it is like the ideal marriage where each Partner is trying their best to bless and honor and give and serve and outdo one another in reciprocating and expressing extravagant love to the other. This furious dance of fellowship is woven into the very fabric of life itself.

God is not lonely, pining away for friendship, becoming vengeful towards us when we do not provide for his need of love and worship. God doesn't *need* us. We are not doing him a favor by receiving him into our lives. It's for our good, not his, that he calls us to himself. He created us out of overflow, not out of lack. He made us only because he loves us. He invites us into an overflowing Fountain of Inexhaustible Love that doesn't depend upon us. We simply dive into the flood that has been forever flowing. Just enjoy participating in the loving adoration the Son has for the Father. Feast at the banquet the Father has thrown for the Son.

We humans, created in the image of God, are also relational by nature. We are incomplete alone. And our interaction with God is our most important relationship, which all other relationships depend upon. The Trinitarian God provides the pattern of love that breathes life into our friendships. His self-contained love is the wellspring we can draw from to quench our own thirst for love and also to give away to everyone we meet! There is no danger of running out! We don't need to understand the Wonders of the Trinity to be able to enjoy the benefits of essential love it provides!

Meditation Exercise
Preparation: Take a minute to try to sense the Spirit of God within you...Can you feel his Holy Spirit bubbling up from deep within?

Scripture: Slowly and meditatively read through **John 14**, paying close attention to the actions of the Members of the Divine Trinity.

1. Consider the process in your life of how you have come to know God... What role did each Person of the Trinity play in this process? Who did you "meet" first? How did you sense him? How did each lead to and reveal the rest of God to you?

2. Think for a moment of how each Member of the Trinity relates to us. We get to know God in three distinct ways. What would be missing if you subtracted one of these Personages? What if God was not our Father? What if God was not the Son? What if God was not the Holy Spirit? How would your relationship to God be different?

Response: Recite the Trinitarian formula of the Apostle's Creed out loud, along with the hosts of saints throughout the centuries, your voice mingling into an immeasurable multitude in joyous adoration... (you may even want to memorize it!) Use your journal to record any insights or questions or prayers or anything else you wish...

"I believe in God, the Father Almighty, Maker of heaven and earth,
And in Jesus Christ, God's only Son, our Lord,
Who was conceived by the Holy Spirit, born of the virgin, Mary,
Suffered under Pontius Pilate, was crucified, died and was buried.
He descended to the dead.
On the third day he rose again.
He ascended into heaven, he is seated at the right hand of the Father,
And he will come again to judge the living and the dead.
I believe in the Holy Spirit,
the holy catholic (i.e., universal) church,
the communion of saints,
the forgiveness of sins,
the resurrection of the body, and the life everlasting. AMEN."

29. God's Incarnation
Divine Logos in Human Flesh

 od became man. Limitless Creator and limited creature, forever fused into one integrated individual. The Absolute absorbed into the flimsy frame of man, somehow becoming One with weakness. Is there any greater mystery in all the sacred writings of the world? How do we make sense of this? Perhaps we don't. Perhaps all we can say is that *if* such an extraordinary event could occur, then there is no better candidate, no more likely person than Jesus of Nazareth. If any human could claim to be both God and man, Jesus is that man. Among all the wise sages of antiquity, Jesus alone makes this outrageous and outright claim.

According to the New Testament writings, Jesus Christ is *fully God* and *fully human-- not* a sort of demi-god (half-god and half-man, with half the attributes of each, but not quite man and not quite God). Jesus was completely, *100% God.* He wasn't just a wise and enlightened man who taught about God. Nor was he just a powerful angel-- the highest created being, but a creature nonetheless. He was, in the timeless words of the Nicene Creed, *"Begotten of his Father before all worlds; God of God, Light of Light, Very God of Very God; begotten, not made; Being of One Substance with the Father, by whom all things were made; Who for us men and for our salvation, came down from heaven, and was incarnate by the Holy Ghost, of the Virgin Mary, and was made man..."* If Christ is not God, then he may have been mistaken about a great many things. If Christ is not God, then our God is no longer our Savior; someone else is. He only sacrificed one creature for another creature, rather than his own precious blood. If Christ is not God, then the distant deity he declares is not worthy of worship, nor are his teachings any better than an educated guess.

119

Jesus Christ must also be completely, *100% human*. He wasn't just a phantom, floating along the street with only the appearance of a human. Nor was he God directing a human body by remote control, without a human soul and mind. Jesus entered fully into the experience of what it means to be a human in this fallen world, *like us in every way, yet without sin*. He felt real pain, real emotion, real temptation, real friendship, real death. If Jesus was not truly human, then perhaps God does not really *know* us, and he remains forever faraway and unknowable. The cross would be only a

lie without substance. As followers of Christ, we cannot deny either his God-ness or his human-ness or we become entangled in an endless web of error.

How could Christ be simultaneously 100% man and 100% God? How could one person live a dual-natured existence? In some fathomless way, this mysterious God-man was the infinite nature of God and the finite nature of humanity converged into a single consciousness. A.W. Tozer says, *"when you think about Jesus, you have to think twice. You have to think of his humanity and his deity. He said a lot of things that made it sound as if he wasn't God. He said other things that made it sound as if he wasn't human."* The Holy Scriptures make some statements about Christ that could only apply to the Absolute Essence of Almighty God. It also makes some statements about him that could only apply to a weak and feeble humanity. Rather than discount the one or the other, we simply affirm this mysterious unity of God and man, exactly as it is taught in the Bible.

Why would the King of Glory become human? Only God could fully answer that question. I would guess that it must be the best way for the Creator God to establish community with created humanity. What must take place for God to know us and for us to know him? Perhaps God must reveal himself in our own vernacular for us to understand him accurately. Perhaps he must enter into our experience to sympathize with our wretched condition. Perhaps he must show us how great is his love for us. Perhaps he must establish common ground with us: a Mediator through whom we may communicate, face to face. Perhaps he must establish a way of discarding the sins that separate us. Perhaps he must establish a link with us through which he may give us all of the resources we will need to fit ourselves to God. Perhaps he must do for us what we could not do on our own. Perhaps we will never know even a fraction of "why" God would do such an outrageous act. But the fact remains— he has done it! So we *must* be eternally thankful for it.

In the opening words of the gospel of John, we read that the incarnate Son of God is God's *LOGOS*, his Word. Ponder the rich layers of meaning of this "Word" spoken by God. *He is the expression, the concept, the idea, the thought, the communication, the Eternal Art, the self-revelation of God himself. He is the Logic, the Mind, the Intelligence, the Reason, the Divine Rationality governing all things, the Unifying Principle behind all of creation* that the Greek Philosophers deduced must exist. He is the *Creative Power*, the *Wisdom* of Hebrew Tradition, through which God spoke the galaxies into being. As the Psalmist writes, *"By the Word of the LORD were the heavens made, their starry host by the breath of his mouth."* Take up the written Word of God and allow it to communicate to you the Living Word of God.

Meditation Exercise
Preparation: Quiet your mind and allow your heart to ask,
"Word of God, speak to me."
Repeat this request in your mind until you feel prepared to hear from God.

Scripture: Slowly and meditatively read through **John 1:1-18.**

1. Ponder the opening words, *"In the beginning was the Word"*.... *"and the Word was with God"*... *"and the Word was God"*... Take each of phrase separately and mull over its meaning... How can this same Word be "with God" and also be "God" at the same time? How would you explain this blatant contradiction?

2. Consider how all of creation was made through this "Word"... Consider why it is called the Source of "life" and of "light"... What do you think it is saying by this?

3. Now imagine how this *"Word became flesh and dwelt among us"*... Does this contradict the previous statements? Try to describe how you picture this happening...

Response: Take a few minutes to ask yourself what you would expect of a person who claimed to be God in the flesh... How would such a Person act or talk? Write out a description of such a Being in your journal.

30. Our Maker
Creative Artist of Origin

od created us for a relationship with him. But *how* are we to relate to him? God uses many different analogies to capture different dimensions of this most central relationship. He is the Potter and we are the clay. He is the great King and we are his trusting subjects. He is our Father and we are his children. He is the Bridegroom and we are his beautiful bride. We will explore each of these facets in the coming chapters. (You may also wish to muse upon the many other intriguing images that Scripture affords us although we will not cover these in any depth: *The LORD is our Shepherd, our Physician, our Friend, our Peace, our Refuge, our Fortress, our High Tower, our Rock, our Hiding Place, our Banner, our Keeper, a Consuming Fire, I AM, the Beginning and the End...*)

First, let us acknowledge him as our Maker. When we unravel the ancient scrolls of the Holy Writings to the very first words of Genesis, we hear this bold assertion of fact: *In the beginning, God created the heavens and the earth.* Pause for a moment in silent meditation upon this simple statement... What are some of the profound implications if such a radical hypothesis proved to be true? St. Paul writes, *"All things were created by him and for him. He is before all things and in him all things hold together."* His hands formed and fashioned the universe, including this tiny blue sphere we inhabit. We bravely venture into the vast unknown reaches of space yet all of it is known to him. He has the schematic drawings for the furthest galaxy tucked away in his files.

Have you ever given serious thought to where everything came from? Have you travelled backwards in your mind from effect to cause, to previous cause, to previous cause, until you arrived at an absolute beginning— *Something* which, by nature, needs no cause? He created all things *ex nihilo*, out of nothing. What existed before the origin of time and space? Even before the universe exploded into being from a tiny singularity of matter, that original dot sprang from nothing... or, at least, nothing like our physical universe. What is *nothing*? What does "nothing" look like? Can you even imagine it? Anything you picture, if even a blackness or a vacuum tends to become *something* the moment you imagine it! It is exceedingly difficult to talk about "nothing" without falling into verbal hypocrisy. Can I even use the word "before" before time existed? God alone is the Uncreated One. He alone is, strictly speaking, *original.* All else flows from him. And because God created all things, he declares all things are good! No thing is intrinsically bad; evil is only good things being misused. *Evil is a twisted good.*

Perhaps we need to stop and rethink the entire world around us. What if every molecule, every quark, every particle in the universe was joyously created by an enthusiastic Divine Artist? The Revelation says, *"You created everything, and it is for Your pleasure that they exist!"* Love is the glue of the universe! It exists only because God loves it! What if the majestic rings of Saturn, the ice moon of Europa, the tumbling Cartwheel Galaxy were actually made *on purpose* because God thought it would be *good*? What if the towering snow-capped peaks and brilliant sunsets are intentionally-crafted works of art? Perhaps it is no coincidence that the Son of God was a builder, a craftsman, being about his Father's business.

"Wait a minute..." you may object—"Aren't these so-called designs just the results of the laws of nature?" Yes, but who wrote the laws of physics to yield such beauty and symmetry? Who decided (not discovered) Planck's Constant? Who enacted the laws of gravitational force? God created both the raw materials and their meaningful combination. Consider the page you are reading, which is only a combining of 26 letters and a few punctuations in various arrangements. In random patterns these letters would be meaningless. God has not only made the basic building blocks of matter, but has connected them in a way that makes sense, that *say something*. Could it be that when looked at from beginning to end, the universe itself spells out a message? The Psalmist David seems to think so: *"The heavens declare the glory of God; the skies proclaim the work of his hands. Day after day they pour forth speech; night after night they display knowledge. There is no speech or language where their voice is not heard."*

Contemplate the beauty and order of the heavens above. God is the Sculptor of Outer Space, the cosmos his art gallery where he displays his wondrous works: the fiery orbs, the spinning spheres, the elliptical paths of icy comets, the distant colorful nebulae, the rotating Milky Way—all declaring with one voice the perfect skill of their Maker. In the words of St. Bonaventure, the whole material world is *"a mirror through which we may pass over to God, the supreme Craftsman."* Tremble at the approach of the terrible and majestic Power that hung the Pleiades. Fall down in worship before the creative Wisdom that designed the elements. Declare in unison with the community of Christ through the ages, *"We believe in God the Father Almighty, Maker of heaven and earth!"*

Perhaps you need to reconsider *yourself.* You have a Maker and you are his masterpiece, fearfully and wonderfully made! Of all his works on the six days of creation, God waits until after creating us before declaring, "It is *very* good." You are *not* just a piece of junk produced at random by an unthinking process without purpose or design. You are God's poem, his crowning achievement of all creation. Can you see this vision of yourself? Or do you insist that God should have made you differently? Until you come to grips with your identity as a work of art worthy of the skilled hands of God himself, *you will never know who you are!*

What is the proper relationship of a painting to its painter? The song to its writer? Is there not a claim of ownership? Is it not their creative property? This is the basis of the claim of God upon all things. We would not exist if not for him! Who owns this spinning blue orb, bursting with life? *"The earth is the LORD's and everything in it!"* Who owns the lanky giraffe of the African plain? Who designed the tiny hummingbird and the humongous humpback

125

whale? Who do *you* belong to? You belong to the One who summoned you into being from the nothingness.

Perhaps creation is still going on. We are not yet finished products. The Potter is still shaping us. The clay is not yet dry. Perhaps like a potter's wheel, this spinning globe is a place of formation, where souls are being fashioned and finished. He is still taking vessels of clay and asking them to submit to his skillful hands. Yet this lump of clay has a will of its own. It can choose to cooperate or it can choose not to... And perhaps, even more astonishing, he wishes to teach us his trade, placing the tools of creation in our hands of clay. Perhaps the whole purpose of our creation is that we partake of the divine nature, becoming in miniature what God is. We become *created creators* called to *"enter into the joy of our Master."*

Meditation Exercise

Preparation: Spend a moment thinking great thoughts of God— worthy and exalted thoughts of your Creator...

Scripture: Slowly read **Psalm 104**, picturing each image.

1. Think about the world's beauty...What does each creature say about its Creator?

2. Imagine being in the workshop of a master potter. See the shelves, the floor, the tools... Watch him sitting at his potter's wheel. He takes a formless lump of clay and slams it upon the wheel, driving his thumb into the center of it. As it continues to spin, it is slowly formed into a beautiful work of art... See the care he takes as he shapes it with various tools and techniques... If you were that lump of clay, what would you say? Are you allowing him to re-create you daily as his heart desires or do you refuse to stay on the potter's wheel?

Response: Spend a minute in quiet, allowing your Maker to shape your soul. Breathe the prayer: *"You are the Potter; I am the clay."*

31. Our King
Sovereign Ruler of All Things

e must receive God as our King or not at all. If you do not recognize God as the utterly majestic Ruler of All, you do not know God. For a God who is *not* breathtakingly magnificent, commanding our utmost respect without uttering a word is not truly God. This is *not* a meeting of equals. God is "far above us," relationally speaking. We are the servants; He is the Master... though he is a kind and generous Master. Many of us order the Almighty around like a minimum-wage employee. We become irritated if he does not do our bidding in timely fashion. Do not insult the Eternal God with such an unworthy idea! God gives the orders, not us. How shameful for us to presume that the Lord of Heaven and Earth should obey us as we bark out commands! Who really sits on the throne of your life?

The odd paradox is that God Most High ultimately wants us to learn to rule with him. He wants his servants to learn to be kings and queens! But the only way he can entrust us with larger parts of his eternal realm is if we prove faithful in the smaller responsibilities we already have. We increase the range of our authority by exercising it in concert with his endless reign. By doing so, we begin to govern our world wisely, like God does.

He is King of Kings and Lord of Lords— *Sovereign over all of Creation*. God not only made the universe, but also sustains and preserves it by his matchless authority. *"Our God is in Heaven, he does whatever he pleases."* Not a single particle of matter in all the vast reaches of the cosmos is outside of his jurisdiction. *God is always in control*. No matter how badly your little corner of the world has been shaken, God is still on his throne. Nothing has ever caught him by surprise nor has he ever made a mistake. He is the technician of tectonic activity and maker of meteorological motions. He is the majestic and terrifying Presence that appeared on the

Mosaic Mountain in thunder, fire and storm! He is the Earth-Shaker! He walks upon the seas, and rides upon the thunderclouds!

We must carefully delineate the God of the Bible from the absentee deity of Deism. God did not set the world in motion and then take an extended vacation. Jesus describes his Father as intimately involved in the slightest details of our every waking moment, having numbered the very hairs of your head! Nothing is outside the reach of God's invisible hand of Providence, which governs the smallest "chance" events, both the "good luck" and "bad luck". This doesn't mean that he is constantly "tinkering" through tiny miracles every few seconds. However, it does mean that *everything that happens is super-intended by God*, regardless how much may be due to his pre-programming and how much requires active intervention. We can welcome even our missteps and mishaps as ultimately allowed by God. He knows the slips and trips that befall us every day-- and still he permits them! He knows when every sparrow falls to the ground... and every sparrow *will* eventually fall to the ground. Each life is in his hands, and he has appointed for all the very hour when it will end.

Our Sovereign God oversees all of the triumphs and tragedies that transpire in our world. He has "veto" power over every occurrence that has ever happened—the fortunate as well as the terrible. Every earthquake, flood, or famine; every war, genocidal dictator, or high school shooting could have been miraculously averted. Yet he has not intervened to stop these catastrophes! (At least for those that actually happened... We have no reliable way of collecting data on disasters that did *not* take place! You may want to pause and consider the calamities that did not happen this morning...) And of course, we never seem to question why good things happen to us (though perhaps we should...).

But why does God allow such appalling atrocities to come to pass? We should not say that these disasters are good—*they are not!* Yet God assures us that he can extract good from even the worst evils. God has an infinitely better perspective than any of us. In our gross ignorance of the trillions of interrelated possibilities and factors that flow into and out of every chaotic occurrence, we would do well not to accuse God of injustice. We may also think twice about demanding a satisfactory explanation for every event.

But why is there *so much suffering* in this broken world? Why so excessive? Perhaps a clue lies in the Genesis story. It tells how God entrusted the rule of this planet to us. Yet through our rebellion, we now reap the bitter fruits of a godless world. The profound pain we feel is both corrective and consequential to a kingdom that has collectively rejected their rightful King. God evicted us from Paradise because we wanted to expel him. Perhaps it is a sign of respect that God allows us to live with our mistakes so that we might learn through the struggle. Maybe this is why it often feels like God is absent from our world... we asked him to leave. The sky looks farther than it should be. The landscape feels empty because God has allowed us the space to hide... at least for the time being. But make no mistake— the King will return.

The good news is that when the Once and Future King returns, he will usher in a new epoch— pain will finally come to an end, existing only as a distant memory. And as we look back on our own story, like every heroic epic, we will see that our conflicts catalyzed a newfound nobility in our character that we never knew we possessed. So, for now, your great and wise Ruler knows the warrior spirit you have within you, and he has placed you in the thick of the battle till you find the strength and courage he has hidden in your heart. We will then be able to appreciate the creative power of struggle, the beneficial effect of all the tension well feel.

Meditation Exercise
Preparation: Spend a moment in God's Presence meditating upon the command: *"Choose ye this day whom you will serve..."*

Scripture: Slowly and meditatively read **Psalm 99**.

1. The following meditation exercise is based on St. Ignatius' "meditation on two standards": Picture in your mind a medieval kingdom with a castle and its surrounding villages... Imagine it is ruled by a good king—courageous, humble and just...

2. Now imagine that an oppressive tyrant has seized the throne from the rightful king. This cruel dictator crushes the people, using lies and threats to control his subjects... The usurper cares nothing for anyone but himself. Consider the effect this has upon the citizens...

3. Imagine the true king is preparing to return to his kingdom. He sits upon his horse arrayed for battle with his standard blowing in the breeze above him...

Imagine that you are a knight whom he has called to join him: "I am coming back to reclaim my Kingdom. Whoever joins me in this battle must be content to live the life of a warrior. I can guarantee you only hardship, pain, hard-fought battles and sleepless nights. But we will taste victory in the end. Will you join me?" Consider your answer...

Now imagine the false king also attempts to seduce you into his service with many fraudulent promises...

You must choose between these two standards. Whom shall you serve?

Response: Is God your King? Would you eagerly rise to the challenge of following him? Would you willingly die for your King? Discuss your answers with the Sovereign God of the Ages.

32. Our Father
Life-Giving Authority

e are the children of the Most High God. More than God's portrait, we are his progeny. When an artist's house is burning down, which will he rescue first—his painting or his child? Perhaps this is the ideal idea of God: a devoted father with his adoring child. The Supreme Ruler of the Universe, at whose command the sky flees, whose footsteps break rocks into pieces, whose voice thunders like rushing waters... The Majestic King of the Heavens gives us the scandalous honor of calling him, "Abba... Father... Daddy... Papa..." He lets us, creatures of clay and water, crawl onto his lap where he sings over us with joy! Can you believe this? What is this world coming to? What kind of wild wonderland is this world of ours-- where the Creator sneaks out of his palace to fraternize and frolic with his creation with child-like delight? And who am I to partake in such a blessed and beautiful realm? With the innocence of a little girl or little boy, I fling myself into the strong, tender embrace of the Everlasting Father: smiling, laughing, crying, playing, learning—this is the intimacy God wants with us!

But for most of us, this picture is smudged and torn, a faded photograph smeared by a negative Father-image. Many have grown up with a father who was self-absorbed, abusive, easily-angered, or absent. And we often imagine that our Heavenly Father is altogether like our earthly father. If your biological father was not affectionate, affirming, capable and otherwise admirable, you will have difficulty relating to God as such. Was your father your hero? Was he always looking out for your best interests? Could you easily trust him with your life? Or was he only concerned about himself? Did he abuse those he claimed to love? Was he weak when he should have been strong? These betrayals are usually projected subconsciously onto the heavens. To see God better, we must discern the good from the bad in our experiences of our own fathers. God won't give us a stone when we ask for bread or scourge us with scorpions when we ask for mercy.

What is a good father like? (Some people have never seen one!) He is a *provider*— giving his children all they need (not necessarily all they *want!*). He provides your basic material needs as well as your basic spiritual needs. Beyond making sure you have enough food, clothes, and shelter, he assures your spiritual survival with an inner grounding, a sense of self. Who am I? Where do I belong? What am I doing here? Do I matter? These are the questions a father is supposed to answer. We all need someone stronger than us to tell us: *You are my precious child. You bear my name. Wherever I am, you will always have a place to call "home". Nothing can ever take my love from you.* These are your Father's promises. Your father gives you a name, telling you who you are. With his identity as your foundation, knowing beyond shadow of doubt *whose you are*, you can then discover for yourself *who you are*. He furnishes his children with a vision for their potential. Before we can assess our own self-worth, we need someone else to tell us what we are worth. He gives *belonging* and *significance* to our existence. And even as he takes pride in our accomplishments, he does not reject us when we perform poorly. Did your father delight in you simply because you were his child?

The ideal father is also a *protector*. His indomitable strength guarantees a place of safety and security in a world of unseen dangers. His authority gives stability to your home, centering you as you learn to deal with your own feelings, questions and fears. You never doubt that he loves you with a love both fierce and true—that he would lay down his life for you! Was your father such a man? If so, you could even trust his discipline. After all, he must protect us from ourselves. Count on it: God cares more about the course of your future than he does about all the paths of the planets in the Pleiades. In our ignorance and immaturity, we clamor after many things which are actually harmful. In such conditions, he often sets aside tenderness to exercise a tough love that commands strict obedience. Only after we submit to his correction can he return to showing compassion. A good father is stern precisely *because* of his love! God loves us unconditionally but he does not treat us unconditionally. *"Consider therefore the kindness and sternness of God: sternness to those who fell, but kindness to you, provided that you continue in his kindness."* God does not tolerate stupidity among his children when he knows we are capable of so much more. But he is patient as he leads us calmly but firmly out of our foolish ways.

We can learn much about our relationship with God by considering the challenges of good parents in raising their kids: How to provide for your children without spoiling them? How to help them succeed without being too hard on them? How to show your children that you love them unconditionally but will punish them when necessary? How to explain concepts way beyond their comprehension? How to protect them without sheltering them from the hard lessons they have to learn? These are the dilemmas every parent faces. Perhaps God faces these same difficulties with us.

Meditation Exercise

Preparation: Quiet your heart before God.

Scripture: Slowly read **Luke 15:11-32**, placing yourself in the story as you read.

1. What was going through the young man's imagination as he set out for a faraway country in hot pursuit of pleasure? Now imagine what was going through his mind when he was covered in pig slop... Have you been sloshing about in any pigpens lately? Which ones?

2. When the prodigal returns home, what kind of reception was he expecting? Imagine how he would have felt when, drawing near to home, he saw his father tossing all dignity to the wind, running to

him, garmenting him in his embrace, and covering him with kisses? After he returns home, does his father allow him to keep playing with the pigs?

3. Spend some time writing in your journal about what your father was honestly like...What was your overall impression of him? How did you feel about him? How was he like the Loving Father revealed by Jesus? How was he unlike this? Can you come to terms with all of the shortcomings and imperfections of your biological parents? Admit that they, like you, are human, all too human...

4. Can you forgive your earthly father and mother for any way they may have wronged you? Can you accept your parents for who they are (or were)-- the good and the bad? Can you extend to them the same compassion and grace that you expect to receive from God? Take some time to consciously forgive your father for all the ways he may have let you down... You may need to write it out in your journal: "I forgive my father for..." Do the same with your mother...

5. Recall that your Heavenly Father does not suffer from the same imperfections your earthly parents did. Go down the list of your parents weaknesses and renounce the lies that God is like this... Acknowledge his absolute perfection...

6. Now ask yourself if *you* have said or done anything wrong to your parents? Have you cherished any wrong attitudes towards either of them? Regardless what they may have done wrong, you still need to confess before God what you have done wrong... Ask God to forgive your wrongs as you forgive those who have wronged you...

Response: Have you acknowledged God as your Perfect Father? Have you thanked him for his provision and protection? Think of the many gifts he has given you: existence, intellect, imagination, emotional capacity, physical sensations, abilities, resources, etc.

33. Our Bridegroom
Heavenly Lover and Prince

ere is the most shocking picture in all of Scripture: God our blissful Bridegroom and we his blushing Bride! The ultimate goal is not to *understand* God but to *love* and *enjoy* him forever! At the heart of the universe is a divine romance of Lover and Beloved! And it is we, the *Ekklesia*, the called-out community of Christ, who is the prized paramour! This is life's deepest meaning, in the mystical lyrics of Misty Edwards: *God is a Lover looking for a lover.* This truth both validates and transcends that desperate longing for belonging that characterizes romance, marriage and sexuality. We look for that "special someone"—a companion both like us yet beautifully, wonderfully different. It is the very fact that a woman is so very feminine that makes her so attractive in the eyes of her husband. And it is man's masculinity that draws a woman to him.

What is this insanity called romantic love? Let us describe this obsession that brings out such passion, life, enthusiasm and energy! It calls forth heroic acts of chivalry, self-giving and sacrifice. A person enthralled by this madness takes such pleasure in simply *thinking* of their beloved. They can think of almost nothing else! They wish to bring *pleasure* to their beloved. They desire to *communicate*, talking for hours about nothing at all, yet hanging on every precious word. They yearn for *closeness*, to be *with* their beloved. Every moment apart they spend daydreaming, longing with knotted stomach for the moment they will again be together. Could this be how God feels about you? Is this how you feel towards him? *"For the Lord delights in his people"* and he asks you to *"delight yourself in the Lord and he will give you the desires of your heart!"* Unlike the image of a child with a father, lovers must *choose* one another. They must *reciprocate* each other's love: *"I am my Beloved's and he is mine."*

This mysterious attraction compels couples to make *otherwise inexplicable* vows of obligation to one another! Marriage is craziness! It is a covenant unlike any other, a freely-chosen debt, to bind yourself voluntarily to another in lifelong loyalty—this is the deep cry of the romantic heart, one we both fear and crave. When this happens, there is a sharing of identity as the bride adopts the name of her husband. This is the debt of delight Christ is seeking!

Even the bride's and groom's possessions are co-mingled: debts or riches, obligations or privileges now belong equally to both. Do you realize what this means? When I enter into matrimonial covenant with Christ, all that was mine is his; all that was his is mine! I give him my weakness, my brokenness, my inadequacy; he gives me his perfection, his strength, his beauty, his glory! He has borne upon himself all my wrongs and punishments. And since his righteousness is greater than sin, sin is conquered! Because his life is stronger than death, death is swallowed up in victory! Because his freedom is greater than bondage, I am set free! Because his cure is greater than my soul's sickness, I am healed! Because his riches are greater than my debts, they are erased! Yet our greatest joy and bliss is only this: *Christ is ours and we are his... for all eternity!*

But so often this enchanted proposal of intimate romance is distorted into what sounds like an insurance sales pitch: "Do you know where you will go if you died tonight? Will you accept Jesus so that you can get into heaven?" Under such an ignoble misrepresentation, we *use* Christ as a means toward our real goal: a ticket into a gold-paved land of eternal bliss. We fail to realize that *he is our eternal bliss!* Our joyous communion with him *is* the happily ever after! Many so-called Christians "accept Jesus", not to spend a life together in loving covenant, but to get an insurance policy with generous benefits and five-star accommodations! Some even openly wonder how much sins they can "get away with" and still take advantage of the offer. This is *not* the gospel of Jesus Christ! Do you wish to spend the endless ages with your Heavenly

Prince in rapt ecstasy? Or do you try to avoid him at all costs except to keep your ticket valid?

Much of the medieval mystical literature uses overtly sexual imagery to describe the highest aspiration of the spiritual life: an experiential union with God. But this is not their innovation, for it appears on the pages of Scripture itself, most notably in the Song of Songs, which is the Song of Solomon. How irreverent and scandalous, almost sacrilegious for God to compare his desire for intimacy with us to a man's sexual desire for his bride! And yet God does not hesitate to use such erotic imagery to impress upon us how instinctive, how "red-blooded" is his desire for you! This is the mystery Paul declares to the Ephesians: Creator and creature wrapped in eternal embrace, a mystical exchange, a One-ness between human soul and Divine Essence. In this experience of ecstasy, you do not, of course, cease to be separate beings. Yet in some inexpressible way, you *lose yourself* in love with him. God desires you; you desire God—can anything in the cosmos keep this blessed union from consummation?

One reason marriage and sexuality are so carefully protected is because of their potency as symbols of our relationship with God. In marriage, we bind ourselves into a sacred bond: the sizzling passion of erotic arousal and the settled give-and-take of daily cooperation, all fitting seamlessly together in a mutual trust between lovers for life. Yet mistrust and hurt often sabotages even the best relationships. Has your picture of marriage and sex been so corrupted that you cannot see them as something honorable? Perhaps all you know of sex is selfish and shameful—an act that is depersonalizing, degrading and disgusting. If romance has held only heartbreak and dishonesty for you, ask God to show you what it was meant to be: an unbreakable vow of safety, intense intimacy and guiltless pleasure. Let God restore your romantic hopes. There is a Perfect Lover...He whispers to you now.

Before your Heavenly Bridegroom, you can bare your soul. Stand truly naked and unashamed. In him, you have nothing to fear.

Strip yourself of all of your fig leaves— the silly props you use to prove your value as a person. What are the things about you that tend to impress people? Remove all your impressive skills, your achievements, and degrees. Lay aside all of your adornments, your false securities: your carefully-crafted image, your reputation, your positions, even your religious performance. Let it all fall to the ground until all that is left is *you*. Trust me... God will find what is underneath most attractive. He is not impressed with your dignified disguises and falsehoods that obscure his creation. Come to him exposed, with all of your imperfections, weaknesses, mistakes, even sins. Look into his eyes of unabashed love, desire and acceptance. Apart from anything you have done, God is absolutely, ecstatically, wildly in love with *you*-- with the real you! He is crazy about you!

Meditation Exercise

Preparation: Prepare your heart. Meditate on the verse: *"As a bridegroom rejoices over his bride, so will God rejoice over you."*

Scripture: Slowly read the **Song of Songs 1-2.**

1. What is your first reaction to all of this erotic imagery? What does this say about you?

2. Consider for a moment how generous is God's offer of covenant: God doesn't owe anyone anything... but he has chosen in his sovereignty to bind himself in union with us in sacred obligation. This is God's intention for his gathered people: *"They will be my people and I will be their God."*

Response: Disrobe your soul before God. What roles, possessions, or achievements do you cling to that prove your worth? Do you think God likes what he sees underneath?

34. On the Mysteries of the Soul

 ow we are going to look into that mystery you are most familiar with: your *self*, your own life, your own soul. We could leave all of the God-talk to the philosophers if not for this swirling cauldron of yearnings and stirrings in our own hearts. You may ignore your questions, stuffing them down, pretending they don't exist, but they will still gnaw away at your mind like an unsolvable puzzle. Your conscience will continue to clamor. Even as you sit in front of the TV or go out every night, trying to numb or feed this need to feel alive, the empty embrace of loneliness always returns. We are a riddle unto ourselves. We are *pursuing* something-- what shall we call it? Happiness? Satisfaction? Fulfillment? Goodness? Beauty? Perfection? Meaning? Truth? Self-Actualization? Eternal Joy, perhaps? It's difficult even to express what this deepest appetite is... but you *feel* it. Whatever this thirst is, your soul craves it as desperately as your lungs crave oxygen. Human nature is defined by *desire*.

Your soul speaks to you, if you will listen. That profound sense of dissatisfaction, that restlessness that has plagued you all of your life... that is the cry of your soul. Why is the experience of joy so fleeting? Why do our desires seem so insatiable? Why does pleasure tease us with unfulfilled longings? Why this thirst for meaning? Why is *homo sapiens'* intellect so curious for wisdom and knowledge? Why do we search so shamelessly for purpose? Why this demanding moral instinct? *What is your soul trying to say to you?!?* It says in a hundred different ways, "*More... more... more...*There is *Something More... Something Beyond* what you see....*Something Greater* than what you have... *Something Better* than anything you have yet experienced!*" It is a bottomless inner abyss that you try your whole life to fill. Yet all the world is not enough! You must have *more* or your soul will slowly starve.

Your soul's hunger is as real as your stomach's—but *what,* exactly, is it hungering for? We cannot ignore our hunger pangs, but when we begin to fill ourselves with the delicacies we crave, we often become sick. What are we to do? No matter how we try to cater to our longings, it is never enough. The law of diminishing returns eventually takes its toll. We gorge our appetites on physical pleasures, yet only increase our craving and our misery. We drink in an ocean of wealth and riches and yet we are thirsty still. We surround ourselves with friends and meaningful activities in our elusive pursuit of happiness... yet we still feel an aching loneliness inside, crying out with muffled sobs. Why is it never enough?

Life has to count for something! We thirst for purpose! If we cannot find some transcendent meaning, we make one up, so great is this instinct! This is our first clue as to what we were built for. What has your heart been pursuing all these long years? Since your childhood, you have been on a journey towards a destination you could not put into words, searching for Something or Someone who would give us meaning, fulfill all of our ideals, all of our needs, all of our desires. *God has set eternity in our hearts*, leaving us longing, thirsting, questing for an experience of the Eternal.

The human soul has a *capacity for the Infinite*. Anything less leaves us unsatisfied. We are small on the outside, a simple shell of flesh and blood, and yet when we gaze inside, there is a gaping void larger than the cosmos. The scarcity of finite resources eventually catches up with us. We were not made for tiny, temporary pursuits. We were fashioned for the Eternal, the Infinite, the Spiritual.

Whether we know it or not, whether we believe it or not, we have always been searching for God. He is your most desperate need, the absolute necessity for the survival of your soul. He is the oxygen, water, food, and rest for the soul. Your spirit runs on the fuel of God's Divine Essence. Here is the hard truth that few will accept: *No earthly possessions, no bodily pleasures, no worldly fame will ever bring lasting satisfaction. God alone can make us eternally happy.* If God were to give us the whole universe, withholding only himself, it would not be enough to silence our cavernous cravings. There is not enough stuff on our entire planet to fulfill us forever! The man who possesses nothing but God has more than the man who possesses everything but God. Without God, it is never enough.

God's greatest gift to us is himself. He is Goodness itself, the Wellspring of Love, the ever-flowing Source of Complete Joy and Happiness. He is Truth, Beauty, Perfection. He is the summation of all we have been looking for. All that we have ever found admirable in a person was simply a faint recognition of the Divine Image shining forth. J.I. Packer tells us that a *"relationship with God is an experience calculated to thrill a man's heart."* We were designed to find our highest fulfillment in connection with God himself. In him we find unconditional acceptance and love. In him, all other things become good. In him, physical pleasures can become truly satisfying. In him, human relationships can become the powerful, life-giving bonds of mutual affection they were intended to be. In him, our works become eternally significant and objectively meaningful. Try as you might, you will never be completely satisfied with anything less than God. St. Ignatius summarizes the foundational facts of life that all must come to terms with: *"I come from God. I belong to God. I am destined for God."* Until we raise our eyes towards heaven, and acknowledge this is true, we are no more than brute beasts in a field.

Meditation Exercise
Preparation: Take a minute to quietly gaze into your soul and ask yourself: *"What are you looking for?"*

Scripture: Slowly and meditatively read **Psalm 16**, pausing upon any phrase that stands out to you.

1. What do you want out of life? Why are you looking for this? Try to honestly assess and express your highest ideals and aspirations for your life... Write down in your journal all of the words that describe

141

your deepest desires... Are they good things? Then list down all the things that the world promises will make you happy...

2. Reflect on the phrase: "apart from you I have no good thing."... Is that your actual experience? Do you honestly believe you can get what you really want without God? Could it be that perhaps God's Presence is the deciding factor between something being bad or good? Can you think of some good things that turn destructive unless regulated by God?

3. Who are those "holy ones", those saints in your life who bring you delight? What are the most meaningful relationships in your life right now? Who are the friends through whom you see glimpses of God's glory? What are their characteristics that draw you to them?

4. Have you tasted the ever-increasing sorrows of those "who run after other gods"?
Reflect on the times you've tried to find goodness apart from God...
Can you honestly say you are happy with the portion God has assigned to you in life? Are you glad for the boundaries and limits God has placed around you? Or are you still hungering for other pleasures or possessions? Do you think you will be more fulfilled if you were to receive more of these things?

5. Consider whether or not you really believe this verse: "In God's Presence there is fullness of joy and at his right hand are pleasures forevermore"... Do you live as if this is true? Why or why not? What could you do to build your confidence in the eternal reality this verse portrays? How would you arrange your life on this truth?

Response: Spend some time talking to God about what you desire. Ask him any questions you may have. Are there any facets of God that you are having a hard time seeing? Ask him to reveal more of himself to you.

142

35. Your Creation
Image-Bearer of the Divine Likeness

 veryone must wrestle with the question: *"why am I here?"* Is there any significance to your existence? Was your birth just an accident, a chance combination of DNA in a moment of blind passion? Were you unplanned? One of the great mysteries of the Biblical histories is that God is able to carry out his plans with or without the cooperation of human intentions. He speaks through the ramblings of sinners. He works through the failures of beggars and kings. His ultimate will and purpose can still be accomplished in the midst of famine, war, disease, sin and other tragedies which are not specifically his desire. Birth is the sole doorway into our universe and God chose for you to enter it! Why are you here? *God intended for you to be.* In his infinite wisdom and love, *God desires for you to exist*! You are *ex nihilo*, something from nothing. Your existence is not necessary to the cosmic order. Strictly speaking, you are superfluous—an overflow of God's abundant joy. *He wanted you* as his child. Has your soul yet come to rest on this bedrock truth? Say it out loud: *"It delighted the Lord to create me."*

Look deep into yourself and you will see the most beautiful sight you have ever beheld. You will see the *Imago Dei*, the Image of God majestically imprinted upon the innermost parts of your soul. Defaced and scarred as it may be, it is yet unmistakable. Deep in your heart, under all the brokenness and hurt, there is the divine likeness, a primal glory, your true self, your deepest identity. You have been bestowed with a unique dignity far above all other created things-- more than the animals, more than the seas, more than the sun itself. All other things bear only the fingerprints of God; the human soul bears also his portrait. This is your original purpose: you were created to shine! You are one pixel on a screen that displays the dazzling face of God! You were fashioned to reveal God's likeness:

his beauty and wisdom, his goodness and power. Your heart is like a magnificent cathedral, a sacred temple, empty and waiting to be filled with the *shekinah* glory of God.

Your entire purpose is found in *God's "glory": the demonstration of the dazzling greatness of God.* The Westminster Catechism declares *the chief end of man is "to glorify God and enjoy him forever."* If living to glorify God does not sound absolutely exciting to you, you probably have a very narrow view of what it is to glorify God. St. Irenaeus declares, *"The glory of God is a human being, fully alive."* Instead of asking, "what can be done to glorify God?" it would be easier to ask, "what cannot be done to glorify God?" John Piper says, *"God is most glorified in us when we are most satisfied in him."* Everything we are, everything we have, everything we do glows with God's splendor— except sin! In fact, *sin*, an archery term, simply means *missing the mark, falling short of the glory of God.* The Spiritual Exercises of St. Ignatius puts it this way: *"you were created to praise, reverence and serve God our Lord and by this to bring about the salvation of your soul."*

Every person is given a miniscule portion of God's unlimited attributes. God is all-powerful; we have been given a tiny measure of *power*, along with the ability to increase or decrease it. God is all-knowing; we are given a tiny pinch of *knowledge*, with the potential to grow in it. God is present throughout the farthest reaches of the physical universe and we are given a little area of physical space, our own body, in which we are *present*. Along with a droplet of authority, creativity, goodness and many other characteristics of God, we've also been given a certain amount of *self-determination--* the freedom to shape our own existence. Being is grace. We did not choose it. But we choose what we do with it. Heed the words of St. Ambrose: *"Know, O beautiful soul, that you are the image of God! Know that you are the glory of God! Know then, O man, your greatness, and be vigilant!"* What a fascinating, terrifying privilege!

We are souls *in utero*, eternal beings in embryonic form. *"You are a never-ceasing spiritual being with a unique eternal calling* to count for good in God's great universe," as Dallas Willard proclaims. God has very high expectations for you-- he expects glory, a soaring greatness from you! He wants your potential actualized. Radiate his glory and in doing so, reclaim your own. *"For we are God's workmanship, created in Christ Jesus to do good works!"* You have been called and commissioned to rule and reign in your own limited sphere of influence.

Ours is a hidden glory, an unrealized glory, given to us in "seed" form. It will either grow to full potential through drinking in the rain of God's Spirit... or it will be wasted, trampled underfoot, stolen away by the birds of the air. God has placed the chisel in your own hand, to make choices that will shape your own eternity. You have been given responsibility to decide for good and against bad. You have been entrusted with the next act of creation, within yourself and this world. The path we choose will lead to either *dehumanization* or *divinization*: our final form either triumphantly more-than-human or tragically less-than-human. Through repeated response to God's leadings, we rise up to become sparkling reflections of God... or through constant neglect, we sink to become no more than animals, hairless primates playing in the mud.

We will never realize our full potential apart from God. It is God's Spirit flowing through you that enables you to become an instrument of peace, an agent of goodness. The further you move from God, the further you are from your own goodness. Only through integration with God do we achieve integration with ourselves and our true purpose. Every decision that moves us closer to God moves us closer to our own ultimate joy and destiny.

Beware! Do not become drunk on the thought of your own greatness. You may become sick from meditating upon your own glory, if you do not keep in mind two corresponding truths: *the glory of your neighbor* and *the greatness of your sin*. All I have said about you applies equally to the most boring, repulsive, irritating person you know. Don't be so arrogant as to think that you alone are created in the image of God but your neighbor is not. The

145

disagreeable masses you pass on the street, the friends you joke with, your irksome family members, and the very person you like the least, all bear the same enchanting imprint of God. You cannot love God and at the same time hate your neighbor. *Sin matters because you matter.* It is the greatness of your destiny that makes missing it that much more tragic. (We will discuss sin in the next chapter.)

Meditation Exercise

Preparation: Acknowledge God's hidden Presence all around you.

Scripture: Slowly and meditatively read through **Genesis 1.**

1. *"In the beginning, God created the heavens and the earth"*... Why does God open with these words? What is implied about all we see?

2. Reflect upon each of the six days of creation...Imagine the forming of each entity...Imagine God's child-like delight as he saw that "it was good"...Consider the creation of the first human soul, the grand finale of the greatest art display ever... Have you yet realized that your existence is a good thing? Imagine God's joy as he looks upon you, hearing his exultant voice declaring of you, *"Very good!"*

3. Think of a time many years ago, before even your parents were born. At that specific time, did you "exist" in any form? Where were you-- your soul, your mind, your spirit, your unformed body? Did God have any knowledge of you at that time? How much did he know about your life? Why did he create you? Why did God draw you out of the void of non-existence to bring you into this reality in which you now live? Do you think God had good intentions for you when he created you? Does he still...even knowing your worst sins?

Response: Are you grateful for your chance at existence? Are you humbled by the fact that every good thing is from him? Are you sorry for any rebellious attitudes? Ask God what he thinks of you...

36. Your Sin
Self-Destruction of the Human Soul

Something has gone *terribly wrong!* What in the world has happened? Perhaps as I have been describing the glories of God and the wonders of his creation, a dissonance has been slowly forming in your mind: If everything is so perfectly good, then *what is wrong with the world?* Why is this world, *your* world, *my* world, so full of pain, misery, and death? Why on earth is each day stained with suffering, hatred and injustice? Why do our hearts ache with such deep loneliness, alienation and dissatisfaction? Why do I so often feel like I've been removed far from God's Presence? Why is my lifescape scattered with the skeletons of failures, broken relationships, and bitter tears? Why can't I consistently do what I know is best for me? How can I simultaneously love and hate the same person (including myself)? We are broken people, living in broken families, part of a broken society—conflicted and fractured. Our world is adrift in a sea of suffering. We dare not make light of the pain and evil in our world. We cannot pretend it does not exist or is only illusion. Has God made a mistake? Has God forgotten us?

The sacred Scriptures sum up the world's problems in one single word: *sin.* Sin is essentially *a disorder of the human soul.* It starts with a disconnect from God; it results in a disconnect from ourselves and from others. The Biblical doctrine of sin is one of the most freeing, hopeful and cheerful truths this dismal world has ever heard! It means that *evil is not our essence!* It preserves the undeniable beauty and worth of a human being even when faced with the often despicable and revolting monstrosity that is human behavior! And it holds out a hope for the healing of the world's hurts. We have already considered the intrinsic greatness of humanity; we must now come to terms with its obvious and total depravity.

We are walking contradictions, question marks with legs. How do we make sense of the statistical certainty that *every human*

147

being, no matter how noble and good-hearted, will intentionally do things they know are wrong? Why do we feel alienated from our Creator, from our world, even from ourselves? How do we explain this universal sense of estrangement? C.S. Lewis, in his masterful book, *Mere Christianity*, claims that every honest and reflective person knows two basic truths— #1: *there is right and wrong*, and #2: *we sometimes do wrong*. Have you ever thought about why any species of creature would ever engage in behaviors that it knew was destructive to itself? Why do we inevitably do things that we know are bad for us? Human experience tells us that a wall has been erected between creature and Creator. So who built the wall?

John Henry Newman describes our predicament thusly: *"the human race is implicated in some terrible aboriginal calamity. It is out of joint with the purposes of its Creator."* This is the daunting doctrine of *original sin*: we inherited a disordered disposition from our forefather, Adam. It is not a *condemnation* against us for a crime we didn't commit; it is an *explanation* for the obvious contradiction we find within! Through some awful primeval tragedy, we have had a falling out with our Father. We now have a terrible inborn tendency to injury. We have fallen from grace, and our fall is magnified by our God-given greatness. We have defiled the very image of God within our own souls! O how the mighty have fallen! Did God create sin? No... not directly. Sin is synthetic, a man-made compound, a misuse of God-given capacities. God gave us the raw materials which we fashioned into the weapons of our own destruction. He gave us rope and we have hung ourselves with it.

Sin is a *separation from God which naturally results in soul-destruction*. It is, firstly, a *relational* reality, a stance of mistrust towards God at the core of our being, a willful rebellion of creature against Creator. We are unplugged from Goodness himself, a self-imposed exile and independence from the Source of Life, a child biting the hand that feeds him. Every mutually-loving relationship requires a certain level of trust-- and we have broken trust with God. This detachment leaves us scrambled, powerless, confused and alone. So the solution to sin is *not* to try to clean up our act. *We must start by being reconciled to God.* Once we fix the relationship, we can begin to cooperate with God as he fixes everything else. This relational disconnection *causes* the practical dysfunction.

Sin is secondly, a *functional* reality. Because we have detached ourselves from that electromagnetic Force that energizes and integrates our souls, we fall apart. So sin is brokenness, a defect in the human machine, an innate inability to do what is best in our daily lives. We are out-of-order, like a faulty grocery cart which automatically goes crooked instead of straight. When we fail to love God, we lose our ability to properly love our neighbor or ourselves. Apart from God, the compass of our heart is disoriented, no longer leads us properly toward what is right and good. *God hates sin like a caring doctor hates cancer.* He doesn't hate the patient. He hates the parts of the patient that are slowly killing him.

Individual "sins" are only symptoms of a soul damaged by sin. Rage, stealing, adultery-- these are outward signs of an overall downward trend of a life severed from its source of direction. The Ten Commandments are a wonderful diagnostic checklist— a few indicators of what a properly-functioning human being should be able to do with no problem. Sins are not a list of arbitrary laws God just decided to thrust upon us! They are dehumanizing behaviors that will destroy us! Every sin is an *act of destruction*, slowly deteriorating both our own souls and the souls of those around us. Like the designer of an amusement park ride, God tells us what behaviors are dangerous (remain seated, please!), not to diminish our enjoyment, but to increase and protect it! Trusting God means believing when he says something is bad for us, *it really is bad for us*, even if we don't understand. God is neither arbitrary, nor mean-spirited, nor stupid when he prohibits certain activities and attitudes. His commands are blessings, not burdens.

As you read this, is your mind continually thinking of the sins of others? We must recognize right from the start that *we are part of the problem.* We each have pockets of resistance towards God in our own hearts. Soltzinytsin tells us, *"the dividing line that cuts between good and bad passes through every human heart."* Have you yet come to the realization that *there is something radically wrong deep inside of you?* Do you *see* that your own soul is mortally sick and in need of a cure? Until you recognize this, you *cannot* follow the Way of Christ! Why? Because the Way of Christ starts with the assumption that something in you is wrong and needs to be made right. *If you don't need a Savior, you don't need Christ.* If you are not convinced that you are in trouble spiritually, then please put down this book and get to the business of saving yourself by yourself. Christ will not "help out" your effort to be your own lifeguard. The Way of Christ is only for those honest souls who can admit unreservedly their own sinfulness.

Meditation Exercise
Preparation: Spend a quiet moment enjoying God's goodness.

Scripture: Slowly and meditatively read through **Genesis 3.**

1. Picture in your mind the idyllic paradise of Eden...Smell the grass, the trees, the earth... Listen to the gurgling rivers and chirping birds...Look at the greenery and the clear blue sky above... Touch the leaves, walk on the grass with your bare feet...
Everything is perfect... God's quiet smile rests upon all you see...

2. Now imagine the confrontation with the crafty serpent... Hear the seeds of mistrust spoken to Eve... How would believing this adulterate her friendship with God?

3. Imagine the first act of disobedience... How did Adam and Eve feel after they had bitten the apple? What changed inside of them?

Response: Is any area of your life filled with shame, blame, or "hiding" from God? Do you feel cheated out of any forbidden fruit?

37. Your Salvation
Restoration of the Human Soul

here is no evil God cannot undo. He is a God of considerable ability. Your Heavenly Father can fix anything! Like a child with their broken toy, bring it to him. What is broken in your life? Your self-image? Your emotional health? Your confidence? Your memories? Your mind? Your body? Your habits? Your family? Your friendships? Your relationship with God? As Dallas Willard reminds us, *"Nothing irredeemable has happened to us or can happen to us." In* God's hands, *everything* can eventually be set right. But we must first admit we are broken.

We cannot fix ourselves. Sin, like a virus in our bloodstream, is too deep, too pervasive. This aggressive soul-disease spreads through our lives, crippling our hands so that we cannot perform the surgery. If you set out to save yourself from the ravages of sin, you will die in your sins. Only a fool would attempt such a hopeless task. You cannot reach the moon by your own strength; you need a power far greater than your own. Turn your human restoration project over to God; He will move heaven and earth to make it happen.

God is an expert restorer of precious art. He alone can bring out the divine image in your soul. He will purge sin with blood and fire. He will wash away years of pain and guilt in the waters of forgiveness. He created us... he can re-create us when we are damaged. No matter how far you have fled from God, no matter how deep the self-inflicted wounds, no matter how scarred and battered your soul has become, you are perfect candidate for transformation! No one on earth is beyond hope! *God has NOT given up on you*! He can begin the healing process right now—this very instant! All he wants is your invitation. He loves you just as you are, but he also loves you too much to let you stay that way. Only repent of your feverish pursuit of nothing before you actually possess it!

151

Since our sin is both a relational brokenness (separation from God) as well as a functional brokenness (disintegration of personal integrity), its cure must also be two-fold. Salvation is *reconciliation* and *regeneration*: restoring our broken relationship with God and restoring our soul's proper functioning. Theologians have expressed these two phases of salvation by saying you are *justified* from the penalty of sin and *sanctified* from the power of sin (these are not so much "steps" as a "cause-and-effect"). You receive *forgiveness* from the guilt of sin leading to actual *freedom* from the grip of sin.

Sin starts with separation from God; it is reversed through a whole-hearted *reconciliation* with God. We must first come to grips with our flight from God before we can turn around and begin our soul's journey home. Salvation begins with a move towards mending our broken relationship with our Creator. And God himself has made the first move! He has literally given his Firstborn to redeem you. The birth, life, crucifixion and resurrection of Christ were all steps towards restoring this ruptured relationship. God has done all he can to invite you back into friendship. Like the prodigal son, come to your senses and come home to your Father! To the degree that something separates us from God, it is sinful. God is more than willing to forgive every offense you have ever committed.

True holiness is true humanity. God wants to renew in you the unblemished purity of a newborn. He wants to restore you to the unspoiled innocence of a child. Allow God to wash away all of the dirt, filth, guilt, and grime that has accumulated over the years. Allow him to pour his healing waters over the open wounds on your soul. On the cross of Christ, he shows in gory demonstration that he will take all of the destruction you have ever done to yourself and to others and bear it all upon his own flesh. He will do whatever it takes to undo sin. Your soul becomes as white as fresh-fallen snow.

The moment the rifted relationship is healed, we can begin the process of *regeneration*, of rebirth from above. The first phase of salvation (reconciliation) happens in an instant, requiring only an invitation; the second phase (regeneration) takes a lifetime and

152

requires our constant co-operation. Once we are reconnected to God, his regenerative power can spread through all areas of our atrophied flesh. With the branch reattached to the vine, the life-giving flow can progressively bring flourishing and fruitfulness. Do not pinch off the flow of divine energies, by saying "no" to the breathings of his Spirit. Sin is addictive. And we are often very slow to surrender our precious poisons. I have to warn you: this can be a painful process. As God begins to inhabit the house of your soul, he will want to renovate each room according to his specifications. Let him dispose of all the junk.

How do we enter into this salvation of our soul? Our *salvation* is by *grace* through *faith.* This means that our restoration to spiritual life, health and freedom comes about only through God's generous, undeserved favor and riches which we gain access to simply by trusting him with child-like confidence. We are made right inside as a result of relationship! That's all we need to get started! An intense faith easily lays hold of infinite power and wisdom from God's storehouses. There are no Herculean works we must do to earn God's acceptance. It is freely given to all!

Faith is an earthquake! *Actually trusting God* alters the entire landscape of life! When you remove your mental foundations from the world of men and replace them upon the Word of God, it changes everything! This one simple decision will send seismic vibrations through all of the structures of life. We will *think differently* and *change our minds and attitudes* about sin, God, money, sex, love, and life-direction—this is called *repentance.* We will also experience such a resurgent influx of God's power and goodness into our lives that good works flow naturally. We cannot help but put heartfelt effort into doing his will once we accept that he only commands what is absolutely best for us. This is the unforced obedience of a friend; not the obligatory obedience of a slave. We follow and obey the One we trust, so *true faith always leads to repentance, good works and obedience.*

153

So here is the crucial question on which your destiny hinges: *do you trust Jesus?* If you answer an unqualified "yes", an entirely new world swings open. Christ himself will be your Way, your Truth, your Life for all of eternity! Here is God's ultimate purpose: *to populate a perfect world.* Its inhabitants will trust and adore their perfect ruler and joyfully follow his perfect laws. But participation must be voluntary; it cannot be forced. So for those who choose to opt out, there will be an alternate site (covered in the next chapter).

Meditation Exercise
Preparation: Reflect on this trustworthy saying: *"Christ Jesus came into the world to save sinners— of whom I am the worst."*

Scripture: Slowly and meditatively read **Romans 8:1-18.**

1. Have you experienced your own profound need for God? Do you desperately need a Savior? Where do you experience guilt, fear and shame? What areas of brokenness do you need to bring to Christ?

2. Have you given up trying to save yourself? Or are you still trying to earn God's favor? Have you renounced your own righteousness and good works as a means to impress God? Have you cast yourself unreservedly into the arms of your Savior?

3. Have you experienced God's acceptance and felt his forgiveness? Are you "in Christ"? Has all condemnation fallen away like autumn leaves? Do you feel this impulse within, deep as your bones: That *you are a child of God?* If so, drench yourself in this amazing feeling! If not, pray fervently for God to show you how he loves you!

Response: Do you really trust Jesus? If so, tell him so... If not, what obstacles, doubts, or fears keep you from trusting him completely? End with Kierkegaard's prophetic prayer, true of every person of faith: *"And now, with God's help, I shall become myself."*

38. On Hell
Ultimate State of Unrestrained Selfishness

ow what of this idea of hell? Isn't this inconsistent with a loving God? Not at all! Hell is proof that God has a profound respect for human decision. *God does not torture people...* but perhaps he will not protect us from the torment we inflict upon ourselves. If we make clear that we don't want him in our lives, perhaps he will grant our request. Hell is *not* God lashing out with wounded fury at a person for spurning him. Hell is Jesus' description of *the inevitable destination of a person's flight from God.* It is God giving you exactly what you want most... if what you want most is not God. All unrepentant sinners eventually find their way into this place of unrestrained self-centeredness and unending hatred. What if hell is only the world that naturally results when God leaves us to our own devices, a self-chosen devolution of humanity? If you consistently choose to go down on the elevator instead of up, you will finally reach the very lowest level. Your "punishment" is just the consequences of your own habitual decisions, the descent of man into darkness.

Heaven and hell are symbol words that represent the spiritual landscape and atmosphere of a life more than a physical location. Heaven or hell could easily exist in a sister universe or our own beloved world at some future time! Hell is the utter collapse and implosion of the godless universe upon itself. It is described in symbolic terms as unquenchable fire, devouring worm and outer darkness—the junk pile of the universe. All roads away from God eventually lead here. Hell is loss... searing loss of all good forgone. It is our being shut out from the Presence of God forever, excluded for all eternity from our own highest good, from our true selves, from one another. What if this rift of separation becomes permanent and irreversible? Self-destruction and the destruction of others become obligatory, not imposed from without but spilling over from within.

155

Before you start down a path, be sure you want to arrive at its end point. If God is perfect Goodness, perhaps his absence will mean the complete absence of Good. What if all that was beautiful and right was sucked out of the world, draining all life and color out of the picture? Imagine an existence devoid of all meaning: pleasure without joy, conversation without communion, ambition without purpose, sex without satisfaction, relationships without friendship, no right or wrong, no one to obey and no one to love, world without end. Does it send a shiver down your spine to think of such an endless cycle of godlessness spiraling on forever and ever?

Consider the severe logic of hell. The Law of Sowing and Reaping tells us that sin produces its own destructive consequences. "The one who sows to please his sinful nature, *from that nature* will reap destruction!" God doesn't destroy sinners— sin does! *If* God honors human choices, *if* human sin is destructive, and *if* human beings are eternal, how could hell *not* exist for those who choose eternally to sin? Ask yourself: *What is a loving God supposed to do with a sinner who refuses to leave the path to destruction?* Should he force you to come with him anyways? Should he extinguish the flame of your existence? Should he allow you to try to live out your life apart from him? Should he put you by yourself so that you don't harm anyone and no one harms you? Or would the loneliness be worse than the measureless mayhem that would result from putting millions of flagrant sinners together? If we say we want to live without God, do we really understand what that would look like?!? Like a 5-year-old who runs away from a loving home, we may find that being on our own is not the never-ending party we anticipated. Is it even possible to participate in a world of perfect goodness if we refuse to live lives of perfect goodness?

Imagine a beautiful garden planet, filled with trees and waterfalls. Now imagine that God has gathered up a multitude of people and deposited them into this ideal setting. Sounds like paradise, doesn't it? Here's the catch: every one of these residents has *chosen* to live a self-centered life, seeking their own immediate gratification at the expense of anyone else. Power-hungry, pride-filled, bloated with lust, driven by greed and envy, living only for the next fix of momentary gratification— all right and wrong has been abolished and there is only gnawing thirst. Selfish desire is the new absolute. But it is never enough to fill the countless empty souls. It escalates—and it always leaves them wanting.

Sin, like acid, dissolves our original goodness. Love and trust become a distant memory. Every interaction would be an exercise in mutual manipulation, using others for your own selfish purposes—and knowing they are doing the same to you. There may be alliances of convenience, but even these could not last long without humility, reconciliation, and forgiveness. It would be a place where anyone could easily take revenge upon enemies... but there would be nothing to stop them from returning the favor. How long would it take before this beautiful planet is transformed into an apocalyptic war zone, a never-ending game of king-of-the-mountain? And not only millions of defiant humans, but perhaps hordes of demonic spirits also in this same state of rebellion and chaotic conflict.

Will there be literal fire in hell? There could be-- set not by God, for he abandoned this place long ago; but fire set by hate-filled people in a raging world of vengeance and grotesque depravity. Every resident will have tormentors aplenty and they will also have the opportunity to serve as torturers themselves. They become walking dead, reaving zombies whose only desire is to feed, to kill, to rape, to destroy. Evil is always hungry. Humans would become ravaging animals—or worse than animals, for animals have not the power that we do. How would such an escalation of evil ever stop with no one around to say, "This is not right"? What if this vicious pursuit of pleasure at others' expense never ended?

Meditation Exercise
Preparation: Spend a couple of minutes soaking in God's Presence...

Scripture: Slowly and meditatively read through **Romans 1:18-32**.

1. Consider how sin begins: *"although they knew God, they did not honor him as God or give thanks to him"*... Why does this start the process of sin?

2. Consider how God punished sin: *"He gave them over"* to the natural result of their sin... What if God allowed reality to take its cut, allowing sin's consequences to compound upon itself eternally? Is there anything unjust about this? What if God stopped trying to contain sin? What if God took all that he brings to the world (love, goodness, etc.) and left? Reflect on a universe which God gave up on... Imagine him closing the door, tears in his eyes, assuring us that he will never bother us again... Imagine there's no heaven... nothing to live or die for... imagine all the people living for today...What would make such a life worth living?

3. Reflect on *a life without right or wrong*-- where everyone just does exactly what they feel like doing... What if all inhibitions were cast aside? How would we relate? How would typical conversations sound? What would marriage or family look like, if it were possible at all? What would work look like? What acts of violence would be done on a daily basis? What sexual perversity would be commonplace? Does this picture freeze your blood with terror?

4. You have already seen hell on earth. Where have you seen hatred unchecked and anger unleashed? When have you seen greed running rampant? Where has uncontrolled sexual lust or insatiable addiction swallowed up entire lives until they were devoid of all beauty and inner vitality? Where has oppression and self-exaltation created hell on earth? Describe some places where hell seems to reign... Meditate upon what beliefs and mindsets cause these hellish conditions...

Response: How would you live if you saw clearly how the flight from God leads straight to destruction? Ask God how you could combat hell right here and now on this planet.

39. On Heaven
Ultimate State of Unrelenting Goodness

Y ou have never really been home before. On this earth, you are only a wandering pilgrim, a stranger in a strange land, with no place to lay your head. Your soul is homesick and you don't even know why. In this life you have had only momentary glimpses of your true country. A. W. Tozer assures us, *"There is another and a better world than this vale of tears we refer to as home."* Perhaps you've experienced flashes of your heavenly homeland: in breath-taking experiences of nature's beauty, in nostalgic longings for a magical memory, in a bittersweet song that transported you beyond yourself, in a fairy-tale world that seemed more real than our own, in the rapturous feelings of falling in love, or in the ecstatic encounter of God's holy Presence that left you wishing you could dwell in that awestruck moment forever. When have you heard those whispers in the wind of the "happily ever after" your heart has always told you existed? Where have you seen these windows of eternity that flash before us for only a brief instant-- and then they're gone? How have you felt this longing to be wrapped in goodness and beauty, not just for a moment, but forever? And yet, no matter how hard we try, we cannot make this feeling last. Before we have truly tasted its sweetness, it is only an aftertaste.

This world is not where we belong. Ours is not the best possible world-- it is the necessary step before the best possible world. Our world is suspended halfway between heaven and hell. It is the fork in the road that allows us to self-select which eternity we are better suited to. We are now becoming creatures who will be fit for either a God-centered universe or a self-centered universe. We will either sink into an existence that can only be described as hellish or we will ascend upon a path that rises to the utmost heights of the heavens. It is your decision to make now. This world is only the trial run. Your afterlife will be an extension into eternity of your ideal demonstrated in this swiftly-lapsing life.

What makes heaven "heaven"? The most important ingredient, the one essential thing is that we will be *"with God"*. It is the full experience of God's immediate Presence, complete union with our Creator, God-in-us and we-in-him. If you have spent your whole life in pursuit of God and his goodness, it will be the complete actualization of your deepest dreams and the fulfillment of your greatest desires. In fact it will exceed our wildest imagination in ways we do not even know is possible! The God-seeker will experience in that everlasting moment the ecstasy of self-transcendence, when faith becomes sight. In the words of Henry Suso, *"What is united on earth remains undivided in eternity."* As we lose ourselves in God, we will finally, eternally, find our true selves. But for the person who has spent their life avoiding God, how could they endure? Do you want to live forever in the full force of God's unrelenting Presence? Do you enjoy being with God?

The word "heaven" may be a bit misleading. More accurately, our eternal destination is *"the new heavens and the new earth."* It is a transformed universe, glorious and immortal; filled with transformed beings, also glorious and immortal... one of whom will be *you!* Perhaps God will give us the keys to play upon the equations of quantum physics to refashion matter at will. Perhaps we may access each tiny filament of energy with our minds for a new potential of creativity. God is anticipating the moment when he can entrust unlimited power to us. But for now it seems, with power so corrupting, God dare not give us unmeasured capacity.

It is difficult to describe the surpassing greatness of the coming reality in the primitive dialect of our current reality. In the Holy Scripture, this heavenly afterlife is symbolized with many diverse images. This union with the Divine Essence will, in some mysterious way, *make us glorious like Christ.* As St. John the Evangelist writes in his first letter, "Dear friends, now we are children of God, and what we will be has not yet been made known.

But we know that when he appears, *we shall be like him, for we shall see him as he is."* As we praise God's glory, we actually enter into that glory and it becomes ours! Our declaration of God's greatness eventually leads to God's declaration of ours! Our quest for Christ will find its destination *when we, with unveiled faces, gaze into the mirror of his glory and find that we have been transformed into his likeness with ever-increasing glory!*

Heaven is described as *a place of feasting and music,* a party that never ends, with God himself, singing and laughing, the jubilant Life of the party! It is a victory parade, a marriage banquet, an awards ceremony, an everlasting holiday! We are not just spectators but central participants in this rollicking romp. It is the celebration of the union of Christ with his people and the final triumph of good over evil! We will be the beautiful bride dressed in white on her wedding day. We will be the battle-scarred warriors honored by all of heaven as heroes. We will be richly rewarded for all our toil, for every tear shed, for each unseen act of kindness. The saints of old shall seek you out to shake your hand and welcome you into their noble company. How long will we celebrate before we really realize *this bliss will never end!* There is no morning after.

And greatest of all, *we will attain God's approval!* Imagine the tears you will shed when God himself declares, in the face of all you have endured, *"Well done, good and faithful servant."* Won't it silence your self-doubts and insecurities forever to have your true Father, of whom your biological parents are only surrogates, smile upon you and pull you tight to his chest in eternal embrace? Does it thrill your heart to think that Someone higher than all the rulers of this world will recognize you for all you've done? From this lofty vantage point, we will finally look back on our earthly existence and all will make sense. We will see how the toughest struggles produced the sweetest victories. We will see how our tiny task fit into God's worldwide work. We will finally put our feet up and enjoy the fruit of a hard life's labor. Let us enter into his *Sabbath-rest.* This is not the boring rest of inactivity and mind-numbing amusement. It is the sacred *shalom* of God: peace, harmony, wholeness and justice—a society without conflict.

And yet in some wild and wonderful way, our work is only just beginning! A whole new world awaits, a world of our own making. We will be swept into a Second Genesis, a re-building of the universe in which we are now co-laborers with the Creator-in-Chief. We will be given responsibility to govern and generate value on a massive scale— of which our earthly works were only practice. In co-operation with our Creator, we will tackle spectacular projects of supreme significance. We were meant to rule the cosmos with Christ as *Kings and Priests* of a whole new reality. This is our re-creation!

With the viral infection of sin completely eradicated, it will finally be safe to know one another: honestly, wholly, without masks. We will see the unblemished beauty of every person. The lion will lay down with the lamb. All will rest in the shade of their own fig tree. So ends all hostility, all pain, all insecurity, all shame. This is the enduring vision God had in mind when he first spoke the universe into being: joy-filled humanity in perfect unity with their Creator!

Meditation Exercise
Preparation: Quietly invite God to flood you with his Spirit. Pause...

Scripture: Slowly and meditatively read through **Revelation 21-22:5.**

1. Meditate upon the imagery and symbols described... What does each image say about the atmosphere of a heavenly after-life? Which images captivate you? When have you experienced heaven on earth?

2. Do you want to spend eternity in the immediate Presence of God? What would that be like? Is your ideal life filled with temporary things or eternal?

Response: Talk to God about how to bring more of heaven to this earth... End by reflecting on the phrase, *"on earth as it is in heaven."*

40. Your Nature
The Architecture of the Soul

To care for your body, you must know your body. The same could be said of your soul. The proper care of the human soul requires at least an elementary knowledge of *how it works*. Just as your body is comprised of digestive system, circulatory system, skeletal system, respiratory system and more, all working together, your soul is an integrated self made up of "parts" (though not in the spatial sense), each requiring nourishment and care. You cannot treat a bruised knee, a heart attack, a brain tumor, and a runny nose with the same medicine. The remedy is determined by the type and extent of the injury. As Christ pours his healing medicine into your soul, you must also cooperate with his restoration project.

What causes this odd phenomenon we call human behavior? Everyone from the counselor to the coach to the advertiser makes certain assumptions about why you do what you do. A.W. Tozer shares with us the secret of the soul: *"human nature is still in formative state, being changed into the image of what it loves!"* We are like wet cement— still capable of being formed, deformed or reformed. Aquinas says, *"all human actions set up a bias towards similar actions in the future."* Christ plans to transform us. So let us decide how we might best become our eternal selves. Using Dallas Willard's framework of human nature, gathered from the fields of philosophy, psychology and theology in his book, *Renovation of the Heart*, we will sketch out the roughly 6 different aspects that make up your life. Each component is inter-related with all the others and a malfunction in one area negatively affects all the others.

1. The first aspect of our nature is the *will*. In the Bible, it is usually what is intended by the words *heart* and *spirit*. This is the core of who you are. Your will's primary job is to direct your life by

163

making choices. It is these uncaused choices, more than anything else, that define you. Every day is a crossroads: you are right now making decisions that will determine what kind of person you will be for the rest of your life... and beyond. Even non-decisions are decisions! Not choosing to do something is practically identical to choosing not to do something. You are a free agent: regardless what you think or feel, regardless of your upbringing or your genetic predispositions, regardless of favorable or unfavorable circumstances, you still have *a deepest freedom and responsibility to decide how you will respond to every choice.* It is in the will that sin resides. It is also in the will that your deepest resemblance to your Creator is found. Therefore, as the Proverb says, *"Above all else, guard your heart, for it is the wellspring of life."*

2. The second aspect is your *thoughts*. Included in this intellectual dimension are your reasoning, beliefs, imagination, knowledge, and memory. Our thoughts are the scouts of our will, constantly searching out every bit of information to evaluate what is true and real and good. They fit things together into pictures and stories. They tell us, to the best of their abilities, *what is, what could be, and what should be.* One "secret" of the spiritual life is that whatever fills your mind will affect the direction of your life in many obvious and not-so-obvious ways. The more you *think* about an action, the more likely your heart will head in that direction. *Your will cannot choose what your mind cannot conceive.*

3. The third aspect is your *feelings*. These incline you towards or against the idea or object you are thinking about. Emotions have tremendous power to move us, to affect us. However, by definition, they are not reasonable. One of the great challenges of the spiritual life is *disordered affections*, i.e., feelings that draw you towards what your mind knows is bad for you. Master your emotions by demanding an account: clarify *why* you feel as you do. Turn loose your reason on unreasonable assumptions. What image, what truth (or untruth), what ideas are they connected to? You will gain a great deal of self-knowledge by constantly asking yourself, "why am I

feeling this way?" Your *thoughts* and *feelings* together compose what is usually referred to as your *mind*. The *will, thoughts, and feelings,* are roughly equivalent to what psychologists refer to as the *ego, superego, and id*, respectively.

4. The fourth aspect is your *body*. Even after you have made a decision, this choice must travel through your physical body, a material object in time and space, to become an outward action. This piece of meat, a mere collection of molecules arranged into a tangled mass of nerves, bones, and muscles must obey properly for you to accomplish anything. Your body is an amazing storehouse of energy, information, and habits. Your body can be trained through repetition to do things without thinking—thus it's power, for good or bad. After all, we are creatures of habit: 99% of what you do is done without reflection or conscious decision. Your body simply takes over and does what it has been conditioned to do. Your brain, the control center of the body, is the primary interface between mind and matter. In the absence of thought or intention, it will continue to carry out previous orders. And yet your body is part of *you*, and you are held responsible for what it does.

5. The fifth aspect is your *social relationships*. A person without some stable, loving relationships is not a whole person. Your friendships are a part of *you*. You cannot truly live as a completely autonomous self. Even if all you have are broken relationships of rejection, abandonment, bitterness and hate, they are still your relationships... and they are still shaping you. And do not forget that your connection with God is your most fundamental relationship, for good or for ill. If this relationship is absent, you are missing the most important part of your *self!* You cannot ignore God and others and still have a well-integrated soul.

6. The sixth and final aspect of your nature is your *soul* itself. This is the subconscious "operating system" that binds everything else into one whole and unified life. A well-ordered soul has been cared for according to God's laws. It will go largely unnoticed, humming along like a well-oiled machine. However, the tragic effects

of violating God's laws will not go unnoticed. Many of the wreckages of human lives we see are simply the dis-integration of soul that results when people are unwilling to live according to God's instructions. We don't have to understand how the medicine works in order to follow the doctor's orders and reap the benefits. When the underlying order of life is disturbed, everything built on it is shaken. This is why we will often use the term *"soul"* to refer to *"the wholly integrated totality of the human self"* which includes all the other parts as well. All of these different dimensions function within a context of God's universal Presence which can interface with each aspect of our lives as he chooses.

Meditation Exercise

Preparation: Quiet your heart with the phrase: *"He restores my soul."*

Scripture: Slowly and meditatively read **Romans 7:7-25**.

1. A question that has plagued theologians through the ages concerns the "freedom of the will". Is your will free or bound? Let's experiment to determine the extent of the freedom of your own will: What are some things you can do by making a clear and determined choice? What are some things that you could never do, no matter how motivated you were?

2. Many obstacles limit our will's ability to do things. What are some of the limiting factors that keep you from following through on what you really want to do?

3. What are the ways in which our feelings stop us from doing what we deeply wish we could do? What are some things that you find yourself doing against your better judgment?

Response: Talk to God about the malfunctions in your own soul. What good intentions seem to elude action? Ask God for help.

The Architecture of the Soul

Adapted from *Renovation of the Heart,* by Dallas Willard. Copyright © 2002.
Used by permission of NavPress, All Rights Reserved.
www.navpress.com   (1-800-366-7788)

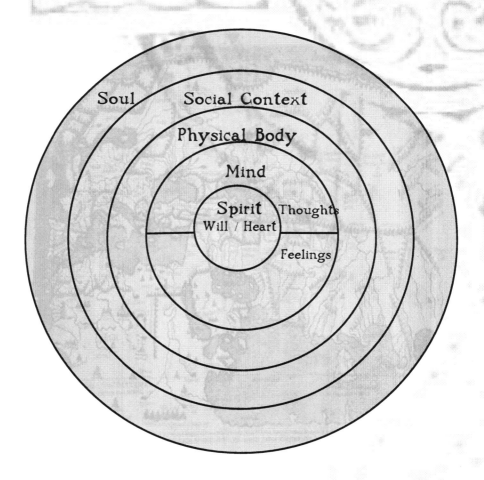

Infinite Environment

Soul

Social Context

Physical Body

Mind

Spirit
Thoughts
Will / Heart
Feelings

41. Your Past
Exclusive Pathway to the Present

s your past a prison? Are you handcuffed by an unbreakable chain of events that you are powerless to change? Many of God's children are trapped in yesterday. Some get stuck in past successes; far more get mired in past miseries. If you are slowed by fantasies of former glories, you may need to discard your dusty trophies in order to press on toward a higher calling. If you are wracked by memories black with pain, these too will need to be swept clean. Do not dwell on past victories. And, by all means, do not dwell on past failures! Both are quicksand. Both keep you from living from the only place you can act in: this glorious momentary flash of freedom called the present. We cannot change the past, but we can change the future.

Do your memories sting your eyes with salty tears of regret, wondering why things didn't turn out differently? In your mind, sift back through the black-and-white images of where you've come from... Do you wish you had a more respectable upbringing, more understanding parents, a better-looking or healthier body, *a different life*? Are you disappointed and miserable with your spouse, your children, or your career prospects? Do you feel like the cruel fingers of fate have dealt you a losing hand in life? Do you ever imagine that you were somehow destined to be a failure from the start? Do you carry a concealed hatred towards someone who has scarred you so horribly that it feels like they have stolen your life away from you? Do you ever find yourself harboring a hidden anger towards God for allowing your history to unfold the way it did?

If you answered "yes" to any of these questions, you will probably find, underneath it all, this tragic fact: *that you hate yourself*—simply for being who you are. And who are you in this warped picture? Someone in the wrong place at the wrong time. Your past is part of you... and *you cannot reject your past without rejecting yourself. And self-rejection is a serious sin, for it is ultimately a rejection of the God who created you.* If your self-image is one of shame, ugliness, disgust, and resentment, then you need to revisit the dark room where you developed these distorted images. Have an honest, uncensored talk with God about what you hate about your past. Does your wounded heart scream out, "*Why?!? Why did you allow this to happen instead of that?*" Do you need to let flow the bitter tears you've been holding in all these years, as your loving Father God presses you close to his chest? Grieve, mourn, cry out to God your frustrations, fears, sadness, and anger. Let the God of all Comfort hold you tight in his warm embrace. We must first accept the past before we can transcend it.

So what are we to do when the reruns return? Do we relive our greatest regrets? *Regrets are not erased by rejecting your past, but by reframing it. We must reframe our horrific past in light of our glorious future!* Face the facts: The past is irreversible...but it is not irredeemable. Refuse to be abused by your past any longer! Though your past is maimed and your present seems marred, the future begins now! Today can be a turning point, a day of reckoning—when you recognize the worst the world can throw at you will never stop God's relentless love from reaching you! No matter how obscene, degrading or shameful yesterday was, no matter how devastating or tragic the events that have transpired today, *even these* cannot foil *God's plans for a glorious you!* See your broken memories in context of the magnificent story God is writing: *"I may have suffered a terrible wrong...but even this cannot stop my Savior!"* Never let the past have the last word!

God does not erase the dark smudges of our past. Instead, he incorporates them into a work of even greater beauty, so that somehow the picture is enhanced by its imperfections! God is a Master of improvisation, generating a work of genius from whatever mess we hand him. He extracts sweetness from bitterness, life from death. Break the shackles of shame: refuse to be defined backwards by what happened. Instead, insist upon defining yourself forward by what God is inevitably making of you: *the likeness of Christ!* What if *you* have done wrong? If so, the answer is not rejecting yourself but repenting of sin. Repentance announces a new intention in tension with the past: *"I did wrong...but this is not who I want to be."* It makes no excuses but accepts the blame. However, it doesn't wallow in the wrong but bathes in the right! Simply invite God to renew and remake this mess you have accomplished.

Here is a truth you must remember: *Your past is the only pathway to your present.* God has wrapped up a wonderful present for you today, and an even more amazing future for you tomorrow— but you cannot get there except through yesterday! Your past, however difficult, has shaped you into who you are right now—the product of your past regrets. *There is no you but this you!!* It is a fruitless fantasy to wonder about such impossible possibilities as: "what if *x* hadn't happened to me?" If *x* hadn't, it would no longer be *you* sitting here today, reading about the furious love of God for you. A different person would exist, with different priorities, doing who-knows-what with their life. And I am quite certain that God loves *this* you, the one sitting here today-- not some theoretical other you that could have existed in an imaginary world where things were different. Christ hung on the cross for *who you are right now!* He desires relationship with *who you are right now!* He has exciting plans of a hope-drenched future for *who you are right now!* And God's plans only apply to the *real* you. You are right now in the right place at the right time for an outpouring of God's grace!

Time is an odd thing. It turns every event into a chapter in a story. Your life inevitably tells a tale, filled with beginnings and endings. But what kind of tale will it be? Is it a sad story or a happy story? It all depends on how it ends! If you allow him to author your future, Christ will guarantee a "happily ever after" ending beyond your wildest dreams! Every story worth telling involves the overcoming of difficulties. No one will sit through a story without any conflict. The most uplifting stories of courage and beauty always contain great sufferings. Here's the common thread in the stories of great saints: they all testify with one voice that it was the hardships that unleashed them, that brought out their best, that made their lives significant. Count on it: if your past entails dramatic pain, then God intends a climactic victory! No hero escapes suffering. A race is marked out ahead of you; run it with all your might! The starting gun has already sounded. Let us make the most of the time before us.

Meditation Exercise

Preparation: Ready your heart for an honest moment before God.

Scripture: Slowly and meditatively read **Romans 8:18-39.**

1. Think back to your earliest images of childhood... the home where you lived... What were your parents like? Are your memories full of joy, hope, and happiness? Or are they full of pain, hurt, and ugliness?

2. Think back over your life... What have been your greatest frustrations... failures... mistakes... tragedies... regrets... Think about your relationships... spouse... children... friends... enemies... Can any of these stop God's redeeming work in your life? Can anything in all the world stop you from communing deeply with God right now?

3. Think about your body... Your looks... your health... your appetites... your sexuality... Have you been nursing a secret hatred for the body God gave you? Have you wished you were someone you're not—coveting your neighbor's life?

Response: Bring to God all that you are... Who is this person God created? Do you see the delight God takes in *simply who you are?* Is your identity, your image of yourself distorted? What is your image of yourself? Describe yourself to God... Now ask God what he sees when he looks at you... Then write in big, bold letters whatever he says! Revise your view of yourself according to his vision!

42. Your Death
Final Reckoning with Eternity

eath is a fact of life. You can try to run or hide, but it will eventually catch you, no matter how fast or how far you run. Consider this disturbing fact: barring the intervention of Almighty God, *someday you will die.* And you probably do not know on which day death will snatch you! Have you given any serious thought to this inevitable fate? Your body will become dust. In your own biological resources, you cannot live forever. The life you live in this body will not last. Ashes to ashes... dust to dust... Are you prepared for all of your earthly dreams and expectations to come to an end? Have you anything to replace them with? This lower life is only our trial run for a higher life. It is the valley of decision, a temporary and decisive interval where we make choices about what kind of eternity we will participate in. What you do with this life will demonstrate what you really want for the next. Are you learning to live with God or without him? Are you spending your time running from God or to him? In the words of Thomas a Kempis, *"How happy and wise is that person who strives now to be in life what he wishes to be found in death."* Who will you be at that moment?

This world is the womb of eternity. Your soul is preparing today for an eternity of God-immersion *or* an eternity of self-obsession. You are in the process of *becoming.* What are you becoming? You are right now practicing the skills that will prepare you for whatever comes next. What are you practicing for? What is your current lifestyle saying about you? As C.S. Lewis says, *"the dullest and most uninteresting person you talk to may one day be a creature which, if you saw it now, you would be strongly tempted to worship, or else a horror and a corruption such as you now meet, if at all, only in a nightmare... There are no ordinary people. You have never talked to a mere mortal... But it is immortals whom we joke*

with, work with, marry, snub and exploit-- immortal horrors or everlasting splendors." You are now being formed into the kind of being you will be forever.

When do you think you will die? Will it be soon or will it be many long years away? Will it be sudden or drawn out? Will it be unexpected or long awaited? We cannot truly know the answer to these questions until we are already staring death in the face. Today could be your Doomsday! Whatever the case, be assured, God already knows the exact time and date when you will draw your last breath. As A.W. Tozer says, *"He knows the name of the driver of the hearse that's going to drive you out to that last place."* And we who walk with God have this assurance: to be absent from the body is to be present with the LORD! And God does not want you to have any regrets. He is doing all he can *now* to lead you upon a path that will result in everlasting joy. But are you following? Are you on a path that will allow you to look back on your life with a smile of satisfaction? Are you living your life now in the light of eternity?

Death forces us to realign our priorities. It is a harsh slap across the face, sobering the heart from the diversions and distractions of a superficial life. What seems so important in the sunshine of life often does not seem so pressing under the shadow of death. Your life will be summed up by a lonely dash between two dates. Once you cross over the threshold of death, only that which is unseen will follow you-- the person you have become and the relationships you have built. Love survives death, for love is stronger than death. At death's door, you will surrender all the toys you have collected: money, car, house, clothes. Your material possessions, your physical pleasures, your moments of fame and recognition, your positions of power and reputation-- all of these things will fade away. Have you stored up the kind of treasures which will last forever? Or have you stored up those which will decay and rot even as your body does the same. Only what is done for love will last. This is why the most important thing you can do with your limited time on earth is to love God and love your neighbor. Live each day

173

with the urgency of one who may die tonight; live each day with the foresight of one who will live forever.

Meditation Exercise
Preparation: Quiet your heart. Use the phrase "Eternal God..." to focus your heart and mind upon the One you are seeking.

Scripture: Slowly and meditatively read through **Psalm 90.**

1. Think about the words "eternity", "everlasting", "infinite", "forever"... How do you picture these ideas? What does it look like? God literally has all the time in the world. How does God perceive time? Consider how God's plans for you are never "short-term"; they extend far beyond your physical death... What do you think God's plans for you include?

2. (Warning: This next meditation may be shocking to those who have not come to terms with their own mortality! If you are unable to deal with this exercise, please talk to someone about your experience and fears...) Spend a few minutes meditating upon your own death. Imagine watching your own funeral... See your pale, lifeless body in the casket... Who are the faces you see there mourning? What would you want people to say about you? Consider the finality, the mortality of your life in this physical body... What would you want written on your gravestone? Look at your cold, gray gravestone standing alone in the rain... What feelings do you experience when you see it? Do you have any "I wish I had/hadn't ____" statements? Do you have any "I'm glad that I did/ didn't ____" statements?

3. Now imagine standing before God as he calls you to account for the life you have lived. How would you answer if he asked you, "What have you done with this life I have given you?" Before God there are no bribes, no secrets, no excuses, no fast-talking

explanations. There is only naked truth. How would you feel standing before God's penetrating gaze? What are the things you wish you could hide? What are the things you wish you had not left undone? What do you think God would say to you? Would he greet you with a joyful smile saying, *"Well done, good and faithful servant... enter into the joy of your Master"*? Or would he say, with eyes full of tears, *"Depart from me... I never knew you..."*?

4. Do you plan to exist beyond your physical death? Does your daily life move you closer to becoming the type of person you want to be forever? What have you spent your life building? Are you getting closer to or farther from the kind of person you want to be for the rest of eternity?

5. What would you do if you knew you were going to die tomorrow? How would you prepare yourself? How would you spend your last hours? Perhaps you need to make time to do some of these things sooner rather than later...

Response: Talk with God about what he sees in your life right now. Ask your Judge to assess your life right now while you can yet make changes. Ask him to point out those things that you should stop now. Ask him to show you those things that you should start doing now. Ask for his help to get started...

Finally, reflect on this fact: for all who die in Christ, the last breath on earth is the first breath in eternity... Suddenly, all sorrows will cease, all pain will vanish, all tears will evaporate, and all sadness will be exchanged for endless bliss...

43. Your Decision
Expressed Intention to Follow Christ

esus' twelve original disciples had a life-altering decision to make-- would they abandon everything to follow him? They did... and the world has never been the same. You have the exact same decision before you today. You cannot follow Jesus and remain the same person. You will be changed. I invite you today to sign your life away. Your use of money, your life goals, your view of sexuality, your place in society-- everything must be melted down and re-forged. The status quo has to go! You were created for God's purposes. Do you intend to fulfill your destiny?

Today you stand in the valley of decision. Bonhoeffer says, *"When Christ calls a man, he bids him 'come and die'."* It is an all-or-nothing proposal. Are you ready to die to this dying world and be reborn into a love-washed world of wonder? Are you ready to flee from this corrupted society and start anew, as a stranger in a strange land? Are you ready to throw reputation to the wind and make a clean break from all the world holds dear? By now you should know enough of the Progenitor of Light to entrust your life into his strong hands. Has the light bulb gone on— that God *must* be your first concern? Have you been "seized by the power of a great affection"? Has he ravished your heart to the point where you are willing to wrap your life around him, forsaking all other gods, to serve him only? If you have been captured by this vision of a new world, a new life, then you must act on it or you will be lulled back into a complacent "life-as-usual". Today if you hear his voice, do not harden your heart. *Choose. Choose! CHOOSE!*

The defining characteristic of the human spirit is its *ability to decide*. It is beneath our dignity to be only effects, never causes. You can choose this moment to *go with God—* to rise above all of your hurts and fears and *become truly original...* or you can sink back down into the mud and mire of the world, becoming simply a product of fermentation and erosion. Originate reality! Step off of dry land and walk on the water! Exercise your will right now— call upon the Living God to empower what will-power cannot do. Receive God's resources so you may push down the pillars of human effort once and for all! Live the rest of your days beyond your own abilities... by the transcending power of God's Spirit within.

PLEASE DO NOT FINISH THIS BOOK until you have made this firm and final surrender deep in the core of your being: to follow Jesus, to re-orient your life around God. Unless you abandon yourself completely to Christ, the rest of this book will do you no good. In fact it may even be harmful. It will turn you into a performer, acting out a life that is not truly yours. The remainder of the book is a tool for shaping a Christ-centered life... if that is your deepest desire. Read over "My Resolution" at the end of this chapter. Ask yourself if you would be willing to sign this sacred covenant in utmost seriousness before God. After this, I will take for granted that you have taken the plunge into the depths of God. If you have *not* come to this place of firm intention to pursue Christ, do whatever it will take to decide *for* or *against* Jesus. If you have any outstanding doubts, questions, fears, or other obstacles, don't move on until you're convinced. Soak yourself in the New Testament, find a mentor and a community of disciples who can help you. But do not hesitate too long with one foot in the lifeboat and one foot on the sinking ship! We are dying—our tomorrows are dwindling away.

Once you have made this your covenant, we will undertake a pilgrimage both difficult and liberating. The first stage of this journey is the *Contemplative Life* in which you will learn to flee each day into the hidden temple where you may immerse your soul in the pulsating Presence of Christ. It is not far, I promise. The next stage is the *Communal Life* where you will join a counter-cultural society, a Brotherhood and Sisterhood of Blood, an underground movement in common pursuit of Christ. Then you will embark on the *Interior Life through the Illuminative and Purgative Way.* Here you will learn a

177

sweet collaboration with God which will so transform your inward character that others begin to notice the very qualities of Christ in you. The virtues within you will be illumined until they shine like fire and the vices within you will be purified with holy fire. Finally, in the *Active Life* of Mission, you will enlist in a worldwide revolutionary mission, functioning in this world with the same love and power and purpose that Christ exemplified, carrying on his transformative work on the earth.

And, with few exceptions, all of this can be accomplished while you still live in the same house and work at the same job and maintain many of the same relationships you currently have. But don't be fooled. Your life will be utterly changed. It will be like night and day. It will take on a whole new hue of meaning and glory. It will become a very different species of life. Are you ready for this?

Meditation Exercise

Preparation: Quiet your heart. Hear Jesus' question,
"Who do you say that I am?"

Scripture: Slowly and meditatively read through **Mark 8:27-38.**

1. Imagine you are one of Jesus' disciples sitting at his feet as he teaches... Reflect on his bold statement, *"If anyone would come after me, he must deny himself, take up his cross and follow me."*... What is Jesus saying to you? How does it make you feel?

2. Meditate upon the question, *"What good is it for a man to gain the whole world, yet forfeit his soul?"*...Are there any temporary pursuits that would keep you from placing your entire life in God's hands? Is there anything in this world you still want more than God's will?

3. Now imagine again Jesus' dusty sandaled feet walking along the rocky, dusty terrain of the Judean hillside... Spend a minute just watching his feet walking, walking, walking, his hands reaching

down, touching the lepers, healing the blind... Now as you look up, you see that it is actually *you* whose feet these are! It is *you* walking after the footprints of Jesus, teaching, loving, serving, along the way to your own cross, upon which you will lay your life down for others... Do you want to live that kind of world-defying life today? What is this cross, your greatest joy and greatest pain? How will you pour out your life in the service of Christ?

Response: Consider the Resolution below... Are you ready to commit to learning this life? If so, pray this Resolution out loud with all of your heart before God... Sign your name on the blank below it... Now talk to God about what this may mean in your life...What will it cost you? What are your expectations? You may also want write out your own personal resolution.

My Resolution:

By God's grace, here is my resolve, the declaration of my lifelong intent:
I now resolve with the rest of my earthly life, to pursue a new way of
life patterned after the Way of Christ. I am a follower of Jesus Christ,
bought by his blood, filled with his Spirit, soaked in his Word,
committed to his people, deployed on his mission.
I will not live as the world lives. I will not waste another day of my life
pursuing the empty and selfish goals of pleasure, power, possessions,
and prestige. I have a higher allegiance:
I am a citizen of God's kingdom and a child of the King.
I will love and serve God with all my heart, mind, soul and strength and
love my neighbor as myself. With complete trust in God's goodness,
I now surrender myself to the will of God in all things.
My greatest desire and intention is to please God, to bring him glory.
I will live out God's purposes on earth
and not even death itself can stop me.

_____

(sign your name)

179

CHRIST-CENTERED

SPIRITUALITY

A HANDBOOK OF *CATECHESIS*
for
the training of novices
in
THE WAY OF CHRIST

PART III. SPIRITUAL EXERCISES
for the elevation of the soul

44. On the Practice of the Contemplative Life

he Law of Sowing and Reaping is woven into the fabric of the universe. Consequences are stubbornly consistent. The person who puts little or nothing into cultivating their spiritual life will get little or nothing out of it. The person who pours their entire energy and effort into the pursuit of a friendship with the Almighty will, from that friendship, reap great rewards. So how, exactly, does one "*seek God*"? How do we interact with the intriguing and radiant Reality we have been reading about? If you aim to actively pursue God's Presence and purposes, these are the two wings upon which you must fly: *the contemplative life* and *the communal life*. Cultivate a life that is deeply *contemplative*: a 24-7, life-saturating awareness of God that bleeds into everything we do. Cultivate also a life that is richly *communal*: intimately connected with a body of people who mirror Christ to us.

Is it possible to become so accustomed to experiencing God that we sense his constant Divine Presence on a daily basis, hour-by-hour, minute-by-minute? I assure you it is, but it is not an easy quest. I am going to ask you to rearrange your life to make room for God. If you will pour your life into these exercises, you will over time begin to see and feel God's Eternal Being everywhere! Through practice, you will elevate your soul into a different kind of existence in which encountering God becomes reflexive, almost effortless.

We will now attempt some *concrete exercises for cultivating a life of Christ-centered spirituality.* Don't get mired in mediocrity! Until we have specific practices that actually show up in our everyday routines and our weekly schedule, we are in danger of being hearers but not doers, theoreticians rather than practitioners. Like a person who tries to learn martial arts through watching movies rather than joining a dojo, we may "know" a lot about following Jesus while knowing nothing about following Jesus. Many of us want, as A.W. Tozer describes it, the *fruit* of the righteous without the *root* of the righteous. We covet an outward life of love, power, joy, and purpose yet we refuse to practice the inward life of prayer, self-denial, and community that makes it possible.

In the following pages, we will begin a regimen of *spiritual exercises,* a reliable path which many saints have walked upon their journey into the heart of God. Many practices are flagrantly physical: we must become animal trainers, and the species of creature we are training is called *homo sapien.* We are after all mammals, a tangled mass of cells and nerves, wedded to an immortal spirit of dazzling potentiality. Spiritual exercises not only shape the spirit, but they also form the flesh to cooperate and rightly respond to the rule of the spirit. This section is your arsenal, your toolbox. Take each practice and try it a few times. Then you can begin to experiment with them. The ensuing set of disciplines will take a soul thirsting for the living God and bring it to the cool mountain springs at which we may drink deeply of his living water.

Enjoy yourself! You may see ways to customize these methods to your own unique disposition, occupation, limitations, and circumstances. Some may work better for you than others. You may also find that in different stages of life you will rely more upon one than another. Don't expect to use all of them all the time. When you feel the spark of holy desire kindled through a particular discipline, fan it into flame. Don't feel guilty for neglecting some exercises in favor of others. Guilt has no place in the practice of spiritual exercises! The goal of archery is not flawless technique, but to hit the bull's-eye.

What is the goal of the contemplative life? It is *an integrated life of uninterrupted awareness of and interaction with the Invisible God.* It is constant communion, connection, and co-operation with God, culminating in an experiential union with God, where you are so attuned to and surrendered to his will that you begin to function as one with your Creator. It is obedience to the command, "pray continually". Prayer is, at its simplest, *communication with God.*

182

Just as there are diverse forms of communication, there are diverse forms of prayer: verbal and non-verbal, talking and listening, questions and statements, emotional and informational, repetitive and spontaneous, words and silence, body language, requests about us or others, and many other subtle forms too numerous to list. I include many different species of prayer not to overwhelm you, but to throw open a spacious landscape to explore. This is by no means all there is out there, but it includes much that historically has proved most useful-- some easy, some difficult.

I have a few important cautions. Whenever we begin to speak of specific methods of seeking God, we also run the risk of treating them as absolutes. The river of relationship runs through many channels. These *exercises are means to an end,* not ends in and of themselves. Their usefulness is connected directly to their ability to bring us into closer contact with God himself, to lift our souls into a place of receptivity and attentiveness to the breathings of God's Spirit. Without the intention to love, know, honor and please God, they are useless! One person may persevere in prayer out of love for God, another out of desire to impress others, still another is guilt-driven, while another prays out of a compulsive perfectionism, but only that which leads to union with God proves useful in the end. These are ways of cultivating and cooperating with the Christ-life already flowing through our veins. Remember, successfully practicing these disciplines won't make God love you more; failure to practice them won't make God love you less. Don't bring perfectionism into the pursuit!

However, don't completely give up on a particular method just because it's too hard! Of course it's too hard — that's why it helps you to grow. An exercise regimen that is easy and comfortable is not doing its job. We all fall down many times as we learn to walk, so don't be discouraged by failure after failure. Also, don't stop just because you don't see immediate, direct results. You will not always be able to see the direct correlation between the exercise and the growth in your life or your drawing closer to God, just as a child does not see the obvious relationship between eating vegetables and living a better, healthier life. We rarely see the fruit of prayer during the prayer time itself. The beneficial results of prayer are more clearly seen in our patience and cheerfulness in our daily life.

Be on guard against using these disciplines in mechanical or superstitious ways. If we're not vigilant, we may fall into depersonalizing God into a vending machine or a magic genie. We start to expect "this-for-that" transactions with God where if I pray x amount of minutes, I get x amount of blessings today. This kind of thinking will choke all life out of our relationship with God. He becomes a means to an end instead of the Ultimate End. That's no way to treat a living Person! It would be truly tragic if we wanted God's blessings more than we wanted God himself.

Meditation Exercises

Preparation: Become aware of God's fiery Presence. Ask him to speak to you.

Scripture: Slowly and meditatively read through **Exodus 3:1-14**.

1. Imagine Moses' wandering the spacious plains of the wilderness... Hear the winds blowing, the bleating of the sheep... Feel the hot wind on your cheeks... See the bush engulfed in flames but unconsumed...

2. Reflect on how Moses felt, conversing with the Almighty...

3. Consider the global effects of this encounter with the glorious "I AM"... How did Moses' life change? What would have happened if Moses had not turned aside from his usual routine to hear from God?

Response: Write down some of your first-hand experiences of God. When and where have you felt close to God? What helps you to hear God, feel God, see God? How do you best communicate with him?

45. On Solitude
Finding Space to be Alone with God

he most strenuous exercise a God-seeker must learn... *is to do nothing.* Step off this dizzying carousel of human activity and achievement, this swirling blur of doing, doing, and more doing. We are suckled on superficiality, marching in lockstep with the parade of people without ever bothering to ask where it is headed, like lemmings to the ocean floor. It seems the more labor-saving devices we buy (so-called, "modern conveniences"), the more we must labor just to get by. Free yourself! By God's outrageous grace, we don't have to *do anything* to earn his love. God is already head-over-heels in love with you! There is nothing that you can do to change that for better or for worse! Just stop everything and learn to enjoy it!

The odd truth is that we often engage in wrong action simply because we cannot stand inaction. As Blaise Pascal wryly observed, *"One of the great causes of human misery is our inability to sit quietly in our own room."* If your momentary choice were between "doing the wrong thing" and "doing nothing", wouldn't you want to be well-trained at doing nothing? Cease striving and *simply be.* Soak in God's reality. Our souls crave solitude, silence, and stillness.

The first step to an acute consciousness of God is *solitude—* the *momentary physical withdrawal from human contact.* Escape from life-as-usual, this sensory overload of constant motion and movement, noise and numbness, busyness and boredom. Leave behind the hurries and worries of the world. Get away! Flee from civilization into the lonely places of the desert. Follow the example of your Savior, who often went out to solitary places where he prayed. Every saint has a fortress of solitude, a chosen loneliness where they can withdraw to meet with their Lord. It is when we are truly alone, and attentive to our alone-ness that we begin to sense that haunting and holy Presence-- and we finally *experience* this powerful truth:

We are never really alone. He is your hiding place, your refuge of total security. Descend with your mind into the sanctuary of your heart and there commune with God, unhindered. As we arrange for significant periods of time away from the crowds around us, following the Spirit into the desert, we will return full of the power to help people in a way we could never do on our own. Activity before stillness is worthless; activity after stillness is indestructible.

Prepare the setting for a God-encounter. Each of us must conduct our own first-hand research on an elusive species: *Deus Absconditus*, "the hidden God". What would you do if you actually expected a visit with your Creator today? What if we awoke each day with an expectation that God wanted to meet with us today? Make room, prepare space for God to fill. God rarely competes for our attention. God will not often raise his voice or cry aloud in the streets. He waits to be wanted. Like the nameless innkeeper of the nativity, you must ask yourself, "Do I have room for Jesus?"

We complain that we cannot feel God, yet our senses are so numbed with shallow pleasures and trivial pursuits that nothing short of a well-placed kick in the hindquarters could get our attention. Thankfully, God sometimes stoops to such crude methods! But it is not his favorite means of communication. If you want to cultivate a close relationship, give him ample time simply to speak, to whisper, to touch. If we're ever going to find our bearings in this eternal universe, we must hide ourselves, find ourselves in the firm, quiet embrace of our Father. Bury your face in his chest. Listen to his strong, steady heartbeat, like the crashing ocean waves against the rocky shoreline. A seeker of God cannot be afraid of solitude and silence. In fact, we must intentionally make time for it. Watch the sunset instead of the TV. Listen to the gentle music of the wind instead of the radio. Take a long walk to nowhere in particular. Set aside blocks of time just to be... alone.

If you are unfamiliar with the practice of solitude, it may be shocking how difficult it is. You may find yourself kicking and screaming for something to do, conjuring up every possible excuse to get out of it. You find yourself justifying why you are too busy to spend a few hours in healing solitude but you have ample time to numb your mind in front of the television. *Why would doing nothing be so hard?* Theoretically, it should be very easy to stop doing things. You just... stop. But once you subtract the noise, the music, the places to go, the people to see, the important work to accomplish, what are you left with? This can be a very frightful experience for a soul that has managed to evade an honest look at what's really going on below the surface. In solitude, you will *come face-to-face with what really drives you.* The practice of solitude turns you inside out. You will be unable to run from your fears, your insecurities and inabilities, your restlessness and boredom, your need to achieve, your lack of inner peace. But as you allow the practice of solitude to do its severe work, it will slowly forge a strength of soul that is obvious. You will become comfortable in your own skin, with who you are. You can finally master the unruly thoughts and desires of your own mind. The recalibration that takes place in your soul frees you from manipulation, anxiety, loneliness and other forces that control you.

Exercises

1. Silence Exercise: Put this book down, sit comfortably with your back straight, close your eyes, and practice being silent for 10 minutes....Now!   (Silence)

2. What did you experience during the time of silence? What did you become aware of? Could you sense God with you? Or just your wandering mind? Your many tasks? An itch in your back? What do these things tell you about what is lurking below the surface in your life? What are some of the things that drive you?

(Warning: Some people find solitude filled with consuming darkness and sheer terror: as soon as you quiet your mind, you find feelings of anxiety, guilt, despair, depression, or anger begin to overwhelm you. If this is your experience, know that these sources of sorrow have been stealing your joy for many years. Try to put into words all of these feelings and fears that appear in solitude. Ask God why you are feeling this way... Also, talk to a trusted friend about it...)

3. Set aside a four-hour chunk of time in the next few weeks to spend in solitude. Take a leisurely walk outdoors, go hiking, or just sit and enjoy the quiet of nature. Leave your work behind and go to the forest, to a lake or seashore, to the desert, or just stroll through the streets of your neighborhood. Take time to actually feel the textures, the bark of trees, the crunch of leaves under foot, breathe deeply. Look at the stars at night. Find the quietest place that you can. Flee the artificial. Remove yourself from life-as-usual routines. Try to sense the Sacred and Silent Presence that has been there all along. Could you take a weekly time of Sabbath rest? How often can you fly from daily life and recalibrate your heart? Could you set aside a weekend alone every few months? Make whatever adjustments you need to in your calendar to schedule in what's most important.

4. If you have not already done so, set aside *time* each day (a half-hour? an hour?) as a part of your regular routine, when you can escape to be with your King. Etch in stone this sacred meeting time (or block it out in your daily planner/calendar)!

5. Find or create a *sacred place* in or near your home where you can seek and encounter God daily, a refuge from distraction. It may be a porch, a window, a special rug, an area of the floor, a chair, a desk or even a home altar. Or it may be a place outside your home, but it must be easily accessible to you on a daily basis: a laundry room, a park bench, a coffee shop, a playground, a roof, a pool area-- the closer to nature the better.

6. **Meditation Exercise:** Read meditatively through **Genesis 28:10-22** in the manner you have been shown. Imagine the sights, sounds, and feeling that you would have experienced if you were there. Respond to what God is saying. Record anything significant in your journal.

46. On Silence
Bathing in God's Sacred Presence

ilence is God's first language—so says St. John of the Cross. Are you listening? God enjoys speaking with us... but he also enjoys silence with us! The next step in our freedom from the prison of the senses is to bathe our souls in silence. Silence is the de-contamination chamber of the soul-- it purifies and cleanses us from distraction, worry, stress, agitation, frustration, and other debris that interferes with the heart on a quest to find God. Empty yourself in expectation. God loves a vacuum; immediately he comes to fill it! Silencing your heart may be the most difficult part of prayer, but once you have done that, all else becomes exceedingly easy! Trying to pray without first quieting your soul is like trying to load your valuables into a knapsack that is already filled with bricks.

Where is God? He is all around you and deep within you. But it is usually too noisy to hear his Voice or sense his Presence. It's sadly ironic that most of us cannot "find" God, especially in light of that simplest and most indisputable of scriptural truths, the Divine Omnipresence: no matter where you are, *God is always there*. The challenge is to experience this reality. It's hard to pay attention to a world imperceptible to the senses when the world of the senses incessantly assaults us. Teach your heart to enjoy silence and your mind will become sharper and your words more potent. Wisdom will not be canned... it yields only at a very high cost.

Too much noise, sensations, speed, flash, words-- these are the enemies of a contemplative spirituality. When our attention is focused on the immediate sights and sounds around us, it's hard to sense the quiet, hidden Presence just behind the thin veil of the visible world. Push aside this three-dimensional curtain before your eyes— enter into the Holiest Place, where the Unseen God dwells in glory. Subtract all distractions and immerse yourself in sheer silence until you can hear, even feel, his quiet whispers. Once God has captured your attention, prayer comes naturally. Don't hold out for the spectacular and sensational. God speaks often to the quiet soul.

We need to learn to *breathe* again. Breathing inhabits that curious gap between the voluntary and involuntary: Unlike our heartbeat or digestion, we can control our lungs if we choose to. This basic action of physical life can either be a distraction of huge proportions or a calming rhythm that creates silence within us. Learn to breathe with your stomach instead of your chest. Your body at peace is designed to take full, deep breaths using the diaphragm muscles of your stomach instead of taking shallow gulps of air with your chest. Also, your nose was created to breath; your mouth to eat and speak. Ideally, you should try to inhale with your nose, if possible. You will probably find that breathing properly tends to relax you while breathing improperly keeps you tense, anxious and distracted. Don't take it for granted. Whenever you pray, it may be helpful to take a minute or two to make sure you're breathing properly. Drink in the rich gift of oxygen, the innocent incense of living things always ascending to God's throne. (Do you feel uneasy about breathing exercises and one-word prayers, having associated them only with Eastern religions? I assure you, these practices have been part of the Christ-centered tradition for many centuries! See Chapter 58, "On Breath Prayers" for further explanation)

A wandering mind can be a terrible distraction in times of silence and prayer. How do we quiet our stray thoughts, which chatter endlessly on, clamoring for attention? There are a few strategies for dealing with them. If it is an important thought that you need to remember, write it down so that you can forget about it. It would be wise to keep your "to-do list" or daily planner nearby so that you can record anything important. For all the rest of your distracting thoughts, the best thing is to ignore them. But in order to ignore them, you must learn to focus your mind on one thought, and use that one thought to protect you from all others. Choose a sacred word or phrase which embodies your desire for God and fix your mind upon it ("God," "O Lord," "Jesus," "Spirit," "Love," "Joy," or

"Mercy"). When distracting thoughts run through your mind, don't chase them around like monkeys in a banana tree! Instead, ignore their chattering and turn away. Simply re-turn your attention back to your anchoring thought, fixing your mind upon that one word, allowing everything else to fade quietly away.

If you have tried to ignore distracting thoughts, but one specific anxiety keeps overpowering you, you may need to switch strategies: Stop and face it head-on. Make it a topic of conversation with God. Ask, "why am I thinking about this so much? Is there anything that needs to be dealt with here?" Become aware of what your wandering, worrying mind might be telling you. Where do your thoughts drift off to when they have freedom to roam? This is one of the best indicators of your idols, the "gods" competing for your attention. What are some of your possible idols?

If you find that your environment has too many distractions, you may use quiet, meditative music to drown out the noise and help you focus. Soak yourself in God's Presence with calming, peace-inducing instrumental or worshipful music. But don't become overly dependent upon it. It is more like training wheels that you may use to help you to get started but you should eventually be able to do without. After becoming accustomed to the practice of silence, you should be able to find it in the midst of any situation.

Exercises

1. **Breathing Exercise:** Sit quietly for a minute with your back straight and your eyes closed... Now become aware of your breathing... Don't try to breathe differently. Just pay attention to it... Does your stomach expand with each breath or your chest cavity? Are you breathing through your nose or your mouth? Are you taking full breaths or half-breaths? Is the air cool or warm? Spend a couple of minutes just breathing...

2. **Meditation Exercise:** Meditate upon the story in I Kings 19:1-13 in the way we have practiced. Talk with God about what it says to you.

3. Listening Exercise: Sit quietly for a minute, eyes closed, no slouching... Now listen carefully to all of the background sounds around you right now. Some sounds may be loud or faint, near or far, constant or sporadic, comforting or distracting, obscure or obvious: various hums, buzzes, conversations, etc. Then as you become aware of each sound, spend a few seconds isolating that sound in your mind and hearing it. Then move on to the next. By doing this, you can peel back each layer of noise, inspect it for a moment, and lay it aside. Once we are aware of a distraction, naming it explicitly and acknowledging it, it loses much of its manipulative power. Once you have heard all the noise around you, spend 10 minutes in this "silence"...   (Silence)

4. What are the thoughts that popped into your mind while you were in silence? Try to recall as many as possible...What do these thoughts tell you about yourself?

5. Thought Exercise: Learn to quiet your mind through concentration on one thought. First choose one word: *God, Jesus, Love, Fire, Spirit, Joy, Goodness*, etc. This will be the thought you will practice fixing your mind upon. Spend a few minutes with only this one thought before you...

Now practice this exercise with one phrase of adoration or thanksgiving or request: *Christ in me, the hope of glory; My Lord and My God; Maker of heaven and earth; Awaken my heart*, etc. Look through the Psalms for one line that you could pray. Now spend a few minutes with only this phrase in your mind... Now try it with a single image in your mind: *a cross, a shepherd, the sea*, etc....

6. How long can you go without speaking (other than when you are asleep)? Take time in the next few days to see how long you can keep quiet (without being rude)...

192

47. On Stillness

Physical Expressions of Receptivity

our body is speaking: what does it say? We must now learn to quiet our physical bodies. Sit still and let the universe wash over you. Much of our communication is non-verbal, praying through our body language. Our bodies are constantly describing the unspoken contents of our hearts. We express our actual internal state and attitudes more accurately through our facial expressions, eyes, hands, and postures than through our words. *Your body is a temple of the Holy Spirit, the dwelling place of the Living God--* and yet it is one of the greatest sources of distraction in prayer. Learn to honor God with your body. Through our physical posture, we can show God our readiness and expectancy... or we can show him we are bored and uninterested. What does your body usually say when you pray?

Stillness can prepare our bodies as well as our minds for prayer. Jesus manifests himself willingly to the heart that enthusiastically desires him. The Knower of our Hearts often responds in kind to the fervor of our seeking: "If you seek me, you will find me, if you seek me with all your heart." Show him your desire! How can you express yourself? At different times, you may want to "say" different things through different postures. As Ignatius of Loyola writes, *"I will enter upon the meditation, now kneeling, now prostrate upon the ground, now lying face upwards, now seated, now standing, always being intent on seeking what I desire...If I find what I desire while kneeling, I will not seek to change my position."* Make every effort to draw Almighty God closer to you (or are you drawing yourself closer to him?)

Many different *postures* of prayer are mentioned in the sacred Scriptures. Moses stood with arms outstretched. Solomon kneeled with bended knee. Mary sat at Jesus' feet. John fell facedown as one dead. You can even come up with your own ways of expressing yourself non-verbally to God. You may bow your head reverently or raise your eyes to the vaulted heavens. (There is no rule that you must close your eyes in prayer!) Some may find walking to be best, but don't let it be an excuse for not stilling the soul! Some may find lying prostrate to be useful, but don't let this lure you to sleep! When sitting, make sure your back is straight and you are not slouching which never makes for attentive prayer.

Use your *hands* to express receptivity to God. We can say a lot with our hands: hold them cupped out in front of you to receive the Living Water of his heavenly fountain. Raise your hands above your head in surrender or exaltation. Place your hands upon your heart, clasp them together before you in pleading supplication. Clench your fists in agony. Open your hands as you let go of all your cares, surrendering them to God. The ancient Celts practiced a *cross vigil,* stretching out their hands like a cross in total abandonment. It is true that our spirit can worship God in any bodily posture, but we cannot ignore the effect our body has upon our spirit.

You may also prepare yourself for prayer by the use of *symbolic physical objects*. You can train your body to respond to certain sounds, sights, sensations, smells or tastes as cues of consecration. Often something as simple as lighting a candle or grabbing a cup of coffee is enough to set apart a time for a God encounter. You can use incense, a prayer shawl, a rosary, prayer beads, a special prayer rug or some other ritual object to draw boundaries around this time of active seeking. If you have a cross, you may grasp it to your chest, or just gaze upon it to focus your mind on Christ. Hold a nail in your hand as a physical reminder of Christ's sacrifice for you. Use physical objects as symbols to help you to experience the spiritual reality it represents. You may even decide to fast from a meal as a physical declaration of your hunger for the Bread of Life. Make extravagant preparations for meeting with God and see if God does not respond extravagantly.

Images strike us with the force of a fist. Illuminate the walls of your house and the walls of your mind with sacred *art*. Look through the vast archives of art to find pictures that portray a particular facet of the spiritual life that is dear to your heart. Put them up on a prayer altar, your bookshelves, your desktop, anywhere they can turn your heart to the Lord. Meditate upon the scenes of the stories of Scripture made by Rembrandt, Da Vinci or Michaelangelo (or perhaps you need to create your own!). You may use an *icon*, a picture of Christ or the saints which, like a window into another world, immediately convey a whole storehouse of truth and mystery. In all of this, let us *avoid the idolatry of images* by keeping in mind that any physical object or picture is a symbol meant to lead you to the Unseen God, and it is he that you worship, not the symbol itself. It is God himself who has the power, the blessings, the efficacy, and not the material object itself, which is only an aid to devotion.

Our bodies are instruments which can be well-trained at doing good or doing bad. Just as we may drive home without even thinking, much of our physical actions are simply habits beyond our conscious choices. Our bodies are often poised and prepared to sin automatically at the slightest trigger. How do we break these unexplainable patterns of behavior? Through re-training our bodies, we may disrupt the sinful and unhealthy habitual responses stored up in our muscle memory. Do you have the rare ability to compose yourself and just sit there? We often smuggle into prayer a lot of nervous tension. This needs to be identified and surrendered. Let the river of time wash over you.

Exercises

1. Stillness Exercise: Sit comfortably upright. Try not to move any body part except the natural rhythms of your body. Can you sit still without fidgeting? Close your eyes for one minute.... Now, without moving, ask yourself, what are you *feeling* right now? What are you tasting? Smelling? What temperature do you feel on your skin? Is there any wind? Do you feel any nervous tension? Do your muscles feel relaxed or tight? What kind of emotions are you feeling right now? Try to become aware of what you already feel...

2. Posture Exercise: Now try to express exactly *what you are feeling* in a physical posture. Hold this posture for ten seconds... Now try to express *what you want to be feeling* in a physical posture. Hold this posture for one minute...

3. Physical Sensations Exercise: Sit comfortably upright. Hear God's soul-searching question, *"Where are you?"* Now starting with your toes, become aware of what each body part is feeling right now. Focus your attention for a few seconds on the sensations of each part of your body: your feet... your legs... your thighs and buttocks against the chair... the touch of your clothes on your back and chest... your shoulders... your hands... your head... Now close your eyes and sit still for a few minutes, seeing if you "sense" God's Presence...

4. Now spend a few minutes offering the members of your body to God. Go through each major body part (your brain, your ears, your eyes, your mouth, your heart, your hands, your genitals, your feet) and tell God that it belongs to him. Talk over with God what he expects of them. What will or won't they be doing from now on?

5. Meditation Exercise: Meditate upon **Psalm 131** in the way we have practiced. Feel the mood described in the passage... Imagine the experience of an innocent child at peace in his mother's loving arms... Now that you have practiced solitude, silence, and stillness, you know: *this is not a quick-fix spirituality!* We do not force mystical experiences. We do not come to our Father expecting excitement and ecstasy. Instead we simply look to him in quiet admiration. I really think God prefers the subtle to the sensational. If he wishes to grant us some extraordinary experience, we gladly receive it. But usually, we are simply glad to have spent a silent moment in his extraordinary Presence...

196

48. On Vocal Prayer
Learning the Vocabulary of Prayer

ou have learned to be still; it is finally safe to open your mouth. But when we finally open our mouths to speak to God, what do we say? What kind of things to do you talk to the Almighty about? Children first learn to speak by imitation, babbling copies of the words they hear from others. As we learn the language of prayer, it would be wise to become steeped in the prayers of the ancient Scripture and of others more proficient than ourselves. *Vocal prayer* is *taking someone else's prayer and make their words our own*, taking them upon our lips and speaking them from our hearts.

Don't be afraid of repetition, unless it is done for outward show or to try to earn God's attention. When it is not done to *get* something from others or from God, repetition can be a wonderful way of taking the wild stallion of your thoughts and bringing it firmly into submission. Our minds get scattered so easily that it is comforting to have a reliable discipline to help restrain it. As wax in a mold is hardened into the desired shape, our thought processes can be intentionally directed along certain desired courses until it becomes habitual through constant repetition. Any neurologist, elementary school teacher or parent can tell you this is true. Martin Luther tells how he would kindle his heart into flame when he lost the joy in his prayers: *"I take my little Psalter, hurry to my room...I say quietly to myself, and word-for-word, the Ten Commandments, the Creed, and if I have time, some words of Christ or of Paul, or some psalms, just as a child might do."* We would do well to follow the example of this and countless other men and women of God, and learn this child-like way of reciting the prayers of others.

Begin with the crown jewel of vocal prayer-- the ancient *Paternoster*, the sacred *"Our Father"*, spoken from the lips of Christ himself to his own disciples. This was his elementary lesson on prayer, the outline of a prayerful heart. The Lord's Prayer is only the very tip of the iceberg, but it imprints a pattern that repeats itself into ever increasing depths. Every disciple should approach Jesus with the humble request: *"Lord, teach us to pray."* Then learn by heart this initial lesson, each line of which is an abundant feast for the soul, to be savored and meditated upon at length. Beware: ingesting this most dangerous prayer regularly may radically overturn the usual order of your life! Besides the explosive "Our Father", I would recommend memorizing at least a few other prayers or psalms that are especially meaningful to you—this puts them within arm's reach at any time. Or try reading one psalm each day, meditatively chewing upon it and turning it into your own prayer.

Some may find repeating vocal prayers restrictive instead of liberating. There is nothing wrong with that. If you find pre-written prayers boring, then just learn the "Our Father" and go no further in this arena for now. However, if you find that these prayers are more meaningful to you than spontaneous prayers, bringing you reliably into contact with God, there are many resources that can be used to continue exploring this path. The *Psalms* are a wonderful collection of honest, open-heart exchanges with God. Look through them and match your mood with a prayer. There are sad psalms, happy psalms, angry psalms, fearful psalms—spanning the full landscape of human experience. There are also many *other Scriptures* that you can take and turn into a prayer directed to God, such as the Ten Commandments, the Sermon on the Mount, or I Corinthians 13.

You may also mine the rich history of the prayers of the global community of Christ. Read out loud or even sing with the saints of ages past! Turn to the historic Creeds and Confessions of the Reformed Churches. Use *The Book of Common Prayer* from the Episcopal tradition, or its excellent re-vision, *The Divine Hours: A Manual for Prayer* by Phyllis Tickle, for a pattern of prayer at fixed intervals throughout the day. Or check out the Catholic tradition, chanting along with *the Weekday Missal* or try out *The Prymer: The Prayer Book of the Medieval Era Adapted for Contemporary Use* by Robert Webber. Look through *The Celtic Vision: Prayers, Blessings, Songs and Invocations from the Gaelic Tradition*, edited by Ester de Waal. Find *The Valley of Vision: A Collection of Puritan Prayers & Devotions*, edited by Arthur Bennett. Or just break open a good hymnal from any church and pray along with its timeless lyrics.

Psalms, hymns, and *spiritual songs* are a particularly powerful form of vocal prayer. Through music, rhythm, melody, and poetry, songs have the ability to stick to the walls of your mind and heart, making them easily accessible. Find songs that resonate deeply with your spirit, expressing your deepest feelings, thoughts, and intentions. You may find that singing along with a worshipful recording can be a reliable way to enter into the Presence of God. I have two cautions about praise songs, however. First, make sure you choose it for its lyrical meaning before its musical beauty or entertainment value. Songs with catchy melodies but paper-thin content may lift your emotions but they won't draw your heart closer to the Spirit of God. And secondly, the most beautiful song can lose its meaning if overused or used carelessly, as a distraction or diversion. However, when used intentionally with a constant remembrance of the meaning, worship songs can be a wonderful way to *enter his gates with thanksgiving and his courts with praise.*

Exercises

1. Song Exercise: Think of one of your favorite songs of worship to God. Spend a few minutes singing this song out loud to your Lord... Now just say the words instead of singing them... Which phrase of the lyrics is the most important to you?

2. Memorization Exercise: Spend 10 minutes repeating and memorizing the Lord's Prayer, line-by-line. Start from the beginning and see how many lines you can memorize in the allotted time...
Then throughout the day, as often as you can remember, recite this prayer in your mind or out loud:

Our Father who art in heaven,
Hallowed be Thy Name.
Thy kingdom come,
Thy will be done on earth as it is in heaven.
Give us this day our daily bread.
Forgive us our trespasses as we forgive those who trespass against us.
And lead us not into temptation but deliver us from evil.
For Thine is the kingdom, and the power, and the glory,
forever and ever. Amen.

3. Meditation Exercise: Spend some time meditating on each phrase of this primal prayer. Repeat each phrase slowly, inquiring to yourself what it means...

a) *Our Father who art in heaven* - What does this say about the Person we are addressing? What is implied in our relationship to him? The idea of "heaven" includes both the farthest reaches of the universe, the realm of spiritual reality, the "throne room" of God's glory, as well as the very air surrounding our bodies-- do you recognize God's Presence in each way?

b) *Hallowed be Thy Name* - This expresses a desire for God to be "hallowed": to be glorified, honored, treated with respect, recognized as holy. Is your deepest desire for God's reputation to be upheld?

c) *Thy kingdom come* - Is your consuming passion for your world to experience God's reign, his governance, his overarching Presence as fully as possible?
What features of God's Kingdom do you long for here on earth, in you and around you: His justice? His peace? His joy? His love?
Can you offer yourself as God's instrument for accomplishing this?

d) Continue through the rest of the prayer this way. In your journal, write out your observations, insights, or questions for each line.

49. On Sacred Reading
Immersing the Mind in Scripture

our Bible is alive! It is a swirling vortex of opposing forces in dynamic tension, a Spirit-breathed whirlwind designed not simply to inform you but to pick you up and transport you into a whole new world! Let the jarring activity of the living Word of God fill your thoughts-- expanding, challenging, refining, crushing and cleansing. As you consistently immerse yourself in the story of God, observing his interactions with specific individuals in actual human history, you find yourself becoming part of the continuing story, the timeless community of God's people. The same Jesus who walked the wave-washed shores of Galilee centuries ago walks beside you today.

The greatest need of humanity is to know God; the most perfect instrument for attaining this need is the Holy Bible. It contains all that is needed for salvation! If you wish to know God, to hear God, to touch God, to see God— allow the sacred Scriptures to seep through you, shaping and forming the architecture of your mind. Approach the ancient text with reverence. Open the book! Blow the dust of the ages from its worn and tattered pages. Study them, learn them, understand them, absorb them until your thought processes have been diverted into new patterns— rather the oldest patterns, tracing the very paths of eternity. The Scriptures will subtly train your senses by constant use to see what was there all along. You will begin to see God everywhere! You will discern good and evil where, before, all you heard was meaningless chatter.

The Holy Bible has an authority unlike any other books or writings. It provides us with a standard, a yardstick by which all other spiritual writings are measured and evaluated. The unchanging words of the Bible will help to anchor your ever-changing experience of God in actual, verifiable reality rather than floating away into the empty speculations of the human mind. Dedicate your

201

intellect to searching and understanding everything you can about the Living God! Learn his ways, his likes and dislikes, his personality— see what he is capable of! Behold your God! Watch how his people lived in concert with him, how they talked with him, how they wrestled with him, obeyed, worshiped, argued with, and honored him. Do we dare attempt a familiar friendship like this?

Read first to *understand;* then to *apply*. We cannot act on what we don't truly understand; but we do not truly understand if we will not act on it. *Knowing* and *doing* are the left-foot, right-foot rhythm of your journey into God. When you open the Bible, ask the Author to speak to you. Carry on your reading in the conscious Presence of God. As you read, pay attention to any word or phrase that jumps out at you. Why does it stand out? Is it confusing... encouraging...disturbing? Then pause and chew on this phrase, slowly turning it over in your mind, savoring the different facets of its meaning. Repeat it over and over with your lips or your mind. Restate it in different words. Think of some definitions, synonyms or associations for the key words. Reason out the logical conclusions implied in each statement. What opposing ideas are *not true* because of this? Feel the tension in the text. Try to understand the intent of the inspired writer: *What are they trying to get across? What does it mean? What do I do about it?* How would my life look if I believed this with every bone of my body? Question! Question! Question! Send your mind on a quest for understanding. And as you interrogate the text, allow the text to interrogate you. Even when our questions remain unanswered, we will have stretched our intellect far beyond its previous knowledge. After you feel you have extracted the full flavor from this word or phrase, pause and ask God if he has anything further to say to you. Then calmly move on.

Interpreting these ancient writings is not always easy. In fact, it can be downright confusing at times! We live in a vastly different world from those textured and colorful cultures of the Biblical eras. We will sometimes make mistakes as we strive to grasp the meanings of these God-breathed texts. Because of this, we will need the assistance of other travelers further along the road to address our questions and bring clarity to our misunderstandings. We do not need to become Biblical scholars to understand the Bible, but we must also be humble enough to admit our need for help. *Proper interpretation is more than just getting the facts right-- but getting the facts wrong will inevitably lead to inaccurate interpretations.* Feel free to use a good Bible dictionary, commentary, or concordance to provide much-needed background information, but don't get distracted by these study helps.

Many find that they have scarcely covered a short paragraph in an hour's time. Others will finish several chapters. Don't worry and don't rush! Never read just to get thru *x* amount of chapters in a day. Take the time necessary to search out the meaning even if you may not completely understand everything. It is commendable to read large quantities of the Bible but never sacrifice *quality* for *quantity*. Aim for depth of understanding, not length of coverage. Like running breathlessly through a museum at full speed, many people sprint through the Bible and wonder why they do not "get anything" out of it! I would rather immerse myself in one gospel for a year, entering into every moment until I truly knew it and knew Jesus through it, than to trample through the whole Bible over and over again and have only a superficial understanding of any of it. Sad to say, such shallow knowledge will not transform a life.

Never stop with intellectual knowledge! Correct information must always lead to interior transformation or it breeds prideful arrogance. Knowledge about God without love of God becomes a deadly toxin, swelling the ego. Do not allow intellectual curiosity to substitute for a life-giving encounter with Almighty God. Do not just fill your head with information about God but rather *commune with God using the Scripture* as your concrete reference point. It is your lifeline, a leash to keep you from going overboard. Your goal is not just to know the Bible-- it is to *know God* through the Bible. There are many Bible experts who have never met the Living God. The Bible is a means, not an end! These sacred texts have a unique ability to communicate the very Presence of God to those who seek him in its reading. This is why it is so important to read slooowwwly. Learn to nourish the craving of your soul for the Divine. It is absolutely tragic to become an expert in the writings of the Bible without ever meeting the Living Deity who fills its pages! Stop right now and resolve before God never to fall victim to this fatal preoccupation with the lifeless letter of the law!

We must study. We must learn. We must acquire knowledge. But always remember that understanding the Bible is the beginning, not the end, of the contemplative life. Thinking correctly about God is not enough. It must be followed by feeling, picturing, responding, praying, worshiping, interacting, living and loving. Otherwise you become a person who knows exactly what you *should* do in your mind, but is unable to carry it out in action. You will know what you are *supposed* to believe, but your heart will remain far from God.

We should probably start with the easiest parts. I recommend beginning your reading in the gospels (*Matthew, Mark, Luke and John*). These four books are the central core of the Bible and perhaps the least likely to be misunderstood. A slow and prayerful reading of these very reliable biographical sketches of Jesus will imprint his likeness indelibly upon your heart, mind and soul. A suggested pattern for reading is included on the **Lectio Divina Bookmarks** in the appendix.

Exercises

1. **Meditation Exercise:** Read through the lengthy **Psalm 119** for 20 minutes, pausing to chew upon any phrase that grabs you... Don't worry if you didn't finish! Now, allow reading to turn to prayer: ask God to give you this same deep love for his Holy Scriptures...

2. Go to a bookstore and pick up a simple Bible dictionary. Every time you come across a word that doesn't make sense, look up its meaning and significance.

204

50. On Meditation
Exercising the Imagination unto Godliness

T he pages of Scripture are your window into a new world! Lean over the edge of the page and tumble headlong into its depths! John Calvin describes how "we feel a divine energy living and breathing in it." Inhabit this new reality until you become accustomed to it. We delve more deeply into the Scriptures by the practice of meditation, which engages not only your intellect, but also your imagination, your emotions, your memory, your heart. You must penetrate further than a surface understanding of the sacred text. It must begin to bleed through your entire soul. Allow the words to stir your affections, to elicit a visceral reaction. Seek not just to know the facts but to feel the emotions that this Scripture evokes. Your sacred imagination is one of the most powerful ways of seizing your scruffy emotions and redirecting them. So when you don't "feel" it, reflect on it, dwell upon it, mull it over, chew on it until you taste it.

Your imagination is a dynamo! Learn to *exercise your imagination unto godliness.* Count on it: *whatever captivates your imagination will dominate your life!* Your daydreams will be either your greatest foe or your greatest ally in the spiritual life. An undisciplined, untrained, unbridled imagination will distract you, assault you, and entice you with many suggestions and temptations of sin, causing pictures, feelings, memories, and plans to stir up in your heart until you find sin irresistible. Followers of Christ must harness this same colossal driving force to fuel a furious pursuit of God instead. Allow yourself to be "tempted" and allured into righteousness. Let God tantalize you with his enticing goodness.

Learn to read the Bible in *pictures* and *feelings.* As you read the various story narratives of the gospels and the rest of Scripture, first try to picture in your mind in vivid detail the setting where the event is taking place, "seeing in your imagination the material place

205

where the object is you wish to contemplate," as instructed by St. Ignatius. This is called the *composition of place*. Visualize the length and the breadth of the landscape, the valleys, the hills, the roads, the buildings, the vegetation, down to the littlest details. You may ask: isn't this speculation liable to inaccurate pictures? Of course! But every story begs for its hearers to fill in the unsaid details from their own experience! Stories are always vicarious. They invite you in, to become a part of it! Does it really matter if Peter's face didn't look exactly how you picture it? Or if the boat was a slightly different shape than you imagine it? *As long as the details we don't know are consistent with the details we do know,* don't worry about being completely accurate (although you want try to be as accurate as possible). Transport yourself back into another world and dwell there awhile. As you learn to encounter the Eternal Father there, you will be more likely to recognize this same Unseen Entity at work in your own world even now.

Apply your five senses, trying to experience the various physical sensations that accompany the narrative. See in your imagination the various sights, paying attention to each character, what they wear, how they carry themselves, reading their faces for anything left unsaid. Hear the background noises, listen to the conversations, noticing both the words and the tone of voice. Do they sound sad, excited, fearful, boastful? Imagine reaching out your hand to touch and feel the various textures and objects. With the sense of smell, perceive the various aromas. Savor the bitter, salty, tangy, or sweet tastes that you would have experienced had you been there. Take a few moments to let each sensation sink in to your consciousness, paying attention to any memories or emotions they may evoke. Try to make the sensations as real as possible, stretching your creativity and exercising your imagination in the service of your Sovereign Lord.

Now, *enter the inner world of the different characters.* Contemplate what they may have been *feeling*; observe the *thoughts* going through their heads; consider what their past was like and how

206

it affected their perceptions of the event recorded. Alexander Whyte counsels the reader, *"...by your imagination, that moment you are one of Christ's disciples on the spot, and are at his feet...with your imagination anointed with holy oil...at one time, you are the publican; at another time, you are the prodigal."* Feel the revulsion at the sight and smell of the putrid leper. What would it have been like to have been Peter at the Mount of Transfiguration? Listen in on Mary's stream of consciousness at the tomb. Stand with Jesus' disciples as he taught them and imagine your gut-reaction upon first hearing these words. Or become an innocent bystander, blending into the crowd. Ask God to help you to actually feel the emotions they were experiencing, whether sorrow, or joy, or compassion, or shame, or fear, or excitement, or pain. The gospel stories speak to us on an intuitive level that makes sense even to children.

If you are reading more conceptual parts of Scripture, such as the letters of Paul or the Hebrew prophets, try to picture every word that you can. When an object or analogy is used such as shepherds or clay jars, stop and try to picture these things. Think of some characteristics of these objects that are relevant to the passage. When the writer encourages or condemns certain actions or attitudes, stop and picture specific instances of these virtues or vices. Also, find out about the actual people involved in the writing of this particular document, so you can imagine the interchange between the writer and the original readers of these letters of spiritual instruction. Picture Paul's face as he writes. Is he excited, angry, calm? What is his tone of voice? Then picture the faces of the Corinthians or the Ephesians, their reactions to the words being spoken. Does it feel like an encouraging pat on the back? A slap in the face? A vehement warning of danger?

Finally, *reflect on yourself* that you may reap some fruit from it. The more you can picture and feel the Bible stories, the more likely you will correctly apply it to your own life. Ask yourself: What do these things signify in my own life? What points of similarity do I have with the main characters? When have I experienced these same emotions? What needs or hungers of my own soul does this speak to? Is it consoling? Is it distressing? What sickness in my soul needs healing? What words spoken long ago in the text are being spoken once again by the Spirit directly to my heart? *What is God saying to me today?*

Don't let the Scriptures fall by the wayside. It can, it *must* penetrate your heart! If you come away from your reading with only new information, you may have done yourself a disservice, absorbing the knowledge which puffs up without growing in the love which builds up. This doesn't mean you have to feel happy or different as a result of your meditation, but it should have broken beyond your intellect. If you feel dry, dull and unaffected, then this may be a topic of conversation with God which could bear some real fruit.

Meditation Exercise

1. Application of the Senses: Go through **Psalm 1** visually: Try to picture each image in vivid detail and color... (i.e., What would it look like to be blessed? What does wickedness look like? Picture every detail of the tree planted by the streams of water, from the color of its leaves to its roots system, etc.)

Now go through this psalm with your hearing: Attempt to hear each sound (What do the whispers of the wicked sound like? What do they ask you to do? Hear the wind blowing the chaff...)

Now go through it again using your imagination to touch, to smell, to taste...

2. Now try to experience the emotion of each line... Why would someone stand in the way of sinners? What does it feel like to be influenced into doing evil? How would it feel afterwards?

Use your imagination to picture your own life lived in each of these two paths... Allow yourself to be wooed into a life of righteousness and drawn away from a life of wickedness... Do you imagine sin as repulsive? Or do you imagine sin as sweet? Ask God to persuade your heart of the long-term benefits of living right...

51. On Conversational Prayer
An Honest Dialogue with God

od is always listening. If you open your mouth right now and speak to God, or even speak inaudibly in the secret places of your interior world, the Heart-Knower will hear you. There is nothing you can say or write or think that God will not pay close attention to. He is used to sorting out your jumbled, unprocessed thoughts, so don't worry yourself about having to pray perfectly. Just open up the floodgates of your heart and let it all come rushing out-- unvarnished, uncensored, raw emotion. Let the Holy Spirit take your imperfect prayers and translate them properly. Do you have doubts? Tell God about them. Do you have fears? Your Father is listening. Do you have dreams or desires? Ask him to provide or guide, strengthen or correct. Discuss matters of mutual interest. Talk to him about anything that's on your mind. Anything that is important to you is a worthy topic of conversation with God (although maybe not for the reasons you think).

Good relationships require honest communication. Never fear to express negative emotions to the Unchanging Maker of Worlds-- he can handle it. After all, he already knew how you felt before you said it! So there is no point in trying to deny or disguise it. You will never find a better partner with whom to practice honest communication! With God, always say what you mean and mean what you say. As you read the Psalms, you will see that this is the way King David and many of God's closest friends spoke to him. Try not to speak words in prayer you don't mean. Be attentive to what you are saying. Assume God is carefully listening to each word; the least you can do is the same. If you ever feel like you're just babbling in prayer (not an uncommon occurrence for most of us!), stop and ask yourself, "what do I *really* want to say to God?" And don't be afraid of silent moments in prayer. Sometimes the best thing you can say is *nothing*.

Never be afraid of simply asking the Provider of All Things for what you desire. Learn to bring your every request to God. Your generous Father loves when his children ask him for what they want! Ask and it shall be given. Seek and you shall find. Knock and the door shall be opened for you. Asking is the rule of all mature, free and respectful relationships— not demanding, not manipulating, not expecting someone to just know. Asking allows them the honor of exercising intelligence, love and choice. God may say "no" to your request, but be assured: it is always for good reason. How would you reply if Jesus asked you, as he did his first disciples as they followed him home, *"what do you want?"*

It is important to direct prayer properly. Your prayers will be derailed if you forget Who it is you are talking to. You will only end up talking to your self, to the wall, or to no one in particular instead of addressing the Lord of all Creation. Because God is invisible, it can be difficult to carry on a conversation with him. Sometimes visualization techniques will prove useful. St. Francis de Sales counsels you to *"place yourself in the Presence of God"* before you begin praying, by one of the following means:

a. Reaffirm in your mind the truth of God's omnipresence-- that he truly is here, and that he is listening. Take a moment to visualize, feel, and be convinced of this unchanging fact.

b. Recognize that the indwelling Spirit of God is especially present within you, enlivening your heart. Take a moment to affirm, consider, and sense this reality. You may even picture an Inner Light glowing from within your body.

c. Remember that Jesus has promised his disciples, "I will be with you always." Use your imagination to make visible what you know to be invisibly true. Imagine Christ standing next to you or behind you just out of sight. What would you say if Jesus was standing before you in bodily form? Or perhaps you need to picture him hanging on the cross in front of you. What better place to offer a

210

prayer than kneeling at the foot of the cross? Some find that speaking aloud helps them while others find the whispers of the heart more effective. St. Ignatius of Loyola counsels us to *"speak exactly as one friend speaks to another, or as a servant speaks to a master, now asking him for a favor, now blaming himself for some misdeed, now making known his affairs to him, and seeking advice in them."*

Let your reading and meditation lead naturally into a heart-deep conversation with God about what has been revealed or stirred up. *Respond* to what God has spoken through the Scriptures. What is he saying to you specifically in your reading? Has he given you concrete instructions to carry out? Do you need to ask for his assistance in a particular area? Do you need to break into worship,  giving thanks and praising him for a particular grace or blessing? Do you need to make a resolution before him, announcing your intention and asking for the grace to carry it out? Perhaps you need to take the words of Scripture and turn them into a prayer.

What topics do we tend to talk about? Here are some typical conversation patterns that you will find come up again and again with God: *confession* (contrite admission of wrong things you have done), *adoration* (joyful celebration of who God is), *thanksgiving* (grateful acknowledgment of what God has done), *oblation* (surrendering and offering of yourself to God), *petition* (humble requests for God to act on your behalf), and *intercession* (compassionate requests for God to act on someone else's behalf).

One very useful tool for conversing with God is *a journal.* Your journal can be a series of written prayers just to help you keep your mind on track while praying. Many people find that the concrete-ness of writing helps to focus their thoughts and words to better express themselves to the Inexpressible Logos. You may want to write in it often, as a daily discipline, or only on special occasions, to record significant transactions with God. Your journal can be a record of your resolutions to God, prayers and their answers, things you are thankful for, even pictures. Or it may be a *rapiaria*, a grab-bag collection of what your Divine Lover has spoken to you, your favorite verses of Scripture, insights he has shown you, or quotes you have heard or read. Use it to keep track of both sides of your ongoing conversation with God. And as you look back through it over time, you may find it to be an accurate diagram of the shape of your soul.

You can carry on a conversation with the Absolute anytime and anywhere, not only during your set time for prayer and spiritual exercises. Try to interject a little conversation with God at the oddest times of the day: when driving, when using the bathroom, when standing in line, anywhere is good (as long as you don't frighten people who think you are out of your mind!). However, it is also good to have a regular appointed time of focused interaction that is not distracted.

Exercises

1. Meditation Exercise: Read slowly through **Psalm 22** trying to feel what its author is going through...

Is it shocking to hear this kind of bold complaining in prayer? How do you think God responds to this kind of honesty? Have you ever prayed like this? Is it legal to pray like this? Did you realize that verse one is the same prayer that Jesus himself cried out on the cross?

2. Picture Jesus standing before you... Imagine hearing his voice saying, "tell me your sorrows..." Take this opportunity to unburden your heart of sadness, frustrations, confusions, doubts or fears.

52. On Contemplation
The Wordless Gaze of the Heart

Can silence speak? The prayer of contemplation is the lofty mountain peak of the ascent of the soul to God. I have led you as far as I can with words. The *wordless prayer of the heart* is something I cannot really explain how to do. Contemplative prayer is done with your heart, not your mind, transcending both thought and feeling. Words can be an aid to prayer or a distraction. At some point, prayer should move beyond the confines of concepts and ideas, into the realm of spirit-to-Spirit contact. Deep cries out to deep, soul touches Soul, and in that touch a profound and wondrous transaction and union occurs. We cease striving— the gaze of our heart fixed upon the unseen God. It is a *restful enjoyment of just being with God*, like sitting in your Father's lap as he sings quietly over his child. And yet it is not simple passivity; it is also awakened activity.

How do we attain this species of prayer? Theophane the Recluse says, *"to pray is to descend with the mind into the heart, and there to stand before the face of God, ever-present, all-seeing within you."* Let your heart cry out its yearning to God without having to describe it to him. Leap with your invisible soul into the mysterious depths of the invisible God. Project your earnest desire towards God like an arrow and let it fly. The unknown author of *The Cloud of Unknowing* puts it this way: *"Lift your heart up to the Lord, with a gentle stirring of love desiring him for his own sake and not for his gifts. Center all your attention and desire on him and let this be the sole concern of your mind and heart. Do all in your power to forget all else..."* At some point, all of your hard work in meditation, study and the like finally ignites a spark... and an intense love catches fire in the heart. Then you have only to rest in his Presence and allow the kindling fire to burn.

Many people cannot really grasp this type of prayer until they have walked some distance with God. So do not feel bad if what I have written above makes no sense to you! Don't try to force it. God will lead you there when you are ready. And usually, it is a dark path-- when you feel like you have exhausted yourself in trying to draw near to God, yet you still feel far away. It is when you have grown in discipline and holiness-- but it is still not enough. Various forms of prayer which nourished you in the past may leave you feeling dry and empty. You may feel disillusioned, even depressed, at your experience of God. Often this pain of longing is accompanied by *intense* encounters with human suffering and broken-ness, either in your own life or the lives of those around you. At this point, some feel they are back-sliding, falling away from God. Actually, this is the time when your soul is expanding its capacity for the Infinite Spirit, requiring more advanced techniques (or perhaps a laying aside of all technique) for drawing near to him. Your Teacher is leading you into a divine darkness of the senses in which all of your inadequate ideas give way to *a pure and naked will towards God*. It is in this dark night of the soul that we learn to pray with our hearts, to love him without any external props. Although it may not feel like it, this is a very good place to be in!

If you have found yourself being led unbidden upon this road, try your best to humbly surrender yourself completely to whatever God is doing in your life. Let yourself be stripped of all your ideas and ideals. It is when your mind runs out of ideas that your spirit may truly learn of the Ineffable One. It is when your emotions fail that you learn to enjoy God even when feelings of happiness are far away. It is when your imagination runs dry that your spirit transcends images into the imageless void of God's unimaginable and infinite Goodness and Perfection. When this happens, begin to make more and more room for this *"prayer of the quiet." Learn to just sit with God.* Many find that the further they travel with God, the less need be said. This communication-beyond-words with God becomes more frequent and more satisfying the more history you have built.

You may also want to find a copy of such classics as *The Dark Night of the Soul* by St. John of the Cross, St. Teresa of *Avila's Interior Castle* or the anonymous *Cloud of Unknowing*. These will help you along the twists and turns of this often treacherous inward journey.

Here are some beginner's steps in contemplative prayer. Think of it as *listening prayer*. Spend a few minutes quietly resting in God's Presence, listening for his voice. God speaks to the listening heart in many ways. But as long as we are talking, we are not listening. God loves to illumine passages of Scripture to our consciousness by making it jump off the page and strike our hearts. God also loves to speak through the still, small voice deep in our souls. God may speak to you with crystal clarity or through vague sense impressions. He may speak often or rarely—both of which are fine, as long as you are waiting upon him attentively. But I hope that, as *you listen intently, you find that even the silence in his Sacred Presence does something to you.* And you may find that it is not his voice you are seeking as much as his Presence, his heartbeat.

Another wonderful aid to praying in your spirit is *glossalalia*, praying in *spiritual language*. This calling out in unknown dialects, whether of men or of angels, is another very useful and edifying practice, expressing the inexpressible wonders of God without the distractions of having to think. It is super-rational, far beyond our own comprehension. I will discuss this more in the last section of this book, so do not worry if you are unfamiliar with it.

The best way of learning the art of contemplative prayer is to faithfully practice all of the other forms of prayer until God leads you further. The transition from active methods like reading, meditation, and conversational prayer to passive contemplation is much like the eagle soaring on the wind. First it flaps its wings until it catches the wind (or the wind catches it). Then it must cease moving and allow the wind itself to carry it, resting in motion. Use whatever means you need to bring yourself to a place of being caught up with God at which point you may discard the exercises and simply float upon the current of God's Spirit.

Exercises

1. Silence Exercise: Spend a few minutes in quiet before God with this one phrase on your mind: *"Be still and know that I am God."* When distracting thoughts appear in your mind, do not try to wrestle them down. Simply ignore them. *"Look beyond them-- over their shoulder, as it were-- as if you were looking for something else, which of course you are."* (Cloud of Unknowing, ch.32) Then gently withdraw your mind from engaging them, returning your attention to this simple phrase... How long can you keep this silence before God without your mind wandering all over the place? If you can just remain silently resting in God's Presence for the next half hour, don't even worry about covering the rest of the exercises...

2. Meditation Exercise: Slowly and meditatively read **Luke 10:38-42** as we've practiced, picturing the places and faces... Are you more like Mary or Martha? Is it easy to simply sit at Jesus feet with your attention fixed upon him? What gets you worried and distracted?

3. Imagery Exercise: Find a place of rest. Close your eyes, seeing yourself in one of the following Biblical images: You are a child resting in the lap of your Father; or you are a sheep snuggled upon the shoulders of your Shepherd. Or kneel before God like a servant, waiting in reverence and affection, whispering to him, *"Here am I."*

4. Listening Exercise: Now ask God to speak to you: *"Speak, LORD, for your servant is listening."* Give him a few minutes of quiet attention, listening intently to the stirrings within... He may speak... Or he may not... Does a word, phrase or picture pop into your head? If you are not sure if it is God or just your own thoughts, try to ignore it... Does it stay with you quietly but persistently? Is it in agreement with the Holy Scriptures? If so, it is very likely that this is God speaking to you. Write it down or describe it in your journal. You may want to test it by asking your spiritual director about it.

216

53. On Lectio Divina
A Regular Spiritual Workout Routine

T here is no discipleship without discipline. Every great athlete or musician knows the value of a daily practice regimen. Proficiency only yields to the disciplined. Are you an undisciplined person? If you are, I must be frank—unless you change, you will waste your potential. Learn to be disciplined in the art of prayer. You won't follow Christ very far if you insist on always taking the easy way out. If you are not willing to do the things now which will bring about good things later, you will not reliably get good things later. Starting today, begin a daily regimen of spiritual exercises. If you've followed this book, you have already been practicing.

Set aside a substantial amount of time every day for your spiritual workout, perhaps an hour (although even as little as 15 minutes would probably do you a world of good). Choose a time of the day that you can withdraw from the world to your place of solitude with Christ. Many say that the early morning is best, soon after you awake. However, you must decide for yourself what time of day is most conducive to a regular appointment with the King of the Universe. For you, it may be in the evening. It may be at lunchtime. Whenever during the day you choose to have it, this is your time of total "God-immersion." Soak yourself in God's healing Presence. This will make it easier to connect with him at all other times.

Now that you have tried each of these forms of prayer, gather them up into a *regula*, a rule or pattern of living. One of the most helpful patterns is the ancient art of *lectio divina*, or *sacred reading*, practiced since the earliest centuries of the desert fathers and mothers. It follows the fourfold path of *lectio* (reading/studying), *meditatio* (Scripture meditation), *oratio* (conversational prayer/journaling), and *contemplatio* (wordless

217

contemplation/restful silence). With a smorgasbord of options before you, you may find yourself drawn immediately into a specific kind of prayer. But the structure of *lectio divina* will give you a "balanced diet", making room for you to connect with God through your body, your emotions, your imagination, your intellect, your spirit, your entire soul. However, after you've tried it a few times, you can then adjust accordingly.

This exercise can be tailored to suit your own profile by increasing or decreasing the time spent in each activity. Through practice, discover what best fits your personal preferences. Do you reliably encounter God's Presence whenever you open the pages of Scripture? Then set aside generous portions of time for this. Are you more inclined to sense him in silent contemplation? Do you tend to hear him when you are writing in your journal? Do you feel at home in the simple repetitions of the Lord's Prayer or the Psalms? Put a lot of time into the types of prayer that you are more comfortable with— but try not to completely neglect those that are not as easy for you. Build on your strengths but don't ignore your weaknesses. Whether you revel in routines or wish to soar with spontaneity, having an elemental structure as a guideline will keep you from getting lost or disoriented. Practice working your way through the steps in order. Then you may depart from the pattern anytime you feel so moved. Don't feel constrained by the form but use it as it helps.

Begin each time of *lectio divina* with a short period of *preparation.* Once you have found a place of solitude, a posture of stillness and have become accustomed to the silent Presence of God, the rest of your time of prayer is practically guaranteed to be rich and fruitful. Many people flounder in prayer because they have not taken the time to get themselves ready! They stumble through the Bible, and mumble through many words without any sense of having contacted God-- like talking on the phone when all you hear is a busy signal! Don't neglect or short change this very important step which sets the tone for all that follows. You may need only a minute for this or you may need 15 minutes. Do whatever it takes to *make yourself present to God,* to focus your entire heart, mind, and soul on him. Then ask God boldly for what you desire from this time of prayer. Use any breathing exercises, physical sensation exercises, vocal prayers, songs or anything else to still and silence your soul in conscious awareness of God. Then you may begin climbing the *"ladder of divine ascent"* known as *lectio divina*.

Once you have connected with God, let him speak to you through his Holy Scriptures, receiving the nourishment for your mind and heart that it provides. First, engage God through reading, studying, and questioning with your intellect. Then, open up your imagination, feelings, and will through meditation until you are thoroughly soaked with God's living word. Don't leave the pages until you have gotten a sense, however slight, of what God is saying specifically to you. Leave no part of your soul untouched. Then, respond to God's action by talking to him about it, initiating a relational interchange. Finally, before you go, give him some time to work on you as you rest quietly in his embrace. Then as you leave this time of spiritual exercise, you may want to transition back into your other tasks by gathering up a "spiritual bouquet" from the garden, taking with you a word, a verse, a phrase or insight to ponder for the rest of the day. In this way, you can take the atmosphere of prayer along with you wherever you go.

Meditation Exercise
Turn to **John 15:1-17**. Use the *"Lectio Divina"* structure of Sacred Reading written on the following page to guide you through your meditation.

Lectio Divina

Preparation: Place yourself in God's Presence

- Find a place where you can be undisturbed (a desk, a park, etc.)
- Quiet your soul before God, who is all around you and within you.
- Recognize, invite and try to sense the Presence of God within you.
- Slow down enough to listen to your own breathing.
- Ask God to reveal himself to you: "I want to know You more..."

"For a few moments, I think of God's veiled presence in things: in the elements, giving them existence; in plants, giving them life; in animals, giving them sensation; and finally, in me, giving me all this and more, making me a temple, a dwelling-place of the Spirit." – *Ignatius of Loyola*

I. Lectio (Read/Study)

- Slowly read and re-read a small portion of Scripture. *Don't* rush!
- Pause and reflect on any word or phrase that grabs you or stands out.
- Write down any questions, observations, insights, summaries, pictures, ideas, or random thoughts...

II. Meditatio (Reflect/Meditation)

- Enter into the story with your imagination.
- Imagine the setting by applying all of your senses: tastes, smells, sights and colors, hear the sounds, feel the textures, etc.
- Imagine you are a character in the story: What are your thoughts, feelings, and motivations? What kind of life have you lived? What do you personally have in common with this person?
- Hear Jesus' words to you. What is he saying to you specifically?

III. Oratio (Respond/Conversational Prayer)

- Converse with Jesus as if he were standing right beside you, as you would speak to a friend. Is he speaking back to you?
- You may want to use a prayer journal to write a letter to God.
- Ask God to help you to live this out today.

IV. Contemplatio (Rest/Silent Contemplation)

- Rest quietly in a sense of God's nearness.
- Feel God's warm embrace as you have encountered him.
- Soak yourself in his Presence. You're with him; He's with you.

54. On the Practice of the Presence of God
Unbroken Communion with God

Every moment is sacred; every second significant. The spiritual life is a life lived consciously and constantly in God's glorious Presence. After you have learned to set aside a daily period of time for intense spiritual exercises, your next goal is to turn every second of every day into one continuous experience of God-saturation. Create a context in which *each moment* is drenched in a pervasive awareness of God's nearness. Allow the fabric of your daily life to be slowly submerged in the Spirit of God so that each "mundane" activity sparkles with new purpose. The continual practice of the Presence of God will so dramatically transform the substance of your everyday transactions that they take on a decidedly new meaning. Learn to live in a kind of "Enoch friendship," in which God is your constant Companion, where it is your actual experience that *"He walks with me and talks with me"* all day long.

Paul gives three interlocking commands for a fulfilling, God-pleasing life: *"Be joyful always. Pray continually. Give thanks in all circumstances."* Perpetual prayer! Indiscriminate thankfulness! Unspeakable joy! Could this be the subtext of your daily existence? Contrary to popular belief, continuous prayer does not need to distract you from the countless tasks of ordinary life. Interacting with God can become your preoccupation 24-7 without ruining everything else. In fact, God's involvement can actually *enhance* each moment of your day. Incidentally, this is one reason it's so important to practice prayers that don't require you to be talking. You can be "in touch" with God as you work on math problems, converse with co-workers, eat your lunch, read books, watch movies, and play with children. *Nothing* in life is better accomplished by stepping out of awareness of God's Presence. No endeavor requires that you unplug yourself from God to be more effective (unless you count sinning).

Is this an idealistic pipe dream? No... as long as you leave perfectionism out of this! Once again, I must remind you that, as in every spiritual exercise, the pressure to perform perfectly will crush you. If you are convinced that you are already a huge disappointment to your Father in heaven and that through these spiritual exercises you may be able to earn back some of his favor, you will live a miserable life based on a lie. Please believe me: God absolutely loves being with you! He is thrilled at *every* little attempt of one of his children to snuggle closer to him! Get used to feeling and knowing God's total acceptance and affection before you begin working at a discipline. Are you convinced before you even start, that God is insanely in love with you? That is the absolute truth of God's heart! If you've lost sight of your heavenly Father's love, you are blind! Stop right now and go back to regain your vision of the God who is so fiercely committed to your well-being, that he was willing to spill his own blood just to be with you! Then you will be motivated, not by fear, but by gratitude and affection, able to enjoy God's Presence rather than endure it.

Practicing the Presence of God is a habit not easily developed. But after you have worked hard to form the habit, the habit will work hard to form you. Its intensity requires that we have fallen hopelessly in love with the King of Glory. No ruthless slave-driver god will be able to sustain this mind set constantly on God. Through the methods you have already learned in previous chapters, you are developing the "muscles" of your spirit to the point where this kind of God-soaked life becomes possible. Your intentional practice times each day for silence, Scripture reading and meditation, conversing with God, and wordless prayers start to spill over into everything else. You will begin to talk with God not only during your set times of prayer but also while you brush your teeth, along the way to work, or waiting in line at the store. You will begin to meditate upon the glory of Christ not only as you read the Bible but as you recite Scripture passages in the bathroom, as you look into the eyes of a loved one, or as you watch a funny commercial. You will sense the supernatural proximity of God when you hug a friend, eat your breakfast, or even while your boss is yelling at you! Your heart will begin to "see" God everywhere. You will begin to feel his joy-filled gaze fixed upon you at all times. The skills that you are learning through disciplined, direct effort will soon become habitual patterns of behavior that will serve to form in you the kind of love-fueled life that Jesus lived.

Here are some ways to start this process: You may find that *music of praise* is a tool for injecting God's involvement into your humdrum routines. Songs have the ability to lift the spirit with little distraction or conscious effort. Fill your morning with song, allowing your favorite hymns and choruses to rise from the depths of your heart and echo throughout the day, lodging themselves deep in the hidden recesses of your subconscious soul. Cultivate a perpetual flame of worship throughout the day with psalms, hymns, and spiritual songs. Choose your musical collection and playlists intentionally to support a habit of God-attentiveness.

Practice *meditation on the ordinary*. Find God behind every leaf or blade of grass. Assume that everything you see or hear is the veiled face of God. The medieval mystics (who called this "occasional meditation") declared that *"the Creator is seen in his creatures"*. It is like playing hide-and-seek with the Father of Light throughout the day. He hides himself behind the "usual stuff" you see each day and you try your hardest to spot him. Be forever alert to his movement. You will see a sparrow and instead of thinking, "oh...there's a sparrow", you will see grace...in the meticulous care that God has for this insignificant little bird. You will see an old man sipping coffee and it will make you think of God's goodness...and you won't even know why. Let every sight remind you of God: sun, clouds, trees, all of creation can become allusions to their Creator. This search for God becomes easier as your sensitivity to his Spirit and your knowledge of his word increases. Like a lovesick teenager, let everything you see make you think of that special Someone. And whenever you spot him, send up a spontaneous burst of prayerful adoration. He will be delighted at the attention. We erroneously assume that "mystics" constantly see supernatural visions of God, when really they simply see God constantly through the natural.

Play Frank Laubach's *game of minutes*. Take a second out of every minute to turn your mind towards God with a quick "hi" or "I love you" or just a knowing look of your soul. See how many times you can turn your mind to God throughout your day, even just for a brief instant. Ask yourself every hour if you have remembered God's Presence throughout that time. Use little things as reminders: the hourly chime of your watch, the color green, or the phone ringing. Don't be discouraged that you will not be very good at this game at first, failing more than you succeed. Keep it playful and familiar. God is not disappointed in your failures and he is overjoyed at your successes. Just keep trying. The recalibration of your mindset will not happen in a day. In fact it will probably take a long time for this practice to become second-nature. You may also pick up the little classic, *Practicing His Presence*, a compilation of Frank Laubach and Brother Lawrence for further instruction and inspiration.

Exercises

1. **Song Exercise:** List some of your favorite songs to your Savior. Sing one right now... Try to sing it often throughout today...

2. **Meditation Exercise:** Meditatively read **Luke 24:13-35**, putting yourself in the place of these disciples... How could they walk so far in Jesus' Presence without realizing it? Why did Jesus "change his mind" when the disciples invite him to stay with them? Could Jesus already be walking beside you now without you recognizing him?

3. Think about whatever activity you will do immediately after your reading and exercises today. Try to imagine keeping God in mind throughout that activity. Now go to it. Attempt to keep "in touch" with God throughout it.

55. On Morning Prayer
A Daily Renewal of Vision

Don't wake up with your eyes closed. If your aim is to live every waking moment in the awareness of God's Presence and purpose, this should start with your first thoughts of the day. If you will just take a minute at the dawn of each new day to recalibrate your life with eternity, you will find your entire day takes on a different hue, an eternal glow. Seek daily renewal. As soon as you wake up, whether you are still lying in bed, or if you need to crawl onto your knees beside your bed, or stumble into the shower, make it a habit that as soon as you have a moment of clear-headed thought available, spend just a couple of minutes offering your life, your day, your very self into the caring hands of God. Don't let your mind begin to wander. Set your mind firmly on God each morning.

Use the crucial moments of daybreak to renew your vision of reality: of God, yourself, and the world. Who is God? What is he like? Who are you? What are you doing here? Why are you doing what you're doing? What do you want most out of life? Have these questions settled before you start doing anything. Don't waste a minute trampling roughshod over these holy moments of your life without a firm purpose. Otherwise, there is really no reason to be up and about. Make it a habit each morning that your first thoughts are of God and his will for your life. Wipe the sleep out of your eyes with a word of thanks. Capture a clear vision with which to walk.

Why is this so important? Because *we so easily forget what is first in life.* We so quickly allow secondary goals to turn into primary goals-- undermining our highest aspirations. Thus God's repeated reminder in Scripture: *"Remember..."* Our simple need for basic necessities (food, shelter, clothing...) subtly becomes an all-consuming drive for wealth if we are not constantly reminded of what is most important. We sacrifice our most significant

225

relationships for temporary pleasures. We allow daily problems to take our eyes off of the finish line, and then we wonder why we have drifted so far off course. If you don't want to waste your life away, don't start a single day without a firm grasp of your goal. Surrender yourself and your day into the hands of God.

Start each day free. Shake off the shackles of yesterday. If you begin the day weighed down by yesterday's failures or intimidated by tomorrow's unknowns, you will only go down from there. Make this your aim: *a single day well-lived.* Forget what is behind, both the guilt of past sins and the glory of past victories. Lay aside both the mistakes and successes of the past, both of which may be a hindrance to your race today. Begin each day with the humble mindset of a beginner, regardless of proven proficiency or previous inadequacy. There is a time for revisiting the past, but it is no place to live your daily life. You may have fallen with a great crash, but now you must pick yourself up and continue to run. Don't keep looking back or you may stumble again! Release yesterday; embrace today. Refuse to allow past mistakes to excuse your present slackness. Otherwise, cynicism will dim the sparkle in your eyes— you will become jaded. *"Today is the day of salvation!"* This day is God's gift to you, a special mission from the King, a present waiting to be unwrapped. Reset the default setting of your mind from despair to hope.

Embrace each new day as a God-given privilege, a new start. Every morning, rise from your grave, rejoicing in your rebirth. Today is the first day of the rest of your life! Do you accept it gratefully? Gratefulness is always pre-requisite to joy. Give thanks! Let child-like wonder flood your heart. St. Athanasius wrote of St. Antony of the Desert, *"He himself gave no thought to the bygone time, but each day, as though then beginning his religious life, he made greater effort to advance."* The old is gone, the new has come. As a newborn infant, begin following Jesus all over today as if this was the first day of your rebirth. Live it with all the vigor of a mighty warrior preparing for battle. *This is the day that the LORD*

226

has made. Rejoice and be glad in it! God's mercies are new every morning-- grab them before they get away! Rise like the sun, like a champion rejoicing to run his course. What if you didn't have to worry about the failures of yesterday... What if you were given a clean slate, a chance to be born anew this very morning... How would you live today in honor of your great God?

Offer yourself to God today, surrendering a new day into the trustworthy hands of God Almighty. Intentionally align your fickle will with the fixed will of God *"Thy will, not my own be done."* Ask him to take control, to lead you and to guide you, acknowledging that he alone fully understands all that is meant to happen today. Release control of the events and people you will encounter today. Surrender your schedule to God, giving him the right to bring changes, people, circumstances unbidden across your path, amending your precious plans if need be. Prepare yourself to do the good works which God has been preparing in advance for you to do. Is there a challenge before you today? A battle you need to fight? A task you must complete? Prepare yourself mentally for them, asking God for the grace not only to survive, but to thrive in the midst of it. Then happily receive from God all that he has chosen for you today.

Your morning prayer should not be too long or complex. It should only take a minute, but it should reset the compass of your heart to true North before you head out the door. It should settle in your mind God's central place in your life. Fix your eyes upon God, remind yourself why you love him. Fall in love with him all over again. Embrace your place in the universe. Then we can order our lives on two levels: the surface level of noise, conversations, and activity, and a deeper level where we carry on a continual, quiet communion with the Indwelling Fire from the Skies.

Exercises

1. Meditation Exercise: Slowly and meditatively read **Psalm 23** as you have been taught, visualizing each richly-woven image... Spend a few minutes resting in the peaceful, dependent mood this passage produces in your heart. Wouldn't this be a good attitude to start every day with?

2. Now you must decide on a morning prayer... It should not be too long and it should sum up what your life is all about. It may be to recite a vocal prayer like Psalm 23, the Apostles Creed, the Lord's Prayer or another favorite Psalm or a saying of Jesus. Or maybe it will be a few key areas to tie down each morning (i.e., worship God, release your anxieties, receive today's challenges). Perhaps it will be your resolution to follow Christ or simply a verse of Scripture. Maybe there is a song or hymn that will awaken you to what's most important in life. Or perhaps it will be a simple thanks to God for another day of life. Perhaps it will be a list: receiving one by one, the fruit of the spirit, putting on the armor of God, or listing out your blessings. Maybe you want to surrender your body to the God who created your hands, your feet, your lips, all for his glory. Maybe you want to have several options to choose from each morning. This is fine as long as it works for you, but start with one thing and expand from there.

3. Once you have decided on your morning prayer, write it out on a 3x5 note card or a scrap of paper.

4. Now place it as a reminder to yourself so that you can do it tomorrow morning. Set it on your alarm clock, tie a string to your finger or tape it to your bathroom mirror. Place it in the first place you will look after you wake up. Then when you see it, take a minute to pray your morning prayer... Continue to leave the reminder there until you begin to do it without being reminded...

228

56. On Evening Prayer
A Daily Examination of Conscience

Let your pillow be your altar. After you have learned to begin each day with God, you must learn to finish your day with him as well. Your day will probably be filled with some high points and some low points. Try to end each evening with a brief evaluation session with God. Every night, before you go to sleep, spend a couple of minutes talking with God about how you used the last 24 hours. Make your way back through the day's events, hour by hour, task by task, person by person, and assess, *without self-condemnation* how things went today. Take inventory of your inner life: Did you keep "in touch" with God throughout the day? In what ways did you experience God today? Did you love the people God put in front of you? Did you fall into any major sins today? Were you offended by anyone today? What blessings did God provide for you today? Was God trying to get through to you but you were inattentive? Now is the time to release it all back to him.

These last few waking moments of each day are your chance to take a quick *look at the state of your soul.* Learn to ask your soul for its daily report: How do I feel about today? What is the state of my emotions? Why do I feel this way? What was my mind fixed on today? How were my decisions? How did I respond to temptations? How did I respond to God? How were my spiritual exercises today? How were my relationships? What sins of omission did I commit today, things I should not have left undone? What sins of commission did I commit today, things I should not have done? Or ask the classic refrain from Ignatius of Loyola: *What have I done for Christ? What am I doing for Christ? What ought I to do for Christ?* Explore the uneven terrain of your own interior world under the illumination of God's light. *Watch over your heart with all diligence for it is the wellspring of life.* If your heart grows cold, there is *nothing*, no priority more urgent than rekindling that fire! This does not mean that we must be on a constant emotional high. Our emotions wax and wane like the moon, but if we find that something, *anything* has eclipsed the face of God from us, we must take immediate action to eliminate the impediment.

This is your chance to seriously consider how wonderfully God has blessed you today. As the old chorus exhorts us, *"Count your blessings; name them one by one!"* How often we ignore or forget God's involvement in our lives! Take some time each day to recall the ways that God has shown up: Has God been there for you? Has God provided for you today? Has he done any miracles, great or small? Has he strengthened you to accomplish good things today? Has he given you the grace to show forth Christ-like character in your life? Be careful not to look upon your own progress with self-exalting pride when it is only by the free grace of God that you are able to become more like Christ. For every victory and every good work, give thanks to God for his generous help.

Practice routine repentance. George Whitefield took time every single day to repent of sin and rekindle a resolve for righteousness. Take a second to seriously consider how you are progressing in your battle with a particular sin or fault that you are concerned about. Conduct continual course corrections. This is not time to punish yourself! It is time to "chart your progress" in this area and compare it with previous days. Analyze what interior moods and exterior triggers led up to your downfalls. Ask yourself: "How often have I fallen today? What was my emotional state? What thought processes contributed to my sin? What people, places, or other circumstances seemed to start up the sin cycle?" Then ask for the specific grace to say, "No" to this sin tomorrow. But don't let self-condemnation ruin this exercise! Use this time to turn from sin and let God wash your conscience clean. This is no time to feel dejected about how depraved you are. Guilt is not supposed to be wallowed in and "enjoyed." It is meant to be unpleasant enough to push your soul into the shower! Stand under the cleansing cascade of

God's overflowing, ever-flowing forgiveness. Let the healing waters of repentance wash over you, soaking your soul in the crystal-clear current of grace. Take Brother Lawrence's breezy approach to success and failures: *"When I realize I have failed, I acknowledge it and say: this is typical; it's all I can do! If I have succeeded, I thank God and acknowledge that this grace comes from him!"* No self-flagellation, no stress.

Your evening prayer doesn't need to be a highly-structured exercise. You may do this while you lie in bed, as long as you don't fall asleep in the midst of it. Or perhaps pray while you shower or brush your teeth or carry out some other bedtime hygiene ritual. You can cover specific areas each evening or just review what stands out to you. Or let God set the agenda: ask him the simple question, *"How did we do today?"* and let him put his finger on anything he wants to address. If all you hear are negative things and continual criticism, you may have a mental roadblock that does not allow you to hear good things from God. To clear aside this obstacle, spend extra time meditating upon the love and grace of God. You may need to structure your examination of conscience to spend time in both *thanksgiving* for the good and *confession* for the bad.

As you finally drift off to sleep, cast all your cares into the capable hands of God— he cares for you. Fill your mind with thoughts and images of God's peace, rest and goodness. Geerte Grote, founder of the *Devotio Moderna* movement, counsels, *"with whatever thoughts a man goes to sleep, he will also rise."* Don't go to bed worried or angry—or you may wake up under the same cloud.

Exercises

1. Meditation Exercise: Slowly and meditatively read **Psalm 4.** Enter into it with your emotions, listening to anything Christ says to you.

2. Open your journal to a blank page and draw a line down the center dividing the page into two columns. At the top of one column, draw a happy face and at the top of the other, a sad face.

231

3. Fill in the happy column with all the good that happened in the past 24 hours. Think about the good things you experienced today, physically, emotionally, spiritually... Blessings you received, simple pleasures you enjoyed, people who made life a little better for you... Think about the basic things that God has given you: life, breath, existence, health, etc... Think about the things you have that others may not... Give thanks for all of these, since *every good and perfect gift comes from above,* from your generous and ever-attentive Father... Think about your good deeds, ways you blessed others, your accomplishments... Give thanks for these, for *it is God who works in you to will and to act according to his good purpose...* Think about God's glorious attributes that have been in effect all day long... No matter how bad your day was, you should always be able to find many blessings if you look hard enough!

4. Now fill in the sad column with the bad that happened in the past 24 hours... Confess any bad things you are responsible for: "There I go again. That's just how I am without you." Tell God about the bad things that happened. Ask for his help or comfort. Could you even give thanks for the bad things, acknowledging that God can use even these things to accomplish something good in your life?

5. Before you go to sleep tonight, maybe right before you turn off the lights, spend a couple of minutes examining your day in this same way. If you need to, place your journal next to your bed or on your pillow as a reminder. Tell God about the good things, tell God about the bad things.... Examine your interior state throughout the day. What have you been feeling?

6. Lastly, paint this final image in your mind before you fall asleep— you in the loving embrace of the Good Shepherd. Use this phrase to anchor your busy mind:

> *The LORD is my Shepherd; I shall not want.*

57. On Task Prayers
Transforming the Rhythms of Life

What if work was worship? You have learned to start your day and end your day in conscious interaction with God— now we must attempt to integrate God's involvement into each activity between these two bookends of our day. If you are now living for the glory of God, even the most mundane routines of your life have new meaning. There is a divine significance in *everything* you do. It's in the multitude of little details that make up your life that provides the richest opportunities for living *"in Christ"* and *"Christ in you."* If God is uninvolved in the many "insignificant" moments of your daily life, then there is precious little left for him to be involved in! How would we bring God into such boring moments as walking up the stairs, brushing your teeth, drinking a cup of water, or taking out the trash? What higher purpose could be served by sitting in traffic, paying the bills, or blowing your nose?

Let us learn to make holy every task of our day. We turn every act into a prayer by one simple thing: *"Purity of Intention,"* as Jeremy Taylor puts it in the classic work, *Holy Living*. Remember: *it is the "why" behind the action that makes it holy or profane*. Reflect on the words of Paul to the Corinthians, *"Whether you eat or drink, do it all for the glory of God."* A sacred act like prayer can be made profane by impure motives; a common act like reading the newspaper can be made sacred by pure intentions. Teresa of Avila writes in *The Interior Castle*, *"The Lord doesn't look so much at the greatness of our works as at the love with which they are done."* The right reason sanctifies every action. When our goal is the glory of God, every meal becomes a blessed sacrament, every bath a sacred baptism, every chore a priestly duty!

A first step towards this practice is to stop and re-evaluate why we do each task of our day. A.W. Tozer reminds us that it is not *what* you do that makes your work sacred, but *why* you do it. Think of your daily household chores. What is your motive? Why are you washing the dishes? Do you think God wants you to do it? Probably he does! He doesn't want you living in a pigpen. If the Shepherd of the Stars wants his child to do this basic chore, you can actually please him by washing dishes! And when it is done to honor him, it becomes a holy work, a pleasing offering to the LORD! By refocusing your aim, you just turned a boring, household task into a divine calling! Chances are if you went through your day, most of what you do without thinking (hygiene habits, chores, etc.) is stuff that God *wants* you to be doing. You have been doing God's will without even realizing it's God's will! When you got dressed this morning, you were clothing a child of the King, preparing to go forth upon a sacred mission of God's kingdom in this world! Think about it: *God actually wanted you to get dressed this morning.* So pour your heart into these daily tasks knowing that you are carrying out the will of God! Paul reminds the Colossians, *"Whatever you do, work at it with all your heart, as working for the Lord, not for men."* Ask yourself as often as you can throughout the day, "What does God want me doing right now?" Or even the trite "What would Jesus do?" With every new task, ask yourself, "Can this be done for God's glory?" And when you find that it can, do it with religious fervor and enthusiasm.

This also requires, however, that we change our behavior when we realize what we are doing is *not* what God wants us to be doing. When we find that we have been honoring God through eating a great meal and then consider that God probably would not want us to eat that second helping of decadent dessert, we cannot, in good conscience, do it for God's glory. I do not want you to fall into an excessive scrupulosity, always worried and paranoid about whether each little action will put you in the wrong. And I definitely don't want you to feel that any time you seek pleasure in your actions, you have stepped out of God's will. God loves to see you enjoy yourself-- so any joy you experience that is not somehow

234

harmful could very easily delight God as well. Allow God to sharpen your discernment in these matters so you have a healthy appreciation for the broadness of God's will. Even entertainment and recreation can be a work pleasing to God!

The Celtic monastic communities of the early centuries prepared specific prayers for milking the cows, kindling the fire, and getting dressed. Use this ancient practice to turn the most boring elements of your daily routine into profound experiences of prayer. Walk through the different activities of your morning and prepare a short prayer or meditation that flows naturally out of the action. For example, while brushing your teeth, pray something like: "Fill my mouth with words of life and not of death, words that build and not  tear down, words of truth and not of falsehood." When you shower, ask for God's cleansing of sin, or ask God to drench you to the bone in his rushing, surging Spirit. When you brush your hair (if you have any!), ask God to sanctify your mind for his purposes, filling it with good and emptying it of evil. If you drive to work, your car can become your sanctuary of prayer and worship. Or turn your daily commute into a time of intercession for your co-workers. On your journey back home in the evening, turn your thoughts and prayers towards the needs of your household.

Your workplace should become the temple where you serve the Living God. There are few occupations that you could not do "in the Way of Christ." Remember, Jesus himself was a blue-collar worker, a craftsman who made a living with his hands. There was nothing unspiritual about his work as a carpenter. If you do manual work that requires little thought, rejoice and be exceedingly glad! You have hours to commune with God, to worship in rhythm with your body. The janitor can mop his way closer to God. The dishwasher can say with Brother Lawrence, *"in the kitchen with pots and pans I am just as much in the Lord's Presence as at times of prayer."* If you do creative work, ask God for his Holy Spirit to flow through you, expressing his primal creative energy through your holy hands. If you work with people all day, use it as an opportunity of flashing a quick prayer at every customer, client or co-worker you come in contact with. Then do your best to bring God's compassionate and caring touch into their lives as you serve them with kindness and affection. Ask yourself with every greeting, "How can I build this person up right now?" Become a fountain of God's blessing, an emissary of Christ to each person you meet. Resurrect every dead moment in your day by bringing the touch of God into it.

Exercises

1. Meditation Exercise: Meditatively read **Ephesians 6:10-20.**
Every day you enter a spiritual warzone. How can you arm yourself for battle each morning, during your everyday routines?

2. Write down the routines that you repeat every morning: getting dressed, washing your face, brushing your teeth, flossing your teeth, brushing your hair, eating breakfast, going to work, etc....Now list the tasks you do every evening before you sleep (coming back home, eating dinner, checking your email or mail, taking a shower, etc.)...
Then next to each activity, write out a short prayer that would naturally accompany such an action....

3. Now consider your average day at work or school... What are the usual activities you would be doing? Who are some of the people you will probably see? What projects will you be working on? What challenges you will be facing? Prepare a short prayer for each...

4. As you go through the next 24 hours, try your best to pray these prayers as you attack each task.

58. On Breath Prayers
Receiving God's Grace like Oxygen

Can you make your every breath a prayer? One action you will inevitably do for the rest of your life is breathe... when that stops, it's over! Now, if your aim is to interact with God as often as possible, you would do well to explore how breathing may be able to aid or hinder this goal. Since breathing is a reflexive, involuntary physical action, you can do it without thinking. What if you could *attach* a spiritual exercise to your breathing, thereby getting a free ride out of it? What if you could turn even your breathing into a form of prayer so that you could actually pray as often as you breathed? What if prayer could become as reflexive and involuntary as breathing?

Perhaps you feel a bit uncomfortable with breathing techniques, having associated them with Hinduism, Buddhism, or New Age nonsense. Am I smuggling a secret syncretism into our spirituality? God forbid! Breath prayers (as well as silence, meditation, imaginative visualization, contemplation and other more experiential practices) have been the rightful property of the historic Christ-centered tradition for centuries, and only recently forgotten. Followers of Christ have been practicing various controlled-breathing exercises for hundreds of years (see the writings of the Eastern Orthodox Hesychasts and the Spiritual Exercises of St. Ignatius). I would also remind you that you *will* be breathing one way or another, either breathing well or poorly. It may also be worth looking at the rich, earthy language of the Hebrews that makes up the Old Testament. The Hebrew word for "spirit" is *ruach*, "breath". Also, the word translated as "repent" or, alternatively, "comfort", *nacham*, literally means, "take a deep breath." Try reading Isaiah 40:1 with this fuller meaning. Or read the New Testament, using "breath" every time the Greek word, *pneuma*, or "spirit" appears. As we seek to offer our bodies as living sacrifices to the glory of God, we would do well to offer the functioning of our lungs to God and learn how to use this most basic of bodily actions to glorify God.

One very effective method of breath prayer is through the use of *"The Jesus Prayer"* which has proven a treasure of the Eastern Orthodox Church for many centuries. It is a simple repetition adapted from the parable of the Pharisee and the tax collector, *"Lord Jesus Christ, Son of God...have mercy on me, a sinner."* Or try the shortened version, *"Lord Jesus Christ... have mercy on me."* With every breath you draw in, whisper with your lips or in your heart, *"Lord Jesus Christ [Son of God]"*; breathing the grace of God into your soul just as your lungs inhale life-giving oxygen. Then as you exhale the carbon dioxide from your lungs, release the confession of your own impurity and need, *"Have mercy on me [a sinner]"*. This is difficult at first and requires disciplined, deliberate periods of practice. Then as your body, mind and soul become accustomed to the repetition, it will flow much more naturally, almost effortlessly. With practice, it can become almost as second-nature as breathing. Pick up the anonymously written classic, *The Way of the Pilgrim*, and read the inspiring accounts of one man's journey towards continuous prayer using the "Jesus Prayer". You may also try other in-and-out breath prayers such as John the Baptist's prayer, *"He must increase...I must decrease"* or Jan Johnson's vibrant variation: *"More of You...less of me."*

Another useful breathing exercise is to use your intake of air as a symbolic action to accompany specific requests. *"Breathe in"* the *Fruit of the Spirit* in turn. With each inhalation, fix your mind upon the character quality you are asking for, letting your breath become the non-verbal expression of your desire to receive. Use the breath itself as an implied plea that the Holy Spirit might fill you with this virtue. Each time you breathe in, repeat the request silently or out loud, "Love... Love... Love..." Repeat this until you feel satisfied that you have made your request known to God and received by faith what you have asked. Then move on to "joy", allowing the joy of the Lord to wash over you from head to toe, like light flooding through your being. Then "peace", "patience" and so on. You could also try a form of prayer recommended by St. Ignatius in which you take *the Lord's Prayer* and slowly read through it, saying one word with each breath. As you pause upon each word, reflect on and visualize all that the word means to you.

You can come up with your own favorite phrase that briefly sums up your aspirations for your relationship with God. Try the prayer of St. Francis: *Deus Meus et Omnia*— "My God and my All!" Or perhaps, "you and you alone", "in Christ alone", "I am yours", or "I belong to you." Or try a confession from Scripture, such as: "My Lord and my God", "O God, you are my God", "Lord, you know me", "the joy of the Lord is my strength" or any other of a variety of possibilities. It may be a phrase from a Bible verse (the Psalms are especially helpful) or a line from a favorite song of worship. As we embed this prayer through repetition into our subconscious mind, it can go humming along in the background even as we carry on with our daily tasks, talks, and thoughts. The shortest, sharpest word can pierce the heavens when hurled from the heart. Traverse the infinite spaces with a single petition.

After having practiced joining words to your breathing, *turn your breath itself into a language known only to you and God.* When you know someone well, even a sigh, a look, or a nod can *mean something* to you. Words are symbols—can't breaths be the same? Since God knows the thoughts and desires of your heart, you don't really need words to communicate with him. Take all of your desire and longing for God and wrap it all up in a single inhalation. You could start by quietly whispering, "I love you, Lord", putting your heart into this request. Then after a minute of this, subtract the words and just breathe, letting the intake of breath, like draughts of golden sunshine, symbolize all that you long for from God. Speak your wordless worship, adoration and love to God through the simplicity of a breath. Cultivate an insistent impulse towards Christ.

Here's an important caution: In breath prayers, as in any spiritual exercises, be careful not drift from *symbol* to *superstition*.

Symbols are physical representations of spiritual realities. Symbols (pictures, rituals, objects, actions) are very useful in that they strengthen our participation in and understanding of the actual spiritual truth-- but they are never essential to it. Symbolism turns to superstition when we start thinking the symbol itself *is* the reality. A wedding ring can be a powerful reminder of a marriage commitment, but the ring itself should never be thought as more important than the spiritual connection it points to. A parable about seeds can make the kingdom of God so much more understandable, but we must never mistake the picture for the real thing. The usefulness and significance of a symbolic act is determined not by anything intrinsic in the act itself but through our recognition of the invisible reality it signifies. Often a wise use of physical symbols (like breathing) can make our spirituality much more tangible and experiential. But don't fall into any sort of superstitious nonsense about breathing in actual energy fields or mystical particles and such! A breath is just a breath-- but it can be infused with all sorts of spiritual significance through our using it to express something beyond itself.

Exercises

1. Meditation Exercise: Slowly and meditatively read through **Psalm 150**, the final overture of the Book of Psalmody. Look at all the non-verbal expressions of worship! Try to see and hear each of them... How could blasting trumpets or clashing cymbals (or symbols?) communicate love to God? What would be necessary of our hearts?

2. Take a period of 5 minutes to practice the Jesus Prayer. With each breath cycle, whisper the phrase, "Lord Jesus Christ, have mercy on me" or an alternative phrase...
In the next few days, when you find yourself waiting in line or stuck in traffic, use that time to practice this prayer habit...

3. Open your Bible to **Galatians 5:22-23** and take each of the fruit of the Spirit and spend a few minutes "breathing in" each one...

59. On the Practice of the Communal Life

Spirituality is not a solo flight. An essential part of learning to follow Christ is restructuring our lives to make room for spiritual community. You need others and others need you, a caravan of companions in the desert of this world. You cannot fulfill your mission alone. It requires connectedness, cooperation, community. Just as you have learned to know God individually through the *contemplative life*, you must also learn to relate to God corporately through the *communal life*. A healthy, full-bodied spirituality integrates practices of both the individual and the social dimensions. Rugged individualism will suffocate your soul, choking out all the vitality of a spiritual life.

Human beings are profoundly social. For better or for worse, your relationships are a core part of who you are. You are more than just an individual. You are a member of humanity, a franchise of human life, and a participant in the future of this world. We are intrinsically interdependent, influencing and influenced by others in obvious and unseen ways. The individualistic culture of the West (itself an ironic, socially-driven mindset!) has blinded us to the way we construct our lives, our behaviors, even our ideas, in response to the accepted social norms around us. Most of our thoughts are borrowed! Even "rebels against society" tend to follow the same boringly repetitive forms, gathering in their own counter-cultural enclaves where they all carefully conform to the same lingo, dress code, values, rules, and acceptable behaviors.

Because of our essential need for solidarity, it is of utmost importance that we plug ourselves into a social construct that supports and strengthens our freely-chosen direction. Find a gathering of disciples who are genuinely seeking to follow the Way of Christ. Then immerse yourself in this learning community-- this *"school for the Lord's service,"* this *"workshop of the spiritual arts,"* as St. Benedict describes it. The most effective education is by example. In this gathering, you will have the opportunity to work with and learn from many other followers of Christ with vastly different gifts and callings. Also, in this protected environment, you can practice the relational skills you are learning among people at various levels of maturity (and immaturity!). How do you really love your neighbor in flesh-and-blood? What do healthy marriages look like? How would Jesus handle an irritating person? What does Jesus' mission look like in our world today? It is in your community of faith that the tires touch the pavement. This is where we can observe real-life examples of what a Christ-centered life actually looks and feels like in living color.

This *ecclesia*, the called-out community of God's people (a.k.a. the "church"), is in some mysterious way the physical body in which the Spirit of Christ dwells. The incarnation of Christ is still taking place! We can "see" Christ, even just dimly, through his reflection in the faces of his people. And you also, as a participant in this fellowship, become a mirror of Jesus to others. We become the hands, the feet, the mouth of Christ in this world today. When we gather with other disciples, Christ-in-me touches Christ-in-you and something almost mystical happens: we *become* Christ to one another. Wherever two or more followers of Jesus assemble for the purposes of God, we can be guaranteed that Christ is present in a very significant way. When I give you a warm hug or enthusiastic handshake, it should be as if Jesus is physically present to you through these transactions. As I speak words of encouragement to you from my heart, it is as if the voice of Christ himself is speaking through me. And the more attentive a person is to God's Presence, the more pronounced this effect upon others will be.

The "church" Jesus speaks of is not a specific building or weekly event, but the gathered people of God. No matter its size, it is a living entity, a social unit unlike anything else on earth. It is like a little pocket of God's kingdom, an imperfect but radiant colony of heaven on earth! By the cross of Christ, we become blood brothers and sisters with kinship stronger than death. This counter-cultural community provides a necessary social structure that strengthens us to stand firm against the sweeping current of the world so that we can bring healing instead of more disease. Through our involvement in a society of peaceful revolutionaries, we are empowered to live in a way deeply dissonant from the world around us.

How do we find this kind of spiritual community? You might find a healthy spiritual community in a nearby Christian church-- or you may not. Perhaps you have been burned or disillusioned by organized religion. Maybe you have run into church groups that have been anything but Christ-like. *The answer to unhealthy community is healthy community, not isolation!* Don't stop looking just because you found a few rotten apples. Instead, search all the harder. Despite her many sins, Jesus' church, like a weathered warship battered and beaten by the wind and waves continues to float through the raging ages, through countless cataracts and course corrections—an ark of safety, a zoo of faith. It will be messy. Remember, a good spiritual community will be filled with sinners! What good is a hospital that isn't filled with sick people? Don't be alienated by your own unrealistic expectations. This gathering of people will *not* do everything exactly the way you want it. It will not be perfect and it will necessarily have many people in their midst who are very wounded and broken. If they only allowed perfect people, would you be allowed to participate?

Here are a few tips: First, look for an assembly of people who looks to Jesus Christ as their standard. This necessarily requires them to take the sacred Scriptures of the Holy Bible very seriously. The atmosphere of their gathering should be overflowing with unconditional love and complete acceptance. They should demonstrate a real concern for one another's well-being. No matter what someone looks like or smells like, what sins they are mired in,

243

they should be welcomed with arms wide open. Like God, they should hate sins but absolutely love sinners! You should be able to sense the Presence of God's Spirit in their midst. It should *feel* a little like you think being around Jesus would feel. The leadership should prove humble and trustworthy— not driven by ulterior motives. They may be of any denomination or style. There are vibrant spiritual communities among boisterous, hand-clapping Baptists and shameless Pentecostals, or among solemn and serious Episcopalians and grave Roman Catholics.

If you have found a living community of Christ, cling to it with thankfulness and loyalty. This living resource of Christ-centered spirituality is one of the greatest gifts God has given you. It may be only a small handful of people or it may be a huge crowd-- no matter the numbers, *it is the Life of God in their midst* that counts. Wherever you choose to get connected, I warn you that it will be far from ideal. But it will have within it all that you need to practice the relational side of the Way of Christ. While there may be times it is appropriate to find another spiritual community, it should never be done lightly or without much prayer for guidance.

Exercises

1. **Meditation Exercise:** Slowly and meditatively read through the description of an ideal spiritual community in **Romans 12**. Which of these characteristics are most important to you?

2. Have you found a Christ-centered community to be a part of? If not, make it your top priority to find one ASAP! Search diligently until you find one... If you are part of a group of disciples, take some time to give God thanks for it... Also, spend a few minutes in prayer for those who lead it...

3. Honestly assess your spiritual community by the ideals in Romans 12. Where are they weakest? Where are they strongest? How can you contribute to improving your gathering in its weakest areas?

244

60. On Spiritual Direction
Seeking Guidance from a Mentor

Every disciple must be a good follower. This goes against the grain of a world that exalts leaders and scorns followers. Our society has sainted the self-made man and the independent woman. We admire the staunch individualist who won't let anyone presume to tell them what to do. However, if you are a disciple of Christ, you must rebel against this rebellious society! Deflate your bloated ego by learning the art of joyful submission. Are you humble enough to voluntarily submit yourself to an experienced teacher? If you truly want to make progress in the spiritual life, you will need a coach. Place yourself willingly under the authority of a spiritual director. A *spiritual director* is *a mentor in the spiritual life, a shepherd for your soul.* Just as a beginner in physical fitness will need a personal trainer to show them the proper techniques and tools, you will need a spiritual trainer to help you get spiritually fit. Find an experienced guide who can personally walk you step-by-step through the Way of Christ. As Eugene Peterson writes, *"For most of the history of the Christian faith, it was expected that a person would have a spiritual director."* At times, you will need guidance, teaching, prayer, encouragement, support, wisdom, perspective, instruction or even correction. Are you correctable? The inability to receive correction always increases our need for it.

Everyone needs personal coaching because everyone is different. Each disciple has their own story, their own style, their own unique path that they must walk. The Way of Christ cannot be mechanized into a one-size-fits-all approach. There are too many complexities, too many twists and turns in the road. We also need individualized attention because of our startling capacity for self-deception. We desperately need a spiritual director to free us from the grips of denial. As Bernard of Clairvaux used to say, *"He who makes himself his own teacher becomes the student of a fool."* You could follow this book to the letter or even the Holy Bible itself and yet still be moving away from God instead of towards him. It is vital to choose a seasoned follower whose life exemplifies the qualities of Christ to help lead you through the swamps and snares of your own journey. We all have blind spots— we need a mentor who loves us enough to tell us the truth. We need to respect and trust them enough to listen and learn.

There is a simple but very important test to use when searching for a spiritual director: just ignore their words for a minute and look at their life. It is imperative that they bear the distinguishing mark: *Christ-likeness.* Simply compare their life to Jesus and see if there is any resemblance. Regardless how smart they sound, how charismatic and convincing their words, how magnetic their personality-- the character of Christ should be radiating through their personal life. How do they treat people? Do they love people with reckless abandon? Do they regularly make God the highest priority in their decisions? They do not need to be perfect, but it should be obvious that they have made some progress in the spiritual life. They do not necessarily have to be more intelligent or even more spiritually mature than you. But they should have first-hand experience of God, not second-hand information. You should notice a growing humility, an inward peace through trials, an honesty about their own failings, a basic respect and kindness towards all kinds of people, and a real enthusiasm about God. Don't waste time listening to a teacher who does not set an example worth following.

Here are a few cautions: Beware especially of patterns of manipulation and control, power trips and other signs that they are using people to boost their own ego. Also watch out if they demand unchallenged obedience, or don't like to be questioned. It's often wise to have a spiritual director of the same gender to eliminate any mixed or hidden motives from the relationship, especially in the beginning of your walk with Christ. Also, be careful not to put your spiritual director on a pedestal or to become too emotionally

246

dependent upon them. If you find that you begin to feel insecure without their approval, or you need them to be instantly accessible, you may need to examine your heart. You may be the victim of a subtle form of idolatry: looking to a mortal for what God alone can provide. No human being can live up to these expectations. They will eventually let you down.

Throughout your spiritual life, you will need all kinds of spiritual directors, who will play different roles at different times, with various levels of involvement. While you may have many mentors and teachers in your life, there should always be a person who knows explicitly that you have placed yourself under their spiritual authority, and they have agreed to carry out this responsibility. It may be the leader of your small group, maybe just a friend with spiritual maturity, maybe a pastor, or even a monk or nun at your local monastery. In the beginning of your life with Christ, a spiritual director is more like a teacher, an instructor in the Way of Christ. During this stage, you may need lots of hands-on involvement and support. Later on, you may need someone more like a counselor who helps you to discern God's voice as he points out areas of brokenness that need to be dealt with as you seek to become a fully-integrated human being. They can help you to work through the various "issues" that surface upon your journey to wholeness. The more you mature, the less involved this person needs to be, but no matter how far you go, you will always need some kind of spiritual direction to help you to pay attention to God's voice. It is especially important when you get to the place where you begin to mentor others in the Way of Christ.

It is your responsibility to find a spiritual director. Don't wait for them to approach you. Instead, you take the initiative. It was said of St. Antony of the Desert that for every area of weakness in his life, he would seek out someone who exemplified the trait he wanted to improve in. Then he would watch and learn from this person until he had been tutored in how to live that way himself. Soul care is too crucial to leave to chance.

Exercises

1. Meditation Exercise Read slowly and meditatively over the story in **I Samuel 3**, imagining each detail. Try to envision it through the innocent eyes of young Samuel. How did the salty old priest Eli provide spiritual direction to this young boy, inexperienced in the ways of God?

2. As you look around your spiritual community, is there anyone who is already playing this significant role in your life? If so, pick up the phone and thank them for this arduous responsibility they have undertaken on your behalf...

If you are not quite sure if someone is providing spiritual direction for you, it may be useful to clarify with them your expectations and see if they are willing to take on this role...

3. If you do not have a spiritual director, look carefully for someone whom you would respect as a mentor in your spiritual life. Pray and ask God for discernment in finding the right person. When you think you know who might be a good fit for you, approach them and humbly ask them if they would be willing to be your spiritual director.... Don't feel bad if they say "no." Keep in mind that if they are already mentoring many people or they are busy with many other responsibilities, they may not have the time to be an effective mentor to you. However, there is no harm in asking.

61. On Small Groups
Sharing Life with a Handful of Disciples

Don't drown in the human ocean. One pitfall of larger churches is that we tend to become just one more unknown face in a swimming sea of humanity. Don't get lost in the crowd! How do we avoid faceless, voiceless anonymity? If your spiritual community consists of more than 12 people, it is probably already broken up either formally or informally into smaller groups. We cannot be "close" to everyone, so we must find a handful of disciples whom we can share life with. Find those few who you can really open up to, who will truly *know* what's going on in your life. This little gathering should be somewhere between 3 to 20 people or someone will start getting squeezed out. There is no need to be rigid about the specific number, but once anyone feels left out of the conversation, it is already too big. Join with a little band of traveling companions who will caravan with you across deserts and support you every step of the way. We need to be surrounded by a small group of disciples who will stand by our side even when all the forces of hell are arrayed against us! We need fellow-soldiers who will go to battle with us and for us. You cannot fight the war alone!

Be forewarned: *True community will cost you.* It is never convenient. You will have to sacrifice your own wants for one another. If you are only looking for a support group that "meets your needs" but doesn't require anything, you will not find soul-deep community. Self-serving gatherings of mercenaries ultimately leave you feeling even more isolated. It creates a narcissistic cult of consumerism that barters "friendship" at bargain prices. If you expect your fellow pilgrims to be there for you through thick and thin-- you must be willing to make this same solemn commitment to them. Real friendship requires give-and-take reciprocity.

Sharing life takes time. Cultivating a close camaraderie and commitment takes extra large helpings of time and effort. It will not

249

sprout overnight. It won't fit nicely into an overcrowded schedule. In our rushed and harried society, you must ruthlessly carve out valuable hours to dedicate to your small circle of friends. Perhaps you need to meet once a week-- maybe more, maybe less. Whatever the frequency, make sure you've established a solid sense of devotion to one another— where you have the freedom to call one another any time you need anything. Each member should be willing to drop whatever they're doing to be there for each other when needed. Let this become like a second family to you.

What exactly do we do in these little gatherings? It should include some sort of praying together, learning the Bible together, eating together, but the most important ingredient is *conversation*-- sharing in each other's lives. Regardless of the specific structure, you should discuss the intersection of God and your lives. We learn each other's stories well enough to help them to see God's unseen hand in the midst of it. Learn to *really* listen, to bear one another's burdens. We all need a shelter where we can process our pain without everyone trying to "fix" our problems with unwanted advice.

Are there people you can turn to when you're feeling broken, depressed, or angry? Is there anyone who will listen to you when you cry? We must be able to share our strength and weakness with one another. Each participant should have the opportunity to bring out into the open the deepest issues of life and receive love, prayer, validation, and encouragement. A close community amplifies the effect of our prayers. In the surprising math of heaven, one may chase a thousand but two will put ten thousand to flight. We increase our effectiveness exponentially when we ask our brothers and sisters who know us and love us to join us in our request. They provide confirmation, clarification, and, at times, correction.

This band of brothers and sisters must be a place of mutual honesty and trust. Everyone needs a place where we can let down our guard and just be ourselves, where we are always welcome, where we belong. We all hunger for a fellowship of friends who truly know us and still love us-- like God does! It is a refuge from

250

rejection, where we don't need to impress anyone. It should be a safe place to be completely honest about our struggles, weaknesses and failures, and yet still find enthusiastic acceptance and grace. Another requirement for building trust is that we must learn to listen without judgment. Let's be realistic: even though our spiritual community is enlivened by the Spirit of God, it is made of sinners like us, who still have a long way to go. We can help people heal by showing that we care about what they're going through, by validating their feelings. Can you simply hear them out without offering advice? Are you a safe person to open up to? Can you just be there for others without having to impose all of your great ideas upon them?

Don't get me wrong: there is a time for honest feedback and firm correction. But confrontation is only helpful when there is a bridge of trust already built. Confront someone for their benefit, not for your own. They must be receptive to a rebuke and only one who loves them can really discern this. Truth-telling is a necessary part of community, even when it hurts. Don't hurt them out of anger or frustration— but also recognize that some healing conversations may be painful at the time. Strive to be as kind as possible. Looking out for someone often means gently but firmly leading them away from harmful patterns in their lives. We must become mirrors to our close friends-- we should help them to see the things they do that hurt others. As a rule, confrontation should never be enjoyable. If you like pointing out others' faults, you are probably not ready to do so.

In order for true fellowship to happen, gossip must stop. There is safety in confidentiality-- when you know that your dirty laundry will not be passed around to others. Never break a confidence through gossip! A person who cannot keep their mouth shut will sabotage the honesty in any gathering. Slander is a cannibalism of the soul. Keep conversations from degenerating into gossip and slander with a simple question. If someone is "venting" about their frustrations with others, then ask them: "What should we do about it?" This question refocuses the discussion on a loving response, not just complaining about someone else's sin.

251

Your spiritual community is a wonderful place to learn to forgive sins and love the unlovely. Wherever sinners gather, there will be many misunderstandings, hurt feelings, disagreements, and offenses. These relational breakdowns are *essential* for a healthy group to function. In fact, most healthy fellowship gatherings have at least one very immature and irritating person who is difficult to love. This is good! It sharpens everyone's relational skills and patience. If everything is always smooth, there is a good chance that either you have not broken through the polite superficialities which keep your souls from intersecting or you have not welcomed people who were too different or disagreeable to you. Only false community is easy; real community always involves some difficulty. Do not use the excuse that there is no group that is good enough for you or that you do not "fit in" anywhere. You must be willing to do what it takes to fit yourself in. Do not waste your time on the never-ending quest for the perfect group. It does not exist.

One last bit of advice: No spiritual life is complete without the essential *discipline of fun*. Make sure you have lots of it! Eat, drink and be merry! Christ was not averse to enjoying parties and pleasures! Celebrate, sing, dance, play games, watch movies, go to the beach, go camping together! Enjoy life more abundantly! Your small group is a great place to practice partying in the Presence.

Exercises

1. **Meditation Exercise:** Meditatively read through **Acts 2:42-47**. Imagine what this community looked like... List the different things they did together... What would this look like in today's world...

2. Are you a part of a small group of disciples right now? Why or why not? If you are, on a scale of one to ten, rate your gathering on level of trust... How open are people with one another? Describe the dynamics in your fellowship. How could you help improve it? Start by planning something fun! (If you're not involved with a small handful of disciples, make it a priority to find one ASAP!)

62. On Spiritual Friendships
Connecting with a Fellow Pilgrim

riendships are not optional in the spiritual life. We all need at least one deep spiritual friendship. Christ always sent out his disciples two-by-two, knowing that iron sharpens iron. The ancient Celts called this person *anamchara*, a "soul friend", while the old Methodists referred to them as "twin souls". Is there someone in your life who is always there for you, someone you can be completely honest and open with?

Even in the safe confines of a small group, it may be necessary to limit how much you share. But within your web of relationships, you should have a confidant who knows you completely, whom you can share anything and everything with. Is there anyone you trust to freely reveal your deepest, darkest secrets to? The path of Christ can be a wearying journey—it's good to find a friend along the way. How lonely it is not to have a best friend (or two, or three)! A man without a friend is only half a man. The writer of Ecclesiastes observes, *"If one falls down, his friend can help him up. But pity the man who falls and has no one to help him up!"* He also says, *"Though one may be overpowered, two can defend themselves. A cord of three strands is not quickly broken."*

Love all people, but choose your friends wisely. Indiscriminate love does not require indiscriminate friendship. We become like those we are closest to. Hope and joy are contagious! Unfortunately, so are discouragement and grumbling. Find like-minded disciples who bring out the best in you. These profound bonds of brotherhood or sisterhood take time to grow. We cannot force trust or affection. We can only discover it and nurture it when we find it. Arrange for lots of time to spend with those few life-restoring friendships that you treasure. Spiritual friendship is built on the solid foundation of affection for one another and passion for God. This means you both actually enjoy spending time together. It

253

also means they take the Sovereign God as seriously as you do. You are *not* required to give up your friends who do not share your love for Jesus Christ. Your zeal for Christ shouldn't set back your relationships. Participation in a spiritual community shouldn't isolate you from other friendships. In fact, a Christ-centered spirituality requires that you make people a higher priority. We need to make lots of room in our lives for all sorts of friendships to grow. Following Christ would only require us to cut off a relationship if it is clearly harmful to us and could not be made healthier without such a drastic action. It must also be clear that such a separation is *never* a rejection of a person's worth but only a protective measure for the well-being of everyone involved.

A close spiritual friendship is the ideal setting for *mutual confession* and *accountability*. In some ways, this friendship will resemble our relationship with our spiritual director, who also knows the sins we struggle with-- except this is a peer relationship of mutual sharing. As we are brutally honest with them, they hold us accountable to becoming the person we want to be. Some find that this kind of accountability is best aided by a set of honest questions covering the most difficult temptations in your life. Through such an open and transparent transaction, they become your safety net that can catch you when you fall. They can be your prayer partner who lifts you up constantly before God in persistent petition like a perpetual flame. They can be your cheerleader, rejoicing with your victories and crying in your defeats. They can be your heart medicine that keeps you going when you lose courage. But how can anyone help you if they don't really *know* you? You must be willing to reveal your true self.

We cannot keep the fire burning within us unless we have other keepers of the flame on whom we can rely. Think deeply about how you can stimulate in your friends the wisdom and energy to accomplish greater acts of beauty and goodness. Through our physical and spiritual proximity to one another, our hunger for God should rub off on one another. As we listen to what God is doing in another person's life, we should catch the contagious love of God from one another, infecting those near us with this hope and trust. Through honest sharing, we gain prayer, encouragement and support. *"Even the strongest stumble and fall, even youths grow tired and faint."* When we are weak, we need someone who will come along side and strengthen us. And when we are strong, we can be there for them. No one is so strong that they never need help.

True friendships are able to handle all the serious stuff of life. But they shouldn't only be serious. *Fun is not a foe of serious spirituality.* In fact, it is our divine obligation! When we take God seriously, we no longer need to take everything else (including ourselves!) so seriously. It is the truly mature adult who can return to the essential discipline of "play time." The most important ingredient in fun is not pleasure— it's togetherness. A crust of bread shared with laughter among friends is more fun than a full-course meal eaten in silence among strangers. Without a friend to share it with, pleasure ends up only intensifying your loneliness. Loneliness and pleasure are a truly sad combination. Make time to have fun together. Go fishing, hiking, shopping, watch sporting events together, read together, go to a museum or a amusement park together, watch movies together and by all means, eat together. Meal-sharing was a cornerstone of Jesus' strategy. Do things you both enjoy, realizing that this, too, is worship.

A quick caution: be watchful over close friendships with the opposite sex. These often innocent relationships sometimes turn subtly into romantic interest (which is fine if you are both single and ready for such a relationship). However, it can be excruciatingly painful if the desire is not reciprocated. If you are married, confiding in someone of the opposite sex can be downright dangerous, especially if you start sharing your marital difficulties. So keep a watchful eye on the state of your heart in all such friendships.

Are you without a soul friend? We all desperately long for friends who we can count on to be loyal to us, who will always watch our back. You can keep dreaming of this kind of camaraderie, but you won't find it unless you are first willing to extend it to someone. Our transitory society makes it harder and harder to find true friends. But there are also many interior obstacles that keep us from connecting more profoundly with others. Perhaps we are insecure, fearing to be known, to be exposed as a failure. So we hide ourselves behind a false image. Or perhaps we have so much disdain and contempt for most ordinary people that we only want to make friends with the popular, powerful or perfect. No one is good enough for us. We may be so self-absorbed or needy that no one wants to get to know us. It is important in all of these cases to remember that there is something beautiful and valuable deep inside of every human being (including ourselves!) that makes them worth getting to know. The best way to find a dependable soul friend is to start being one.

Exercises

1. **Meditation Exercise:** Read the bittersweet story of the parting of two soul friends, David and Jonathan in **I Samuel 20**. Write out any specific things you see in the story that demonstrate their strong love for one another...

2. Do you have a deep spiritual friendship? Why or why not?
If you do not, write out a list of the 5 closest people to you... Who might you build a closer friendship with? Give them a call and see if you can spend some time together... If you do have a soul friend, give that person a call and tell them what a great blessing they are to you... Plan together to go out sometime soon and just have fun together...

3. Write up a few questions that you could cover with your spiritual friend that would keep you accountable to the kind of life you want to live... Then ask your friend to do the same... Commit to checking up with each other on these questions as often as is necessary.

63. On Reading Spiritual Classics
Learning from Ancient Masters

it at the feet of men long dead. Don't limit your spiritual community to those physically present and alive today. Having established the Holy Bible as your primary source of spiritual instruction, you may supplement your reading of Scripture with the classic writings of other saintly women and men throughout the hallowed halls of history. Even today, you can sit at the feet of St. Augustine, St. Patrick, St. Francis, Julian of Norwich, St. Ignatius, St. Teresa, Martin Luther, John Calvin, Jonathan Edwards, or John Wesley. Draw deeply from the experience and fervor of these or other spiritual masters of antiquity. Adopt one of these old saints as a secondary spiritual director to bring greater depth and breadth to your training. The rich diversity of personality and perspective among these ancient writers brings a grounding to our spiritual formation as they display what authentic devotion to God looks like in vastly different times, cultures and circumstances from our own.

You may want to start with some of the easier works. For beginners, I would recommend starting with Thomas a Kempis' *The Imitation of Christ*. This invaluable resource has been the definitive handbook on devotion since it's writing almost 600 years ago. Another accessible book for novices is Madame Jeanne Guyon's classic work published under the name, *Experiencing the Depths of Jesus Christ*. Or peruse Oswald Chambers' *My Utmost for His Highest*. Or follow John Bunyan's *Pilgrim's Progress,* a quaint little story of the spiritual journey. These writings require slow meditative reading. Don't blast through them at the speed of light. Read just a little and then pause, allowing them to sink into your mind and heart.

If you want to learn what a God-immersed life looks like, take up and read the simple little book, *The Practice of the Presence of God* by Brother Lawrence. This humble brother was a cook in the monastery kitchen where he learned to commune with God amidst the clatter of pots and pans. Or pick up *Practicing His Presence* which includes the aforementioned book along with selected writings of Frank Laubach, a modern mystic who sets a more recent example of a minute-by-minute relationship with God. (Laubach's example is especially instructive in light of his tireless work in international politics and literacy education, which were not hindered but enhanced by his constant attention to God.) Another classic in this vein is Jean Pierre de Caussade's *Abandonment to Divine Providence*. Or explore the use of the Jesus Prayer with the anonymous *The Way of the Pilgrim*. These books will instruct and inspire you further in your aim for a 24-7 spiritual life.

Although most modern books lack spiritual depth, there are some real treasures that can awaken your desire for more of God. If you cannot quite swallow the older writings, read some of the better writers of the last 100 years. I would recommend first and foremost, the works of A.W. Tozer, C.S. Lewis or Dallas Willard. All three of these brilliant thinkers and deeply spiritual writers are sources of real nourishment for the intellect and the soul. Pick up A.W. Tozer's *Pursuit of God* to kindle your passion for God or Dallas Willard's *Divine Conspiracy* for an insightful overview of the spiritual life from a contemporary philosopher. C.S. Lewis' *Mere Christianity* gives a well-reasoned defense of the Way of Christ. Other modern writers with a deep understanding of the spiritual life are Richard Foster, John Piper, Larry Crabb, John Ortberg, Philip Yancey, Eugene Peterson or Henri Nouwen.

As you sharpen your mind, try out other classic writings on the spiritual life including Julian of Norwich's *Showings* or *Revelations of Divine Love*, St. Francis de Sales' *Introduction to the Devout Life*, Jeremy Taylor's *Holy Living*, William Law's *A Serious Call to a Devout and Holy Life*, or the *Sermons* of Johannes Tauler. Or explore in greater depth the mysteries of God with some weightier theology such as Anselm's *Proslogion*, Thomas Aquinas'

Summa Theologica, Calvin's *Institutes*, or Jonathan Edwards' *Religious Affections*.

Use the biographies of exemplary followers of Christ throughout history to see the person of Jesus Christ reproduced, albeit imperfectly, in different shades and hues. Check out the *Confessions* of St. Augustine to see how this worldly young man was inwardly transformed into the towering spiritual titan he became. Or start with St. Francis of Assisi, a firebrand whose beautiful, fanatical devotion to Christ is chronicled in many books. From there, move on to the life stories of St. Antony of Egypt, St. Patrick, Henry Suso, St. Teresa of Avila, David Brainerd, John Wesley, St. Theresa of Listheiux, Hudson Taylor, Charles Finney, or even the more recent Mother Teresa of Calcutta. Or find a collection of the Lives of the Saints, Foxe's Book of Martyrs, or The Lives of the Desert Fathers and the Desert Mothers. As you get to know them through meditative reading of their life stories, you will in a small way get to know Christ better. Let their stories inspire you to greater heights in your own life even as you sift out some of the obvious extremes peculiar to different eras.

After walking for a while with Christ, you may need further guidance along the way of suffering and contemplation (Why do these two seem joined at the hip? Perhaps someday you'll know...). If that's where you are, try the anonymously written *Cloud of Unknowing*, St. John of the Cross' *Dark Night of the Soul* or St. Teresa of Avila's masterpiece, *The Interior Castle.* Or perhaps read Michael Molinos' controversial book, *The Spiritual Guide* or Thomas Merton's *New Seeds of Contemplation*. Each of these can give further instruction in ways of communing with the Divine beyond understanding.

These writings are not to be digested with the same readiness as the Sacred Word of God. We are not free to pick and choose which parts of the Bible we agree with or disagree with. However, in these subsequent spiritual classics, we need discernment to discard ideas that are misguided or just plain wrong. Use the Spirit-inspired

259

Word of God and our Spirit-infused reason to help us to filter out the wheat from the chaff. Many of the best spiritual classics are part of the monastic movement which has flowed through much of the history of Christianity. You do not have to be a monk in order to ignite your heart's fire at their flame. You can glean rich spiritual insights and wisdom if you "translate" their passion and practices into your own state of life. Always look firstly for a real passion for the person of Jesus Christ. They may be Catholic, Protestant, Eastern Orthodox, Quaker, or something else, they may have different doctrinal slants, different emphases or different writing styles, but they are indelibly unified in their intense love for God revealed in Christ.

As you become familiar with Christ-centered spirituality, you may also learn from other writings as well-- but exercise caution that you do not uncritically adopt beliefs or practices that are opposed to the Way of Christ. With eyes of discernment and wisdom, you can profitably look into the great works of other religions, philosophy, literature, psychology, the sciences, poetry, education, economics, politics, business and history—Augustine's statement rings true: *"all truth is God's truth!"* Learn to draw a line in your mind between what aligns with Christ and what doesn't. There is no antagonism between real faith in Christ and reason. A disciple must be a seeker of truth, wherever it may be found.

Exercises
1. **Meditation Exercise:** Slowly and meditatively read **Job 28.**

2. Go to a local bookstore and look through some of the above-mentioned spiritual writings. Select one that you will begin to read to expand your wisdom of the spiritual life.

3. Keep a notebook nearby as you read. Write down statements you particularly agree with. Also pay attention to what statements you don't agree with and try to reason out why.

64. On Communal Worship
A Sacred Encounter with Mystery

oin the empyrean orchestra! All the universe worships God—are you playing your part? *Worship* is the act of *expressing the glory of God* which often results in *experiencing the glory of God!* One vital facet of communal spirituality is worshiping together with our community of faith. Join regularly with other disciples in *ascribing to the LORD the glory due his name.* Through song and silence, Scripture and sermon, symbol and sacrament, we retell the story of redemption with our minds, our bodies, our emotions, our whole souls. Through creed and creative expression, visual arts and physical actions, we routinely remind ourselves of what we already know to be true, and of what, or rather Who, we are living for.

Where can mere mortals born of the dust go to stand in the Presence of Divine Mystery? Where can seekers of the Inner Fire venture to find the Temple of the Living God? Where does God dwell? Wherever we, the blood-washed people of God, assemble to worship in reverence and in awe, there you will find the *Holy God, Holy and Mighty, the Holy Immortal One,* revealed in their midst. It has always been the practice of Christ's community to set aside a sacred space and a sacred time to seek together an encounter with the Almighty. And we are not the only ones seeking. God himself is seeking with anticipation to find such gatherings of worshipers who will worship him with passion and precision. And when he finds them, he gladly seats himself upon the golden throne built of living adoration, joyfully inhabiting the praises of his priestly people.

Therefore, we gather expectantly each week to worship the LORD in the splendor of his holiness-- declaring his terrifying glory, his wondrous beauty, his glowing perfection. We do this, not to bring pleasure to ourselves, but to bring pleasure to God. Did you realize that God pays close attention when you express yourself to him? Did you know that he notices when your heart is not in it? You can bring a broad smile to the face of God by lifting your voice to him in heart-born praise! And though God doesn't *need* our worship, he does *want* it... he delights in every whispered word. He doesn't need our money, but it thrills him when you give it as a freewill offering. So we gather to give, not to receive.

However, as with all things done for God's sake, worship works to our advantage as well! So while we participate in order to bless God, we find that we also are blessed. As we seek God, he seeks us. Worship has a snowball effect: when we pour out our love to God, We find his love poured out upon us! One of the most reliable ways to "sense" God's Spirit (although not fool-proof!) is to enthusiastically join with others in proclaiming out loud the glory of God. He loves to show up in full force when we are all together in one accord calling out to him.

As we assemble as one, each of us reaches down into the depths of our interior being and finds that underneath all of our differences, there is one core passion, a deepest love upon which we are all deeply unified. Like members of an orchestra, we are all on the same page: bringing our individual parts and finding their greater meaning in the whole of a grand symphony. It is significant that we not only hear our own voice but the voice of the woman or man next to us. In the context of communal worship, we feel the reality that our highest purpose is found as one piece of the most perfect puzzle ever assembled-- for it is a picture of the unseen God. As we together speak the *amen*, declaring, "so be it" to each prayer of the individual, we add our voice and our heart to theirs. It is only in and through the worship of our Creator that the fragmented and broken pieces of jagged humanity are brought into unity, a majestic mosaic, the embodied image of the invisible God.

Every community of faith develops a *liturgy, an order to their expression.* Some are formal while others are casual. Most will include the singing of songs, the proclamation of the Word of God, the Eucharistic meal or communion, and prayer. Different cultures and different communities have a dazzling variety of elements in their worship gatherings. Some have stately robes, architecture and adornments; others are stark and simple. Some revel in incense, icons, candles, and bells; others use only a Bible. Some rejoice with loud singing, clapping, and dancing; others sit in reverent, holy silence. The Holy Scriptures do not endorse one style or taste over another. God loves this rich diversity! I hope you do, too.

Your job is not to critique but to participate. Surrender your individualistic preferences and become part of a larger body. A liturgy is a communal mysticism. With a variety of different personalities and styles involved, it is very unlikely that you will find everything in the liturgy exactly to your liking. You may actually find some elements of it insufferably boring or trite! There is always going to be some repetition and redundancy when week-to-week you find the same words. This strengthens our familiarity. It is always important to remember that you are not here to enjoy yourself but to offer yourself to your Creator in loving adoration. We have an audience of One. It is *not* for your entertainment but for God's enjoyment.

All worship must have an Object. Everyone worships; but not everyone worships the right thing. The only proper object of worship is the One True God. Always be careful that your worship is directed solely at him. Never allow the focus of your worship to subtly drift towards the music, the people, the building, your own feelings, the church-- all of these are only servants. Let them direct your gaze to your Master. A .W. Tozer describes genuine worship as *astonished reverence*. Worship should include several key ingredients: *admiration, honor, fascination, and love*. If this is not your response in your worship gatherings, reflect on this: Whom do you most admire? Whom do you hold in highest honor? What fascinates you the most, inflaming your imagination with wonder?

Let us put all we are into our worship, offering *our all* in response to the God who gave us his *all*. It should be a full-body message: we use our eyes, ears, nose and mouth along with our hands

263

and feet to tell God how madly, how deeply we love him! If there is any place in life to be immoderate, uninhibited, undignified, this is the place to show the full extent of your extravagant and ecstatic love. Put your heart, mind, soul and strength into it! Why do we look approvingly on a man "going overboard" in showing love for his sweetheart with lavish gifts, outrageous gestures, making a fool of himself-- and yet we frown upon the person who is "crazy" about God? So feel free... put your whole body into this transcendent transaction! Sing psalms and hymns and spiritual songs, declaring God's praises to him, to others, and to yourself. Use rich visual imagery to create things of beauty to reflect your Creator! To extrapolate Augustine's dictum: *all beauty is God's beauty.* Stand rapt in adoration. Put your reason and intellect into high gear as you ponder, study, learn and sleuth out his mysterious ways. Lavish your material resources upon God as you place hard-earned money into the collection plate. And even when feelings lag, it is not hypocritical to enter fully into passionate expression of what we know to be true. There is always reason for worship, even when we don't feel it. Let God's perfect nature and loving acts, of infinite worth and inexpressible beauty, determine what authentic worship will look like, not your own feeble and fleeting emotions.

Exercises
1. **Meditation Exercise:** Read slowly and meditatively **Psalm 100.**

2. Write out some of the reasons why you love God.... What are some things that God has done that you can worship him for? What are some attributes of who God is that you can worship him for?

3. The next time you gather to worship, come ten minutes early and prepare your heart... When everyone is singing together, ask yourself if your heart is being expressed in the words of the songs? Pause for a minute just to hear the praises of others... Meditate upon the fact that God pays close attention to each and every voice and heart...

65. On Eucharist
Participation in the Mystical Body of Christ

You have been invited to the Lord's Table—will you join him? At the last supper, Jesus shared a symbol-laden meal surrounded by his disciples: Peter, James, John...and *you*. Although you may not find your likeness in Leonardo da Vinci's famous painting, be assured that you have a place at the table-- in the glorious communion of saints. The Eucharistic Meal was instituted by Christ to make sure that every spiritual community of his disciples could partake in his Last Supper with him. And even if we were not with him at the historical event, we can still participate in the sacramental event. A *sacrament* is a *symbolic and sacred act in which Christ's mysterious Presence becomes real to us.* These sacred mysteries speak to our souls in ways that words cannot.

The communion is always a communal activity of the gathered community. It never involves just one person. This ritual reinforces the collective aspect of our faith, that *"we who are many form one body, and each part belongs to all the others."* The spirituality of Christ stubbornly refuses individualism, instead demanding a healthy interdependence upon one another. In ancient

265

times, the underground societies of Christ shared, in the shadows, the *agape*, or *love feast*, a family meal that constantly reinforced Jesus' command, *"Love one another as I have loved you."* Before participating, the warning would be issued: *"let no one have any quarrel against another. Let no one come with hypocrisy."* They practiced radical reconciliation in imitation of their resurrected Lord.

Rituals of worship are moments of recollection... to remember, to rehearse, to recreate those rending events that affect us most deeply. While Christ-centered spirituality should not degenerate into dead ritualism, we must not despise those few, reverent rituals which imprint more deeply upon us God's living image. Our communal gatherings culminate with the re-presentation of the Christ's Passion. At the Lord's Table, we replay the supreme sacrifice of the Christ for our sake. We recall once again the flayed flesh of the Lamb of God draped upon the bloodied cross 2,000 years ago. In our human forgetfulness, we dare not lose sight of the one essential fact, that crucial moment in history upon which all of our hope hangs—Christ and him crucified. We re-live the gruesome spectacle: the torn and beaten body, the dark red blood poured afresh before our eyes. We choke down the broken fragments of *the body of Christ, the bread of heaven.* We taste upon our tongue the bitter tang of *the blood of Christ, the cup of salvation.* We attend once again the memorial service of the man who gave his life that we might live. We shall never forget the steep price that was paid for the ransom of our God-forsaking souls. And we proclaim once again the Mystery of Faith: *"Christ has died; Christ is risen; Christ will come again!"*

And yet not just *remembrance* but *participation*! We are what we eat. By eating the body of Christ, we become the body of Christ. Christ's physical Presence on earth is now mediated through his apprentices... gathered and dispersed throughout the world! By receiving the cup of Christ, we receive the only antidote to the crippling effects of sin: a transfusion of Christ's untainted blood drawn from his veins by rusted nail. And yet by drinking of this bitter cup, we also volunteer to take up our own cross and follow our Lord all the way up that path to Calvary. When Jesus asked the sons of Zebedee, *"Can you drink the cup I am going to drink?"* in their blessed ignorance, they answered, *"we can."* Jesus confirmed that they would indeed drink from his chalice of sacrificial sufferings. We are the flesh-and-blood display of Christ now! We are his hands and feet! The church becomes a sacramental community, fellow soldiers, participants in the Great Insurrection which Christ began, crucified with Christ on Calvary's crown.

Different denominations have had difficulty describing the Eucharistic event in philosophical categories to the satisfaction of other traditions, yet this is the symbol of our unity (How ironic that a symbol of unity could bring such division!). Yet every tradition still celebrates this act of awe, partaking of the bread and the wine as the body and the blood of Christ (regardless of their differing definitions). We together are the men and women who drink the blood of God.

We gain a greater appreciation for the words and actions of Jesus when we consider the Jewish culture that formed his context. This was not just any supper, this was the Passover Seder meal, celebrated for centuries by the children of Abraham in commemoration of the Exodus event. This traditional family meal is freighted with rich symbols of salvation and freedom, hope and expectancy... encapsulating the whole Jewish identity as a liberated people, a chosen people and a messianic people. During this feast, they look back in figures upon the bitterness of slavery, the bricks and mortar they were forced to build with, the ten plagues through which God conquered each of the false gods of the Egyptians, and the miraculous sojourn through the Red Sea. They also look forward to the coming of the heralded Messiah. So when Jesus took the unleavened bread tucked away in its three-in-one pocket, the hidden messianic hope, and said "this is my body," it included a whole history of meaning. When he took the goblet of judgment, and proclaimed, "this is my blood, shed for you and for many," there was no mistaking his claim that he was the Passover Lamb, whose blood on their doorposts protected them from the judgment of death which passed over them. Jesus whets his disciples' appetites when he concludes with a promise that he will drink the last cup of wine with them in his eternal kingdom.

Exercises

1. **Meditation Exercise:** Slowly read through **Luke 22:7-30**, paying attention to the cadence of communion in that upper room long ago.

2. The next time you receive the Eucharist in your community, reflect on all the ways Christ is embodied to you in this ritual... As the presiding elder speaks the words: "This is my body," they represent Christ to you. As the elements are received, these also are the Presence of Christ. As you ingest them, you yourself become the body of Christ as the physical particles of the meal merge with your physical flesh.

66. On Baptism
Initiation into the Sacramental Community

ave you yet drowned to death? Your first response to receiving the new life of Christ is to "be baptized." Every disciple should receive this sacramental induction into the spiritual life (unless there is some substantial and exceptional reason why you are not able to). This is one of the first acts of obedience to Christ, your new Master. The word baptism literally means *immersion*. It is a soaking, a sinking, a dunking, a bathing of an object in a liquid that surrounds it on all sides and saturates it through and through. Thus, in the first century, the word "baptizing" would have been appropriately used of washing dishes, dying cloth so that it absorbs a new color into its fibers, or sinking a ship down to the depths of the tossing sea.

Baptism is a physical immersion, a spiritual immersion, a social immersion, and an intellectual immersion. As a physical act of going through the waters, it is a symbolic statement that marks our

entry into the Life of Christ. In many ways, it is like a wedding ceremony that denotes the specific date, the very moment in time when this spiritual bond is sealed, even though the love and commitment may have been there before. This formal ritual becomes the enduring reminder of a lifelong promise: that you will follow Christ, embracing his kingdom and prioritizing his purposes above all else. And while a wedding does not "make" a marriage, it does start it off on the right foot. This is the point of no return, the line in the sand. There is no going back to life-as-usual after you have taken the plunge. Throw away all you have ever known and step over the edge into the vast unknown.

Baptism is also a spiritual immersion, saturating us in the surrounding Spirit of the Living God. It is a rebirth into a new life, the initiation rite of death and resurrection. As our bodies are brought beneath the surface of the water, we die to our old natural life. The flesh falls into its grave. We enter the waters of baptism as a portal into a new world. Let us not forget what Dietrich Bonhoeffer reminds us, *"When Christ calls a man, he bids him, 'come and die'."* This is an invitation to crucifixion! But it is also an invitation to resurrection. You cannot have the latter without the former. As our bodies are raised up again, it is our entry into a different kind of existence, where we breathe the pure air of heaven even as we walk the face of the earth. We become inter-dimensional beings, nurtured both by the physical resources of the visible world around us as well as drawing from the unseen reality of God's penetrating Presence. Only the dead may join this sacred kinship; we enter through the doorway of death. Yet we emerge fully and finally alive! Baptism is both our tomb and our womb.

Baptism is also a social immersion, symbolically enacting our entrance into a new community, a new social arrangement. You cannot baptize yourself. You must submit yourself to the hands of another. There is no private faith—it is always lived out in communion with others, with a common language, common customs, and common stories. Most tribal cultures had initiation ceremonies for entry into adulthood, a rite of passage that signifies that you are ready for the rights and responsibilities of full participation in the community. It identifies us with a peculiar people, a nomadic family, a wandering tribe of wayfarers in a wayward world, the children of light in a land of darkness. This is your moment to take your place among the Twice-born, the People of the Presence. We are the madmen who speak of the death of God... and his spectacular resurrection! We are the jesters of the world, a festival of fools marching with comic delight in the opposite direction of the stampeding mob of society. Baptism marks us as members of the revolution.

Baptism is finally an intellectual immersion, a renewal of mind that leads to a transformation of character. During the earliest period of the church, baptism was integrated into a process of *catechesis*, a period of intense training during which the catechumen learned a new Way of life. It was a divine re-education to be able to function properly in this God-soaked world.  Just as a novice scuba diver needs to be taught many new skills, priorities, and equipment usage to thrive in their new aquatic environment, the novice disciple needs to be taught to think differently and act differently under this new vision of reality. All someone needs to begin is that initial burst of insight, a seminal faith which says, "Jesus is the greatest! I will follow him! He is my Master! *Jesus is Lord!*" Then from this starting point, they must begin the ongoing process of learning to live and love like Christ. Every spiritual community is responsible for the instruction of beginners in the Way of Christ. And the disciples most likely to advance to proficiency are those who see themselves always as beginners.

We must relearn life and love. Our moral re-formation is similar to a child's first formation. What starts as external compulsion eventually becomes internal compulsion. We need our elders to teach us how to do what is right. The girl who is compelled to read by her teacher becomes a woman who is compelled to read by her own inner thirst for wisdom. The boy who is forced to wash his hands "because Mom said so" becomes a man who is forced to wash his hands by his own understanding of cleanliness. Obedience leads to abundance. Do you want to become a person who *has* to do what is right? Do you want to become a person who *loves* to do what is right? They are one and the same! When you learn to love always what is good, you are forced into it by your own desire. The goal is inward transformation, an internal obligation to the good. We must acquire a taste for it!

The process of *catechesis*, culminating with baptism, establishes you in a new identity. Some cultures even give you a new name at baptism to emphasize this fact. You have been crucified with Christ, and you no longer live! The old man who went down in baptism never comes back up. Instead, a new man, a Christ-animated being, comes up in its place and begins to live out a new life of Biblical proportions. From this point on, you have found yourself, your *true self!* You are no longer of this world. You are other-worldly, extra-terrestrial. Enter the baptismal grave as a wretched sinner; emerge from the baptismal womb as a new creation. *The old has gone! The new has come!* This is your birthday on which you are reborn from above. No one truly tastes life until they've tasted death.

Exercises

1. Meditation Exercise: Slowly and meditatively read **Romans 6:1-14.** Consider the interplay of "life" and "death" described in this passage. Each time each word is used, try to understand *what* specifically is dead or alive?

2. Can you imagine yourself "dead to sin" and "alive to God"? What would this look like in your daily life? How would this feel—to love justice, to enjoy goodness, to hate selfishness? How would you like to instinctively do the right thing?

3. What are the sins, the fears, the vices that you would like to leave behind in the waters of baptism?

4. What are the strengths, the character qualities, the virtues that you would like to bring up with you from the waters of baptism?

5. Have you been baptized yet? If not, go to your elders and tell them you wish to be. They may have an instruction process they would like for you to go through in preparation. If so, enter into it wholeheartedly.

CHRIST-CENTERED

SPIRITUALITY

A HANDBOOK OF *CATECHESIS*
for
the training of novices
in
THE WAY OF CHRIST

PART IV. The Practice of
INTERIOR
CHRIST-LIKENESS

67. On the Illumination of Christ-like Virtue

ll of God's desires for your life can be summed up in one richly hyphenated word: *Christ-likeness*. This has been God's consuming passion, his constant purpose for you since before you were born, to form you into the kind of perfect humanity Christ displayed. What kind of person do you hope to become? Every man is less than a man who is not like Christ. God has always wanted to regenerate in you a life of the same quality as his Beloved Son, Jesus. It is sketched on your original blueprints! He only waits for your permission and cooperation. C.S. Lewis puts it this way: *"The real Son of God is at your side. He is beginning to turn you into the same kind of thing as himself. He is beginning, so to speak, to "inject" His kind of life and thought, His Zoe, [spiritual life] into you; beginning to turn the tin soldier into a live man. The part of you that does not like it is the part that is still tin."* When Christ infuses his spiritual DNA into the human bloodstream, it begins to effect changes, re-ordering the inner life and re-creating the image of Christ in new skin.

This transformation does not turn us into an army of clones or robots. Rather it elevates our own life into a whole new realm of potentiality and diversity. The genetic sequences of our souls are purified of harmful defects, breathing new life into vestigial organs within your own unique personality. Your individuality without Christ at its core is incomplete, flawed, stunted, and broken, a work of art defaced and vandalized. Only in Christ can you become the masterwork God intended, functioning at full strength. There is no better way to live. You will never be more free to become your true self than when you are living like Christ.

How can we tell if we have made genuine contact with God? How do we know that we know God? *True union with God always changes a person.* It will (super) naturally result in our becoming more like Jesus. Being *like Christ* is a byproduct of being *with*

Christ. Spiritual exercises are only a means to this end. Unless they are resulting in a transforming friendship that leaves our souls changed, they are a waste of time-- useless, dead religion. Spiritual maturity is not measured by hours spent in prayer or chapters of the Bible read. A disciple is mature only if their prayer and Bible knowledge has enabled them to become a more loving, patient, self-controlled kind of person. The forging of Christ's character in our souls is the true measure of our spirituality.

This part of the journey is properly called *the interior life*-- the change must happen on the inside if it is to have any real value. Dressing a bulldog in a tutu doesn't make it a ballerina. We humans judge by outward appearances but God looks into the depths of the heart. He is not impressed by someone who acts loving when their heart is still full of hate. He desires truth on the inward parts. External changes are valuable only if they are the result of, and are resulting in a heart that is being changed. Our aim is to alter our inner life; let the outer life take care of itself.

Christ-like character requires two things: *the illumination of virtue* and *the purification from vice* in the soul. Wouldn't any personality be improved by the addition of virtue and the subtraction of vice? A *virtue* is a *strength of character prepared by habit to live rightly*. A *vice* is a *weakness of character accustomed to habitually do wrong*. The character qualities of Jesus are described in what has traditionally been called *the Theological Virtues* (faith, hope and love) and *the Fruit of the Spirit* (love, joy, peace, patience, kindness, goodness, faithfulness, gentleness, self-control). The obstacles to Christ-likeness are described in *the Seven Capital Sins* (pride, envy, anger, greed, lust, sloth and gluttony). (How words change over time! The old word "virtue" used to mean *strength*, springing from the same root as "virile"— now it seems to imply a purse-lipped pusillanimity! The word "vice" used to mean a *trap or bondage* that holds you captive-- now it seems like a "harmless habit" to laugh about and wink at.) The pursuit of Christ-likeness is a cultivation of strength and an escape from bondage.

275

The practice of interior Christ-likeness is a gift of God's grace from first to last. Please do not read this as a self-help project of mechanical techniques to be mastered. Following step-by-step will *not* guarantee perfect results! It is much more like the cultivation of a seed: preparing the soil, watering and protecting it as the life potential contained within bursts into actuality. It is God's project from beginning to end; He is the Author and Finisher of our faith. We participate in the process, not passively but actively receiving new inclinations being made available into our hearts. I can teach you what virtue is, but I cannot teach you virtue. This must rise up from the inside as the volcanic force of the Christ-life within pushes up to the surface. When you invite the Holy Spirit to take up residence in your soul, you gain new energies for goodness. As God freely grants these capacities, it will require struggle to unlock the potential through practice. And as we expend our greatest efforts, they acquire for us an effortless excellence with which we live.

Your Creator has entrusted you with the terrifying privilege of self-creation. Your soul is still being shaped! St. Thomas Aquinas tells us: *"All human actions set up a bias towards similar actions in the future."* That is why I have included with each virtue a *spiritual discipline* that tends to encourage and energize that particular trait. An athlete does not wait until the race to begin training. Instead, he disciplines his body regularly so that on the day of the race, he is completely prepared for peak performance. In the same way, do not wait until the temptation presses upon you, but proactively prepare for the race through daily exercise. Use the means available to you, but don't fall into legalism. Apply these disciplines with discretion according to what makes the most sense for your particular situation. As with every discipline, use

them when they're useful, discard them when they're not. And never deceive yourself into thinking you did this by your own superior strength and intellect.

Would you like to become like Jesus? Is it your deepest desire to learn to live like Christ? Can you even imagine yourself striding across the landscape of your life with the confidence, peace and power that Jesus had as he walked upon the earth? Can you see yourself with the same determination, endurance and purpose under trials that our Lord exemplified during his passion and crucifixion? Will you allow him to liberate you from the bondage of sin and free you to become a man or woman overflowing with love, forgiving offenses as naturally and instinctively as breathing? Among the

warring wishes battering your reborn soul, you may find this deepest desire: *that I would respond to God as my hand responds to me.* Do you hate every tendency that hinders this total, unreserved obedience? When Christ enters the dwelling of your heart, he will begin to redecorate the interior, but he insists on securing your agreement and assistance with each stage of the renovation process. Will you give him free reign, a *carte blanche* commitment to have his way in your life? Is this is your lifelong goal?

If you are committed to becoming Christ-like, brace yourself for a steep climb. Let us follow Christ up the slopes of the sacred mountain of transfiguration. It will be a difficult ascent, with many falls and bruises. The butterfly will tell you: transformation is a laborious, bewildering, often painful experience. But if we keep at it, we will finally discover our true form. We cannot even fathom the mystery of what we shall be. *But we know that when it is made known, we shall be like him, for we shall see him as he is.* If you love

277

what you see in Christ, you will love the restoration you will begin to see in your own soul!

1. **Meditation Exercise:** Slowly, meditatively read **II Corinthians 3**.

2. **Journal Exercise:** Write out a description of "the Christ-like you" going through your daily challenges. Take your personality, your skills and opportunities and animate them with Christ's glory radiating from within: all your strengths enhanced, your weaknesses rendered irrelevant, and your sins eradicated. What would this "ideal you" look like? How would it feel to be that person?
Imagine yourself consistently living out love, joy, and peace. What would your face look like in the mirror? Imagine yourself treating others with unfailing patience, kindness, and goodness. How would your voice sound when you speak?

Is this what God wants? Is that what you want? Agree with God that this is your goal as well as his...

3. Give yourself irrevocably into the hands of God. Pray in the first lines of the great hymn: "Take my life and let it be consecrated Lord to Thee"...
Ask God to form the character of Christ in you...
Offer your interior world to God: your intellect, your imagination, your memories, your thoughts, your desires, your will, your relationships, your soul...

68. On Faith
Complete Confidence in a Trust-worthy God

 aith is the spark that will set your world on fire. It sets off a chain reaction in your soul that changes everything. The initial step on our journey towards Christ-likeness is faith. As A.W. Tozer says, *"Faith is all-important in the life of the soul. 'Without faith, it is impossible to please God.' Faith will get me anything, take me anywhere in the kingdom of God, but without faith there can be no approach to God, no forgiveness, no deliverance, no salvation, no communion, no spiritual life at all."* A broad smile breaks over the face of our Heavenly Father when his beloved children throw themselves into his open arms with simple, uninhibited trust. *Faith* is *trust.* We will define *faith* in this context as *unshakable confidence in a trust-worthy God.* Every life-giving friendship is built upon trust, especially with a God you've never seen. The kind of faith the Bible commends is primarily a relational word but it relies upon a specific picture of reality that undergirds it.

Everybody has faith-- everyone has beliefs about reality that affects the way they live. Even the most hardened and hateful soul may believe that God exists. The real issue is "What sort of God do you believe in? Do you trust this God? What or who do you really trust?" If the kind of God you believe in is *not* trustworthy, than it is not a god worth believing in. Of course, trust cannot even begin unless we believe that a certain kind of God exists and that he is the kind of God who rewards those who earnestly seek him.

Examine your assumptions about reality, God and yourself. Have you come to the conclusion that our world is animated by a wondrous God of staggering power, unfathomable wisdom and unimaginable love who is more than willing and able to generously reward and bless those who rely upon him? Or do you think our universe is ruled with iron fist by a cruel, sadistic god who enjoys watching humanity suffer? Or is he watching us from a distance, uncaring and unconcerned? Or perhaps you find belief in any such "divine being" far-fetched or unintelligent? If you truly think "God" is either non-existent, evil, uncaring, uninvolved or impersonal, I dare you to try to live in complete alignment with this belief! See where it takes you. Is it live-able? Is it practice-able? Does it match what we see in our souls? Faith is *not* accepting something as true that I don't really believe, as if opposed to reason. That would be foolishness. It's what I do after I have become convinced of a truth: reminding myself of its reality and acting upon it.

Faith is a one-two punch of *belief* and *action.* The first step to increase our faith is through greater acquaintance with the object of our belief. Your faith in God grows as God grows more faithful in your mind. Starting with a simple conviction that there is a God who is truly good and trust-worthy, our faith, like a tiny mustard seed, can grow into a life of on-going personal interaction with this incredible Being. We increase our faith capacity through meditating frequently upon God's communication with us, chewing upon and digesting the mysteries of God's infinite power, wisdom and goodness, pondering the real-life stories of men and women who lived lives of interactivity with God. As we become more and more persuaded of God's matchless greatness, our faith potential automatically climbs with it. Trust becomes the only sane response to this irresistible God we've come to know. In fact, we would be foolish not to abandon ourselves completely to such a God. As great as your God is, so also is your faith. In fact, you could gauge the accuracy of your picture of God by the vitality of your faith in him.

The second thing we can do to increase our faith is to act upon it. Our faith is proved genuine in the furnace of actual experience. Beliefs without action degenerate into a fantasy world in your mind, detached from real life, a retreat from reality. To study the articles of faith without actual attempts to venture into this theoretical reality will leave you with a mind full of inactive, inert information. Our world is a faith gym. Without exercise, our faith becomes a lifeless corpse without energy or ability, a skeleton without substance. To turn a tiny seed of belief into a virile faith, you must begin to experiment by stepping out recklessly and risking it all on God's promises. Ironically, faith grows best in a dark environment. Darkness obscures sight enough that we must depend with naked trust upon the quiet inner whispers of a faithful God to guide us, fixing our eyes not on what is seen, but on what is unseen. When things don't make sense, when God seems far away, when we don't understand why something happened, we are standing in the nursery of faith. Faith is not the absence of doubts; it is acting according to your core conviction in spite of doubts. Faith never feels safe-- it feels like foolishness. It is as counter-intuitive as quantum physics! (Does it really seem like the walls before us are made of swirling swarms of electrical charges?) But we must begin to act upon this growing vision of God's greatness until it begins to weave itself into the very fabric of our daily lives. As the new paradigm is confirmed in various experiments, we will find it easier to believe than not to.

True faith fuels courageous confidence! The man or woman of fully-formed faith is fearless, bold as a lion in the face of danger and uncertainty. They are able to live confidently, act decisively, and pray enthusiastically. They do not get anxious and agitated by unexpected changes or intimidated and overwhelmed by challenging obstacles and risks. Instead, they remain quietly confident that their God shall supply all their needs. Too often we seek for courage in the wrong place, relying upon *self-confidence* instead of *God-confidence.* We foolishly misplace our confidence when we try to find sure footing within our own imperfect abilities and incomplete wisdom instead of reaching for the hand of the Almighty God. When the flood surrounds you, pray with the psalmist: "Because he is at my right hand, I will not be shaken." Faith is the only kind of courage that is not built on an illusion. True faith inspires initiative and motion; only pseudo-faith provides an excuse for limpness and laziness. Here is a discipline (not a law!) for exercising your faith:

The Discipline of Tithing - Perhaps the most accurate measure of our faith is our use of money. He who does not trust God with his money does not trust God. In the Law of Moses, God expected each of his people to give a *tithe*, one tenth of their gross income to the work of the LORD. Is your faith up to the challenge? Can you give away money you cannot afford to give? This is your faith challenge: *For the rest of your life, give no less than 10% of the money you make to God and his purposes.* And the more make the more of it you can give! Give to your spiritual community, to the poor, to your neighbors, all as an exercise of faith, an expression of confidence in your Creator. Say with joyful confidence, *"My God shall supply all my needs, according to his riches and glory in Christ Jesus."* If you reject this discipline as too radical, too demanding, your faith will be stunted like a bonsai tree, a miniature of what it could be.

1. Meditation Exercise: Read through **Hebrews 11** and jot down the key elements of faith. What attitudes or actions does it inspire? What results does it lead to? Is a life of faith easier or harder than a life without faith? What would heroic faith look like in your life? If you were a man or woman of great faith, what would be different?

2. Gauge where your faith is at...What is the temperature of your faith? Is it at the boiling point? Or is it a lukewarm fizzle? Where is your stress level-- how troubled is the pond of your soul by fears, doubts, and anxieties? How boldly do you pray? How confidently do you live? Pray honestly: "Lord I believe. Help my unbelief!"

3. Calculate 10% of your gross monthly income. Write a check to your spiritual community for this amount. Give away at least this much every month from now on! If you are too timid, try this experiment: do it for 3 months— see if God does not make ends meet somehow. Or start with 1%, then each month increase it a percentage point till you reach 10% (or 20%! or 50%! even 90%!) Just begin to stretch your faith and see how far it can go!

69. On Hope
Optimistic Expectancy of a Glorious Future

The next rung on this ladder of divine ascent is the virtue of hope. *Hope* is all about *expectation.* It is defined by Dallas Willard as *"anticipation of good not yet here, or as yet 'unseen'."* The hope of Christ is not a half-hearted "wish" for something, as in "I hope it turns out okay." *It is an assurance, an ironclad guarantee that after all of our adventures and hardships, there will be a "happily ever after"* from which we will see every past difficulty as a necessary part. *"God is able to make all things work for the good of those who love him, who are called according to his purpose."* As followers of Jesus, this is our bedrock assumption: *God will ensure that every single thing that happens, every moment of our lives moves us closer to a wide world of untold wonder and joy which God has prepared for us.* At some point in history future, *"the earth will be filled with the knowledge of the glory of the Lord, as the waters cover the sea!"* Nothing can stop the churning momentum of the wave of God's sovereign goodness from breaking over our universe! Even though you are not responsible for completing the project, every building block you contribute to God's kingdom will leave your fingerprints on the final product. No best effort is ever futile. No love-borne work is ever wasted. If you are pressing towards the same ultimate purposes as God is, absolutely nothing can get in your way! This hope lifts our eyes to the horizon, filling our souls with optimism, our bodies with energy, and our minds with meaning.

Through hope, every follower of Christ should be filled with limitless vision. Our sight is conditioned by our expectations. We see what we *want* to see, what we *expect* to see. So the fearful person sees endless possibilities of harm. The angry person sees offenses, insults, and disrespect in every pair of eyes they pass. The thankful person sees a multiplicity of reasons to worship their Creator lurking behind every rock and tree. We should be able to look at our lifescape and see some very real opportunities for God's goodness to burst forth. Hope turns all of life into a God-theatre. We wait in anticipation to see how God's story will unfold in the darkness. You can only act upon what you can envision. Your line of sight determines your future. Through a constant gaze upon God and his spectacular vision of goodness for our universe, your entire life will be brimming with light.

Despair thrives only when we lose sight of God's ongoing plans and purposes. If you close your eyes to God Most High, all you will see is darkness in every direction. When hope dies, all else dies with it. Hopelessness causes gloom and despair to pervade every nook of your existence-- your facial expression, your moods, even your physical health. Don't bother trying to drive away despair with a broom. Simply open your eyes to the radiant hope of restoration God reveals and despair will wither away. We tend to color our present in light of our future. Human beings can endure almost any manner of suffering as long as we know there is an ultimate purpose that it is leading towards. Despair thrives on fear and uncertainty about where your path is leading. Hope assures us that the end is unquestionably good, no matter how grueling the climb is right now. Are you willing to be swept up into his breath-defying vision of eternal goodness?

Hope even enables us to look unflinchingly at all of the ugliness in ourselves and in the world without losing heart. We can face the awful reality of where-we-are without losing sight of the awe-inducing reality of where-we-shall-eventually-be. Our sins, no matter how filthy, will be washed away. And God can even use our past sins for good purposes. Every manure pile can fertilize a new and bountiful crop. As Julian of Norwich wrote in her *Revelations of Divine Love*, *"Sin is behovely [i.e., inevitable]. But all shall be well, and all shall be well, and all manner of things shall be well."* We can honestly examine the festering open sores of pain and suffering in our hurting world without shrinking back from the monumental task of healing. It is idealism unmarred by realism; it is realism unclouded by idealism. When you look at our tattered and battered world, are you eaten away by a consuming despair? Or do you see this broken globe brimming with possibilities of perpetual renewal? The difference is hope.

Hope increases the capacity of ordinary people to brave new levels. What are your expectations of the people around you? What are your expectations for yourself? People tend to live up to (or down to) our expectations of them. One of the first gifts Jesus gave some of his disciples was a new name, a new identity to raise their expectations of themselves now that they were citizens of his kingdom. It was hope that allowed Jesus to see an unreliable, wishy-washy fisherman and proclaim to him —"You are no longer Simon [a reed] but Peter [a rock]." He declared James and John the "Sons of Thunder". At Jesus' calling, the greedy tax collector, Levi, became Matthew, the "gift of God". He declares things that aren't as if they were, calling into being what does not exist. As he did with Gideon, he declared them mighty warriors— then didn't settle for anything less. Read Jesus' rebukes of the disciples in this light: they were convinced that Jesus wanted to make them champions! It was the reproach of a coach who set impossibly high standards because he knew his boys would ultimately reach them. Hope also enables us to

receive correction and criticism with thankfulness. Through eyes of hope, we can honestly acknowledge exactly where people are without being discouraged or judgmental. It gives us very high standards for ourselves and yet it refuses to keep punishing ourselves for our shortcomings and failures. What does the Almighty God see when he looks into your future? What name would he speak over your life? Do you need to re-name someone who has been a hopeless failure in your mind and speak hope into their life?

Hope can only grow to the level of your faith. The credibility of your vision for the future rests upon the credibility of the God who promises to make it happen. Unless he is working behind the scenes to bring about a good end to everything, it is a vague wish-dream, a wisp of smoke without substance. Our expectancy is based on our God's goodness and power, not a naive idealism that expects everything to be easy. Hope must be forged and tested in the infernal fires of human experience. Either this world is the only glimpse of light you will ever see in an eternity of consuming darkness-- or it is a brief moment of darkness before an eternal sunrise. Which picture will you choose? Either could be true... depending upon Whom you place your trust.

The Discipline of Scripture Memorization- One of the biggest obstacles to hope for the Christ-inhabited soul is simple forgetfulness. Day-to-day worries distract us from the hallowed history we are a part of today. Remember... every promise will come true! Steep your mind in the timeless texts of the Scripture, allowing his promises to become permanent residents in your mental architecture. In the swirling confusion of sadness and suffering, we need something solid to tether our hearts to. God's word of hope is an anchor for our souls.

Perhaps you feel you have neither the time nor the skill to memorize a single Bible verse. May I ask an irritating and intrusive question? If you were to fast from the TV, the internet, and video games for a week, how much extra time would you have to devote to cultivating this or other mind-transforming disciplines? The tentacles of technology quietly entwine our minds until we are hopelessly enmeshed in its web. And we resent any suggestion that we may be controlled by its puppet strings. Do you need to cut yourself free from its cords with a decisive slice?

1. **Meditation Exercise:** Slowly and meditatively read **Psalm 42**. Honestly ask the question of yourself, *"Why so downcast, O my soul? Why so disturbed within me?"* Do you ever get depressed? Discouraged? Downcast? Despairing? What things bring you down? What areas of your life disturb you? What fears or conflicts sap your soul's energy? Write these out in your journal...

2. Now receive the prescribed antidote: *"Put your hope in God, for I will yet praise him, my Savior and my God."* Apply this encouragement to each and every area...
Can you acknowledge by faith that God will eventually bring good out of this? Are you absolutely certain that this darkness will soon be a dim memory?

2. **Memorization Exercise:** Memorize the following verse from **Jeremiah 29:11**:
*"'For I know the plans I have for you,' declares the LORD,
'plans to prosper you and not to harm you, plans to give you a hope and a future.'"*

Repeat it over and over again. Then see if you can repeat it without looking. Recall it often throughout the day.

70. On Loving God
Passionate Commitment to God's Glory

ove, like breathing, is the inflow and outflow of our souls. To be fully human, we must do two things: *love* and *be loved*. But how do we survive on the streaky streams of weak and imperfect human love? We need much, much more! We need access to the endless rushing reservoir of life-giving Love that is God himself. *God is Love*... essentially, infinitely, perfectly. God is the initiator of this wild cosmic love affair—you need only realize and respond. Don't even attempt a life of virtue and good works until you have been knocked over, brought to your knees by this staggering realization: *God is absolutely, inexhaustibly, and hopelessly in love...with you.* Have you ever really experienced being totally and completely loved? Until you have known it in the deepest part of your soul-- tasted it, felt it, found yourself, lost yourself in this breathless, profound mystery, you have no idea what it feels like to be alive! This is the most important thing about you: that *you are God's Beloved*! Without this, nothing else matters! Stop everything! Seek this treasure, worth more than all the worlds! Pause and ask God: how much do you love me? Until we've received this mind-blowing kind of love, we can never expect to give it. *We love because he first loved us.* Love responds to love.

When we are truly awakened to this life-consuming, soul-transforming, spirit-intoxicating love of God, we can't help but respond with a bit of enthusiasm. We begin to crave the Living God as our lungs crave oxygen. The God-captivated soul will seem insane to a self-absorbed world. As St. Francis of Assisi's biographer noted, *"This man of God was out of his mind in a most delightful way!"* We will "go overboard", go nuts about God. It will seem the height of foolishness to build our lives around a Presence invisible to the rest of society. This "crazy" kind of love compels us to joyfully sacrifice all things, to recklessly abandon ourselves to his pleasure, turning our souls inside-out for God's greater glory! The whole system of Christian devotion is only explicable as the lunacy of a lover! We must fall madly in love with our Lord, becoming love-sick, love-drunk! No dreary and dull religious duty can sustain the devotion necessary for a Christ-centered spirituality. It must consume us like fire! (If you think such a God-fixation would be unwise or psychologically unhealthy, you have obviously not understood God's primacy in the created order: He is the only reason anything exists!)

This is the central burning core of Christ-centered spirituality. *Loving God is unquestionably the most important activity in the universe, the beginning and end of the spiritual life.* Without this vibrant, essential relationship, all miracles, good works, nice words, self-improvements, and religious rituals are just irritating noise. With it, even the smallest act of service takes on an eternal glow. Our so-called "righteous acts" are disgusting and sickening to God unless enflamed by love! When asked, "what is the greatest commandment in the law?" Jesus answers unequivocally, *"Love the Lord your God with all your heart and with all your soul and with all your mind and with all your strength."* If you get this wrong, you get everything wrong! If you get this right, everything else will end up right! However, Jesus' definition of "love" is light-years removed from what passes for "love" today.

Love is not some soft, sentimental, "secondhand emotion." It is not a mushy feeling of desire but a muscular, flint-like, decisiveness of heart. *Love* is defined as *an act of the will in which we choose to seek the good of another-- "will-to-good"* for short. It is the will that gives love substance and permanence! Can you tell your *will* from your *desires*? Your desires (feelings, emotions, affections, wants, likes and dislikes) come and go; your will (the part of you that chooses, decides, commits) can stay fixed no matter what. Our desires may incline us towards an object but it is our will that chooses to act with or against our feelings. Lasting love must be intentional. It may start as a spark of desire but it is sustained by steady decision. Usually love begins with a flash of insight or a feeling of affection, but it is fanned into flame as a firm and furious commitment to act *for* this person. We feel affection; we decide to love. A spark does not make a fire, unless it finds fuel.

Love must express itself— it grows through each expression. Once your soul has been ignited with love for God, there is much you can do to kindle it to perpetual flame in your deepest desires. If you have chosen to love God above all else, begin to act on this love in every way imaginable. "How do I love Thee? Let me count the ways." There are infinite opportunities to express the acts of love. Love *touches*-- it seeks closeness with, wants to join with, to have and to hold, to be with, to interact with its Object. Love *speaks*-- it wants to communicate, to exchange, to whisper and listen, to write, to call, to tell, to reveal, to converse. Love *looks*-- it gazes, pays attention to, watches, thinks about, daydreams, imagines and imitates. Love *gives*-- it shares and creates, it serves and sacrifices, it offers itself. Love *enjoys*-- it plays, smiles, spends time, wastes time, gets excited, scheming to bring pleasure to its Beloved. Even the hottest fire will eventually die if it runs out of fuel. You cannot build a relationship on warm feelings alone. Cultivate closeness with God! Without daily investment, your spiritual life will be inconsistent—a shallow and unstable affair, blown and tossed by the wind.

With love, the more you give, the more you get. If you regularly express extravagant love to God, you will consistently find you have more to give. Unexpressed love quickly turns to nothing. Write a love letter to God, take time away from all else just to be with him, read stories about him in the ancient writings, tell him your secrets, draw a picture for him. Worship him in song! *Anything done for love of God will be joyfully accepted by him!* Does it delight you to think that you can give Almighty God a unique display of affection he will receive nowhere else in all creation? Make your own exclusive contribution to the undying joys of God! Let your mind muse upon the glory, the greatness of God, recalling his infinite perfections. The more time you spend with God, the more convinced you will be that he is the most worthy, love-able Being in the universe. Here is today's "to-do" list: 1. Love, 2. Be loved. If you have done these two things, it has been a good day.

The Discipline of Sacrifice - One of the strangest characteristics of love is that its strength is measured best by how much you give up for it. The cross of Christ is the most profound expression of love in all of human history-- because it was the costliest. Here's the all-time high-water mark for love: *"Greater love has no man than this-- that he gave up his life for his friend." "This is how we know what love is: Jesus Christ laid down his life for us."* Are you willing to lay down your life for him? Thousands throughout history have literally shed their blood for his name. While you may not have the high privilege to die for him, will you live for him? Will you present you body as a living sacrifice, holy and pleasing to him? Passionate love must be expressed in passionate ways. Break open the bottle of your love and pour it out lavishly upon the feet of your Lord, the Lover of your Soul! Give your very self to him. Don't hold anything back, worrying about whether you will have any left for others! He will surely provide abundantly for the one who has given all to him. Do something outrageous, something radical out of love for him. Give God an entire paycheck of hard-earned money! Give up valuable things out of love for God! Practice "vigil" by staying up an extra two hours just to worship God... or wake up a couple of hours early to worship him. Or give up a favorite indulgence (TV? Meat? Lunch? Coffee?) each week.

1. **Meditation Exercise:** Slowly and meditatively read **I John 3.**

2. Do you feel truly loved by God? Do you feel absolutely accepted? Have you experienced that you belong to him? Do you feel fully forgiven? If you don't, explore why this might be so.

3. Do you have a deep, unquenchable love for God? If you *really* wanted to express extravagant love, how would you do it? Is there something of great value you could sacrifice for God?

71. On Loving Others
Self-Sacrifice for our Neighbors' Needs

ere is the one infallible proof that you are a disciple of Christ: *that you love one another*. Loving God inevitably spills over into the rest of our relationships, permeating them with this unearthly quality. Does your heart really surge with love for God? It will result in that same bursting, enthusiastic response to the spirit of another human being! Without this verifying characteristic, we can be sure that our "love" for God is counterfeit, a cleverly disguised worship of Self. The man who fasts constantly and prays for hours with many eloquent words, yet despises his fellow man is farther from God than the common prostitute. Spirituality is no substitute for love. Don't just *act loving*! *Actually become loving* on the inside!

Love is the crown jewel, the summary of all virtues, the one-word definition of Christ-likeness. It is the wellspring of joy, peace, patience, kindness, goodness, faithfulness, gentleness and self-control. Authentic love is the combustible fuel for the human engine— inspiring heroic deeds, bursting forth in overflowing virtue, propelling us into joyful sacrifice that springs naturally from within rather than forced from without. This is God's commandment: *"Love your neighbor as yourself."* This is not a safe, theoretical love of humankind in general. It is a *demanding, practical love for the specific individuals* who happen to cross your path each day. Don't even talk about *loving all humanity* until you can *love the specific human sitting next to you* right now! God calls us to act for their best interests just as you act for your own best interest. Do you have this *will-to-good* for your neighbor?

God is easy to love— he is absolutely perfect! But what about all of these imperfect people? Some of them are just plain evil! *How do we love those we do not even like?* Love begins when *we place extreme value upon a person* and act in accordance with that value. It awakens when we recognize good in someone. And if we believe God, *there is some good in every person...* and it's worth fighting for! We love them because we love him. After gazing awestruck at the Source of Love Itself, our eyes become accustomed to noticing the value in every human being that crosses our path. When we are familiar with Christ, we begin to recognize his indelible image stamped on the spirit of every person, no matter how ruined or defaced that image may be. We discern the inestimable worth of the individual that God has already placed upon them. We develop what Albert Schweitzer calls, *"reverence for life"* because all life is God's handiwork. Does this seem impossible? Why would Christ command you to do something, unless there is some way to actually begin to do it? If you honestly cannot bring yourself to love people, go back to square one— a love relationship with God in which we are both receiving and reciprocating that love with our Unseen Father. God is our inexhaustible wellspring of pure and selfless love. Fill up before you pour out. Don't leave home without it! Ask God to flood you each morning with an overwhelming love for people. Without this selfless species of love, all good works and good words ring hollow.

Love must be moved from within. God's love is self-initiated and unconditional. It doesn't wait for you to become worthy. God loved us *before* we were "worth loving." While we were still rebellious sinners, Christ died for our ungodly souls. We didn't have to measure up first. How dare we demand that others measure up before we love them! Unearthly love does unworldly things: it serves sacrificially, it sheds blood,

293

it lends without thought of return, it is kind to the unkind, it blesses enemies, it respects the disrespectful, it wastes time listening to the "unworthy". And yet who is unworthy? Does not God place immense value upon the worst of sinners? Are not the most useless human beings of unspeakable worth to God? After all, he paid a premium price. Does not God command us to love? And would you disobey his command? Are you worthy of love? Are you love-able because of the Image you bear or because of your many admirable acts? One unspoken barrier to loving the unlovely is that deep down, we actually think we *deserve* God's grace! If God had treated us as our sins deserved, where would we stand?

The Discipline of Intercession - Love provokes action. It cannot sit by passively. Unfortunately, there is not always something obvious we can do for those we love. So the easiest first step in loving anyone is to pray for them, lifting up their needs before God and asking for his blessings upon their life. Try the old Quaker practice of "holding them in the Light." Bring different faces and names before God. Ask him to meet their needs, to draw them closer to him, to give them whatever is best for them. Ask if there is anything specific you should pray for. Some wonderful intercessory prayers are found in Colossians 1:9-15 or Ephesians 1:16-19. Put the weight of your whole heart behind each request, truly willing their best. In doing this, many of the submerged obstacles to love may surface: an unresolved hurt, a subtle jealousy, or a judgmental spirit. Then you can deal with it nakedly before God, confessing and asking for his promised forgiveness and purification. As you pray, you may also find that God will assign you specific tasks so that you become his hands or his mouth to them. The true intercessor must be willing to *ask* according to God's will and then *act* according to God's will. You may also intercede for any groups of which you are a part of including your church, your neighborhood, your school, or your family. Daniel 9:1-19 shows a brilliant example of standing in solidarity with our surrounding community, shouldering their sins in confession as "ours", giving thanks, and making requests.

1. Meditation Exercise: Slowly, meditatively read **I Corinthians 13.**

2. Journal Exercise: List in your journal the specific people God wants you to love.

a. Start with the people nearest you, your "neighbors". These are the people you see most often: your family, friends, co-workers, classmates. Who will you see every day this week? Who will you see at least twice this week? Who do you see once a week? What is something you could do today to bless your own household?

b. Next, think of the members of your spiritual community. Jesus said this was the verification of his message: the authentic love demonstrated in the gathering of his disciples. "Practice" loving in these safer environments.

c. Then move on to those who are most difficult to love. Think of the "least of these", the neediest people around you: the poor, the mentally ill, the irritating, the irresponsible, the social misfits, the alcoholic and the drug addict— those who have nothing to offer you. Is there someone in your social circle who is the object of gossip and ridicule? Is there a homeless person who bothers you on your way to work? Ask God to point out at least one needy person whom you are called to show love and respect to. Then begin to talk to this person; ask them to join you for a lunch or coffee. Ask God to show you an act of extravagant love you could do for them.

d. Finally, learn how to love your enemies... Who are the people who have harmed you? Who are those you have wished would drop dead? Do you have a relative who has ruined your life? Ask yourself, what is one thing you could do to bless them? Start by forgiving them and praying for them. Then maybe offer a kind word or even an invitation to reconcile. Can ordinary people do something this radical? Not without God's miracle-working love flowing through your veins! Here is a caution especially important in loving the needy and our enemies: loving someone does *not* mean trusting them or giving them whatever they want. It means you give them what they need. There is a big difference! *Love is an act of the will in which we choose to seek the good of another.* They may be stuck in a destructive pattern and love may mean doing exactly opposite of what they want. It doesn't mean giving them the opportunity to hurt you again or take advantage of you over and over again (that won't help them one bit!) Instead, we must try to move them towards what is ultimately best for them.

3. After writing this list of specific people you are called to love, spend 20 seconds per name interceding on their behalf... With each name, ask yourself if you really want the best for this person.... Try to set aside time each day or at least once a week to intercede with God on behalf of those closest to you. You may want to make a prayer list of your priority relationships. Or you may just ask God to bring faces to your mind as he sees fit, that you may pray according to his list.

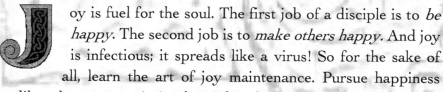

72. On Joy
The Experience of Ultimate Satisfaction

oy is fuel for the soul. The first job of a disciple is to *be happy*. The second job is to *make others happy*. And joy is infectious; it spreads like a virus! So for the sake of all, learn the art of joy maintenance. Pursue happiness greedily-- but pursue it in the right place! It is incredibly near-sighted (almost blindness!) to think that a million dollars, a gorgeous boyfriend or girlfriend, a keg of beer, or a mansion on a hilltop will bring lasting happiness! Have you been seeking such shallow and short-lived solutions to your eternal need? If all seek happiness, why do so few find it? *We must find an indestructible happiness:* substantial... permanent... universal... impenetrable! It must be able to survive intact through whatever sorrows life throws at us, never giving up and never giving out! Don't settle for anything less.

This rollicking, robust version of happiness is called Joy. *Joy* is defined as the *experience of good— the pleasure of possessing what is truly best*. It is the fulfillment we feel when *we have what we want* and *we want what is good*. There is contentment when our deepest desires correspond precisely to our greatest good. You are seeking joy— and Joy is also seeking you. One often overlooked aspect of Jesus' life was his fantastic, bombastic joy! It drew children flocking to him. It made him the life of some very flamboyant parties. It drew criticism from stuffy religious types who called him the first-century equivalent of a "party animal." It enabled him to say without a hint of irony, "that my joy may be in you." If you cannot picture a smiling Savior, perhaps you are not seeing him in proper focus.

Our problem is not that we are pleasure-seekers; our problem is that we are seeking eternal pleasures from temporary sources. We confuse inner satisfaction with outward pleasure. God refuses to let us live in dependence upon temporary physical pleasures that only survive under the most delicate of circumstances. Yet for many of us, these shadowy wisps of superficial pseudo-joy are all we have acquired a taste for! This sickly species of satisfaction demands more and more just to keep us afloat from one day to the next. And yet the law of diminishing returns guarantees that we cannot keep this up forever. And yet we try. So we go through life in pain-avoidance mode and pleasure-acquisition mode which turns us into incredibly self-centered people. Yet true joy keeps eluding our grasp.

We cannot quite comprehend that the Eternal God actually wants us to be eternally happy... because he keeps urging us to let go of our empty pleasures. As C.S. Lewis writes, *"Our Lord finds our desires not too strong, but too weak. We are half-hearted creatures, fooling about with drink and sex and ambition when infinite joy is offered us..."* Now don't be mistaken: pleasure itself is not bad-- God created it! Our bodies were intentionally fashioned with thousands of taste-receptors in our mouths and nerve-endings throughout our bodies, extremely sensitive to touch. God formed us to feel pleasure! But the fleeting pleasures of a passing world will not do for an eternal soul! Complete contentment comes when we have *enough*-- and nothing will satisfy our heart's ever-increasing thirst but the inexhaustible Fountainhead.

God himself is the infinite reservoir of true, soul-deep joy that freely flows into open hearts. There is really no way to describe God's drenching, joy-filled Spirit, like ice-cold spring water against the skin of your soul! The greatest gift God could ever give you is himself. *In his Presence is fullness of joy! At his right hand are pleasures forevermore!* Have you yet tasted and seen God's inexpressible bliss as an actual reality? Our Lord is overflowing, abounding, bubbling over in pure, undying joy! Do you not see that God is perfectly happy? Can you feel his absolute pleasure in life, his deep delight in all he has created? He was filled with exuberant excitement long before our world was created and he will still be deliriously happy long after our time-bound planet has passed away. *Our God is in the heavens; He does whatever he pleases!* Raise your voice in festive song: *"Joyful, Joyful, we adore Thee, God of Glory,*

Lord of All." Delight yourself in the Lord—He will give you the desires of your heart! Do you realize the only things that make God angry are the things that keep his children from boundless, boisterous joy? Obey God's command: *"Be joyful always!"* What kind of Deity would order us to enjoy life endlessly-- elevating "joy unspeakable" to the level of primary virtue? Father, Son and Holy Spirit— Joy-mongers all! Could you really enjoy or love a "god" who is irritable and depressed? If your portrait of god is a gloomy, grumpy tyrant, proceed quickly to the nearest trash can and dispose of this insulting caricature.

Suffering and joy are not mutually exclusive. The Biblical writers assume that suffering and joy can co-exist in the same person at the same time. Pleasures and pains will come. But God-born joy thrives through pain. That doesn't mean we will be constantly smiling, laughing and "having fun" (although these also should have a prominent place in our lives!). But even when things go terribly wrong, and sadness covers the surface of life in a fog, we find a subterranean joy like an underground spring flowing underfoot, ready to burst forth like a geyser at the next opportunity.

There is always reason for rejoicing. *Sorrow is temporary; joy is forever.* At times, you may feel depressed, empty, alone-- but these do not have the final word. Cry, mourn, grieve, but do so in the context of joy everlasting. We patiently endure a night of weeping, knowing that the darkness will end and we will eventually awaken to an eternal

morning of endless joy. During times of discouragement, do not allow the poison of self-hatred, bitterness, and shame to seep into the inner core of your heart and stop it from beating. Depression will drain all energy from your soul until you feel like lying down and giving up. Do not give in!

Joy will return with a vengeance! *Good is always bigger than bad— for God is very good, and God is very big.* Any particular bad is always dwarfed by its cosmic context of unconquered, uncompromised goodness, stretching beyond the horizon in all directions. *Joy is the only logical response to this all-pervasive, limitless goodness well-secured.* Sorrows must always be seen against the colossal backdrop of all-encompassing joy. Beyond the stormy cyclones that shake our lives to the core, the starry heavens continue to twinkle with an undisturbed joy that will continue throughout eternity. When fortune smiles, give thanks. When catastrophe strikes, bear it courageously... and give thanks that even this cannot derail a son or daughter of the King from their appointed arrival into eternal bliss. Joy appears when we forget about ourselves; sadness returns when we forget about God.

The joy of the Lord is our strength. We must have access to this hidden source of energy to live a Christ-centered life. Joy makes us immune to the soul disease of despair and is the first line of defense against sin. Temptations are most appealing when we are feeling alone, dissatisfied, inadequate, listless or angry. Joy propels us to accomplish a life-full of worthwhile deeds, whether we are spit upon or embraced, honored or insulted, whether we fail or succeed, whether hungry or well-fed. Even feelings of emptiness can be welcomed as a longing for more of God! Recognize it as a love-sickness, the tension of unfulfilled desire. Jesus reminds us that we are blessed when we hunger and thirst for righteousness; it is the prelude to the banquet. When you are unsatisfied with your prayer life, when you don't feel God's Presence, when you remember wistfully the times when you worshiped God with greater fervor, this reminiscence too is a joy. For you know it will be all the more satisfying for the seemingly endless wait. When God does not speak, hiding his face from your gaze, enjoy the silence-- your Divine Lover is preparing a place for you.

The Discipline of Thankfulness - Only thankful souls may enjoy simple pleasures. This world is sprinkled with little splashes of sparkling joy, if you will lift your face to the heavens. Thrill your heart upon the matchless excitement of mere existence! Exult in the profound pleasure of being alive! Worship with St. Clare: *"Thank you, Lord, for having created me!"* Every luminous breath is a blessing; every swift second, a generous gift of grace! Luxuriate in the prickly, tickly touch of green grass under bare feet, of cool water on parched lips, of the gentle swirling song of a tree-full of birds, of a pleasant phrase dancing across a page. You cannot be sad while you are giving thanks! Make a daily habit of giving thanks for each miniscule pleasure. Thankfulness is such a powerful discipline, it can change your entire outlook on life by steady practice!

1. Meditation Exercise: Slowly and meditatively read **Philippians 4.**

2. Journal Exercise: Write a list of the countless little blessings you have received just today... See if it doesn't lift your spirits with each new blessing named... Try to give thanks at least once a day, especially when you feel down.

73. On Peace
The Restful Freedom of Complete Surrender

veryone is crying, "Peace! Peace!" Yet there is no peace. Our world is frantic and fearful, restlessly running along this ragged road, searching for inner peace. Our minds are conflicted and confused, our families filled with misunderstandings and mistrust, and our planet is plagued with wars and rumors of wars. What is wrong with us? Why can't we all just get along? Long before the automobile, the computer, or the electric light were invented, Augustine wrote the following prayer: *"You have created us for Yourself, and our hearts are restless until they find rest in You."* This is our most accurate diagnosis for our stressed-out, burned-out world. We will always be tossed about, inwardly off-balance until we have come to rest on the only firm foundation in the universe: a mind-transcending peace that the world cannot give... and cannot take away. *Peace* is defined as *the rest that results in true, well-secured good*. It is the security we feel when we are sure that everything will work out for the best in the end. We can finally breathe a sigh of relief when we are convinced that our Father has everything under control. We cease striving and simply know: *He is God... and we are not.*

True rest finds us when we stop trying to control the world. We believe the myth that through sheer will-power, we can force the world into submission by controlling other people, controlling circumstances, and controlling each outcome. We try to control everything except the one thing we are supposed to: ourselves. Like Atlas, we carry the weight of the world on our shoulders, straining every sinew and muscle, lest everything come crashing down. Do you ever feel this way? And yet Someone else, the Prince of Peace, has already offered to take the governing of the world upon his broad shoulders. Yet we don't trust that he will secure the outcomes that we want... so we continue to grunt and sweat under a burden we were never meant to carry. Stop waiting for perfect circumstances to be at peace. Find peace here and now--- or not at all.

The password to peace? *Surrender.* Surrender yourself to the rhythm of the universe. Abandon yourself into the strong and loving arms of God. Evelyn Underhill defines peace *as "a calm willed acceptance of all the conditions which God imposes upon us."* Obviously, *all un-surrendered sin* robs our tranquility, for there is no peace for the wicked. But we must also release *all un-surrendered outcomes* to God as well. This hands-off approach is best expressed in the prayer of Jesus through blood-soaked tears in the crushing darkness of Gethsemane: *"Father, if you are willing, take this cup from me. Yet not my will, but Thine be done."* After wrestling alone over the portion chosen for him by his Father, Jesus committed his spirit into the hands of Divine Love. Thomas a Kempis instructs, *"Give up your desires and you will find rest."* Once you can forgo a desire, you are no longer controlled by it. Peace departs the moment we want something and will not be without it! Until that decisive moment of detachment, you will feel the stomach-churning terror of looking over the edge of a precipice into a bottomless abyss. But once you step off of solid rock, you will find yourself weightless, suspended in perfect peace that defies understanding. This is not where you begin to fall but where you learn to fly. It is only when we let go of the earth that we find ourselves safe in the arms of our Father, the safest place in the universe.

Surrender does not make us passive fatalists who sit back and accept anything as God's will. Draw a sharp line between the two great arenas of life: what-we-can-do and what-we-cannot-do. God's arena consists of what he alone can do. Our arena is defined when we ask God this most dangerous question, "What can I do?" *God rarely does for us what we can do ourselves.* And he often seems to think us capable of more than we think. Like a good coach or teacher, God gives us tasks we feel unable to accomplish. Then he helps us to do what we never thought we could do. In the process, he stretches us to become more than we ever thought we could be.

Once you have a clear idea of what you are supposed to do in your arena, there is no reason to hurry or worry. If you're working on part of God's plan, don't you think he will see it through to completion? Just roll up your sleeves and get to work. Pour your passion into it. You can work calmly but diligently, knowing that God himself wants you to be doing this work. If God has called you to it, he will give you enough time to accomplish it. Take it as a fact: *You have all the time you need...to do everything he wants you to do.* (How could this statement be untrue if God is all-knowing?) The same applies to money and other resources. With God, you will have all you need...but perhaps not all you want! Do you feel you don't have enough time in the day? Or enough resources? Perhaps you are squandering it on distractions that are not part of God's plan. Or perhaps you need to get started obeying anyway and let God provide the rest when it is needed.

When it comes to God's arena (what-we-cannot-do), we are the cheering fans, praying hard, but recognizing that he is the one who controls the outcome. Never take upon yourself the crushing burden of that which you cannot do anything about. This only breeds anxiety and angst which will choke the life out of your soul. In the midst of any disquieting problem, pour out every drop of your heart in prayer, asking him to do what you think he should. Then let go. Abandon all your concerns and worries at his feet, knowing that he cares for you more than you could possibly imagine. Once we have divided our arena from God's arena, all life-draining stress turns into either energizing work or enthusiastic prayer.

Worry is an insult to God. We have no business being anxious. *"Do not be anxious about anything, but in everything, by prayer and petition, with thanksgiving, present your requests to God. And the peace of God, which transcends all understanding, will guard your hearts and minds in Christ Jesus."* Your stress level will tell you how much you trust God. Anxiety, stress, worry, and insecurity: all are forms of fear. Tell your heart the truth: *you are afraid of many things.* Dallas Willard defines *fear* as *anticipation of harm.* We fear we will lose something we cannot do without. We fear we will not be able to secure an outcome that is essential to our contentment. But this is a fact: *if God does not secure it, we can live without it!* We fear we will suffer irreparable harm. We fear pain, and run from it like jackrabbits. Yet here is the gospel truth: *In Christ, pain cannot harm us. In Christ, there is truly nothing to fear.*

The Discipline of Journaling - Whenever you find yourself overwhelmed by stress, sit down with pencil and paper and clarify your fears. Exterminate anxieties by exposing them to the light: "What am I really afraid of? What if I fail? Does that make me a failure? What if the future turns out different than expected? (It most definitely will!) What if tragedy strikes? Won't God still be there to pick me up and dust me off? Won't he still lead me into undying glory? Can anything at all derail God's plan to bless me for all eternity? What if people get angry at me? Does that make me any less of a person? What if people find out I am flawed and imperfect after all?" (Trust me, they've already figured that out!) Embrace your weakness! You are not all-knowing or all-powerful! Explode the myth of control: You are not in control of anything except your own response to a big, big world! Our souls are disturbed by the specter of fears unexpressed. Worries turn to monstrous shadows in the dark. And yet the light reveals them as harmless. As long as we are rushing around, afraid to face our insecurities, they retain their power of intimidation. Journaling will help you to slow down, sort through your feelings and thoughts, reflect on your life in God's Presence, and present your requests to God. Prayers written often have more permanence and impact than prayers merely spoken.

1. **Meditation Exercise:** Slowly and meditatively read **Ephesians 2.**

2. **Journal Exercise:** Turn to your 'fear list' from chapter 25. Anything to add? How do fears look from God's vantage point? Imagine yourself free from fear... How would it feel?

74. On Patience

A Spiritual Toughness that Endures Pain

ife hurts. Get used to it. It's time to grow up and accept that suffering is unavoidable in this fallen world. God's children are not exempt. You will drink from this bitter cup. Pain is the price of greatness. There is no victory but through struggle; no glory but through pain. We cannot run from pain all our lives if we want our lives to stand for something. Don't misunderstand me: God does not enjoy watching us suffer-- but he does warn us that we will: *"In this world you will have troubles. But take courage. I have overcome the world."*

Endurance. Toughness. Perseverance. Fortitude. Tenacity. Longsuffering. Stamina. These words are virtual synonyms for the *patience* the Bible speaks of. Watch Christ stumble along the *via dolorosa*, the road of suffering, and remind yourself that you are summoned to follow. Will you walk with him wherever he leads? Even to death and beyond? *Patience* is defined as that *indispensable ability to persevere towards a goal despite suffering*. It is a fighter's tenacity, a stamina of the soul, a spiritual toughness that presses on. It is the courageous commitment to carry the cross through the dirt, despite bleeding wounds, fatigued muscles, and the cruel taunts of the opposition, until "it is finished." Following Christ is not for the faint of heart. Disciples must find inner strength, a warrior's heart. But how do we develop such a staunch battlefield courage?

Never forget: *your soul is indestructible!* God has given the gift of an impenetrable, steel-plated soul to every disciple. As St. Justin Martyr taunts his tormentors, *"You may kill us, but you can never harm us!"* The only foe that can ultimately injure you is yourself! The only weapon capable of destroying the disciple is *unrepentant sin,* an incorrigible inner rebellion, a self-inflicted wound. Apart from sin, nothing is ultimately harmful; therefore, nothing is ultimately fearful. Aquinas quotes Aristotle in offering this

306

definition of cowardice: *"A man is a coward when he fears what he should not fear."* We need not be rash or reckless. Feel free to flee a charging rhino or an armed gunman, but do so remembering the eternal perspective: these may harm your body, but they cannot harm your unconquerable, eternal soul!

Pain cannot harm us! Pain is not the ultimate wrong in the world. It is a warning light, an indicator of what is really wrong. Pain has a purpose. It is our protection, for health and well-being. It is "the gift no one wants," as described by Philip Yancey's perceptive book, *Where is God when it Hurts?* God gave us nerve endings in our skin so we could sense when something is wrong and move to remedy it. God also gave us emotional pain receptors in our souls. When our relationships are damaged, when we are estranged from God, when we are mutilating our own spirits, we need to *feel* how harmful it is. If we couldn't experience pain, how could we tell what is wrong? What would happen if God were to eliminate all pain from the world? Would we continue to touch the hot stovetop? Or should God just turn off the stove permanently? If so, how could we cook? And what would be the purpose of a stove that didn't cook? Without pain, we would be like lepers, numb to the damage we are doing to our bodies, continually subjecting ourselves to self-mutilation without knowing it. Sadly, most of us only learn the hard way. Getting hurt is the alarm that wakes us up to what is bad for us. C.S. Lewis says, *"Pain is God's megaphone to a deaf and dying world."*

Now we must know the difference between good pain and bad pain. Hurt is often a warning of impending harm, but they are not identical. Discernment is knowing the difference between what is only *hurtful* and what is truly *harmful. Hurt is a temporary painful sensation; harm is a long-term blockage to well-being.* An athlete knows well the pain that is necessary for muscle growth. This is the pain that they expect, ignore, push towards, and in some cases, even learn to enjoy. But there is also the pain of a torn muscle, the pain of damage. This cannot be ignored, it must be fixed. Don't stop the symptoms with a painkiller; treat the root cause.

Do you want to accomplish something worthwhile with your life? Then steel yourself for the hardships ahead. It is the universal testimony of the saints: *suffering is a necessary part of the path to blessing.* You must pass through the desert, though bruised and bone-weary, to get to the Promised Land. Agony is the womb of both grief and greatness. Think of the many good things that only come through hardship and struggle: birth, growth, maturity, humility, change, victory, awareness, compassion, wisdom, patience. Would mountain-climbing, football, or puzzles be any fun at all without a degree of difficulty? Could people grow deep? Could marriages last if we left when it got hard? Could children be born and raised? If we cannot cope with pain, we cannot cope with life.

Beware two parasites that poison perseverance: *quitting* and *complaining*. When you are doing what you know is right, never, never, *never give up!* A farmer who quits before harvest time will see all of his work wasted. You need a resilient will that won't turn aside at the first sign of opposition. Patience only grows in soil that normally produces impatience! Situations that try our patience also build our patience. So resist the urge to abandon ship when storms hit. Complaining is also useless. Grumbling is the quitting of our hearts before the quitting of our feet. It only extends our stay in the wilderness. Don't bounce from job to job, from relationship to relationship, from church to church looking for a perfection that will not be found this side of Eden. Count on it: there will be times when you feel like giving up. The key part of the process is precisely when we feel like we've come to the end of our resources. When we are fatigued and everyone is worn out, this is the time of metamorphosis! This is the moment when the blood of Christ begins to pump through our veins. We can go the extra mile only on a different fuel source.

The Discipline of Embracing Suffering - Receive every challenge as a chalice given by God for the perfecting of patience. Don't shrink away from these unique opportunities for growth. Let God stretch your pain threshold through the simple tests of daily life. I am not talking about a sadistic self-infliction of pain! After all, each day has enough trouble of its own, without having to seek it out. Just to make a living without taking shortcuts, to make a marriage work, to pour out your life in sacrifice for others takes incredible emotional fortitude! Whenever you feel frustrated, recognize that you are in the gymnasium of the soul. Work out unseen muscles by welcoming discomfort as discipline. Feel the burn! Learn to enjoy waiting. Claim each unexpected delay in your day as God-given time to learn patience; practice the Presence of God. Embrace difficult, irritating, socially-awkward people. If you don't know any, find some.

Trials are part of a process that yields great results! Jesus' little brother James had seen this cycle work so well, he writes, *"Consider it pure joy, my brothers, whenever you face trials of many kinds, because you know that the testing of our faith develops perseverance. Perseverance must finish its work so that you may be mature and complete, not lacking anything!"* The tougher the trial, the more effective! When you are treated poorly, rejoice! When you are stuck in traffic, rejoice! When a project fails, rejoice! This is your training. Now this *doesn't* mean that we don't stop our suffering, when possible. If you have aspirin to stop your headache, by all means, use it. Take all right and reasonable measures to make life more bearable. But after having done all you can to alleviate pain and it persists, don't complain. Flex your patience muscle instead.

1. Meditation Exercise: Meditatively read through **James 5:7-20**.

2. Journal Exercise: Write down all your trials and frustrations... What areas of your life are just not working out right now? What difficulties do you just wish would go away? What people try your patience? When do you feel like giving up?

3. Imagine Jesus stands before you... He tells you he has a special mission for you which will entail great hardships... Would you accept this mission? Now consider this: Would you endure your current afflictions if you knew it was part of God's assignment for you?

309

75. On Kindness
A Friendly Attitude of Unconditional Respect

ow much is one life worth? How do you determine the value of a soul? Their net worth? Their usefulness to you? Their fame? Their physical beauty? From a cosmic standpoint, human beings are either near-worthless clumps of molecules on a little clod of dirt circling an insignificant star-- or each and every person is of more value than all the stars glowing in the heavens. There is no middle ground. We must begin to see the infinite worth of every human being in the eyes of their Creator, not because of what they do, but because of what they are: the work of his careful hands, stamped with his divine image, redeemed by his precious blood. These are walking treasures! When your eyes are enlightened to see everyone through this lens, you cannot help but honor one another above yourself.

Kindness is the natural result of a God's-eye-view of persons. *Kindness* is defined as *unconditional respect for everyone* you meet. It is *a gracious disposition that makes us easy to get along with, friendly, cheerful, agreeable and pleasant towards all kinds of people.* It is an enthusiasm for individuals, a passion for people, a generous joy that shares a smile with everyone. Kindness is not the bland "niceness/ politeness/ tolerance" that is so prized in our world. We are called to something far more costly than mere tolerance: we are called to love. Kindness is truer than political correctness, for it will not be faked. God has no use for plastic smiles behind which lurks hateful thoughts. God looks upon the heart. True kindness sees beauty in every face, regardless how misguided they are.

Think of someone you admire, whether for their expertise, fame or wisdom. How would you treat them if they were sitting here? Aren't you careful not to needlessly offend or insult them? Don't you tell them how much you appreciate and admire them? Wouldn't you be fully present to them in conversation, listening carefully, not allowing your mind to drift? Now... what if you were to treat everyone with that same dignity? What if every person is a VIP? What if everyone is a celebrity (someone worth celebrating)? Is it possible to live without partiality towards those deemed "more valuable" to society? In every interaction, whispered this reminder to your heart: "for this creature, the Lord of Glory gave his life!" Would we dare treat them with contempt? What if we honored the poor, the prisoner, or the outcast as we would honor Christ himself? Kindness does for others what we wish they would do for us. Do you quietly hope others will notice you? Then notice others! Do you love it when others express appreciation for your work? Then express appreciation for theirs! Do you wish others would listen to your opinions? Then listen to their opinions! Honor them! Compliment them! Light up when you see them! Greet them warmly! Get excited about what they say! And we practice all of this vicarious blessing, not to get it back from them, *quid pro quo*, but just because we know, if we were in their shoes, we would be glad to receive it. For it is more blessed to give a blessing than to receive it.

There are two opposite responses towards the wounds and weaknesses of others: *contempt* or *compassion*. We see the sins and shortcomings of others as reasons to despise, dislike or even hate them— or we can allow our hearts to break for them. Don't judge them self-centeredly... as inconveniences to our precious little plans. Let your heart well up with tears for the frailty of your fellowman. Turn your eyes from the cosmetic to the cosmic. Has someone been angry or mean to you? Look beyond your own wounded ego and let your spirit ache for their wounded soul. Is someone socially awkward? Consider how deep the loneliness they must feel! Has someone caused their own misery? Reach out a hand of rescue-- not a fist of retaliation! Why disdain the man whose life has already been ravaged by his poor choices? When you're at your worst, how would you like others to approach you? Heal their hurts and hear their hopes. See the person they could become! Tease out the flickering potential hidden within them!

Nothing kills kindness like a judgmental heart. How disgusting for a disciple of Christ to be mean and self-righteous! How, in the name of the Crucified Christ, could we who bear his name become even more critical and condemning than the rest of the world? We should be the most hospitable, accepting people in all of society— not approving of their actions but completely thrilled with their existence! We live in a world where people are starving for  genuine affection, for someone to tell them that despite their sins and imperfections, they are still lovable, still worthwhile. In a world of hatred and shame, the Brotherhood and Sisterhood of Christ should stand out like a city shining upon a hill, renowned for welcoming the stranger, for lifting up the weak, for comforting the sin-scarred. Jesus' mission statement quoted from Isaiah 61:1: *"...to preach good news to the poor...to bind up the brokenhearted, to proclaim freedom for the captives, and release from darkness for the prisoners, to proclaim the year of the LORD's favor."* Is this your mission? We should be known for *who we are for* more than for *what we are against.* Jesus touched the lepers of society-- how can we, his blood-washed brothers, kick them when they're down?

Conflicts are no longer something to be feared. It is an opportunity to see through someone else's eyes and hear someone else's heart more deeply. Kindness makes us listeners and empathizers. See the other person not as an enemy to be conquered but as an ally to be strengthened. Even if you still do not see eye to eye, decide never to hold a grudge. Do not allow unresolved conflict to calcify into a permanent feature of your soul. Never take revenge by throwing back poisoned darts at the one who has harmed you. Be a cause and not an effect! Don't return an equal and opposite evil for evil. Instead, return an outrageous, unexpected blessing and joy! Become an energy source that catalyzes and creates good in others. Every time you lash back verbally, you are acting inconsistently with the Lamb who was led to the slaughter yet didn't open his mouth.

What does your facial expression communicate? Do you have a "yes" face or a "no" face? Your face either welcomes people, setting them at ease in your presence or it warns people like porcupine quills, to be careful and keep their distance. Practice hospitality in your countenance, showing a warm, welcoming, inviting attitude to everyone. Give people the gift of undivided attention. Listen with your eyes as well as your ears. Assume a posture of interest. Try smiling at people and see how it improves your friendships! It might even make you feel better, too! You can't become best friends with everyone you meet but you can be friendly with everyone you meet. Every culture has its own manners, its own way of showing proper honor and love to others (i.e., Do we bow, hug, kiss or shake hands? How do we address our elders? What do we do with our hats?!?). Such customs are kindness enshrined in social norms. So while we need not fuss over stuffy and pretentious politeness, we should be practiced in "good manners" which express a robust and routine respect for others.

Your tongue has the power to kill or to heal. Are you easy to get along with or easily offended? Do you blow up like a land mine when someone triggers one of your sensitive issues? Do people have to walk on eggshells around you, careful not to say or do anything that might upset you? Or are they free to be themselves? An explosive temper demolishes years of kindness in a few senseless seconds. Think before you speak. Ask if your words will build people up or tear them down. Speak worth into everyone you meet. Otherwise we harm people face-to-face with insults, attacks and verbal jabs or we wound them behind their backs with gossip, slandering their reputation to others. Avoid gossip by asking yourself a few simple questions before engaging your mouth: What is my motive for saying this? Will it help someone or to put them down? Will it harm their reputation? Am I taking responsibility to help this person? Or am I just satisfying curiosity? Whenever you talk about other people's problems, if you are not part of the solution, then you are part of the problem.

The Discipline of Speaking Blessing - Make it a habit to leave every person that you interact with feeling built up. Try to speak a blessing within the first minute of your conversation with anyone. Give them a sincere compliment. Verbalize their value. Encourage them, strengthen them, show them honor, acceptance, affection and enthusiasm. Search carefully for the image of God peeking out of this person's soul and let them know the good that you see. By doing this, you are putting fuel on the fire of godliness in their heart. Try extra hard to do this for those who may dislike you (and perhaps you dislike them?). You may even find yourself actually enjoying that person! Then, after blessing them to their face, go and bless them behind their back. When you finish your conversation, as you walk away, breathe a three-second prayer of God's blessing upon them. Practice "reverse-gossip": make it a habit to mention in conversations all the wonderful things you can say about others, especially the more difficult people.

1. Meditation Exercise: Slowly and meditatively read through **Romans 12:9-21.**

2. Journal Exercise: Write down names of some people you have the hardest time showing respect to...Ask God to show you the beauty in them...Think of a compliment or something encouraging you could honestly say to them... Now go bless them.

76. On Goodness
A Courageous Determination to Do What's Best

hat is God's intention for his children? Is God delighted when we live muddled, mediocre lives of squandered potential? Absolutely not! Your Father wants the best for you: beauty, brilliance, excellence, glory! Isn't that what you want? God's expectations for each of us are literally sky-high! He wants us to shine like constellations of stars glittering in the night sky. God doesn't just want to lead us out of the land of slavery; He wants to lead us into a land flowing with milk and honey! He is determined to make the most of your life... Do you share this ideal? The virtue of *goodness* is defined as your own *commitment to doing what is best for you and for others.*

Doing good always has a high cost. The road to the Promised Land is not the easiest road. In fact, it may be the path of most resistance! Do you have the fortitude, the determination, the guts to do whatever it takes to seize "the good life" God has prepared for you? Be strong and courageous! God will be with you as you take possession of the Promised Land, but you still have to fight for it. You have to slay the giants you find there. You have to cultivate the ground. Some very real "goods" can only be acquired through painful toil and conflict. Don't let fear keep you stuck in the barren wasteland of "what might have been."

What is "the good life" God wants for you? Most of us confuse *what-is-good* with *what-feels-good* or *what-makes-us-look-good.* While there is nothing wrong with feeling good, you must aim higher! For so many foolish souls, the ideal life is a fantasy of self-indulgence and physical pleasures of food, sex, comfort and entertainment. Is this really the highest life you can imagine? I'm sorry, but seeking such a sad ideal will shrivel your spiritual self until all that is left is an animal self. Do not waste your life sitting in a

corner eating your cherry pie, imagining this is the good life! Pursue earth-shaking, divinely-recognized, eternal greatness— not the tiny spotlights of temporal fame. Partake of pleasures that are both *long-term* and *universal.* We dream selfish, myopic dreams of self-exaltation at others' expense. God desires a selfless, heroic greatness of self-sacrifice for the good of others.

In God's eternal economy, true goodness is always reciprocal. What's ultimately *good-for-you* is always *good-for-others, good-for-our-world,* and *good-for-God.* What is bad for our world is bad for every inhabitant of it. It is only an illusory goodness that sees me benefitting at another's expense. When I harm others, I am really harming myself. And whenever I harm myself, I am sowing the seeds of destruction for others. So part of seeking what's best for yourself includes helping others to do what's best for them. And the best way to lead others into their Life of Promise is to simply live out your Life of Promise yourself. The best instruction is always by example. For this, God became man.

Are you your brother's keeper? Absolutely! God wants you to fiercely contend for the highest destiny of those around you. Take responsibility for helping those around you become the most beautiful specimen of God's dazzling glory they can possibly be-- just as God wants you to be. As a team player, you are called to draw out the best in those around you. And while they must do their part, never let it be your fault that they did not have the help and support they needed. We cannot change people but we can give them every opportunity to change. God tells the prophet Ezekiel that we are to be like a watchman on a wall. If we sound the alarm and they do not listen, then we have done our part and they are responsible for their neglect. But if we fail to do our part of alerting the person to their danger, then we are held responsible before God. Ironically, sometimes what is best does not always appear kind. And what seems kindest is not always best for them. *The twin virtues of kindness and goodness must work hand-in-hand; they are two sides of the coin of loving conduct to others.* Kindness without goodness is only sappy sentimentality that would rather watch someone destroy themselves than upset them. Goodness minus kindness can degenerate into a harsh and bossy fault-finder.

The Discipline of Loving Confrontation – Fear of conflict constricts our ability to do good to one another. We end up confronting only when we're angry and we back down when we are peaceful. God wants precisely the opposite. We must be just as committed to truth-telling as we are to cheer-bringing. We cannot afford to cheat our brothers and sisters of opportunities for Christ-likeness by telling them lies. Learn to speak lovingly and truthfully, even when it means correction and conflict. Be ready to call it straight. But please do not take this as permission to become the nagging sin-police of the world, pointing fingers at everyone for their bad behavior! Paul's letter to the Ephesians gives a concrete plan for how God's inter-dimensional community is equipped to reach the full stature of Christ-likeness. He gives these directions: "Instead, *speaking the truth in love*, we will in all things grow up into him..." Love is the container; truth is the contents. A cup of sparkling cool water is a blessing; that same water poured without its container onto your lap will ruin your entire night. And an empty cup is just plain useless. In the same way, we must make sure that our attitude of love provides a suitably large container for our words of truth.

Here are some guidelines for deciding whether we should even bother to open our mouth with a correction. First and most importantly, consider your motive. Ask yourself, do I truly love this person and want what's best for them? Do I see a vision of their glorious potential or do I just dislike them? Do I want to hurt them with my words? If you cannot speak in love, please do us all a favor and shut up! Until you are motivated by genuine concern, you have no right to speak truth. We must learn to silently bear other's faults and weaknesses before we can safely open our mouths. Secondly, consider their receptivity. Will they receive this correction from me as an act of love? Are they a disciple working towards Christ-likeness as I am? Do I have enough of a history with them to show that I am a true friend? Or do I still need to lay some groundwork to convince them I am on their side? *"For the wounds of a friend can be trusted, but the kisses of an enemy are multiplied."* Lastly, consider the timing and urgency of the correction. How necessary is it to confront this particular sin? Would it greatly improve their life to remedy this habit? Choose the best time to talk about it. Or ask God to engineer the ideal time for this conversation. Gain their permission by asking: Can I speak with you privately for a minute? Can I offer you a suggestion?

Prepare your correction before you deliver it. Like Nathan confronting King David, consider the best way to say it. Express yourself compassionately and concisely. Decide beforehand what specific action needs correction. Don't just give vague feelings and random impressions-- that won't help them improve. Instead, try to say in one sentence what, precisely, is wrong. You may give a few concrete examples of what behaviors are inappropriate and what negative effects they have. But please don't spend more than a couple of minutes harping on all the things they are doing wrong. We never really know the whole story, so be ready to listen to their side of it. If they agree that they need to change these behaviors, offer a few positive, concrete steps they may take to begin to make some progress in it.

Always consider what they need to hear, not what you want to say. Never try to override their God-ordained ability to make

318

their own choices, even if they choose their own destruction. Surrender the manipulative weapons of control and condemnation: yelling, name-calling, shaming, rage, threats, embarrassment and accusations. You can get away with all sorts of truth when you wear a friendly face instead of a frown. Just smile and state the facts as you see them. No matter how heated the disagreement, you can always offer continued friendship. As much as it depends upon you, try to reconcile when you have crossed swords with anyone.

1. **Meditation Exercise:** Slowly and meditatively read **Joshua 1.**

2. **Journal Exercise:** In what area of your life do you know you could do better?

3. Is there someone close to you that you know could also do better in some area? If so, write out in your journal their specific behaviors that need correction...

Write down how it makes you feel when they engage in this behavior... Write out what they should do instead... Now decide if you should deliver this bite-sized piece of correction... Perhaps you should ask God to arrange a time to talk to them...

77. On Faithfulness
A Consistent Habit of Reliable Character

ho are you today? Do you go from Jekyll to Hyde overnight? Your character is what you are consistently, not occasionally. The Way of Christ must become *your* way, a habit you wear at all times. As dearly loved children, we imitate our immutable Father in his flint-like faithfulness. God does not change like shifting shadows. His emotions respond exactly as they should every time. His intentions for humanity remain constant, from creation to conflagration. God's purposes and priorities are entirely predictable. But his startling and surprising methods keep us forever guessing. He will, without fail, do good. *Jesus Christ is the same yesterday, today and forever.* His character was etched deeply in his heart, not brushed lightly upon the surface. *Faithfulness* is defined as that *Christ-like constancy of character which invites trust.*

Learn the art of strategic stubbornness. There are times to compromise and there are times to be uncompromising. How do we know the difference? We must set our hearts unswervingly on God's perfect will. The faithful person possesses a certain Christ-like tenacity-- the steadfast ability to set their face like flint towards a God-ordained target and not allow anything to knock them off course. The richest rewards require, in the words of Nietzsche, *"a long obedience in the same direction."* If we give up or change course every time the weather changes, we will never get very far with anything. If our life trajectory is a constant up-and-down emotional roller coaster, we will never arrive anywhere. You cannot live a productive life or a reliable life without becoming resolute. If you lack this quality, any skills or strengths you have are wasted. Any work you do will bear little or no fruit. Each time we run from hardship, we train our souls in cowardice.

Occasional goodness is not true goodness. We never get a vacation from Christ-likeness to "do our own thing." Trust that took years to build is torn down in a day without consistency. A husband who does not commit adultery for all but one day a year is not a faithful husband. The cashier who only steals from her company a couple of times a year is still a thief. The man who looks at pornography only once a month is still a porn addict. Nothing encourages humility like taking a good, hard look at our own worst moments. In our best moments, we seem like saints in our own minds... if only we were like that always. Do you have a sober-minded self-assessment? When developing your self-portrait, don't only see your sociable, smiling self. See also the negative exposure: your darkest, depraved, distorted self. Even the most horrific criminals have their good moments. But when we see ourselves at our worst, we can only come to one conclusion: we are sinners. We all stand in need of grace to stand before God's holy face. It is God's goodness, not ours, that enables us to draw close to him. Never lose sight of this!

Let honor follow honesty. Followers of Christ should earn a reputation of reliability. How does one gain a trustworthy reputation? *Not* by trying to gain a trustworthy reputation! The most reputable people are usually not concerned about their reputation at all. *Repair your character and your reputation will follow.* Learn to be who you are at all times. A major component of faithfulness is complete honesty. Our word can be trusted if we establish a track record of truthfulness. The dishonest person will eventually be found out-- and the greater the deception, the greater the distrust that results. It is a dangerous thing to become skillful at deceiving people! Your greatest victim will be yourself. Try never to tell a lie or to intentionally mislead people, even in small matters. You may find it more difficult than you thought! The next time you are tempted to tell a lie, ask yourself *why* you want to cover up the truth. What are you protecting? What do you hope to gain? The true priorities of our hearts are revealed by what we would lie for.

Become someone whose words have substance. *Take responsibility for every word* that carelessly drops from your lips. Does your "yes" mean "yes" and your "no", "no"? Let every word be a promise, unbreakable within reason. Let your commitments control your circumstances rather than your circumstances control your commitments. Every broken commitment is a statement of disrespect to the person whom you have casually disregarded. Take your promises seriously and be honest about your inabilities. Are you able to make and keep promises promptly to yourself and others? There are times when extenuating circumstances prevent you from keeping your word, but these will be obvious and rare.

Make it your goal to master your emotions so that you can make good choices, without being swayed by the fickleness of feelings. *Our feelings are wonderful servants but terrible masters.* Use your feelings for gathering intuitive information. Use them for assessing the impact of actions. Enjoy them when they embrace what is good. But never, ever surrender to them. The person who gives their feelings the steering wheel will find that they overreact drastically. To avoid one obstacle, they toss themselves in the opposite direction and hit another obstacle. They accelerate too quickly and decelerate too slowly, pursuing pleasure far beyond its proper place and usefulness. They are tossed to and fro by the waves, changing direction like the winds. We need a well-kept mind to keep them in line. While we are not called to be unfeeling Stoics, moodiness and emotional instability are not fitting descriptions for Jesus' disciples. Even our anger should be reliable— directed always toward injustice, not just a random outburst because we had a bad day. The same thing angered Jesus in the beginning of his ministry as at the end: the misuse and abuse of God's holy dwelling place.

Faithfulness must be global. God is no respecter of persons. We, too, should show no partiality. Nobody trusts the two-faced creature, who shows one face to the rich and powerful and another to the poor and powerless. The true test of trustworthiness is how we treat those outside our circles of trust: the poor, the stranger, even our enemies. Some of the most monstrous men in history were quite kind-hearted to their own kinfolk. We, the children of light, must go the second mile and show a sincere respect towards all humanity. And while we will obviously have extra responsibilities and loyalties towards our family and closest friends, it is completely unacceptable to be irresponsible and unkind to those on the outside.

The Discipline of Stewardship – Your life is a treasure house. How do you invest these treasures? God has entrusted you with time and money. He expects you to use them wisely. Your King watches to see how faithfully you steward these precious resources. Do you responsibly use your "stuff" to do good? Or do you squander it all on selfish, worthless pursuits? *A schedule is a spiritual document. A budget is a blueprint of our soul.* We are often so concerned about what we *don't* have, that we never make full use of what we *do* have. Your Divine Master waits excitedly to commend you as a *"good and faithful servant"* for maximizing your gifts. If you are a good caretaker of God's resources, he may reward you with more responsibility. All you have belongs to God. You are not even the owner of your own physical body. You are its manager and its primary user. Paul declares to the Corinthian church, *"You are not your own. You were bought with a price. Therefore, honor God with your body."* Have you come to grips with the fact that all of your stuff is not *your* stuff? Are you using it all for God's glory?

1. **Meditation Exercise:** Slowly read through **Matthew 25:14-30.**

2. **Journal Exercise:** List all of the resources you possess... material possessions... strengths... abilities... advantages... relationships...
Look over the list: Do I really think God gave all of this? Have I given God all that I am and all that I have?

3. Fill out your **Monthly Budget** (in Appendix).

4. Fill out your **Weekly Schedule** (in Appendix).

78. On Gentleness
The Unforced Freedom of Real Humility

These last two virtues are especially important: they are the two planks of the cross upon which our sins are crucified! With the twin crossbeams of *gentleness* (i.e., *humility*) and *self-control*, you will find that every opportunity for vice becomes an opportunity for virtue. The first three of the seven deadly sins (the irascible sins of the chest: *pride, envy* and *anger*) are slain by true humility. And the bestial power of the last four vices (the concupiscent sins of the gut: *greed, lust, laziness* and *gluttony*) is broken by the practice of self-control (more in the next chapter).

You may notice I am switching words on you. The words "gentleness" or "meekness" have come to imply softness, timidity, even weakness. The Greek word used in Galatians 5:23 (The Fruit of the Spirit) is *prautes,* which is probably more accurately translated as *"humble"* in today's world. It means lowly, grounded, and stands in polar opposite to arrogance and pride. Oddly enough, "human", "humility", and "humor" all come from the same Latin root *humus,* which is "of the earth." It is what Augustine was pining for when he exclaimed, *"If only humans would acknowledge that they are human."* We are truly self-aware when we learn the glorious paradox of our existence: *we are dust of the earth; we are daughters and sons of the Most High God!* Humility is defined as *the recognition of our true place in this world.* We see ourselves as *nothing more* and *nothing less* than God

created us to be. We can finally leave behind that consuming human drudgery of self-justification! We rest our self-worth on God's word, not our good works. Quit trying to prove to everyone that you are such a good person! Your occupation of self-exaltation was a dead-end job. Tell your overworked ego to take some time off. Stop overstating your performance trying to boost your perceived value. Stop scheming to justify your existence. It's already been justified by One who overrules all other judgments! Your price tag was affixed with nails to the wood long ago.

Do not mistake false humility for the real thing. There is nothing Christ-like about self-hatred. *False humility is self-conscious, self-absorbed, self-justifying, self-condemning, and self-rejecting.* It keeps our eyes fixated on our selves: our weakness, our inadequacy, our shame, our worthlessness. *True humility is self-forgetful.* C.S. Lewis describes it like this: *"Do not imagine that if you meet a really humble man he will be what most people call 'humble' nowadays: he will not be a sort of greasy, smarmy person, who is always telling you that, of course, he is a nobody. Probably all you will think about him is that he seemed a cheerful, intelligent chap who took a real interest in what you said to him. If you do dislike him it will be because you feel a little envious of anyone who seems to enjoy life so easily. He will not be thinking about humility: he will not be thinking of himself at all."* True humility makes us confident in who we are! We rest in God's estimate, not our own. We don't need to prop up our shaky self-assessment with the support system of "self-esteem": a flimsy structure where the subject of evaluation is also its object (who would trust an author's review of their own book?).

Our eyes have seen the glory: the dizzying immensity of the Infinite God! We have seen all creation dwarfed to insignificance by its colossal Creator! We have lost the ability to be impressed with human egos—except when we glimpse, as through a pinhole,

325

Eternity's Flame flashing through them. As the stars become invisible at the rising of the sun, the most magnificent creature is swallowed up in the scorching glory of its Majestic Creator. Pride, envy and anger melt away when we finally see the staggering vision of God! We can no longer be self-centered; we must be God-centered. How can we worry about our own worth when we are lost in worship of the One who, alone, is worthy? In Christ, we love each human being not because of what they do but because they are loved by God... and this applies to us, too! Love yourself freely as God loves you— just as you are. With no false ego to protect, the humble person can finally be honest with themselves about themselves. They are never threatened by others... they have no false facade to uphold! Undisturbed by compliments or complaints, they are free to *rejoice with those who rejoice and mourn with those who mourn.* They have a tone of gentleness, grace and respect with others, having no need to control people or force their way. Humility is the only view of oneself that enables one to live a life of love.

It is so refreshing to talk to someone who is unconcerned with managing appearances, someone without a mask. There is such liberty in being free from the oppressive opinions of others. Humility doesn't care what others think of them, whether praised or blamed. It serves freely without worrying about who may be watching. It has no image to maintain and puts on no airs or pretenses. Humility brings a blissful disregard for all the silly games that people fret about. Imagine never having to defend yourself! Put-downs do not penetrate the hide of a humble person. Vicious verbal attacks do not vex them. In fact, they are almost incapable of feeling insulted or slighted. Have you been stung with harsh, condemning words? The antidote is radical humility. If there is any truth in the correction, receive it thankfully as if the messenger had been sent by God. If they remind you that you are imperfect, you may cheerfully agree! If they have mistaken your motives, rejoice that your confidence rests not on their approval but on God's.

The true litmus test for discerning fraudulent humility is when you fall into sin. False humility wallows in self-pity trying to atone for its sins through misery. Such camouflaged pride refuses to receive forgiveness since, "we don't deserve it." If you insist on punishing yourself a hundred times over to try to pay for your sins-- you are indulging pride, not humility. Of course we don't deserve forgiveness... and yet we are so confident in God's outrageous forgiveness! Hate the sin and love the sinner— in this case, yourself! The truly humble person has no illusions about their own perfection. They can easily admit their wrongs with a breezy confidence, knowing that God's love was never conditional upon their performance in the first place.

The Discipline of Secrecy – Here is a wonderful way to work out your "humility" muscle: *do your best to keep your good works and good qualities secret.* Flee human praise. Do good as quietly and unobtrusively as possible. Make others look good. Deflect every compliment you can. In this playful endeavor, don't lie, deceive, or deny truth; just try to avoid notice. While everyone else scampers after first place, seize the last place. Enjoy obscurity! Count on it-- the moment you do something selfless and noble, you will feel like telling the whole world, with trumpets and banners. This is pride trying to creep into your spirituality. Many good deeds and godly disciplines are sabotaged by such shameless self-seeking. Beware: the fruits of virtue often produce seeds of pride! Instead of calling attention to your good deeds, which is the instinctive reaction, do those tasks which are less noticeable. If you are sincerely complimented, don't be pretentious or deny it (hoping they will admire your humility!); just receive it thankfully and move on to more important matters.

Revel in your hidden communion with God, far from the bright lights of human recognition. The purest devotion to God always takes place under cover of deepest darkness— unalloyed, untainted by motives of earning human praise. Give, pray, fast in the secret places that you may look upwards and ask your ever-watching Father, "Was this pleasing to you? It was for you and you alone." Use each act of hidden worship to build a bridge from your spirit to God's Spirit, a hidden path where lovers meet. Begin to gather exclusive interactions, just between you and your Divine Lover. Serve secretively, as a gift for the eyes of God alone.

1. Meditation Exercise: Slowly and meditatively read through Matthew 6:1-18.

2. Journal Exercise: Examine your life for signs of pride: Do you look down upon certain people? What "good works" are you doing? Would you still do it if no one ever found out? What offends you? What is the worst thing someone could say about you? What are the things that you do to try to impress others?

3. Take a moment to survey your strengths... Where do you excel? What sets you apart from the crowd? Who gave you these gifts? Rejoice in these gifts! Give thanks to the Giver of these good things! Now, think of someone who is more gifted than you... Can you also give thanks for their gifts? Can you reverence God's glory in others?

4. Do something impressive this week... and make sure no one else ever finds out... (anonymously give money to someone in need, fast a few meals, spend a couple of hours praying for people, clean some toilets, sweep floors, pick up trash, eat lunch with a homeless person— your treat, of course!)...

79. On Self-control
A Disciplined Life of Self-Mastery

ake your decision: you will master your desires or your desires will master you. Which will it be? Whatever has the power to command you, this is your god! The mass of humanity are slaves to their bodily appetites, spinelessly subservient to the tyranny of their ravenous cravings. The followers of Christ must revolt against this raving dictator. St. Paul declares his defiance: *"Everything is permissible for me. But I will not be mastered by anything!"* A disciple must learn self-discipline. We live on purpose: doing what we know we should do... and not doing what we know we shouldn't. Just as patience is the ability to endure pain, self-control is the ability to forgo pleasure. *Self-control* is defined as *the indispensable ability to say "No!" to any desire: sex, drink, comforts or pleasures.* Self-mastery, like tempered steel, is an inner strength needed to deploy ourselves with exactness toward what we truly want. It is the preparation of soul and body necessary to live up to your best intentions. You have a noble mission ahead of you. Self-control is simply getting out of your own way.

Our greatest battle is against ourselves. No one sets out to destroy their own lives. So why does it happen so often? We find our highest aspirations stifled by our own lower appetites. The apostle Paul, a spokesman of God, diagnoses our subconscious suicide: *our flesh wars against our spirit.* Our self-centered bodily desires have taken us hostage! Perhaps you can relate to the inner conflict described in Romans 7: *"I have the desire to do good, but I cannot carry it out. For what I do is not the good I want to do."* We *want* to eat healthier, but we also *want* to eat large quantities of gooey, chewy doughnuts. Which *want* will win the day? A man *wants* to be a good husband and father... but he also *wants* to have casual sex with the lovely lady living three doors down. And so the road to hell is paved before us... and we must find a way to turn our best intentions into reality. Here's the good news: by God's grace, we can rig the contest! Prepare yourself for these battles. Make sure the right "want" triumphs every single time. Steel your spirit and starve your sensual desires. You can beat your body into submission using fasting, solitude, and other forms of self-denial— until it obeys without question the slightest command of your God-ward will.

In order to say "yes" to the right things, we must become accustomed to saying "no" to the wrong things. The self-controlled person is poised and prepared to choose rightly in any situation. They have the wisdom to know what to say "no" to and the strength to follow through on that "no". Stare down your fiercest drives and desires! With a firm command, make it go lie down in the corner. Do you have this self-mastery, this authority over your own life? Jesus issued the following warning to his followers: *If anyone would come after me, he must deny himself, take up his cross and follow me."* John Calvin names *self-denial* as the summary skill for the Christ-life. If we pursue every whim and pleasure, we forfeit our soul.

This necessity for training in self-denial is one reason why many of the spiritual disciplines in this book are *"subtraction" disciplines*-- fasting, chastity, silence, all sorts of "going without". We can learn to be fine and fulfilled even when many of our desires are not being met! Never let your physical appetites command a lifestyle that is contrary to goodness—it will fashion your own self-made hell. So we practice saying "no" to each and every appetite, even in situations where it is perfectly lawful and permissible. The last four of the seven deadly sins (greed, lust, gluttony, and sloth) are only normal physical desires that have gotten out of control. They won't take "no" for an answer. There is nothing wrong with the pleasures of food, sleep, sex, or possessions. But if you do not master them, they will tear you limb from limb in their search for gratification. Even such worthwhile goods as family, health, success and honor can become excessive and obsessive. Resistance is essential for freedom.

Self-control is, thankfully, not just avoiding the wrong desires-- it is also embracing the very best desires. It is finding and discerning the deepest desires of your soul and then shaping your lifestyle to pursue these goals with reckless abandon. It takes discipline to prune away the distractions and aim your life in a consciously-chosen direction. Choose your habits wisely because once you form them, they will begin to form you. Seek first the dreams and drives that align with God's eternal kingdom: every other good thing will fall into proper place. Food, drink, clothes, and other provisions will be ideally provided for the person whose life is careening forward at full speed toward their God-breathed calling and destiny. When God is your top priority, there is a divine order and symmetry to the chaos of life, even when we can't see it.

Daily discipline is the path to greatness. Without practice, your potential lies unused, untapped, unknown. Exercises are absolutely essential to success in fields such as music, athletics, education, business or the military. No one wakes up one morning just knowing how to play the works of Beethoven or shoot 90% from the free throw line. You cannot expect to become a good athlete or musician without putting in the long hours of practice. And the better you want to become at it, the harder you have to work. It is the same with matters of the soul. No one just wakes up one morning being able to forgive their enemies, to defend the poor and broken, to withstand temptations, to live like Jesus. We all need practice.

St. Paul exhorts his young protégé, Timothy, *"Train yourself to become godly. For physical training is of some value, but godliness has value for all things, holding promise for both the present life and the life to come."* Spiritual fitness will ready you for any challenge that life throws at you. Practice tapping in to your divine source of strength—the indwelling Spirit. Flabby, out-of-shape spirituality will make you into an easy target for the enemy of your soul. Don't wait until you're in the heat of battle to begin using your weapons! Let God equip you and prepare you for feats of strength! Let God train your senses through constant use to distinguish good from evil! Then

331

Christ, whose noble blood runs through your veins, can send you as a fearless and battle-hardened warrior on twisted roads treacherous to tread, on those missions that make heroes.

The Discipline of Sabbath – When is target practice? We must take careful aim at our objective of self-control. We will not drift into a disciplined life. Our lives, like our universe, tend from order to disorder. We will need to set aside a regular time to re-focus and reorder our lives. The ancient Hebrew discipline of *Shabbat* forces us to rest from feverish activity. Step back from life-as-usual once every seven days and yell, *"STOP!!"* Slow down, breathe... and just enjoy life for even one second. A full day of Sabbath-rest is best. But even half a day would prove immensely helpful. Your weekly schedule is the picture of your priorities. If your lips say something is important to you yet it does not appear prominently on your calendar, it is your calendar that speaks the truth.

Life revolves around relationships-- with God, with family, friends, with our own souls. Yet relationships do not clamor for our attention like bills, projects, telephones, and other clutter. Take time to take care of your priorities. Who are your priorities? Take time to seek God. Worship with your spiritual community. Spend hours with your family and friends. Take time to do whatever recharges and relaxes you: Sports? Reading? Walking? Sleeping? Exercise? Working with your hands? Make time to do it! In this, as in all disciplines, be harder on yourself than you are on others.

1. **Meditation Exercise:** Meditatively read through **Hebrews 12:1-13.**

2. **Journal Exercise:** List some activities to feed each need:
Spiritual Needs: What could you do to get closer to God?
Physical Needs: What could you do to energize your body?
Social Needs: How can you strengthen your closest relationships?
Emotional Needs: How can you recharge your emotional batteries?
Fill out your **Rule of Life** (in Appendix). Then carve out a Sabbath in your **Weekly Schedule** (in Appendix) to take care of your priorities.

80. On the Purification from Sinful Vice

here is only one obstacle between you and a radiant Christ-likeness: *sin*. Do you want to live with an effervescent joy, effortless goodness, and indiscriminate love? Then break free from destructive patterns that hold you captive in a self-made prison. The wounds of sin are self-inflicted. Face it: if you cannot stand up to a particular vice with a defiant *"no"*, then *you are a slave to that sin*. You will not taste true freedom while fettered to these restless compulsions of your flesh. If you wish to reach your fullest potential as God's treasured child, remove the ropes that trip you up, one-by-one. Like an Olympic runner, *"let us throw off everything that hinders and the sin that so easily entangles, and let us run with perseverance the race marked out for us."* We will now examine each of the *"seven deadly sins"*, so we can slip out of their tightly-wrapped coils. These seven species of sin are golden calves, false gods that promise fulfillment but ultimately fill our mouths with ashes. Like so many dead-end paths that plunge us over the precipice, these proverbial thought-processes seem right to a man, but in the end, they lead to death.

Here is God's diagnosis: your soul is sick, your heart disfigured by the poison of the serpent--selfishness, anxiety, mistrust, doubt, shame, fear, insecurity, hatred, blame, and ultimately, unbelief and rebellion against God. This viper's venom can be vomited from one victim to the next through vicious words, spewed through the air with an acidic look, or passed through skin-to-skin contact with violent or selfish acts. It produces a progressive deterioration of the soul, even being passed from generation to generation as a genetic defect, through corrupted sequences of spiritual DNA. This is the state of the soul gripped by the wasting cancer of sin. The epidemic has gone global and you are exhibiting its symptoms.

The good news is that there is a universal cure. The bad news is that the disease itself makes us loathe to receive this cure. The untainted blood of Christ is the antidote, his broken body our nutrients, circulating through our system, releasing pent-up toxins, and bringing life, healing and restoration. Have you taken your medicine? If so, you have already been forgiven. *Now it is time to be purified.* Jesus gave his life not only to free you from the guilt of sin, but also from the grip of sin. Let us begin *the Way of Purification*.

But first, please consider this question: Do you *really* want to be free from sin? Or do you feel you might be missing out on something fulfilling? As you learn to "trust Jesus", you will begin to believe that he knows better than you what is really good for you. He sees the ravaging effects of our sin! Can you trust the great Physician of your soul to inform you of what is healthy and what is unhealthy to your inner life? As long as we're convinced that sin is a harmless pleasure, arbitrarily forbidden by a "wet blanket" God who doesn't want his children having too much fun, we will not live free. Even if we forsake sinful actions, we will still be enslaved in our hearts. Like the Israelites who fled Egypt with their feet but whose stomachs were still longing for the tasty morsels that captivity provided, we can be chained by the affection for sin even while we abstain from it. When he draws a line in the sand, are you really convinced it would be best not to step over?

Our eyes have been damaged by sin. We are so deceived about the nature of reality that we actually think sinning might improve our lives! *Sin is never worthwhile* when seen with a wide-angle lens. However, with our poor, myopic eyesight, we cannot see far enough to identify the connection between our sugar-coated sins and their nauseating results. By definition, *all sins are damaging, to ourselves and to others*. No sin is harmless. If a habit were truly harmless, it would not be sin. *Every sin leads to misery*. And Plato was correct: it is even worse to do wrong than to suffer wrong. The murderer does greater harm to himself than to his victim! The oppressor will suffer more than the oppressed. Second-hand sin can be confined to this life; the sin of our own hands will follow us into the next.

Jesus commands, *"Go and sin no more."* Will you obey him? Decide! From the innermost core of your being, cry out: *Sin shall no longer be my master! I died to sin; how can I live in it any longer?* Don't tolerate sin's tyranny! Count yourself dead to sin but alive to God in Christ Jesus. Re-paint your self-portrait: By God's grace, you no longer need to sin! All your needs can be met solely by the providence of God. Learn to see yourself as dependent on God and independent of sin, instead of vice versa. This *change of mind* is what the Bible means by the word, *repentance*. It is an alteration in your way of thinking, a change of direction, intention, mindset and attitude. Until you make a firm decision to repent, you will be unable to access God's vast resources right under your nose.

Can you imagine yourself free from sin—unselfish, unashamed, undaunted? This is your true self! Can you see yourself going to bed each night with no regrets about how you lived today and excited about tomorrow? What would it feel like to easily turn your best intentions into action? Imagine the joy, the stab of exhilaration you would experience decisively conquering each temptation that came your way! Picture all of the good things you could accomplish if you were not mastered by the opinions of others or the insatiable appetites of your own body. Does it seem possible or enjoyable to consistently do what's right? Or are you still duped into thinking that you need sin to keep things interesting? The more captivated we are by the glorious vision of a sin-free life, the easier it will be to get there. That is why we must keep the life of Christ always before us! Are you convinced that you must leave the land of slavery? Are you ready to begin the arduous journey to freedom?

Freedom is costly. We will pay a price for our exodus. Our slavery is also our means of security. Are you willing to give up your own reliable methods of medicating your pain with your drug of choice? Could you rely upon God to help you through your suffering instead of taking matters into your own hands, taking the shortcut? Sin is the easy way out: the credit card for the hopelessly in debt, the alcoholic's bottle, the sex addict's pornography. It temporarily eases the pain, but injects more infection into your bloodstream, ultimately increasing your pain and withering your soul. Are you ready to fight for liberation? Like removing a splinter, this will be an excruciatingly painful procedure. Our dysfunctional inclinations do not go quietly.

You cannot break the vice-grip of sin over your life by yourself. The first step to overcoming sin is to *give up trying to do it on your own.* We are imperfect, broken, weak and powerless to do what we know we should do. Oddly enough, the biggest obstacle to conquering sin is a "can-do attitude" built on the wrong foundation. Recognize from the depths of your heart, that *apart from God, you can do nothing!* We must humbly admit that our lives have become unmanageable; we are in need of new management. Place your trust in Christ, relying upon his power to do what you cannot do yourself. We can do all things *only* through Christ who strengthens us. Do you truly believe God has the power to free you from your sins? That he can restore you to sanity? If so, cry out desperately for deliverance! You need the Mighty Hand of God to turn the water to blood, to send the fire and the hail, to part the raging seas...but you must be willing to walk through it on your own two feet.

1. **Meditation Exercise:** Slowly and meditatively read **Psalm 51.**

2. **Journal Exercise:** As Aristotle says: *"a man who cannot repent cannot be cured."* Write your prayer of repentance: Admit to God (and yourself!) that you are powerless to stop sinning on your own.... Express your trust in God's power to set you free... Ask God from the core of your being to change you...Pray it out loud...

3. In the next seven chapters, we will begin to compile your own catalogue of sins. In the words of AA, "make a searching and fearless moral inventory of yourself." Set aside seven pages in your journal to begin listing out all the different sorts of sins you have committed. Write at the top of each page: "I confess and renounce the following sins:" Then ask God for the grace to remember and be rid of them.

81. On Pride
The Black Hole of a Self-Centered Universe

he primordial sin, which spawns all other sins, is the self-deification called pride. Pride is *a self-centered soul system*, where God is displaced as the gravitational center by a tiny and pitiful substitute: your self. Assuming the role of ruling the universe will ensure your universe ends up collapsing upon itself. We need a complete reversal of our paradigm, a Copernican revolution of the soul. Humility aligns you with reality, when you recognize that you are just an orbiting planet, a satellite; God alone was, is, and always will be the Sun, the Light of Life, the Sovereign Center of all things, the Ground of Being. We do not have the weight, the gravity to anchor and sustain the universe in balance. *Pride* is defined as *the deluded desire to make ourselves the ultimate reference point instead of God.* There is no folly more foolish than to try to live as if God does not matter. *He alone matters!* We are creatures of dust, utterly dependent upon God for life, breath, worth, our very existence.

The essence of pride is when we attempt to sit upon the throne instead of the true King. If the secret hearts of humanity were laid bare, those tearful, fearful lyrics would become clear: *everybody wants to rule the world.* Our ego-centric arrogance puts us in competition with God himself-- a very unwise place to be. *"God opposes the proud but gives grace to the humble."* God wants to be on our side, but it is our own stubbornness that sabotages the alliance. As C.S. Lewis declares, *"pride is the complete anti-God state of mind. It is how Satan became a devil."* Pride is the search for Perfection conducted in the wrong place, mistaking the image of God engraved on our hearts for the Real Thing. Face it. You are an inadequate god, unworthy of worship, unable to control the cosmos. The sooner we accept this indisputable fact, the better off we will be. *He's God; and you're not.*

Of course, we would never openly admit to such self-worship. Few people would ever say "we are gods"...but our actions betray our unexpressed hearts. Why are we so offended when someone puts us down? Why is it so hard to accept that life will not always follow our perfect plans? Why do we hate being corrected? Why must we constantly control, control, control? Pride is the conviction that *I deserve to get my way*. My desires must be fulfilled wherever and whenever I want them to. *My will be done!* And we set about controlling people and circumstances to get our way in the world. We defend our honor, our rights and our wants with religious fervor. It's a lot of pressure, trying to be God.

Pride is the root, the spark, the primal origin of all other sins. Envy, anger, greed, lust, gluttony, laziness-- these are just perversions of normal, God-given desires. They are *disordered affections* that result when we elevate any human want to a divine right that should not be denied. When we allow a simple desire for sex to do whatever it wants, it becomes monstrous. A necessary need for food and drink can turn into a numbing medication for emotional pain when not properly limited. What causes fights and quarrels? Aren't they generated because we cannot deal with not getting what we want?

Sinful pride is *not* the joy we take in the accomplishments of our friends and family. Nor is it our sense of achievement at doing something well (although these are often annoyingly accompanied by pride). Nor is it a healthy self-respect based on our God-given value. Pride is a broken ego-system that blinds us to our own imperfections and weaknesses. It makes us unteachable, uncorrectable, uncaring and unable to admit when we have done something wrong. Our unruly flesh takes every disagreement personally when we have already decided beforehand that *we are always right*. Many of our "communication problems" are just our refusal to listen objectively to the perspective of others. This is the *"will to power"* Nietzsche spoke of, the manufacture of our own moral code, the mindset of a two-year-old carried into adulthood.

Pride gains much of its strength by its invisibility. Like a parasite that thrives in even the most "spiritual" persons, pride avoids detection by mimicking its predators, like zeal, faith, discipline, and love. The most insidious form is that Pharisaical pride in our own righteousness. We become so enamored with our own spiritual maturity that we are blinded to our greatest sin. *Thankfully, there is one dead giveaway to camouflaged pride: judgmentalism.* When we look down on and condemn others for their immaturity

and weakness, we can be sure that pride has been driving us. Like a big "x" drawn in the middle of your forehead, you cannot see your own pride. You can only "see" your pride through the mirror of another's eyes. And when we see this devil's image in others, our first instinct is anger, condemnation, and judgment. Instead, be compassionate, knowing they see it in us as well. Whenever you become offended at the prideful arrogance in someone else, begin at once to ask God to remove it, freshly revealed in your own heart.

Oddly enough, pride is also the cause of our feelings of self-hatred, self-rejection, self-condemnation, inadequacy, and inferiority.

339

Walter Hilton writes, *"Pride comes by night to attack a soul when it is despised and condemned by other men, to make it fall into discouragement and sorrow. It comes also like an arrow flying by day when a man is honored and praised by all-- whether for worldly or for spiritual deeds-- to give him vain joy to rest upon, in himself and in a passing thing."* Overly low and overly high self-esteem are equally pride-induced, as opposed to a humble and sober self-analysis. Self-loathing is the obverse side of self-worship. Whenever your false god (Self) falters in its ability to keep all of the planets spinning, we begin to beat this old god in an attempt to revive it, to save it. Ironically, the way out of self-hatred is humbly owning up to our own inadequacies, our imperfections, our sins. Admit it: *you are not perfect... and you don't have to be.* Embrace your weakness as a constant reminder of your absolute need for God himself, always goading you into his presence. Turn from your worthless idol to worship the one true God. Pride is often cured by a clear vision of the great, high and noble God and a true examination of your own small self.

The Discipline of Confession - Confession is how you distance your soul from the sin itself. In confessing, we declare *"I did this act but it is not who I want to be. This is the part of me I wish to renounce."* It is an invitation to our great Physician to remove the cancerous parts of our soul while leaving the healthy parts intact. "Therefore, confess your sins to each other and pray for each other, so that you may be healed." Strike at the root! Forcefully remove pride by ruthlessly confessing the very worst in you. Give up your cover-ups and let your sins see the light of day! Sin thrives on denial. It must stay under the radar to remain viable. Unless we confess, pride keeps us stumbling about in a dark cloud of denial and self-deception where we can still pretend we're okay. Take responsibility for the specific sins you have committed. Let go of all your excuses, self-justifications, blaming others and circumstances, your attempts at self-redemption through doing good things. Instead, present yourself before your merciful God just as you are. Take drastic measures to exterminate the swarms of sin infesting your soul.

After you finish your catalogue of sins, I am going to ask you to make a General Confession: to confess to God, yourself and another person the exact nature of all of your wrongs. Give or read this list to your spiritual director or a spiritual friend-- someone you deeply trust. Does this terrify you? Why must we confess to another person? Until we are honest with a flesh-and-blood person, we are not truly honest with God or ourselves. Why do you wish to conceal your faults? Why must you hide your shame behind the fig leaf of falsehood? Why fool people into thinking that you are better than you actually are? Does something rise up in you saying, "No, I could not tell *every* sin!"? That very instinct within you is the essence of pride, the inability to admit that you fall so very short of perfection.

1. Meditation Exercise: Slowly and meditatively read **I John 1:5-2:6**.

2. Journal Exercise: On the first page of your catalogue of sins, write "Pride" at the top. Then list down the major manifestations of pride that you see in your life... Don't try to list every time— that would take forever! Also write the name of someone you can confess to. Now write this prayer, if you believe it: *"I am not God. I cannot control the world. I cannot even control myself..."* End the prayer in your own words.

82. On Envy

The Competitive Ambition for Admiration

We all have a God-given drive for personal significance. We want to know we have not lived in vain. As Dallas Willard writes in *The Divine Conspiracy*, "...*everyone from the smallest child to the oldest adult, naturally wants in some way to be extraordinary, outstanding, making a unique contribution or, if all else fails, wants to be thought so.... We were built to count, as water is made to run downhill.*" Every individual was intended to impact the earth. But our search for significance must be sought under God's watchful eye; otherwise it becomes a desperate performance to please the fickle fancies of the world. We are meant to seek greatness *in God's eyes*. He tells us what feats to attempt. He provides the talents to do it. He sets the bar. And he tells us when we have reached it. But when we subtract God from this equation, our quest for glory becomes a *vain glory*, a *selfish ambition for more power, an addiction to admiration.* This we call envy. When we fail to measure ourselves by God's objective vantage point, we can only measure ourselves *by* other people's subjective opinions and *against* other people's relative achievements. *Envy* is defined as *a misguided desire to achieve greatness in the eyes of the world.*

Envy turns all life into a competition. We have an imaginary Olympics running inside our heads. Everything we have and do (looks, clothes, cars, homes, jobs, achievements, fame, etc.) becomes a contest to see who is the queen or king of the hill. Everyone else is a competitor and a threat. We begrudge the person of higher status than us; we despise the person of lower status. Without God, our neighbor is our enemy in a never-ending rat race. We are unable to rejoice in our neighbor's good fortune unless it contributes somehow to our own. A little friendly competition is fine, but opponents too often have hatred seething behind their teeth. Beneath the veneer of polite and plastic smiles, we really view others as combatants rather than teammates. Conversations, relationships, work, even spiritual pursuits, become a game of trumps to prove ourselves better than others. And when we win this pointless match, do we not feel arrogance, condemnation and contempt towards those below us? And when we lose, does it not results in jealousy and hatred towards the one who stands above us, even hating ourselves for not measuring up? Win or lose, we always lose.

Envy sends us scampering on an endless quest for power: getting it, keeping it, and increasing it. We strive and claw for control, trying to impress those above us and oppress those below us. We sink to new depths as we scale the corporate ladder—rather, the corporal ladder constructed of the corpses of those we've tread underfoot. We are consumed with acquiring more of anything that can be used for our advancement: money, reputation, knowledge, position, status, skills, techniques, even people. We begin to look at the world as something to exploit rather than to enjoy. Truth be told, we want to be all-powerful! We want to be looked up to, to be envied. We don't want friends— we want worshipers! Yet even as we strive for the praise of men, we bow our necks to the approval of men, becoming their slaves.

Comparison-based self-worth is a death trap. You will always be stuck somewhere in the middle of your imaginary totem pole of performance. If your identity is based on how well you stack up against others, every second will be filled with fear, anxiety, and self-doubt. Admiration quickly turns to antagonism. So we gossip and boast to increase our standing. But there will *always* be some sorry souls you can look down on for not measuring up to your lofty position; and there will always be those fortunate few more gifted, more beautiful, more skilled, more *anything* than you will ever be. Can you be content with five people on earth who are "better than" you? Or fifty...or five thousand...or five billion? We are noble creatures, great of soul—but we cannot seem to abide equals, rivals or superiors. How do you avoid the crushing feeling of insignificance when you face the fact that there are millions far better than you in almost every category? And even if you find yourself at the highest pinnacle of success, you now have the exclusive and exquisite terror of knowing that all the world is working towards your demise! And they will succeed; no one stays on top forever! It is vanity to base your value on empty comparisons or hollow self-congratulations. "Being better than others" is not the goal— "being your best" is!

Envy enslaves us to external appearances. The Public Eye is a hideous idol. We sacrifice our children, our future, our joy on its altar. We would rather *appear* good than actually *be* good. Do you realize how twisted that is? We find ourselves polishing our public image to shiny perfection while our private self is rotting in maggot-ridden neglect. We use little white lies to "save face," managing our façade and spinning the truth to our advantage. Never waste valuable breath trying to seem holy, smart or successful. Do what is truly honorable, whether or not it will ever be honored. St. Francis said, *"how you appear before God, that you are, and nothing more."* It should make no difference whether others esteem you or revile you. If you are treated like a celebrity, recall how you are nothing apart from God. If you are treated with contempt, recall that the King of Kings gave his life for you.

Here is the hidden secret behind every man's eyes: *all are insecure who look to the world for security.* Some mask their fears with manufactured bravado; others protect their insecurities by withdrawing their hearts from harm's way. As long as our identity is built on the shifting sands of perfect performance and public opinion, we are always one step away from utter collapse. No wonder we are such perfectionists! We are not working to do good for God and others—we are working to validate our value, to establish our very reason for existence! We dwell for a moment in a fool's paradise of high reputation and high achievement... yet tomorrow these may vanish into mist. We seek the favor of lesser gods. Apart from God's approval, *we will never be good enough.* Security only finds us when our source of security is secure. We must be affirmed by Someone greater than ourselves— join the ranks of the "God-esteemed."

Every competition needs an audience. When you look up into the crowds watching your life, who are you trying to please? Whose applause are you struggling to earn? Perhaps your mother or father? A teacher or mentor? A friend? An enemy? A competitor? Someone who wrote you off as worthless that you are trying desperately to prove wrong? Someone who, no matter what you do, will never give you their full approval? We have a stadium full of people to please! Archibald Hart advises, "clear out your grandstands!" Go through the bleachers one by one and escort each member of the audience out of the arena until there is only One left— One who knows and loves you like no other, One who knows what pains you've borne, One who sees you without comparisons, One who died for your destiny, and will welcome you into glory. And he does not grade on a curve.

The Discipline of Submission - Take the initiative to knock the chip off your own shoulder! One of the greatest disciplines to overcome envy is to willingly subject yourself to the authority of another. Submit yourself to a spiritual director, allowing them to speak correction into your life. Commit yourself to a spiritual community, no matter how much they may irritate or inconvenience you. Let go of control and participate in their mission even if it is not exactly as you would choose. Enthusiastically advance the agenda of others: spiritual leaders, employers, even the government (except when what is commanded is contrary to Scripture).

1. **Meditation Exercise:** Slowly and meditatively read **James 4:1 - 5:6.**

2. **Journal Exercise:** Write down the evidence of envy you see inside.

3. Who are your competitors? Who are you most envious of? Who do you try to outdo, even secretly wishing they would fail? Find a way to bless them: encourage, thank, compliment, or serve them...

4. Who is in your audience? Who are you trying to impress? Whose approval are you seeking? Tell God you want to live for him alone...

345

83. On Anger
The Poisoned Venom of Cultivated Hatred

ot all anger is harmful. Without the corrosive effects of pride, *anger* is only *a natural impulse to right a wrong*. Like a pain reflex in your fingertips, healthy anger is a protective, problem-solving instinct that alerts us: *something is wrong!* This unpleasant sensation signals that your will has been blocked, propelling a rapid response to remove the obstacle before things get worse. In an ideal world, *anger should drive the problem-solving process*. How can I most effectively and lovingly fix this situation? *Attack the problem, not the person!* In a well-ordered soul, anger is like an alarm clock, quickly turned off once it has awakened us to action. The sun would never go down on our wrath. Coupled with Christ-like compassion and discernment, we would first identify precisely what is wrong, and then carefully and calmly correct the conflict for the ultimate good of everyone involved. Yet, in the wreckage of our world, we rarely see such reasonable, virtuous anger. Instead, we see boiling hatred and hostility, raging aggression inflamed with pride lashing out spitefully or plotting icy revenge. Such sinful *anger* is defined as *a hate-filled desire to hurt someone for hurting us.*

Anger turns to sin the moment we forget that God is Judge, and we are not. We are not the standard of right and wrong; nor are we the enforcers of justice. But in our self-righteous indignation, we want to punish the transgressor who has frustrated our self-sacred agenda. Hurt turns to hate as we assign a face to our pain, someone to blame. Is God's will thwarted or simply my will? Either way, recall God's warning: *Do not take revenge, my friends, but leave room for God's wrath, for it is written: "Vengeance is mine; I will repay," says the Lord.* Has a true injustice taken place? He is able to maintain cosmic justice without my intervening.

How do we overcome evil without anger? The best way to confront aggressive evil is with aggressive good. When someone is flagrantly cruel and malicious, the only response more viscerally fulfilling than an outburst of anger is an outburst of joy! Instead of escalating the conflict, surprise them with an unexpected shot of compassion and good cheer. Bludgeon a belligerent person with an avalanche of kindness, goodwill, and love. Say with St. Augustine, "Let them say against us whatever they will, we love them even if they do not want us to!" To show excessive warmth and care to an enemy—this is a dish even sweeter than cold revenge. If they still insist on assailing you, you can always walk away. Or even more exhilarating, if you have the guts, unmask their malice by standing with steely resolve and offering your cheek to their fury.

So how do we deal with the anger within us? Much of our anger is only wounded pride. Our fragile egos are so easily offended! Do you feel like everyone is judging you, looking down on you, attacking you with subtle accusations? Are they ignoring you or leaving you out? Sensitivity to such slights is a sure sign of pride. The humble person really doesn't care that others condemn them. When you feel the force of anger rising within, cling to radical humility. Detach your anger from the fuel line of self-righteous pride. Pull the plug on your rage by asking yourself the simple question, *"So what?"* I didn't get what I want... So what? I was insulted and disrespected... So what? Why does this bother me? Has my worth been attacked? Why give them the right to tell me what I am worth, when the God of the universe already settled that question on a splintered cross long before I was born! As John Climacus reminds us in his classic book, *The Ladder of Divine Ascent*, *"Why do you take offense at insults? Is it not your pride that has been wounded? Why not rather be wronged? Why not rather imitate Christ in being falsely accused, mistreated and insulted, spit upon? Can you still say with Christ, 'Father forgive them. They do not know what they are doing'?"* Offenses, insults, derision, these things are poison to an unregenerate soul; to the Christ-dweller, these are anti-venom intended to inoculate us against the disease of pride. Beware when you hear yourself say, "I deserve..." or "I don't deserve...". Do we really want to receive the *'eye-for-eye and tooth-for-tooth'* that we deserve?

How do you express anger? Do you explode with volcanic fury, erupting with a year's worth of pent-up pressure in fits of rage, acts of violence, verbal assaults and other red-faced expressions of hatred? Do you have days where you lumber around like a wild animal, ready to attack and maul anyone who gets in your way? Or do you build up a reservoir of resentment, simmering deep below the surface? Do you display your displeasure in a passive disregard, bitter contempt, withdrawal, an icy "I don't care" attitude? Such subtle attacks of sophisticated meanness can be just as damaging, if not more so. Our emotional coldness may destroy without lifting a finger. When I turn away from you in disgust, when I avoid you, or intentionally leave you out of my life, you will receive my message of disdain very clearly. The serrated edges of our sarcastic remarks may inflict deeper wounds than our fists ever could.

Do you bottle your rage? Sometimes depression is a disguise for anger suppressed or denied. It takes a lot of energy to nurture a grudge, no matter how carefully we conceal it. We act like we are not bothered when, in fact, a fantasy of revenge is seething beneath the surface of our consciousness. And so the venom turns inward and begins to poison our own bloodstream, causing irritability, irrationality, and mysterious bouts of self-hatred. The seeping acid of anger steals our sleep, disturbs our digestion, robs our energy, and eats away our bodily integrity. But if we can't ignore or unleash our anger, what should we do with it?

First, inventory your wrath. Learn to ask yourself honestly: "Why am I angry?" Angry people are almost always hurting, fearful people. We are deeply wounded and we use anger to protect these wounds, masking our secret insecurities with bared teeth. We attack when we feel threatened. What are you afraid of? Who usually provokes your anger? Authority figures? Rude drivers? Family members? Co-workers? Competitors? (Measure the height of your

348

anger at its highest point, not its lowest. Even the most hateful, explosive person may seem gentle and peaceful in their best moments.) We may be able to trace back the roots of our anger to some specific individuals from our past. Perhaps there are a handful of people whom you have been angry at for most of your life. When we fail to rightly resolve our past hurts, anger tortures us, imprisons us, and handcuffs us to those we hate the most. Who are the people who have injured you, whether physically or emotionally? Who are those faces that fill you with disgust, those voices that boil your blood? Who are the objects of your bitterness, resentment, and hatred? We must deal with these hurts if we are ever going to be healed. Joy always abandons a resentful soul. So how do we dispose of all the hurts inflicted upon us?

The Discipline of Forgiveness - The answer to long-term anger is always the same: *Forgive those who trespass against you.* Forgiveness is a healing stream that flows from the throne of God to you and through you, washing away years of hurts and offenses— not excusing it, explaining it, or ignoring it, but eradicating it in the only way that truly frees us. *Forgiveness* is defined as *a decision to renounce the right to receive payment for an injustice committed against you.* It is *releasing your right to retaliate,* even in the smallest ways. Forgiving is not excusing! We excuse a fault because it is no big deal; we forgive a wrong because it is a big deal! Also, forgiveness does not mean you cannot confront someone. However, the purpose of the confrontation will change from retaliation to reformation. You are not yelling at them to gratify your hurt feelings by hurting them back. Instead, you are on their side, offering helpful correction which will bless them (if they can receive it). When we confront in anger, we become the problem! The wrongdoer will not be thinking about how to amend their ways but how to protect themselves from our anger! But you cannot extend forgiveness to others unless you have experienced its cleansing water yourself; and you cannot receive forgiveness if you refuse to give it. Surrender to the floodwaters of God's forgiveness. Freely receive; freely give.

1. **Meditation Exercise:** Slowly and meditatively read through Matthew 18:21-35.

2. **Journal Exercise:** Write down all major incidents of anger that you can remember— both the eruptions of out-bursting rage and the silent, seething resentment boiling beneath the surface...

3. Make a list of all the people you have wronged... Then list all those who have wronged you... Often it is much the same list. Those who hurt us most deeply, we often seek to hurt. How have you gotten back at them, either directly or indirectly?
Now, with God's help, release forgiveness to each person who has wronged you...

Practice the three steps of forgiveness:
First, with clenched fist, *acknowledge* that an injustice was committed against you.

Second, with open hand, *let go* of your right to get back at them. Write down in your journal, "I now choose to forgive (name) for (wrongdoing)."

Thirdly, with open arms, show love and *reconciliation* to them, *when appropriate.* With those people you have wronged, try to make amends, when you can... Use discernment and the advice of a friend... Every time they come to mind, say in your heart, "I bless them in Christ's name."

84. On Greed
The Materialistic Addiction to Possessions

oney is *not* the root of all evil. It is our *love of money* that God pinpoints as the cause of so much strife and misery. *Greed* is defined as *not knowing when to say "enough" to the accumulation of material resources.* You will never have enough wealth while it is your idol. It is folly to rely upon money's scarcity to provide security. The love of money has broken countless families apart through workaholic parents who provide more and more material "stuff" for their children and less and less spiritual resources. Greed has exploited workers and expanded waste to increase profit margins for fat shareholders. What would our world be like if greed wasn't driving our economy?

Our souls are for sale to the highest bidder. People will do almost anything for money. Offer a person a million dollars and they will suffer the worst torment, they will conquer their fears, they will change their lifestyle, they will betray their best friend. This is the essence of worship-- in spirit and in truth. This is what a god deserves. You have discovered the official religion of our planet. Do you worship God or Mammon, the deity of money? *What would you be willing to do for a million dollars?* What sinful habits would you give up? What inconveniences would you be willing to put up with? Now here's the rub: *would you do the same for the sake of Christ?* If we won't do for the love of God what we would do for a fistful of dollars, we have a divided heart. Cry out for forgiveness! Ask God to heal your heart of the disease of materialism!

Why this love affair with Money? It is our most convenient score card for establishing our personal significance. It is our most tangible source of power. We can walk into a mall and purchase status, convenience, admiration, immediate gratification. All our selfish habits are well-provided. Are you able to survive without these? We accumulate more and more "stuff" like our lives depended on it. We cling to our treasures like a drowning man clings to a life preserver made of lead. The entire advertising industry is built on convincing us to covet our neighbors' stuff. Preying on our envy and pride, we use money to outdo others and prove we are successful. We are driven to buy things we never knew we wanted. How often do you buy things based upon the status they convey? *Indifference to wealth* is a surer path to satisfaction than *acquisition of wealth*.

Sometimes it is just the thrill of accumulation that drives us. Shopping becomes our addiction and credit card debt our burden. Greed leads to an inability to live within one's means. Consumerism eventually consumes you. Why is it so exciting to acquire and own something new? If shopping is your favorite pastime, perhaps you need to find something better to do with your time. Perhaps you need to spend some time with the poor. Try feeding the hungry before you feed your obsession for possessions. How much of your life is spent in pursuit of things which will become dust? Cars, houses, jewelry, clothes, and small kitchen appliances! All will eventually disintegrate into nothingness! Watch the life span of all that you own. In a matter of years, moth and rust will turn them into junk. What among your possessions will not rot into the dust? *A man's life does not consist in the abundance of his possessions.* When you strip away all your artificial trappings, what's left underneath? That's the only "stuff" that really matters.

No greedy person ever imagines that they might actually suffer from this vice. We always have a "reasonable" excuse: wanting to take care of family, to be responsible, to be prepared for future economic hardship, etc. And we are always able to point to someone else who has much more money and is much more wasteful than we are. Greed sends us scampering up the corporate ladder at the pace of insanity, in a frenzied attempt to prove our self-worth to the world. We aggressively pursue promotions to higher positions of prestige, all in a misguided attempt for security. The workaholic runs to his place of worship from six in the morning to ten at night. Why work 80 hours a week to provide material things to a family you barely know because you never see them? Thomas a Kempis warns: *"whenever a person becomes obsessed with success and material things, he quickly becomes restless."* Have you felt this subtle restlessness stealing upon your soul?

So is it more spiritual to be poor? Or is it a sign of God's approval to be rich? How much money does God want you to have? Well, for the moment, he wants you to make the most of exactly how much you have right now. What matters is not how much money you possess but how you use what you possess. There is nothing wrong with being either poor or rich-- but to whom much is given, much is required. You can be greedy in any income bracket—or generous. God told his friend Abraham that he would be blessed so that he could be a blessing to the nations. Are you "bless-able"? If God blesses you with more finances, will you be a blessing to others or will you just become more careless and frivolous with your money? Will you "raise your standard of living" and "enjoy the finer things in life"? Or will you invest your treasures in heaven?

Money, like any finite resource, cannot afford happiness. The law of diminishing returns guarantees the more you get, the more you want. It is not "money" that excites us— it is "more money". Pursuing infinite joy through finite cash will send you into a death spiral that will finally crash. What are you are aiming for financially? How much money would be ideal? When would you be able to say, "that's enough. I have all I need to make me happy?" If you had one million dollars, would you not want just a little bit more? Do you know any rich people? Have they gotten enough to be ecstatically happy? Are they? What exactly would you spend all this money on that would make your life so perfectly wonderful? Would you spend it on yourself or others? How exactly would owning a nice house or a nice car make you happy? Would someone in a poor "third-world" country consider you filthy rich? Is money a means to an end or an end in itself? And if a means, then to what end?

The Discipline of Simplicity - Strive to give generously and live simply. Money only brings happiness when you give it away! Conquer greed with a reckless generosity! Give boisterously, not begrudgingly. When a rich man wanted to become Jesus' disciple, he was instructed to go sell all his possessions and give it to the poor. Then he would be free to follow the Master. If Jesus asked you to do this, could you? Could you give away everything? How about 50%? In the chapter "On Faith", I already invited you to give away at least 10% of your income to the work of God. Have you begun doing this? Make a decision right now that money will not be your master. You may possess it but it shall never possess you. Do you need to set up a "giveaway" account? Will you regularly set aside money to give away and then ask God to show you who he wants to bless with it? Make a habit of giving away money and possessions regularly. As a general practice, buy for need rather than want. There is nothing wrong with having quality products, but never buy for the status conferred. Commit to yourself: "I will never again make a purchase to win admiration from anyone." There may be times to splurge, but try not to indulge yourself with the unnecessary until after you have given gratuitously to others.

Avoid debt like the plague. Debt and savings are polar opposites. Debt borrows money from your future; saving lends to your future. If you are already caught in a sticky web of debt, take immediate steps to extricate yourself from its tricky threads. If you need help, ask your spiritual director. Save regularly... even if you're not sure what for. Keep a budget in order to learn to live within your means and steward well the wealth God's given you.

1. **Meditation Exercise:** Slowly read **Matthew 6:19-34.**

2. **Journal Exercise:** Write down each incident of greed you recall.

3. Review your **Monthly Budget** (in Appendix). Also write down some basic spending guidelines of how you can practice simplicity.

85. On Lust

The Soul-shriveling Enslavement to Sexual Desire

ex is not only pleasurable; it is *holy*. Human sexuality was created intentionally by God as a creative power entrusted to creation. The male and female body parts were made to fit together in a powerful, unifying act of raw pleasure which produces the miracle of children into the world. Our sexuality is not an embarrassing mistake or an unintended side-effect but a beautiful and profound statement of our union with God, a picture of the human-divine nexus of eternity. As such, we must remember that our *sexual organs and desires are sacred*, and defiling ourselves sexually is just as sacrilegious as sacrificing a pig on the altar of his holy temple. What kind of Deity would make reproduction so much fun? What kind of scandalous God could have invented the orgasm? Couldn't God have created us without such stirrings in our loins? Didn't he know the trouble it would get us into? Maybe God thinks we are capable of doing a lot better than we think we are. The sin of *lust* is defined as *unbridled sexual desire*. G.K. Chesterton observes, *"the moment sex ceases to be a servant, it becomes a tyrant."* Sexual feelings are not the problem-- it is not a sin to be sexually attracted or to have sexual thoughts. It becomes the sin of lust when it gets *out of control* and begins to control us, making our decisions for us.

Sex was meant to seal an unbreakable bond between a man and a woman. This is only achieved through that "old-fashioned" consensual *covenant of marriage—'til death do us part*. That promise makes possible the ideal intimacy—a vow to return to one another, partaking of one another again and again, now and for the rest of your lives. Sex can make someone feel like the most special person in all the world! It is not a right to be grasped but a privilege to be granted. Within the warmth and security of mutually-promised love, wholly *exclusive and permanent*, sexual intercourse becomes the union of souls. An inter-penetration and exchange of spiritual substance is symbolized in the sex act as the differences in male and female anatomy become the source of greatest pleasure. Build a high stone wall around the enclosure of erotic love! Let it be a new Eden, a secret garden to explore together and partake of its succulent fruit. God looks with an approving smile upon lovers' innocent embrace, as they lie naked and unashamed. Isn't that what you want? We sense intuitively such intimate oneness is ideal— but society tells us it is unrealistic. It is not... if we will stop worrying about past mistakes and begin to live now in such a way as to make it possible. Do not settle for less than the best! Both *premarital sex* before marriage (fornication) and *extramarital sex* outside marriage (adultery) will ruin the permanence and exclusivity of this covenant relationship. God forbids these not to spoil our sexual pleasure but to protect it!

Sex is generative power. When restricted to marriage, the sex drive is strong enough to force a young man to grow up. It is the superglue that holds a family together. Don't suppress it; sublimate it! Properly channeled, sexual energy fuels creative impulse and teaches selfless love. Fire is a useful and wonderful force, if properly contained. But the instant it rages out of control, it turns dangerous, devouring anything in its path. Don't ask God to take away your sexual desires— you have no idea how that would destroy your fundamental humanity! Instead, ask God to teach you to master your urges. So... how do we tame this ravenous appetite?

The first link in lust's iron chain is the *intentional look of lust*. Jesus tells us that when our eyes linger on another *in order to cultivate sexual feelings,* we are already on the slippery path to adultery. Our hungry eyes begin to devour the flesh of our victim to feed our fantasies. He was not referring to the unintended sexual thoughts and feelings that naturally arise when we see a sexually attractive person. It is what we *do* with those natural sexual thoughts that matters! Do we continue to stare, our imagination going into overdrive, undressing them and molesting them with our minds? Or can we simply acknowledge our desires as real, recognizing that nothing good will come of pursuing such thoughts and turning away towards something else? These everyday choices to either pursue sexual images in your mind or to turn away, will be known only to you and God, winning no praise or scorn from men. But if you consistently lose this battle, you have already lost the war. The steel chain of lust will begin to wrap you in its cold, empty embrace.

The extreme version of "looking to lust" is pornography, which easily leads you into sexual addiction. *Pornography is any visual image used intentionally to inflame sexual desire,* whether it is on the internet, TV, magazines, books, movies, strip clubs, or even sexually-explicit romance novels. But isn't this just "normal"? What is "normal" is not necessarily good! If you are periodically bathing in the cesspool of pornography, decide right now: *I will do whatever it takes to free myself from this sewage of the soul!* Confess your sin to a trusted spiritual friend. Get rid of your stash of sexual images from home or office. Protect yourself from access to internet pollution. Change any weekly patterns that lead you in this direction. I would be less concerned about masturbation, than what accompanies it. While it is debated whether masturbation per se could be part of a healthy spiritual life, it is probably the least destructive sexual outlet during the de-contamination process. If you are going to masturbate, at least do so without pornography.

Once the mind is softened by cheap sexual fantasies, all that's missing is the opportunity, a "weak moment," that keeps you from a falling headlong into an illicit sexual encounter. Flirtatious glances, playful banter, "harmless" teasing, intimate conversations, suggestive touches, a spontaneous kiss— it is only a matter of time before it crosses over into something you did not intend, injuring all your highest aspirations of intimacy. Examine your friendships: are any teetering on the brink of regret? Is there anyone in your life you might possibly sleep with if given a chance? If so, make sure you never have that chance! Are you already involved in a sexual relationship unprotected by covenant? If so, stop! Pick up the phone and end it now. Stop lying to yourself! Don't even try to salvage the relationship unless you both agree to start over and build on an unbroken foundation. The couple who fornicates before marriage is more likely to find adultery ripping them apart after marriage.

The Discipline of Chastity – Every disciple of Christ must learn the sacred skill of *sexual self-restraint*. Self-control is essential no matter what your status: single or married, young or old, man or woman. Don't allow your sex drive to run rampant, goring at random like a wild beast! How many families are broken or scarred by lust's indiscretions? How much hurt, loneliness and betrayal in our world is a result of lust's transgressions? How different our world would be if sex was properly contained! Is it possible to live a full life within the tension of unfulfilled desires? Actually, it is impossible to live a fulfilled life *without* learning self-restraint! Happy homes are inevitably ruined by an unrestrained sex drive: bonds of trust broken, divorce papers filed, family secrets hidden, abortions executed, diseases contracted, tears shed, love compromised-- all because someone failed to keep their pants on.

Do any of us avoid sexual confusion as we drift to adulthood? I doubt it. Have past mistakes left you broken? Have you been scarred by rape, incest, child molestation or some other perversity? These are not beyond God's restorative power. Do you find yourself with same-sex attractions? This is no reason for panic nor is it an excuse to indulge your desires. Homosexuality is not a special category of sexual sin. It only means you're a sinner like all the rest of us. There is no magic formula for dealing with homosexual desires (or heterosexual desires), but we can find wholeness in the midst of the struggle by clinging desperately to Christ and his guidelines.

1. **Meditation Exercise:** Meditatively read **I Corinthians 6:9-20**.
If you are single, make a solemn oath right now to abstain from sex until married! Ask God for help...
If married, agree together to forego sex for a short period of time...

2. **Journal Exercise:** List all major categories of lust committed.

86. On Laziness
The Numbing Paralysis of Procrastination

he human body needs rest; the human spirit needs recreation. A disciple of the Galilean Lord should not be driven ragged by the matters of eternal significance that they deal with daily. It is a heroic but tragic fantasy to "burn out" in the service of Christ. As Robert Murray McCheyne said before passing away at the frail age of 29: *"God gave me a message to deliver and a horse to ride. Alas, I have killed the horse and now I cannot deliver the message."* Make time for the activities which renew, restore and rejuvenate both body and soul. Do not deplete your strength through neglect. You can't go far on an empty tank. We can only pour out what has been poured in. A worn-out, burnt-out disciple is of no use to anyone. The blessing of Asher is given to you: *your strength will equal your days.*

However, rest and recreation, like any other need, becomes a cruel slave-driver if we do not keep it in its proper place. *Laziness makes rest and recreation into idols.* Even a healthy diversion can take over our lives. The first sign of laziness, traditionally called *sloth*, is procrastination, putting off for later what you should be doing now. This is actually a spiritual problem, a weakness of resolve which fails to follow through on decisions. The Hebrew Proverbs warns against the foolishness of the *"sluggard"* who *"buries his hand in the dish; [yet] he is too lazy to bring it back to his mouth."* Laziness keeps us from doing the things now which will enable us to do more in the future. Laziness is also the reason for many of our *sins of omission* described in Scripture: *"anyone who knows the good he ought to do and doesn't do it, sins."* How many good things do you know you should do but can't get around to doing?

The procrastinator's greatest tool is the *excuse*, an art form among the lazy. We are so skilled at justifying our own behavior! If you think hard enough, you can find a convincing reason for avoiding any responsibility. Your big "but" gets in the way: I should do this, *but*...I am too tired...too busy...it is too risky...I'm not sure...I got distracted...or as the proverbial sluggard says, *"there is a lion in the road."* What are your favorite excuses? One way to deal with excuses is to rephrase them as challenges, replacing your "but" with "even though." Instead of saying, "I need to go to work, *but* I didn't get enough sleep last night" say, "I need to go to work *even though* I didn't get enough sleep last night." Put your valuable time and energy into finding solutions instead of excuses!

The answer to laziness is *not* to just keep busy. *Busyness* and *laziness* are not mutually exclusive! Sometimes they are the best of bedfellows. He who works when he ought to sleep is just as lazy as he who sleeps when he ought to work. *Laziness* is defined as *not doing the right things at the right time.* Failure to do the right thing at the right time will numb your spirit and lead to depression, boredom, and apathy. It drains your energy and strains your nerves with the difficult demands of playing catch-up. The fear of boredom keeps us incredibly busy doing nothing of significance. Boredom is not the absence of activity but the absence of purpose. Some of the busiest people in the world are simply covering up the fact that they have no idea what they want to accomplish in life! We think we have covered great distance when we have only been feverishly running in circles. Learn to ask yourself, "What should I be doing right now?" A great tool for living life on purpose is to formulate and follow a life-vision, a *Rule of Life*. This keeps you focused by constantly reminding you what you're supposed to be doing with your life. Thankfully, as a follower of Christ, you already have a worthy mission. Our life goal is, in the words of St. Ignatius, *"ad majorem Dei gloriam",* we live *"for the greater glory of God."* Is this what you are busy pursuing? Comfort and convenience are priorities only to the aimless.

Time is your most valuable natural resource. All are given the same daily allowance. You cannot manufacture more of it and you cannot rewind, fast-forward or pause it. You can only receive it as it comes and use it wisely. Beware of "killing" time-- you may be murdering your closest ally! The key to good time management is, in the words of St. Francis of Assisi, *"put the bitter ahead of the sweet"* or in today's language, *delayed gratification*. Learn to wait for your rewards. Work hard sowing your fields if you wish to reap bountifully. Once you know what your goal in life is, do everything possible to prepare yourself to reach that goal. Here are two useful tools: a *weekly schedule* and a *daily planner* (or calendar). This helps make the most of every opportunity God gives you.

When it's time to work, work hard and intelligently. Don't rush or do things half-heartedly. When you hurry, you end up making more work for yourself. The best work is done calmly but steadily. As St. Francis de Sales puts it, *"Make haste slowly."* Don't get overwhelmed. One task at a time, one day at a time, one problem at a time. Never give less than your best. Take whatever resources you are given (time, materials, people, etc.) and make the most of them. Don't worry about what you could have done if you had more time or better materials. Instead of complaining, just bring out the best in whatever you are given.

Sleep is a basic need for your physical well-being. Not getting enough sleep at night will leave you unprepared for the tasks of today. Most people need anywhere from six to nine hours of sleep each night to function at full capacity. Although you can't expect to get the ideal amount of sleep every night, you should be getting a restful, fitful sleep regularly. If you are routinely worn out, you need to change your routine. We have many excuses why we do not have time to sleep well, but you could save a lot of time each day by being fully rested. But we must also guard against becoming ensnared by our bed. When you know you should awake, place your feet on the floor and get up. Don't lie there and think about it.

Recreation is helpful and healthful for your mind and body. It is literally a time for the re-creation of your soul. Everyone should have at least one hobby: something they do for fun. Perhaps you thrive in sports or outdoor activities. Or you enjoy reading or music or artistic endeavors. Whatever charges you up should be a regular part of your life. Entertainment can also be a harmless, often healthy use of time in small doses. But beware of excessive amusements that leave you with a mushy mind and a soggy spirit. Movies, television, the internet, video games— all can be useful, informative, even inspiring. A hobby should help you to relax and get your mind off of your usual occupations. It should leave you less stressed-out than when you began. However, TV or video games easily become major time-wasters that shrivel your soul, leaving you feeling drained and sluggish if you do not set some good boundaries. When your "entertainment" leaves you with no time to practice your spiritual disciplines, it has probably become an idol! Remember: *the eye is never satisfied with seeing, nor is the ear filled with hearing!* They are bottomless pits that continue to hunger as long as we live.

The Discipline of Physical Exercise - Everyone should be involved in some sort of bodily exertion on a regular basis. Whether it's through manual labor, sports, cycling, fitness training, running, or just walking, try to break a sweat several times a week. Get your heart pumping, push your muscles a little past their comfort levels and stretch well to keep flexible. Not only is this good for your body but it also is a great way to keep your mind and will sharp. Don't let your muscles deteriorate from lack of use or your body becomes spoiled. Conquer your excuses and plan physical exercise into your schedule at least a couple of times a week. Even this can be taken up for the glory of God. We can be assured from the gospels that Jesus did not lead a pampered and sedentary lifestyle.

1. **Meditation Exercise:** Slowly read **II Thessalonians 3:6-16**.

2. **Journal Exercise:** List how you have been lazy in life.

3. Review your **Rule of Life** (see Appendix) and your **Weekly Schedule** (see Appendix). Are they balanced? Do they reflect your primary purpose in life? Is there time for good works? Do you have time to rest and exercise? Do you have time *not* to?

87. On Gluttony
The Overindulgence of Bodily Appetites

ood and drink are basic necessities of the body. God designed the physical appetites to preserve life. We seek pleasure instinctively, and when indulged naturally, moderately, and properly, most pleasures produce vibrant life (How often would we eat, drink, breathe, sleep, or reproduce without such an alluring incentive?). But do not be fooled: A human being, unlike a slopped pig, requires more than indulged appetite to be happy. Man does not live on bread alone! But we keep looking to the earth to provide what can only come from above. *Gluttony* is defined as the *idolatry of our physical appetites*. I include here not only overeating, but all sorts of bodily addictions: alcoholism, drug addiction, eating disorders, self-mutilation, and other compulsions too numerous to name. Gluttony is whenever we surrender our own better judgment to our own physical hungers. Paul described this enslavement when he said, *"their god is their belly, and their glory is their shame. Their mind is on earthly things!"*

All addictions are idolatry. It is when some physical indulgence takes the place of God. We yield the last word to it, declaring, "thy will be done." When we deal with our brokenness by running to a false god, we become addicts. Some addictions are more socially-acceptable and some are inherently more destructive, but every addiction places a wedge

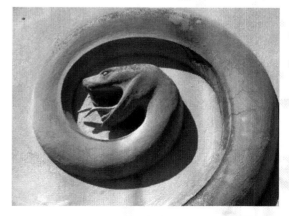

between us and God. (I doubt that smoking cigarettes will be a big issue on judgment day... but they will ensure you get there much quicker! Cigarettes are not only hazardous to our health but are often a symbol of rebellion... and they are just plain gross! So why not stop?) Strangely enough, we often develop a love-hate relationship with our obsessions. Nothing can truly replace God. Nothing else can handle the weight, the pressure of the expectations of deity. Anyone or anything that is put in the place of God will always let us down. Addictions always have deeper roots than their surface manifestations, so they must be handled with the utmost care and sensitivity. There are so many interconnected dynamics, self-deceptions, excuses, and hidden support patterns that it is helpful to find a counselor to help you untangle yourself.

Eating disorders, such as anorexia, bulimia, overeating or obesity are never just about food. Eating (like all addiction) becomes a numbing reflex for emotional pain. We cover our pain, we mask our guilt, we silence our self-hatred by getting one more drink or one more bite or one more hit. But the hurt always returns and so does the hunger. Until you deal with the spiritual roots, you cannot truly be free. To make matters worse, we often derive our identity directly from our physical appearance. If we are thin and physically attractive, we somehow think that makes us a better person. And if we are fat and unattractive, we believe we are worth less. Remember what God said when he chose David as the next king of Israel: *"People look at the outward appearance, God looks at the heart."* Do you believe this?

Your body does not belong to you. It is God's temple and you are its steward. Believe it or not, your diet has spiritual implications. Eat all that you need, not all that you want. A healthy body is not a guarantee of spiritual health but it is often a result of it. Moderation doesn't mean doing just a little bad; it means limiting good things so they don't turn bad. If you regularly consume too much junk food, you are showing a basic disrespect for the God who dwells within. How would you feel if someone trashed the house you let them stay in? Are you filling the body God gave you with garbage? A good diet generally consists of lots of water and foods that actually grow in nature: vegetables, fruits, meats, grains, etc. If you can't even tell what plant or animal this came from, that's not a good sign! Limit sweets and fats so they don't become your enemy. I am not saying that there is no time for occasional indulgences, but how much indulgence is enough? Addiction thrives on the deception that satisfaction is right around the next corner. Moderation thrives when we remember the truth that no pleasurable sensation, however intense, will ever be enough.

Alcohol itself is not sinful... but it can be dangerous. In the Bible, drinking is limited, not prohibited. Christ's followers are not forbidden wine, beer or strong drink. Jesus himself provided more alcoholic

beverages for a wedding that was running low! However, Scripture warns vehemently against the dangers of its abuse and counsels temperance. Alcoholism turns rational men into rabid dogs, robbing them of all self-control and sending them forever panting for more. If you are going to drink, here are three guidelines. First, guard yourself against dependence. Beware when you find that you are looking forward expectantly to your next drink. Set a reasonable limit (a two-drink maximum or something comparable) as a precaution. Be especially careful if you find yourself wanting to push the limit just a little. Secondly, guard against drunkenness. If you tend to overdo things, you may find that complete abstinence is the best prevention. Thirdly, guard against losing your wits to it. If you find yourself saying or doing things that are out of character, start rethinking your drinking. When you do something stupid in a drunken stupor, you are at fault for your ignorance.

Drug abuse is another area where gluttony may rear its ugly head. Obviously, taking illegal drugs is inexcusable, but even prescription drugs, pain-killers, anti-depressants, even cold medicine may also be abused. You may take prescription drugs when you need them, but understand that when manipulating the body's natural chemistry, you are liable to have some very serious side effects. An over-dependence on drugs may show a tendency to take the easy way out.

The Discipline of Fasting - Fasting is one of the best training grounds for exploring the fierce dynamic between your flesh and your spirit. This is where you learn self-denial, where you see the battle you are up against. Test your resolve! Go without a couple meals and see how loudly your body screams for attention. More than anything else, fasting tells your body who is the boss. If you are struggling with any pleasure-seeking sin (sexual addictions, pornography, TV, overeating, etc.), fasting is an indispensable part of strengthening your spiritual muscles.

Here are some practical tips and cautions in the practice of fasting. Anytime you fast from food you must drink lots of extra liquids. Never fast from water. Don't do strenuous activity when on a fast; expect to move a little slower than usual. Start and end your fast gently with a small, light meal of simple, healthy foods. Start slow, perhaps with a two-meal or three-meal fast. Then you can work your way up to a three or four day fast. Check with your spiritual director and your doctor before undertaking an extended fast. Do not fast if you have an eating disorder, are pregnant, or have a medical condition like diabetes or hypoglycemia. You can also do partial fasts such as a bread-and-water fast or a vegetables-and-water fast. That way you can forgo fancy food that gratifies the taste buds without abstaining completely from healthy food that strengthens the body.

1. **Meditation Exercise:** Slowly and meditatively read **Daniel 1**.

2. **Journal Exercise:** List each major manifestations of gluttony you remember. What are your usual addictions? Which is the most harmful?

3. Decide on one day a week that you will fast. It may be only one meal or it may a partial fast, but try to make fasting part of your weekly spiritual exercise regimen.

4. You have now completed your catalogue of sins. Look over the pages chronicling your failures... Are you glad when you wilt before these temptations? Recall how you feel every time you surrender to a sin... Whenever you are weary of battling, remember: giving in to sin will not bring relief! It only saps you of life!
Are you, in the words of AA, *"entirely ready to have God remove all these defects"*?
If so, *"humbly ask him to remove your shortcomings"*...

5. Now take a few minutes to imagine yourself free from all sin...
Can you imagine yourself *not just abstaining from the acts of sin, but free from the desire to sin*?
In your journal, write out a detailed description of "a sin-free you", your unique life unencumbered by the sins that entangle you:
Without pride, envy or anger, you are free from the manipulations of men—you cannot be bought, intimidated, flattered, or insulted!
You have no hypocrisy for you have no one to impress... See your face without a hint of fear—your brow is not notched with all the lines recording your worries...
You are in complete mastery over all of your desires... Without greed, lust, laziness, or gluttony, you are internally at peace...
See your face with a calm, self-possessed satisfaction with whatever you have...

6. Now take your catalogue of sins and confess them to God...
Are you completely convinced of his promised forgiveness?
Now confess them to a trusted friend. Decide how and when you can make this confession... Call them and set up a time to talk...

88. On Temptation
Stopping the Cycle of Sin

any view temptation as a terrible curse. It is actually a great blessing, an essential element in your spiritual formation. Temptation is the gateway to greater power. To become a seasoned champion, we must pass unharmed through this baptism of fire. Every battle is an opportunity for defeat... or for victory! *Every choice to do wrong has a corresponding choice to do right!* And choices are habit-forming; they make us who we will be tomorrow. Therefore, every conquered temptation becomes a crown displaying God's splendor! Every successfully completed test strengthens us in spiritual combat. If the Spirit of Christ dwells in you, then you are of his sturdy stock, born of kings: the Progeny of Light! He trains your hands for war and bestows the strength to bend a bow of bronze! If you aim to stand victorious over the vanquished foe of temptation, you must do two things: *prepare carefully before the battle* and *fight courageously in it.* Equip your mind for the mounting offensive. Then rise up with a warrior's heart and turn loose your aggression against sin's seductions!

Most temptations can be traced back to a lie. Such lies undermine God's perfect goodness, power, wisdom, or love. In the heat of fray, sin makes us terribly irrational. We literally become stupid and foolish when blinded by desire. Such seductive enticements are half-truths from the enemy of your soul. Like bait on a hook, the Arch-Deceiver will show us the moment of gratification and carefully conceal the harmful consequences. Once you take the bait, you can be sure that you will be pulled farther than you wanted into places you never meant to go.

Arm yourself against specific sins by compiling a list of the many reasons not fall into this particular trap. Reflect on its harmful results. Consider how it will ruin God's best plans for you. Decide beforehand that the long-term pain is not worth the momentary pleasure. Memorize specific Scriptures that will fortify you against your greatest foe. Let truth break the bondage of deception. Imagine how you will feel looking back at your life from your deathbed. Do you want to be the kind of person who could not overcome this? Ask yourself what you would tell someone else in your predicament. Disarm your arch-nemesis of his weapons of secrecy and loneliness by quickly confessing your struggle to someone. Enlist them as a prayer partner to provide airborne support.

You can also take measures to remove occasions to fall into sin. The easiest way to overcome temptation is to avoid it completely. Do not overestimate your own strength. If you are trying to lose weight, do not work at a bakery. The blessing of temptation is forfeited when we bring it upon ourselves. Take note of the predictable pathways to disaster: the times, the places, the people, and the circumstances that seem to accompany your downfalls. Pay special attention to your emotional states that make you susceptible to temptation. Once you know when and where you are weakest, you can build your defenses appropriately.

Once the battle begins, be strong and very courageous! God wants to give you the victory over this Goliath. The real battleground is in your mind. Most temptation follows a familiar pattern: It begins with a *thought*: a suggestion, an idea, or a mental picture. It turns into a *fantasy*, filling your imagination with an enticing scenario of how wonderful it would feel to give in. This inflames your *desire* for the sin until you are completely captivated by it. From here you only need opportunity for it to turn into *action*. And the further along this process you are, the harder it will be to stop it. Let's look at this deadly cycle more closely.

It is not wrong to be tempted. In fact, the suggestion to sin is your battle-cry, a call for victory! Do not start feeling guilty and beating yourself up just because a perverse picture popped into your head. It is not a sin to find that you are drawn against your will towards a suggestive thought. It only becomes sinful when *your will*

369

consents to be drawn further in. It is your decision whether you will choose to board this train of thought. Whether sparked by an external stimuli or a random thought, the best strategy is just to ignore it, leaving it out in the cold as you turn your attention to something else. Before the idea has picked up momentum, walk past the "advertisement" and get on with life. When you notice a fantasy of revenge or sex or greed playing across your mind, speak firmly to it, *"that's enough!"* and walk out of the theatre. Turn your mind to its next task. Sever the head of the serpent before it gains entrance! A brief sinful thought quickly dispatched is a *victory!* However, if it drags on and on... the proposal has probably gained your consent.

Once the initial thought gets in, sin quickly seizes you by the imagination. It presents your mind with a fleshed-out fantasy of sin indulged. The tide turns in favor of your foe when your mind starts to conceive delightful details, vivid images, suggestive scenarios and sensations, even plans begin to take shape. Once your imagination is filled with filth, your feelings are easy prey. An overwhelming flood of desire quickly sweeps you away. At this point, it is easy to say that we had no choice because our feelings are so irresistibly strong. This is *almost* true. We cannot control our feelings by direct effort; but, with great effort, we can control our thoughts—and our thoughts will direct our feelings. First, change what you love; what you do will surely follow. Even when hopelessly caught in the current of desire, you can still pull the plug by redirecting your thoughts. Escape the suffocating coils of sin by turning your back on the python: "and now for something completely different!" You cannot dismiss thoughts of chocolate bunnies by trying really hard not to think about chocolate bunnies. Otherwise, all you will be thinking about are the chocolate bunnies you weren't supposed to think about!

By forming a habit of re-direction every time you are tempted, you turn the persistence of the enemy back upon himself. Your desires do not have the final word—your decisions do. *Use every temptation as a reminder to do good, to say "hi" to God, to pray for a friend, to recall to a Scripture, to renew your love for*

Christ, or even to get your mind off of it through some diverting activity. If your imagination is occupied with meditations upon the life of Christ, you will have no room at that time to fantasize about lesser subjects. And we can always call out to our conquering Commander, asking him to quickly come to our aid. The best battle position is on your knees. If each satanic assault only serves to excite more faith, love and goodness, your antagonist will eventually give up (for the time being) since each offensive only hurts him more.

If you lose the inner battle, your will inevitably lose the outer battle. Guard your thoughts! Whatever inhabits your mind for long will lead to action. Even if this process happens instantaneously, the longer you dwell upon a sin, the more likely you will actually carry it out. The murderer has already been murdering people in his mind long before he ever actually picks up his weapon. The adulterer has already slept with countless women in his mind before he ever "falls" into the affair he "never meant to happen". Have you already embraced a sin in your heart? Would you do it if you could? Perhaps you would do it if you knew you would not be found out. Think for a moment of all the things you would do if you knew you wouldn't get caught. In these cases, the idolatry of our reputation, the sins of pride and envy are actually preventing other sins from being acted upon. We know our house is overrun when the only reason we don't have more scorpions is because they are being eaten by the snakes!

1. Meditation Exercise: Meditatively read through **Colossian 3:1-17.**

2. Journal Exercise: Choose the most prevalent sin in your life...
List times, places, people, and occasions that trigger this temptation...
Describe the emotional state you are usually in when you fall: lonely?
Hurt? Angry? Discouraged? Worn-out? Why do you feel this way?
What images or thoughts usually lead you into this temptation?
What lies fuel the fire? What views about God and yourself?
What Scriptures and truths could combat these lies?
What could you turn your mind towards when temptation strikes?

CHRIST-CENTERED SPIRITUALITY

A HANDBOOK OF *CATECHESIS*
for
the training of novices
in
THE WAY OF CHRIST

PART V. Your KINGDOM MISSION of Sacrificial Love

89. On the Active Life of Spiritual Power

Christ's mission is now your mission. As an apprentice of Christ, you have been drafted into the *Missio Dei*, the mission of God to a broken and dying world. Hear the call of Jesus: "As the Father has sent me, I am sending you." We have looked at many *don't's*. Now let us look at the many *do's!* Once we have given up our addictions, our promiscuity, our materialistic pursuits of pleasure, do our days become dull and dreary? Not on his life! If you strive undividedly to disseminate Christ's love daily, life will never be boring! But if you settle for a mild middle-class lifestyle of comfortable Christianity, you will slowly suffocate the Spirit within you. Your soul has found healing; now scatter this healing energy to every soul you encounter! Christ-likeness must become epidemic— starting with us! We are to bring the *shalom*-- the well-being, peace and justice of God's rule into every space we find ourselves in. It is time to walk the prayer, *"Thy kingdom come, Thy will be done, on earth as it is in heaven."* These are your marching orders. Wherever your foot treads, bring about the goodness of God Almighty on every level of existence (spiritual, physical, emotional, intellectual, volitional, and social). You have not been set free for your sake alone. Like Abram before you, *you have been blessed to be a blessing* to the nations. How tragic it would be to live and die without doing anything of permanence. Pursue ambitious goals for the transformation of society, but remember: *whatever is done with and for Christ will last forever.*

We must now, in the words of St. Francis de Sales, *"live Jesus!"* We are to do all things *"in the name of Jesus."* This means we are to walk in his *authority* to carry out his *purposes*. We must have the oil upon our own foreheads, the anointing of the Holy Spirit. Like a policeman's badge, the Spirit of Christ authorizes and obliges us to carry on the work of his kingdom upon the earth. Do not ignore your sacred obligation. Whether you like it or not, whether you feel like it or not, you are now an ambassador of God's reign, an agent of God's

373

love and justice. As his representative, you must now conduct your affairs as you think Jesus would if he were in your place. Like Christ, your life will be filled with sorrows, but increasingly, they will be second-hand sorrows. You will not be feeling sorry for yourself but bearing the burdens of others. We can no longer stand around wringing our hands asking, "Why doesn't God do something about this mess?" We are the body of Christ! We are his hands and his feet! We must do something about this mess! We are to speak the words that he would speak! We are to heal the sick he would heal! We are to serve the poor he would serve! Bring restoration! Bring liberation! Bring transformation to your world!

This *Active Life* of Christ's Mission is the final stage of Christ-centered spirituality. You establish an outpost of God's kingdom on earth right beneath your feet. Supply the presence, power and purpose of God to every room and every relationship you enter, particularly those you spend a lot of time in. Kingdom work involves both the miraculous and the mundane. You bring the experience of Christ to others by bringing sight to blinded eyes or by bringing a cup of cold water to a thirsty co-worker. Both are, strictly speaking, the work of God's Spirit. You are a living example of God's reign, both through specific kinds of actions (healing, prophecy, deliverance, servanthood, evangelism, and making disciples) and by your overall lifestyle (at work, at home, at play, in all your relationships). Expect that your footsteps will be followed by miracles, both miniscule and magnificent.

It is absolutely contrary to the Way of Christ to live a self-indulgent, me-first life. Have you experienced that God surrounds you with an ocean of love? Then invite your neighbors into this inexhaustible flow! *Freely you have received; freely give.* A contemplative and communal life must fuel us towards an active life of mission. Otherwise, our spirituality is only a selfish pursuit of selfish fulfillment. If the Eternal Spirit has truly invaded the inner chambers of our lives with his contagious *agape* energy, we will begin to love our neighbors with the same sacrificial love Christ showed us. The community of Jesus is meant to be a hope factory, established for the manufacture and distribution of this most precious and rare resource! Christ-centered spirituality always turns our eyes outwards: *"lift your eyes to the fields, they are ripe for harvest."* This decaying world, like your own soul, yearns for the healing touch of Jesus. Don't wait around idly for God to rescue you from the world; ask God to rescue the world through you!

Just as Jesus was the light of the world, he now expects you to be the light of the world. After having been illumined by proximity to his radiance, you are to take this living flame from heaven and light up the world like a shining city set on a hill. Pass on what you have received. Jesus began his ministry with the words of the prophet Isaiah, *"The Spirit of the LORD is upon me because he has anointed me to preach good news to the poor. He has sent me to proclaim freedom for the prisoners and recovery of sight to the blind, to release the oppressed, to proclaim the year of the LORD's favor."* Could you take these words as your own life mission statement? The assignment Christ began now belongs to you. This Scripture is now to be fulfilled in your own life. You are to pick up where he left off. However, as you will see, he has not left off at all-- he has simply chosen to work through a new pair of hands! Roll up your sleeves-- you have a job to do.

As you progress in your communion with your Creator, your life will become so deeply integrated with his life, that it may almost be difficult to discern where your own natural abilities, ideas and energy ends and God's begins. Your desires become more and more aligned with God's desires. Your abilities co-operate more and more with Gods abilities. Your very existence becomes more and more caught up in the existence of God. You might almost say that we *"participate in the divine nature!"* The mind of Christ "thinks through you." The words of Christ "speak through you." Through constant practice, the use of supernatural resources becomes habitual, almost second-nature. Perhaps you will find that you have become so enthralled with doing good that little energy needs to be expended on trying *not* to do bad.

The work of Christ is impossible without the same power at your fingertips that Christ had. This is why Jesus warns his disciples *not* to set out on this world-wide revolution until they had been *"clothed with power from on high."* You can't carry out this work naked! Apart from the supernatural activity of God's Spirit through us, we can do nothing. But there is no limit to what a follower of Christ can accomplish when *"the Spirit of him who raised Jesus from the dead is living in you."* Without this otherworldly dimension to our activity, nothing valuable will be accomplished. So our greatest priority must be to keep closely connected to our Power Source, the Creator of Life. We don't do good works *for him;* he does good works *through us!* And, most importantly, he does good works *in us* as we labor alongside our Lord. *He doesn't need us to accomplish his mission,* but he loves accomplishing his mission in and through and with his children!

1. **Meditation Exercise:** Meditatively read **Matthew 9:35-10:16**.

2. As you reflect on this passage, ask yourself how you would feel if you were one of Jesus' twelve disciples sent out on this initiation mission... Would you really believe that you had been given authority over every disease and sickness? Would you really believe that God would provide for all of *your* material needs as you go?

3. Now, look at your own life. Have you accepted the mission he has given you? Talk to God about it... Use your journal to record the highlights of this conversation...

4. Recite this prayer reflecting the spirit of St. Francis of Assisi:
 Lord, make me an instrument of your peace;
 Where there is hatred, let me sow love,
 Where there is injury, pardon,
 Where there is doubt, faith,
 Where there is despair, hope,
 Where there is
 darkness,
 light,
 And where there is sadness, joy.

90. On Spiritual Baptism
Immersion in the Spirit's Power

D on't settle for a powerless version of the gospel. The work of Christ requires access to the miraculous. There was a very real supernatural dimension in the ministry of Jesus *and* his first disciples. If you subtract the healings, the prophetic, the almost "magical" elements from the story of Jesus and his apostles, you are left with a very different story. Throughout the history of Christ's people, we hear strange reports of the same displays of God's power breaking into our present reality! Has it occurred to you that perhaps following Jesus today might possibly mean doing the same kind of "odd stuff" Jesus did? Can you imagine wielding the same cataclysmic power in prayer that Jesus had when he walked through the streets of Jerusalem? Could miracles follow you as they did Jesus? Is that a realistic expectation for Jesus' disciples living today?

Although Jesus was the Only-begotten of God, it appears he lived within the same limitations and constraints the rest of us are bound by. He seems to have gained his power through the same channel (immersion in the Holy Spirit) that he expects us to access. When Jesus sent out his apprentices on their initial mission to the villages of Israel, he deputized them with authority to drive out evil spirits and to heal every disease and sickness. Are we disciples, two millennia later, also so authorized and empowered? Jesus said that *"anyone who has faith in me will do what I have been doing. He will do even greater things than these!"* Could it be that we also are sent out to *"heal the sick, raise the dead, cleanse the lepers, and drive out demons"?*

Perhaps you truly *wish* you had this wonderworking ability, but you honestly don't feel up to the task. Perfect! This is exactly where you must begin. Jesus told his disciples that if they would wait receptively, they would be completely inundated in the active energy of the Spirit of the Living God! In fact, he warned them *not* to go anywhere until they had been filled. This was the great promise and the great priority. This soul-saturation in God's invisible Substance was the secret of the first apostles' supernatural power. Don't look at them as if by their own power or godliness they made the lame walk! It is only by plugging into the electrical current of the God of Abraham, Isaac and Jacob that these works were done through their frail hands of flesh. And we also are promised this gift when we wait expectantly on our Father!

Have you received the full force of this Gift? Have you been empowered to work the works of the kingdom? Have you heard the *Abba*-cry welling up from within? Has the Spirit of Sonship testified with your spirit that you are God's child? Pentecostals are notoriously pushy, trying to pressure people into specific experiences to prove they are "Spirit-filled." Thankfully, you don't have to prove anything to anyone. If you wish to *"receive the Holy Spirit"* as Jesus commanded, seek the Spirit, not the signs! Different Christ-honoring traditions have emphasized, added to, or subtracted various things from this influx of the Spirit. Regardless how you define it, just receive it! Each spiritual in-filling in the Scriptures manifested itself in slightly different ways. Don't get caught up in the details of how it is expressed: joy, boldness, zeal, the power to speak in other tongues, prophecy, heal the sick, teach and proclaim the good news, practice holiness and hospitality-- any ability that could be necessary to fulfill the global mission! The fullness of the Spirit's power is not optional for the follower of Christ. You need it to complete your job. This infusion of supernatural energy equipped ordinary people to do works of the same caliber as Jesus! He releases his Spirit upon us so that we might be his witnesses—those who share their experience of Christ with the world. Your actions become signs, indicators of God's invisible Presence surrounding your life. They are intended to bring a sense of wonder and mystery into our humdrum world. Through this baptism into celestial fire, you are equipped with the means to do *whatever it takes* to represent God's rule on earth.

Allow me to warn you: *supernatural power does not make life easier!* It is not a short-cut to health, wealth and happiness. The apostles did not sit around curing each other's colds and accumulating possessions for a comfortable life of self-indulgence! They were thrust out into a treacherous and hostile world with instructions to transform it. The power is great because the task is great! They were empowered for a massive undertaking the likes of which our world has never known. Light-bearer, you will need all the resources you can get to carry out the work of Kingdom-Come-- on earth as it is in heaven. Do not imagine that you will avoid disappointment and failure in this undertaking. Anytime you step out in faith, there is a risk of failure-- as Jesus' original twelve disciples experienced firsthand. But you will never see miracles if you never attempt the impossible.

Prepare to be amazed! And prepare to be disappointed. When we are directed by the Spirit of God himself, there is no telling what may happen! There will be times we don't see anything happen... and there will be times when the wonders of God burst before our eyes! Get used to the unexpected. Imagine the shock when Jesus healed the blind man with mud made from his own saliva! The indwelling Spirit opens us up to a whole new range of mystery. No longer are we limited by the usual constraints of the natural world. Many movements of God from the early apostles through Johannes Tauler, George Fox, Jonathan Edwards, George Whitefield, John Wesley, through modern Pentecostals and Charismatics have seen shocking displays of shaking, weeping, falling down, trance-like ecstasies, healing, prophecies and speaking in unknown tongues.

However, Jonathan Edwards also warns us in his well-worn work, *Religious Affections,* that such striking signs are neither *proof of God's work* nor *proof against it.* Beware of abuses, distortions, and devilry disguised. One reason many hesitate to embrace the baptism of the Spirit is because of all the obnoxious foolishness done in his name. Every supernatural gift can be counterfeited with grotesque caricatures. Some work up ecstatic experiences and miracles through emotional hype, enthusiasm, or frenzied hypnosis. Some try to force healings with a circus-like atmosphere of high-flying feats of daring. Some see demons lurking behind every mishap or illness. Nothing is quite as sickening as watching someone try to drum up God's power through manipulation and deceit. Such quackeries and trickeries usually focus on the bizarre, glorifying the sensational and superstitious over the supernatural.

379

Don't allow cheap imitations to dissuade you from seeking the real thing! Don't fear that your loving Father will give you a scorpion when you ask for bread. God only gives what will nourish and energize your soul, not something harmful. Clear out the doubts. Ask yourself: Do I deeply desire to be directed by God's Holy Spirit, however he may lead? Think it over. Do you wish to receive from God whatever he wishes to give you? Or will you say, "no, thanks" because you are scared of falling into error. It's actually not hard to steer clear of error: just keep asking yourself whether you are seeking God himself or a specific experience. Open yourself up to whatever God wants to do. Don't place limits on him about what it's supposed to look like. Then let God use you in ways both unassuming and spectacular.

If you want to be whelmed over by the Holy Spirit, probably the best place to go is to your spiritual community. The book of Acts tells of the Spirit being given at the laying on of the apostles' hands (though not limited to that method). Sometimes it required a time of expectant waiting... sometimes it didn't. Maybe you need to tarry with Christ for one hour... or ten days like the 120 at Pentecost in Acts 2... or it could happen spontaneously like Peter's listeners in Acts 10. Who knows? God will give us what we are disposed to receive. How will we know if we are filled? Is there a reliable sensation or phenomenon to guarantee that we are baptized in the Spirit? I cannot say... You will probably sense something of the Spirit flooding your soul, but every person's experience varies. And you will find yourself living beyond yourself. Perhaps it is not so much a binary on-off switch but a floodgate that may open to a tiny drip, a trickle, a growing gush or a non-stop, overflowing downpour into our souls! Perhaps as you attempt the miraculous works mentioned in the next few chapters, you will find a greater and greater release of the Spirit in your life.

1. **Meditation Exercise:** Slowly and meditatively read **Acts 2:1-21.**

2. Spend some quiet minutes with this gentle invitation in your heart: *"Veni, Sancte Spiritus"* (Latin: *"Come, Holy Spirit."*)

91. On Spiritual Language
A New Dialect of the Spirit

ne of the first and most common symptoms of supernatural power has been the fascinating phenomenon of *glossalalia,* or spiritual language. Throughout the book of Acts as well as many times throughout history, various groups of disciples have experienced this ability to speak in unknown languages upon being filled with the Holy Spirit. Using a spiritual language greatly simplifies prayer. We don't need to know what to pray for! Have you ever been burdened to pray for something yet find you have no idea what to say? Perhaps God's will is perplexingly unclear. Perhaps you are praying for a person whose life is a riddle to you. Perhaps you are emotionally overwhelmed and cannot even grasp a single word that seems appropriate. Perhaps you are not even sure why you are praying! At times like these, it is refreshing to know you can pray precisely according to God's will without understanding. Only allow the Spirit to pray through you in his own distinct dialect. Sometimes these tongues are known by other ethnic groups and sometimes they are simply the supernatural vocabulary of the Spirit.

When it is an actual human language, it is a miraculous witness to the international scope of God's mission, extending the worship of God into other cultures and contexts. The unbeliever may, for the first time, hear the praises of God being declared in their own native tongue. The God of all the Earth always meets us where we are, proving to us that he can speak to us in our own words and symbols. That is part of the miracle of the incarnation-- that he comes to us right where we are, wrapping himself in the familiar trappings of our world so that he may show us the strange new ways of a shimmering world of wonder.

On other occasions, the use of spiritual language may be super-rational communication of our re-born spirits directly to God's Spirit. This supernatural exchange takes place on a level of consciousness that can only be described as deep calling out to Deep. It is the unintelligible dialogue of lovers, not speaking words but speaking love unhindered by words. Like a mother cooing at her infant, we can say something much deeper than words through what sounds like a meaningless babbling. Yet it is anything but meaningless, holding deeper meaning than any speech could express-- your own private dialect of worship and wonder.

Why does this mysterious gift of spiritual language so often accompany the outpouring of the Spirit of God? Perhaps it is poured out so liberally because of its self-edifying quality-- it is the only gift you can practice *by yourself* to *build yourself up*. We are not filled with the Holy Spirit once and for all. We must keep getting filled if we want to experience perpetual spirit baptism. You are a Bearer of the Flame! This cleansing fire within has the power to heal the wound of the world! You must keep it burning brightly! Refuel as often as you need. Seek continual renewal. In this way, spiritual language becomes the primary means of filling up the tank of the Spirit anytime you feel empty. It is your means of self-edification. You can use this gift at anytime to kindle more of the Holy Spirit's fiery Presence in your life. You could say that spiritual language is the one "selfish" gift which builds you up so that you can build up others.

In many ways, spiritual language is like training wheels to the other gifts. It helps you to *practice co-operation* with the Spirit of God. It is an exercise in sensitivity and response to the movements of the Holy Spirit. Here's how it usually works: do not expect to suddenly burst forth into an ecstatic utterance like a geyser. *This gift does not bypass your will... only your understanding.* You still have to choose to open your mouth-- God won't open it for you. Once you have become willing to receive this gift (perhaps a difficult step?), you will most likely have a few syllables pop into your head or "on the tip of your tongue", as it were. You will feel silly because it makes no sense (it is, precisely, non-sense), but if you actually just open your mouth and say those syllables, more will come to you.

These words, unlike virtually everything else you say, won't come from your rational thoughts. They will come from... somewhere else. Instead of reaching into your mind to find the words to say, you reach into the inner dwelling of the Spirit. You will be speaking in other tongues as *the Spirit gives you utterance.* This will sharpen your sensitivity to God's Spirit within because you will be regularly using this "pathway" from God's Spirit to your will without having to think about it. By regularly responding to these syllables given to you (by speaking them out), you are strengthening your ability to interact with the Holy Spirit and respond immediately without having to figure everything out. Begin to allow God's Spirit to speak mysteries through your own mouth. This is also a very humbling process. We become acutely aware of the foolishness of God which Paul assures the Corinthians is greater than human wisdom. If you are bound by a fear of looking foolish, you will never be able to function in this capacity.

Spiritual language is not only for private use. It can also be used to edify others. It may be a useful part of a gathering of disciples *if it is properly regulated.* Its interpretation can serve as a sign to unbelievers of the authenticity of God's Presence. When God's Spirit speaks in such a way, they may exclaim, "God is truly among you!" However, if it is done without some kind of order and without being explained and interpreted, it will only convince the uninitiated that you are a stark, raving lunatic.

Avoid the extremes of making too much or too little of this gift of unknown languages. Some groups have made "speaking in tongues" the main focus, the badge of spiritual attainment. Because of this, people are coerced into trying really hard to come up with something-- whether it is from God or not. This also leads to all sorts of attention-getting displays of self-exaltation. We are right to feel uncomfortable about such manipulative methods. If you do not speak in tongues, don't feel guilty and don't let anyone condemn you. Heaven has no second-class citizens. But we must also resist the urge to reject this gift as a knee-jerk reaction. We may fear that this path will lead to backwoods snake-handling and shouting at strangers on street corners. Don't shrink away from any of God's blessings, no matter how much you have seen it used improperly. Don't let false miracles scare you away from all things supernatural. Above all, let us remember that any gift of the Spirit must be used to build up and not to tear down. Paul wisely warns the Corinthians against the offense of spiritual exhibitionism: *"If I speak in the tongues of men and of angels and have not love, I am only a resounding gong or a clanging cymbal."*

1. **Meditation Exercise:** Slowly, meditatively read **I Corinthians 14:1-32.**

2. Have you worked out any emotional or intellectual roadblocks to receiving this spiritual gift? Have you seen this gift abused or are you scared of becoming "one of those weird Pentecostals"? Does it seem like this is not a gift but a curse?
If you have any misgivings, talk it over with God. Tell him why you are apprehensive and see what he says...

3. Invite the Spirit, the "Breath" of Heaven to breathe in you...
Sit quietly before God for a few minutes...

4. Are convinced that your Loving Father wants to give you this gift? Are you willing to graciously receive it? If so, ask God for it...
Then see if the syllables do not appear in your mind out of nowhere, waiting to be spoken... If they do, open your mouth and begin to test drive this wonderful gift...

92. On Prophetic Guidance
The Revelation of God's Voice

oes God still speak to humankind as he did in the days of old? Or has God lapsed into silence after the Scriptures were written? Here is one resolute fact the Bible reveals about God: *He talks.* He communicates. People are starving for divine guidance, hungering for a word from beyond the world. They want to know what God is saying to their world today. They want to know if God really sees them. They want to hear that God cares about what's going on in their lives. *Prophecy* is *the ability to hear from God: first for yourself, then for others.* God wants to use you as his spokesman, his mouthpiece. You can bring God's direction into this world by simply learning to listen to his still, small voice within you.

God still speaks today. And normal people like you can hear him. Are you listening? God made your mind... he has the exquisite ability to get through to someone who thinks exactly like you! Attune your ears to hear his whispers. Listen carefully for that Inner Voice, and when you hear it pay attention! God speaks differently to each person. Some hear God almost every day; some hear him clearly only every few years. You may hear actual words; you may feel impressions. Few hear God as an actual audible voice (although this could happen as well!). *For most of us, God speaks through thoughts appearing in our minds.* They will sound almost like our own thoughts except that they have a certain quality: an authority, a calmness, a gravity, a weightiness. You may have a degree of certainty that a word is actually from God, but only rarely will you be absolutely sure that God has spoken. Prophecy always requires faith. There is usually room for doubt. "Did I really hear from God?" Revelation is meant to bring you clarity, not certainty. Some are gifted prophets, others are not. But we may all use this gift with some profit.

The first step toward hearing what God says *now* is knowing what he already said *earlier.* Become familiar with God's voice by becoming familiar with the *Holy Scriptures*, the written Word of God. This gives us a grid to run every supposed "word from God" through to see if it aligns perfectly with what we already know of God's character. Let the pages of sacred Scripture form an impassable concrete parameter which no prophetic word may transgress. No mystical message in our mind carries the same weight and authority as what has already been confirmed upon the pages of Scripture. Never accept as authentic anything which contradicts the clear teaching of Scripture, regardless how beautiful it sounds. Check with a wise and trusted spiritual friend if you have any misgivings. The more discerning people who will confirm a prophecy, the more likely it is from God. Revelation is ongoing. The Holy Bible is God's *defining* revelation, not his *confining* revelation.

What forms do prophecies take? There are many ways in which God speaks to his people. You may have *visions* or *dreams*. Rarely do visions take the form of "out-of-body" ecstatic experiences. Often they are just pictures that pop into your head. Pay attention to any images that form in your mind's eye as you pray and seek God. These may actually be divinely-ordained visions. If you think it may be from God, ask him about it. Let God reveal what it may mean or if it is actually his idea. If you have any significant dreams that made an impression or left you with a sense that it may have some meaning, spend a couple minutes trying to evaluate and understand it. Has God been trying to say something? You may want to check with your spiritual director or a friend for help in interpreting them. And write down any dreams if you're not sure. You may come back to it at a future time and find that its meaning is now clear.

Prophecies also take the form of *words of knowledge*. These are *facts about reality that are divinely revealed*. God may show you specific information about a person's life that you couldn't otherwise know. God may tell you secrets about someone's past or future, their sins or their strengths, their hidden thoughts, their secret aspirations. If you receive these kinds of words of knowledge about someone, don't use it against them. Be compassionate. Use this information to pray, to

386

counsel, to build them up, not to tear them down or manipulate them.

You may also receive *words of wisdom— godly direction for decision-making*. Wisdom is correctly applied knowledge. It is knowing what to do with what you know. This kind of prophecy tells people what to do about specific situations in their lives. It is as if they were able to ask God himself "what must we do?" and God literally answers them. He may even arrange for "coincidental circumstances" to say something to you. Pay attention to these divine synchronicities.

There is too much craziness that creeps into "prophetic" ministry. Prophetic guidance is an area that needs tremendous discernment, compassion and especially *humility*. Always remember Paul's warning to the Corinthians: *"If I have the gift of prophecy and can fathom all mysteries and all knowledge..., but have not love, I am nothing."* Never use prophecies as a power play, to control or to gain an advantage over others. The ability to accurately prophesy is *not* evidence of spiritual maturity. God can speak through anyone, no matter how mature or immature they are. The Hebrew Scriptures tell how he once spoke through a donkey; He can do it again! Acknowledge your imperfection and inexperience. Pride very easily steals in when someone speaks the words of God, so be very vigilant against this stealthy enemy.

Never pressure people to just believe you because you believe it is from God! Prophecies are weighed by their hearers. We are not required to get people to believe us! That is the work of God's Spirit. Your job is simply to speak. Let God make it ring true to their hearts. It is often best to preface a prophecy with, "I think God may be saying..." or "This is what I think God is showing me..." If it is from God, God will make it clear. If you made a mistake, it will not cause any major damage.

Sometimes prophecies are for the sole purpose of calling you to the work of prayer. We are not always required to tell the prophecy. Perhaps we are to keep our mouths shut and take it to God in prayer. Our intercession for others takes on more authority and accuracy when we've been prompted by God. You are much more likely to see a prayer answered if it is something God revealed because you are praying in line with what God is already doing. If you know God has summoned you to it, assault heaven's gates with a bombastic barrage of prayers!

If you would like to hone your prophetic skills, here is a wonderful way to do it: *practice prophetic prayer among a small group of disciples.* When you come together with others whom you know and trust, give God a chance to speak his guidance into each other's lives. Gather around one person who you will be praying for. You may lay your hands upon them if you wish. Then ask God to reveal something to each of you about how you should pray for this person. Spend some time in silence listening. Try to discern what God may be saying about them. If he places a specific need on your heart, then pray earnestly for that area. If God has spoken a word or phrase or Scripture to them, tell them what you think God is saying. If God gives you an image in your mind, describe to them what you are seeing. Then you can ask them honestly afterwards what was "on" and what was "off". This feedback will sharpen your skills as you begin to see when it worked and when it didn't. Also, continue to practice the *lectio divina* exercises described earlier in this book. Whenever you hear or read Scripture, ask God "what are you saying to me?" Then listen in silence.

1. Meditation Exercise: Slowly and meditatively read **Acts 21:7-15.** In this example of a prophetic word, do you see how Paul and the prophet had different ideas about how to respond to this word from God? This emphasizes the need of discretion in the use of prophecy. How do we avoid misinterpreting a word from God?

2. Have you already heard God speaking to you? Think back through your life: Were there times when you thought perhaps God said something to you? What did he say? How did it make you feel?

3. Take 5 minutes and practice listening to God: *"Speak, Lord, for your servant is listening"*...Write what you think God might be saying... Now think of someone close to you who needs your prayers... Ask God if there is something specific he wants you to pray for... Write it down and ask them about it later...

93. On Healing the Sick
The Restoration of Bodily Health

Healing is not just *proof* of the gospel message; healing is *part* of the gospel message! Before he opened his mouth to teach, Jesus extended his hand to heal. This was his method. Leprosy, paralysis, seizures, fevers, even death itself fled at his word. There is no limit to the kinds of ailments he can allay. Why was the healing of hurts so prevalent in Jesus' ministry? Healing is one way God can express his love to us (although the absence of healing in no way implies a lack of love). Sickness is often the most obvious pain in our lives. By restoring our health, Jesus shows that our screaming needs are not beyond his concern. Healing is a tangible way to bring his audacious, gracious resources to bear upon the real and immediate needs of our world. He truly knows our pain. Jesus doesn't like to see broken bodies any more than he likes to see broken souls— his passion procures a cure for both. But he always presses towards deeper restoration.

Jesus told his disciples to heal the sick... and for hundreds of years, his followers did just that! They assumed this was part of their commission: to bring physical, emotional, and spiritual healing into the world. And while history has seen many gains and losses, Jesus' command has not been rescinded. Healing is now part of your calling. Do you think God wants to heal through your hands? Do *you* want to be used in this way? Healing often opens the doors to the kingdom of God. God's salvation has always been holistic: body, soul, mind, and spirit. However, bodily healing is often the attention-getter, the visible image, an illustrious illustration of God's intention. Show people how God feels about them! God absolutely loves to put smiles on people's faces.

So let us practice the miraculous. Start playing with fire! How shall we begin? If you wish to heal the sick, first ask for the wisdom, faith, and power to be used in this way. Then raise your faith-level by reading the healing stories in the Bible or in more recent history. Not only will this encourage you *that* God can do it, but it also gives real life examples of *how* it's been done. Keep yourself full of faith by talking to disciples who have healed others. But don't wait too long before stepping out there and attempting it. You don't need to know "how" to pray for healing. Just try it. The best way to learn to heal is to start trying.

When you see someone you know is sick, ask if you can pray for them. Most people will not mind-- they probably won't expect it to work either, so don't worry about disappointing them if you fail! You don't have to guarantee anything. Once you have secured permission, ask them exactly what is wrong and where it hurts. You may need to take them aside to a more private place so as not to be distracted or to attract attention. It also helps to have others pray but only if they are also full of faith. You may need to raise the faith of those participating-- perhaps through a quick affirmation of God's ability and desire to heal people.

Then, if appropriate, place your hands upon the sick person. Ask their permission and then lay a hand on or near the area of their body that is affected. Francis MacNutt reminds us that *"touch can be prayer that has power all its own."* For some reason, physical contact is often a means of God's transference of power, almost like divine radiation treatment. In fact, many report sensations of heat, electricity, vibrations or other odd phenomena at the laying on of hands. So, do we have to touch someone to heal them? No...but it seems to help! In the Bible, most healing stories include bodily touch as part of the healing process, although there are instances in which touch and proximity is explicitly excluded. But do not treat this method as a magic formula.

As you begin praying, pause and listen for a moment. See if God's Spirit is saying anything specifically about how you should pray. Look upon the person before you and see if you can connect with God's heart for them. "God, what do you want for them?" God may bring to mind a picture, a Scripture, a word or a phrase for you to speak out. Invite God to heal them unless he leads you in another direction. Sometimes God may give you an extra helping of faith to command the healing. There is no need to raise your voice or shout, but speak to the body and tell it to be healed. One strange feature of Biblical prayers of healing is that most are in the form of an order: *"Be healed." "In the name of Jesus Christ of Nazareth, walk." "Take up your mat and walk." "Be opened."* It almost seems like God wants you to practice using the authority he has already given you. This makes sense if God wants to cultivate a dynamic spirituality of initiative rather than inactivity and idleness. Perhaps God wants to release his healing power into you so that you do it rather than asking him to do it. But please use discernment!

Be sensitive to the person you are praying for. If they seem incredulous, antsy or uninterested, by all means let them to get on with their lives. Don't condemn or scold them but send them off with a blessing and an open invitation for further prayer anytime they need. But if they are desperate, expectant and open, don't be afraid to simply soak them in prayer. Sometimes healing is a process requiring time *and* touch. Your prayer doesn't have to end when you run out of words. You can remain hands-on in prayer, praying silently or praying quietly in your spiritual language, seeking further direction.

After you finish praying for them, stop and ask them if anything has happened. Has anything changed? Did they feel anything? Don't hesitate to try again, especially if you see a partial healing. If they say it feels a little better, it is likely that God is still in the process of healing them so you may need to keep praying until it is fully healed. Healing prayer may be spread over days, weeks or even years! Even Jesus himself took more than one prayer to heal the blind man in the eighth chapter of Mark's gospel. If you pray for people consistently and faithfully, you will probably see some total healings, some partial healings and some total failures! Let me reassure you and set your mind at rest: *some people you pray for will not get healed.* Don't be afraid to fail.

So let us address that haunting question: *Why didn't they get healed?* How do we respond when we pray hard and faithfully...and nothing happens? Do we berate them for lack of faith? Do we deny their sickness as an illusion? Rather than construct theologies that amount to practical Deism, can't we say with honest optimism those three precious, freeing words: *"I don't know"?* We are dealing in mysteries— complexities beyond comprehension. As Job can tell you, God can and does use sickness for a higher purpose: to awaken us from our slumber, to draw us closer to God, to humble us, or other reasons shrouded in the mysteries of God's sovereign will. But as Francis MacNutt reminds us in his classic work, *Healing*, *"by New Testament standards, it should be normative for the Christian to pray for the removal of sickness rather than its acceptance. Redemptive sickness is the exception, not the rule."* Conduct your own experiments in combining various amounts of faith, love, anointing, holiness, touch and time, infused with the catalyst of God's power. Although healing power comes only from God, we can still gain experience at using and co-operating with it. No car can run without power-- but not all drivers wield that power with the same skill. Also remember that the death rate in this imperfect world still hovers at around 100%! And death may be the utter failure of health... or the eternal restoration of perfect health.

One last caution: supernatural healing should not be at odds with natural healing! There need be no animosity between medicine, miracles, psychosomatic cures or natural remedies. Instead we rejoice in anything that brings health instead of sickness, life instead of death! Don't neglect or disparage the many blessings of scientific advancements in health care. Don't make someone stop medical treatment to prove their faith in God! (To be consistent, we should pray our teeth clean instead of brushing them!) God rarely does for us what we can very well do ourselves. We don't need to worry about what is strictly supernatural healing, what is due to medical intervention or what is the body's own built-in recuperative power. God can use any means he chooses, including medicine, the feeling of being loved strengthening an immune system, placebo effects, emotional healing, getting enough rest, or a divine miracle. It all comes from him.

1. **Meditation Exercise:** Slowly and meditatively read **Acts 3:1-16.**

2. Is there anyone God wants you to heal? If so, pray for an open door...

94. On Releasing the Oppressed
Deliverance from Inner Bondage

o many souls are in bondage to compulsive habits that defy reason. No matter how hard we struggle, we cannot break free from the crushing grip of uncontrollable addictions or self-destructive patterns. We may find ourselves adrift in the darkness of a debilitating depression, pummeled by wave after wave of hopelessness, worthlessness, loneliness and despair... and nothing seems to keep us afloat. Some of us may find ourselves panicked by irrational fears, anxieties and insecurities that paralyze us *even though we know better!* We know we shouldn't feel this way, but it doesn't stop the inner turmoil. Where do we turn after we've seen the psycho-therapist, learned the fancy names for our symptoms, taken the medications—yet still find ourselves brutally wounded within, unable to carry on? Is there no hope?

Christ came to set the prisoners free and release the oppressed. Deliverance from all forms of inner bondage is God's gift to you... and your gift to others. Many emotional problems have natural causes (chemical imbalance, mental illness, psychosis, neuro-chemical addictive processes, etc.), but there is also a supernatural side to the equation (inner wounds, strongholds of deception, careless vows, demonic activity, etc.). So feel free to receive any medical or psychological help available: medication, counseling, or other treatments. But do not shy away from the spiritual healing that is also available. There is often a complicated cause-and-effect interaction between the physical and the spiritual. We do well not to discount either side of the human soul.

Blaming demons may sound silly, irresponsible, or downright medieval. But if we believe God is not made up of subatomic particles, then it is not inherently illogical to believe there could be other beings without material form (i.e., angels and demons). The fact that Jesus believed in them should convince us such un-embodied persons are, in fact, real. Images of squalid, dank insane asylums filled with shrieking maniacs used to make "normal" people shrink from admitting the need for psychological help. In the same way, images of vile demon-possessed zombies spewing rancor on pallid priests often frighten us away from the everyday ways demons oppress the average person.

What exactly do demons do? The driving purpose of demonic spirits (including Satan, their commander-in-chief) is the destruction of humanity, by any means possible. Since they have already chosen to oppose God for all eternity, their overriding desire is to strike at God, to wound him, to destroy him. But God sits safely beyond their ability to harm him directly. However, they can still hurt him indirectly... by hurting his children. We are God's treasured creations-- his princesses and princes. That is what makes us such attractive targets to the enemy.

The primary weapon of demonic oppression is *deception.* Demons want to *control* your life; each lie you believe gives them greater control. Lies are Satan's native language. The whispers of the serpent are the poison that kills spiritual life. By listening to lies, we ingest the viper's vomit, and disorientation, confusion and exhaustion sets in. His most common toxin is *accusation:* "you're ugly, worthless, unlovable, hopeless, a failure..." Have you heard this "loser's script" recently? Satan will bury you under such self-hatred, condemnation and shame until you hate yourself almost as much as he does! He not only lodges false claims against you but against God, hoping to separate you: "God hates you. He doesn't care about you. He'll abandon you just like your father." If you listen long enough, he will convince you that God is like Satan: erratic, weak, spiteful, impatient, irritable, and ignorant.

Every negative behavior is built on a lie. When we find a bad habit cannot be broken no matter how hard we try, a demonic stronghold may have taken root. Therefore, the first step towards freedom is *identifying foundational falsehoods and replacing them with truth.* When we latch onto any of Satan's "facts" and begin to live by it, we give our enemy a foothold, strategic leverage to accomplish his terrible purposes in our lives. This doesn't mean we're demon-possessed! It only means that a satanic thought pattern has been established in our minds, which may support all sorts of irrational behaviors such as self-mutilation, sexual perversions, chemical addictions, cultic practices, child abuse, etc. Unexplainable compulsions are often due to demonic chains that have stealthily been wrapped thickly around us over many years. They can spawn severe negative emotions: chronic depression, erratic anxiety and fear, bitter resentment, misplaced rage, suicidal thoughts and apathetic weariness towards life. But these lies are often so tightly-intertwined with wounds, sins, imaginations, vows, memories, and other entanglements that a veil blinds our hearts from even seeing the truth right in front of us. No amount of reasoning can unravel it.

At this point, we may need to delve into the second step of deliverance: *the healing of inner wounds.* Jesus came to bind up the brokenhearted. Demons, like parasites, feed on our wounds causing them to fester. Rejections, assaults, abuse... often in moments of deepest suffering, we reframe the world to cope with it. Our enemy fills our minds with vivid images, still-throbbing wounds, painful memories, hurtful conversations—all of which confirm his diabolical conclusions. Lies are our protective mechanisms to cover our crushed and maimed spirits. Heal the wound, heal the soul. Sometimes we need to ask the question, *"When did all of this start?" "Why did I start believing this?"* Ask Jesus to heal these hurts. Ask him to pick up the pieces of your smashed and shattered soul, and put you back together again. If he reveals any significant instances or images, ask him to show you what is true.

As our great Physician pours his healing balm upon our broken hearts, we must *renounce* anything we have done that has provided an entry to our enemy. Sometimes, gaping holes have been ripped into our souls through occult practices such as witchcraft, Ouija boards, tarot cards, magic charms, spells or other "seemingly harmless" spiritualist activities. We may have put out an invisible welcome mat to unclean spirits through involvement with Wicca, Satanism, animism, shamanism or other religious idolatry. Consciously renounce any such blatant invitations for anonymous spirits to enter your life. We may need to forgive unreleased grudges or repent of past sexual activities which can inadvertently open doors to demonic influence. We may need to renounce any rash vows we made to ourselves or to others (i.e., "I will never let anyone hurt me like that again!" "I will prove them wrong, no matter what!"). Demons are all too willing to exploit these pacts as permission to participate in your stated promise. Often closing these doors on the devil and opening them to God is enough to cause the schematic strategy of Satan to come crashing down. As you gain freedom through taking these steps yourself, you are prepared to be used greatly to minister deliverance to others who are in bondage.

The last step in deliverance, *demonic confrontation*, is necessary only when someone is severely oppressed. Then we may have to do the distasteful task of driving out demons directly. Demons prefer to stay hidden, lulling us into thinking they don't exist. But when ignorance fails, they will try intimidation. Demonic manifestations are meant to *distract* or to *scare you.* You get so fascinated with fighting demons that you ignore God. Or you become immobilized, frozen with fear. *Never fear a demon!* No matter how they rant and rave, they are powerless over the person immunized to their lies. Take refuge in this truth: *Greater is he that is in you (Christ) than he that is in the world (Satan).* Don't do this alone! Great discernment is needed in such encounters. Pray for protection for you and your team. Ask the oppressed person if they want Jesus in their lives instead of the demon—otherwise, there's not much point in getting rid of it! Ask them to renounce any area known of sin. Then confront the demonic entity directly with a command of expulsion: "In the name of Jesus Christ, spirit of self-hatred, go!" Or to paraphrase of Jesus' synagogue exorcism: "Shut up and get out!" There is no magic formula. You do not need to raise your voice... demons are not deaf. So with quiet confidence, be persistent and unyielding— every demon recognizes the superior power of Jesus Christ (though they may try to bluff their way out of it!).

1. **Meditation Exercise:** Slowly and meditatively read **II Corinthians 4.**

2. Do you need to renounce any secret and shameful ways of your past? Is any bondage unyielding? Do you need to ask someone for help?

95. On Serving the Poor
Meeting the Physical Needs of Humanity

as love ever pushed you out the door? Has love ever emptied out your wallet? Has love ever taken visible form? Has love ever worked your muscles to the bone? Has love ever woken you up, bleary-eyed, in the middle of the night? Has love ever left you in physical pain? If not, are you sure love is real? Or is it only a fine theoretical idea? Love takes physical shape when it impels action! Unless its energy converts into motion, you have to wonder whether love has any real substance. Jesus had little tolerance for discipleship without sacrifice. He required each disciple to give up physical resources and comforts, weighing their love on the scales of action. When spiritual substance actually displaces physical objects and sensations, we see its reality. St. John describes the tangible nature of love: *"This is how we know what love is: Jesus Christ laid down his life for us. And we ought to lay down our lives for our brothers. If anyone has material possessions and sees his brother in need but has no pity on him, how can the love of God be in him? Dear children, let us not love with words or tongue but with action and in truth."*

If you are not regularly serving the needy, can you truly say the love of God is in you? Or do you not see the desperate faces pressing in around you? Are you deaf to the cries of the oppressed, the poverty-stricken, the victimized, the dying? Does the plight of the helpless, the hopeless, and the homeless at your doorstep not bother you? Who will feed and clothe the poor around the world? Who will care for the orphans, the widows, the refugees, the lepers, the untouchables? Who will aid the disaster victim? Who will rescue the children out of prostitution, abuse, and sex trafficking? Who will educate the illiterate? If not *you*, then who? If not *now*, then when? It is *central* to the Way of Christ to care for the poor. If you wish to touch Jesus in the flesh, go hug a homeless man! He is sacramental.

Part of the supernatural work of the Spirit does not look very miraculous. It looks like stuff anyone could do. This leaves us without excuse! They are simple acts of servanthood, like the traditional *seven physical works of mercy* of the medieval church: *to feed the hungry, to give water to the thirsty, to clothe the naked, to shelter the stranger, to care for the sick, to visit the prisoner, and to bury the dead.* The ancients looked upon these acts of kindness as spiritual acts of worship. These acts, just as much as  miracles, bring the resources of the kingdom of heaven into our earthly existence. God's power is demonstrated not only in *other-worldly actions*, but in *other-worldly motives*. As an agent of God's work, we have to cultivate a sensitivity to the hurting world around us and a willingness to do something about it. Consistent servanthood is a thunderous proclamation of the good news of Christ.

One reason for the explosive growth of the community of Christ's disciples in the second and third centuries was their fanatical compassion. They rescued the abandoned babies left for dead (a then-culturally-acceptable practice for dealing with unwanted pregnancies). They cared for the sick that others had given up on. They built a loving community of warring races and social classes. They even sold their own possessions to support the poor among them! This kind of outrageous, active mercy towards the hurts of others was one of the most convincing proofs for the transformative claims of the gospel of Christ. Despite many claims to the contrary, such selfless compassion does *not* come naturally. It must come supernaturally, through the Spirit of Christ dwelling in you.

True servanthood requires radical humility. A token gesture of service can leave the ego intact and even a bit self-satisfied. Most people are willing to do a little bit of hard work and sacrifice if they gain some publicity for it. Anyone can help the poor when a camera is there to record it for an applauding world. But it takes a transformed heart to serve silently in the shadows, even when it hurts. This is the true test of a servant's heart: When you have poured your heart into doing good works and receive no recognition for it, how do you respond? When no one thanks you or pats you on the back, do you become bitter? If so, you were not fueled by God's Spirit but by your own flesh. When you worked twice as hard as someone else, yet they receive all the accolades and fame, do you get angry and jealous? If so, you were building your own kingdom and not God's. The best kind of service is in secret. Then we must rely upon the Spirit of Jesus to provide the joy, the strength to keep going over the long haul.

Sometimes you have to force yourself to act loving before you feel loving. If you want to love someone, try serving them sacrificially. St. Francis of Assisi tells the story of how he used to despise lepers, disgusted by their filthy appearance and nauseating smell. Then one day, along the road, a leper approached him and God told him to *kiss the leper*. Fighting back every natural inclination, Francis obeyed and, in that moment, his heart was changed. He found a love and compassion well up within him that fueled a lifelong service to lepers that brought him great joy. Did you realize you can actually enjoy serving other people? But don't wait until it's fun before you do it; instead, do it until it becomes fun.

Practice *xenophilia*— usually translated *hospitality* (literally, the "love of strangers"). Make your home, your office, *your very presence*, a place of welcome, warmth, and acceptance. Here's a good way to practice: pretend you are an employee of a store or hotel that is well-known for its customer service. However, in this case, *the world is your workplace!* You are God's employee and the person in front of you is your customer. Make their stay here as enjoyable as possible. Anticipate what your guests might need right now and give it to them. If there is a mess, take responsibility for cleaning it up. Perhaps this is the mindset Jesus wanted to cultivate when he told his disciples: *"Whoever wants to become great among you must be your servant, whoever wants to be first must be slave of all. For even the Son of Man did not come to be served, but to serve..."*

399

Where do we start to practice servanthood? First, consider how you could serve those around you in everyday life: your family, your spiritual community, your co-workers, or even your enemies. Second, find one group of needy people beyond your usual sphere of influence. Perhaps you are called to serve the homeless in a nearby park, or the elderly at a care home nearby, or the disadvantaged children at your local juvenile detention center. If you really want to experience the Presence of God, spend time with the mentally ill, the drug-addict, or the AIDS patient. It is when you confront extreme need (way beyond your own resources!) that you must depend wholly on God. Or your heart may even stretch around the globe to provide clean water, food, medical care, education or employment in less-developed countries. Among the poor, the neglected, the oppressed, there you will find Jesus.

A caution in the practice of servanthood: We must neither shirk the burden nor shoulder the burden to fix the world. Since the sheer amount of "humanitarian work" needed is far beyond our ability, we are often tempted to just throw up our hands and give up. We say, "It's too big!" and think it a valid excuse for doing nothing. On the other hand, we may be tempted to feel responsible for fixing the whole problem. That is God's job, not ours. We are his instruments. We are only called to do what is within our reach. We must trust God to take care of the rest.

1. Meditation Exercise: Slowly and meditatively read through **Matthew 25:31-46.**

2. Are you currently serving the poor in any meaningful way? What group of truly needy people has God placed on your heart? How can you serve them regularly?

3. How can you serve your family or friends this week? Your spiritual community? Your neighbors?

96. On Evangelizing the Lost
Declaring an Alternate Reality

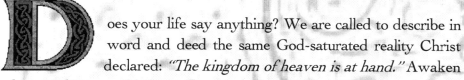oes your life say anything? We are called to describe in word and deed the same God-saturated reality Christ declared: *"The kingdom of heaven is at hand."* Awaken the watching world to God's power and Presence right in front of them! It's show and tell time. Make it clear: the resources of heaven are within arm's reach! God's goodness is accessible to all right here and now in the magnificent person of Jesus Christ! He forgives us! He restores us! He teaches us! He adopts us! He daily interacts with us! This is the *evangel*, the *amazing news*, the sublime vision of Christ and his kingdom. If it is true, it is the best thing this poor world has ever heard!

Message-Bearer, it is your responsibility, first of all, to *embody* this mystery of mysteries. The best way to show others the greatness of Christ... is to *live like him*. In your own limited way, give a living example of what Christ looks like. A life of supernatural power, inexplicable love, indefatigable joy, and radical humility will surely get their attention! Live out loud the love of the Lord! Obviously, we won't do this perfectly. But the closer we get to Christ, the more this new reality shines through. The evangel must be incarnated in our own human skin before it is believed. A demonstration of the Spirit's power is far more persuasive than human wisdom. Our communication must be holistic. Our lives should be synonymous with our message. Don't let your left hand erase what your right hand has written. In the sentiments of Francis of Assisi, *"Preach the gospel always. When necessary, use words."* Jesus *words* had power because his *life* had power. Your attitudes and actions speak much louder than your arguments.

The second thing you can do to show people Jesus is to *listen* to them. Every human being is desperately searching for someone who is *for them*, who is on their side. Though they are probably too prideful to admit it, the person in front of you would be thrilled to find that God values them and cares deeply about their lives, their joys, their hurts, and their concerns. Let them know that God is interested in them by *you* being interested in them. Shut your mouth and actually pay attention to what they are saying! Learn to read souls. Ask questions about the things in their life that really matter. Don't stop with superficial small talk about peripheral issues when every human heart longs to be truly heard, discovered and valued. Gently probe their background, their beliefs, their dreams, their disappointments, their worries, their inner world. And resist the urge to try to correct every misconception that they have. Your motive must be love. Don't look at anyone as a potential convert but as a friend, a beautiful masterpiece of the Creator. I assume that God has shown you how to love someone simply for who they are. Give the gift of real curiosity without ulterior motives. If you listen long enough, it becomes clear as day where their thirst for God is experienced. Question them respectfully, not to trap but to discover them. Be an explorer, not a hunter. If you approach people as a notch on your belt or a project, this dehumanizing attitude will be assumed of God. Let's do the world a favor and stop evangelizing uninterested strangers. Pray for strangers, serve and bless them... but please, turn strangers into friends before you tell them about Christ!

A third method of sharing your faith is simply to *tell your own story*, your own encounter with God, with no additions and no subtractions. What do you really know of God? Tell plainly what you have seen, felt, and heard without embellishment and without running it through a filter. In your own words, describe how God has shown himself to you. How has God's Spirit invaded your life with his beauty and truth? Share the gut-honest truth just the way you experienced it. Please, *please* don't pretend that your life has become perfect since Jesus has come into your life-- we all know it hasn't! Speak with brutal honesty about your own up's and down's in following Christ.

Here's some good advice for the faith-sharer: *Thou shalt not bear false witness.* Resist the urge to lie, exaggerate, or spin the truth. When we deceive, we speak the language of devils. Never give half of the story thinking the other half *may* prove less than convincing. A beautiful lie is never better than the embarrassing truth. Less polish, more passion. If you do not understand something, say so! If you don't know an answer, admit it. If your life is less than exemplary in certain areas, there is no glory to God in faking it. A hypocrite is someone who is putting on an act, whose life does not match up with their talk. The solution to hypocrisy is simple honesty. You can never be called a hypocrite as long as you just tell the plain truth about yourself.

A fourth way to introduce them to Jesus is simply to hand them a copy of the Bible and have them *study one of the gospels* for themselves. Invite investigation! I usually recommend the Gospel of Mark because of its rustic simplicity and power (although scholarly types may appreciate the gentle eloquence of John's Gospel). Study it together or have them read it and take notes on anything unusual they noticed about Jesus. Then discuss it with them later. Here is the main question you want to keep addressing: *"what do you think of Jesus?"*

A fifth way to proclaim the evangel is to actually try to *explain* it as best as you can. Prepare to paint a picture of a God-filled world. Show them its undeniable beauty and inescapable logic. Give them a glimpse of a Christ-centered reality and let the truth seduce them. Describe Jesus' audacious plan of multiplying his Spirit into a vast and radiant community of countless beautiful and noble souls living in effortless harmony. Entice them with rumors of better world. Don't bludgeon them with dogmas; allure them with possibilities. Nowhere is creativity more sorely needed than in evangelism—or more sorely lacking. Avoid clichés at all costs. The moment anything (including a Bible verse) becomes over-familiar to someone, it ceases to challenge their preconceptions and begins to confirm them. Say it new. Prepare to give a reasonable answer to those who ask for the logic behind your hope-filled eyesight. Don't be surprised if it elicits a strong reaction. Our distinct message is also the world's most disorienting message. If it bothers them, they may actually get it! If they do not feel threatened by Christ's message, then (contrary to all appearances) they probably have not really grasped Christ's message.

Watch for faith to be awakened in someone's heart. Until the light goes on in their mind, no amount of pushing or pulling will help. But when you see that spark of interest, when you see desire kindled like a flame, fan it furiously! Never attempt to get them to go along with something they are not convinced of. A lived gospel does not need to be forced upon people. Any time you find you must use manipulative means to persuade someone, you can be sure your message has been distorted. If you must pressure people with fear-inducing scenarios and trap them with clever salesman-like tactics, it has obviously ceased to be good news. *Truth speaks for itself.* We need not hammer upon it; it carries its own weight. We must also respect people enough to let them wrestle with it themselves. There is a time for words and there is also a time for silence.

The final goal of evangelism is to bring them to a place of such *love and confidence in Jesus,* that they are willing to make a life-encompassing decision to follow him. If someone sounds hungry for more of Jesus, let them know that they can begin to follow him any moment they choose to. Invite them to enroll as his student in the Master's class of life. It may help to formally introduce them to Jesus, the way you would introduce anyone to your friend: speak to one, speak to the other, then let them speak to one another. But don't push for premature decisions. Rarely does someone make a life-altering change of direction without putting some serious time and thought into it. Give them time to process their fears and doubts. Let them count the cost.

1. **Meditation Exercise:** Slowly and meditatively read **Acts 8:26-40.**

2. Write out your gut-level response in your journal: If someone asked you why you follow Christ, what is the most honest reason you could give? What convinces you this is how you should live? What have been the greatest benefits? What about the greatest difficulties?

3. If you were intent on getting to know someone and finding out who they really are inside, what are 5 to 10 questions would you ask them? Now look at the **Questions for Sharing your Faith** (in Appendix) for some questions that will help you to explore *their* spiritual beliefs... Underline 5 to 10 questions you would feel comfortable asking...

97. On Making Disciples
Training Others to Follow Christ

ow we reach the ultimate goal of our mission. Making disciples, or students, of Jesus Christ is the last and most important stage of the sacred mission of the Christ. It is our greatest privilege and our most important responsibility. This was Jesus' Great Commission to his followers: *"Therefore, go and make disciples of all nations, baptizing them in the name of the Father, and of the Son, and of the Holy Spirit, and teaching them to obey everything I have commanded you. And surely I am with you always, to the very end of the age."* It is our assignment to bring ordinary people into apprenticeship to Christ, no matter what culture or ethnicity they are, immersing them into the fullness of God's Being, and showing them how to live their lives as Christ would, with effortless love, joy and goodness. This is our most pressing task in this world! We must be about our Father's business of recruiting and training novices in the Way of Christ. I hope that by now you are clear about this fact: *the most loving thing we can ever do for anyone is to help them to follow Jesus.* And the best way to help them to follow Jesus is to love them. We cannot make disciples if we cannot make friends.

Discipleship happens best in the context of community. The Spirit of Jesus is transferred to others through the channels of loving relationships. So when disciples gather, we immerse one another in the nurturing Presence of God-in-our-midst when we worship, fellowship, and reach out together. Foxhole friendships develop as we take on the world together in mission. However, this does not excuse us from making an intelligent effort to teach neophytes how to follow Jesus. A spiritual community that does not work toward making disciples is, sadly, not fulfilling the primary purpose for which it was created. If a can-opener cannot open cans, is it still a can-opener? Or as Jesus more elegantly puts it, *"You are the salt of*

the earth. But if the salt loses its saltiness, how can it be made salty again? It is no longer good for anything, except to be thrown out and trampled by men." I do not mean that every person we reach out to will respond and become a disciple. We leave the results of our efforts to God. But let us not fail to make the effort.

So how do we go about making disciples? Dallas Willard describes the process of disciple-making with the acronym *VIM: Vision, Intention, Methods*. The first step is to bring a person to *see the glorious vision of Christ and his kingdom*. Unless they have gotten a glimpse of who Jesus is and what he offers us, there is *no good reason* for them to jump on board. This step corresponds closely with the work of *evangelism* described in the last chapter. We share the wonders of Christ through living a life of supernatural power and servanthood, asking questions and truly listening to them, sharing honestly our own story of God's involvement in our life, helping them to study one of the four gospels, and explaining whatever we can of Christ's kingdom. *Ravish their hearts with the mind-blowing goodness of God!* You may also need to clear away some intellectual roadblocks that hinder them from thinking *this God could actually be real.* Once they have really experienced the outrageous, audacious love of Christ and trust him enough to follow him, you are ready to help them with the next step.

The second step is to *secure their intention to follow Jesus.* Until they have made a conscious decision to become a disciple of Jesus, you cannot really train them in the Way of Christ. Jesus defers to the desires of our hearts. He doesn't move into a person's life unless they invite him in. They must choose to make Jesus their Master. Until this happens, your job is to continue showing and proclaiming the Kingdom of Christ to them until it ignites their faith. Anticipate and prepare for that blazing moment when their soul bursts aflame and they are ready to dive in.

At this precise point, we begin basic training. When their heart asks, *"what must I do?"* step in to *instruct them in the methods of how to follow Jesus.* Begin to show them the ropes of the Way of

Christ. Teach them those spiritual exercises and disciplines that will strengthen their spiritual life. Once someone has entered the reign of God, they must be instructed in how to conduct themselves in this new kingdom. They need to know what God expects of them. They need to learn how to live in daily interaction with God and practice living out their mission on earth. Help them to understand what God is doing in their souls so that they can rightly cooperate with his transformation project. Help them to see and recognize his voice and his movement in their lives.

How do we teach them these things? Here is a way that I am very excited about: Give them a copy of this book, *Christ-Centered Spirituality*! Ideally, they read each chapter and do the exercises on their own. Then your job would be to assist them, holding them accountable for actually doing what they're reading about, and answering any questions they may have. However, if they are not able to read through it themselves, you can administer the exercises to them yourself (See the "**Novitiation Class**" in the Appendix). To do this, I would recommend meeting with them at least once a week. First, have them read the Scripture and meditate upon it. Walk them through all of the meditations and other exercises from the chapter. Ask them the questions and listen carefully to their responses. Spend some time discussing the passage of Scripture together and what it says about the chapter's main subject. Then you can summarize in your own words any point(s) from my written ramblings in that chapter that you think might be useful.

Obviously, I am a bit biased-- there are many other useful methods of training disciples, including other very effective discipleship books to guide people through this process! One book, however, that is not optional, the most important book of all, *the Holy Bible*, must play a major role in their learning. However, make sure that the emphasis is not only on *knowing* but upon *doing*. Making disciples is not primarily about transferring information to them. It is about transfiguring the inner person to become like Christ. Information, while very important, is only a *means* to the changing of a heart and mind. The training that takes place must be evidenced through action, through living out what you are learning.

Let me be explicitly clear: we make disciples *of Jesus,* not *of us.* They are not *our* disciples, but his. This is why disciple-making should take place in the context of a community of disciples. We do not want to reproduce our own flaws, mannerisms and personality quirks—we want to reproduce Jesus who lives in us, that he might also live in them. Your job is to connect them permanently to Jesus, not to you. At the beginning of the process, you may need to be very involved in their life, but you must also be working towards the day when they will not need you anymore. The most rewarding day of a disciple-maker's life is when the person you have raised up and instructed is now repeating that process with someone else.

1. **Meditation Exercise:** Slowly and meditatively read **I Timothy 4**.

2. In order to make disciples of Jesus, we must first be disciples of Jesus. And the most effective way of proclaiming the good news is to live it out. So before you even start to think about making disciples first ask yourself honestly, "Am I a disciple, a student of Jesus? Am I learning to live more like Jesus?"

3. What specific things can you do to cultivate a life with God that will enable you to guide others?

5. Think of some people around you who might be willing to learn from you the Way of Christ. They may already be followers of Christ and simply need some guidance. Or if they are not followers of Christ, you will have to start with evangelizing them.
Are there any members of your family who may be interested?
Or members of your spiritual community?
Or friends, co-workers, classmates, or neighbors?
Make a list of 5 possible disciples. Begin to pray for them to grow closer to Christ. Look for a chance to invite them into the process.

98. On Your Sacred Calling

esus has a job for you—a specific assignment to reach some specific individuals as part of his worldwide strategy. *Do you know your calling?* Who are you called to serve? He has selected you out of all of his apprentices to reach a strange land filled with savages. Who are these natives restlessly awaiting a man or woman of God to emerge from the darkness, learn their tribal language, brave the inhospitable jungles of an unfriendly culture, and open the Word of God to them? For most of us, our place of mission is precisely *where we already are.* Your calling starts in your own backyard. The Lord of the Harvest has *already* plunked you down in a certain area of his mission field and he will hold you personally accountable for accomplishing some very particular results reaching some very peculiar people: your neighbors. You are a missionary to your street or building! He has appointed a location for your vocation... a place called *here.* Your calling is only an extension of your love— and he has already commanded you to love your neighbor as yourself.

We have looked at the content of our calling; now let us look at the context. We know *what* to do: serve the needy, heal the sick, make disciples, and other miracles, random and routine. But *where*, precisely, shall we do it? The place to perform these works of the Spirit is *in your everyday life.* Don't go and quit your job and become an overseas missionary or join a monastery, thinking these are your only options for living a supernatural life. Your "secular" job becomes a sacred calling because *you are in it.* Your life circumstances become a holy place simply because they are occupied by a holy person.

Imagine a world where Christ's covert ambassadors are scattered throughout society in the common places where ordinary people work and live! What better hiding place for agents of an other-worldly kingdom than as students, housewives, and cashiers at the local grocery store? Your "ordinary circumstances" are part of your mission! If you are a cook, God is in your kitchen and he wants your kitchen to become an outpost of his kingdom. If you are a business person, God accompanies you to work each day and cares deeply about how and why you do what you do. If you are a student, God has enrolled you in a learning process far greater than your teachers know. Whether you are married or single, your home is an embassy. Your heavenly calling starts now... with exactly what you have. The revolution begins at your home address (although where it will lead from there, who knows?).

Dallas Willard says this about Jesus' mission: *"If he were to come today as he did then, he could carry out his mission through most any decent and useful occupation. He could be a clerk or accountant in a hardware store, a computer repairman, a banker, an editor, doctor, waiter, teacher, farmhand, lab technician... he could very well do what you do. He could very well live in your apartment or house, hold down your job, have your education and life prospects, and live within your family, surroundings, and time. None of this would be the least hindrance to the eternal kind of life...."* Your assignment is to learn how to live your life as Jesus would... if he were you. Figure out how the Christ would conduct himself if he were in your shoes today. How would Jesus deal with your family? How would he treat your boss or your friends? How would he conduct himself in your neighborhood grocery store? Where would he eat lunch if he had the same amount of money in his wallet as you do? How would Jesus finish the project you are working on? Would he go about his "love life" the way you do?

Don't make excuses for why you cannot do what Jesus would do. He didn't take any shortcuts. He placed himself into the same kind of boxed-in, limited, imperfect life that you and I have. He had real family problems, a regular job, a lower-class education and financial difficulties. Although he was the divine Son of God, he imposed upon himself the suffocating limitations of the common man... and he thrived in the midst of it! He shows us by example how

410

a disadvantaged individual with no special talents, *"no beauty or majesty to attract us to him"*, could bring the fullness of God's Presence and power into the world around him. He relied on the power of the Holy Spirit in the same way he expects us to.

Let us look at *your life* as your mission field. How do you turn a boring, humdrum life into a sacred calling? The secret of the sacred is in the *intention.* Whatever you previously did out of compulsion or for your own benefit, begin now to *do with the intention of pleasing God.* Take all that you are and all that you do now, with the exception of sinning, and begin to do it all with God's pleasure in mind. You may please God through work and play; through singleness, marriage and children; through school and social involvement. And especially you must find a pocket of needy people in the midst of your life that you may serve. Find a way to live out the Christ-life in the midst of the ordinary world he has placed you in. Look at your relationships and your unique station in life. Function as a representative of Christ to *these people* in *this capacity.* Let people "see Jesus" through your interactions with them. And perhaps you will experience the exhilaration Eric Liddell spoke of in *Chariots of Fire: "when I run, I feel his pleasure."*

There is no qualitative difference between the calling of a preacher and the calling of a plumber. Both should be servants of the Most High God, reflecting his radiance to the world. There is such a vast diversity of callings through which God can be glorified! Whatever your vocation, it is just as sacred as the priest presiding over the sacraments. William Law says that *"when it can be shown that men may be vain, covetous, sensual, worldly-minded, or proud in the exercise of their worldly business, then it will be allowable for clergymen to indulge in the same tempers in their sacred profession."* This means that any behavior you would find unbecoming for a pastor or spiritual leader is also unbecoming for *you.* No matter where your paycheck comes from, you are just as much in "full-time ministry" as the local church pastor. God wants all of you. He is all-

411

demanding because he is all-redeeming! He will take every sphere of your life and remake it for his glory.

Fulfilling your sacred calling will require an eye transplant. You will need to begin to see things differently. Look at people and tasks through the eyes of Christ. When you  see your neighbors, your wife, your kids, or your friends as God sees them, you will begin to treat them differently. The more you *see like Christ*, the more you will *look like Christ*.

Let me remind you before we go on: before we engage in the *work* of God, we must be engaged in the *worship* of God. Christ-centered spirituality must begin with a fierce fixation on Jesus Christ. This transforms us inwardly into people who are able to do outwardly what Jesus would do. Don't get so caught up in doing the work of the kingdom that you neglect the flickering inward flame of fascination with God. Good works without love are worthless! Your sacred calling will fail unless it draws its strength from a deep inward communion with God that is kept always burning afresh.

I must also emphasize that you are sharing joy with people. This requires participation with the world, not protection from it. Our Lord regularly enjoyed food and strong drink with all sorts of unsavory characters— riffraff, rabble-rousers, ragamuffins, and rascals. If we are to imitate his holy example, we should never be too far from a pagan party. Rub elbows with, enjoy small talk with, and celebrate milestones with your neighbors. Do you need to throw a party to get to know those in your apartment building, on your floor, or on your block? If the work of Christ makes you a dour sourpuss who is above "the secular world", it has removed you from Christ!

1. **Meditation Exercise:** Slowly and meditatively read **I Peter 2:1-12**.

2. Reflect of verse 9... What does it mean, practically, to be "a chosen people, a royal priesthood, a holy nation, a people belonging to God"? Write in your journal how you could actually live this out...

99. On Employment
Your Ministry to your Workplace

ork is *not* a necessary evil. It is an essential part of our nature and calling. Through work, we reflect the image of God. Work is a dignity, a compliment to your capacity. As soon as Adam was created, he was given a job description: *"The LORD God took the man and put him in the Garden of Eden to work it and take care of it."* He was also given permission to partake of the fruit of his labor and God's grace. There is nothing evil about making a profit with what God has given us. Before we ever tasted the bitter fruit of disobedience, humankind was already working hard... and enjoying every minute of it! Depending on your mindset, your job can have everything to do with God's kingdom... or it can have nothing to do with it. It's up to you.

You will most likely spend the majority of your waking adult life at work—so it must form a primary context for your spiritual life. If you leave God out of your work, you leave him out of most of your life! Your spirituality must permeate your workplace. Your job should become a gymnasium of spiritual exercise. It is also your primary platform, your pulpit through which your life speaks its message. It is where you live out an active demonstration of the good news of Christ's kingdom. Don't work just for the money! Money is not the reason for your work, but a benefit of your work. The purpose of work is *to bring good into the world.* Of course, we should seek to be paid in a manner which enables us to do this with a roof over our heads and food on our table. But which is more important to you—making a good living or making a good life?

For the follower of Christ, *there is no "secular" job; there is only the sacred.* You must determine how to make your employment into a holy occupation. Turn your workplace into a *divine office.* Start by giving some serious thought to what exactly your job contributes to the world. Most jobs provide a *good:* a valuable product or service to people (unless you happen to be a drug dealer, a stripper, a pornographer or some other job that is inherently immoral). Ask yourself, "What *good* am I doing here?" Jesus happily went about providing quality wooden products to a small village on the outskirts of Galilee's fishing district. There is nothing unholy or selfish in Jesus spending time sawing, hammering and finishing a beautiful and sturdy plowing yoke and then taking money for his masterful workmanship!

Now ask yourself, "If Jesus was working at your workplace, what would he do differently?" (Remember, he was a craftsman much longer than he was a rabbi!) There is a Christ-like way to be a banker, a Christ-like way to be a teacher, even a Christ-like way to be a computer programmer! Would he arrive at work the same time you do? Would his conversations sound like yours? Are there any dishonest business practices he would refuse to participate in? Would the quality of his work be noticeably different from yours? Practice closing the gap between Jesus' work habits and yours. What are some specific things you could change? What keeps you from doing that now? What must you do to get there?

Examine your work ethic. *"Whatever you do, work at it with all your heart, as working for the Lord, not for men."* These are the words of Paul, a humble tentmaker and the heroic apostle to the gentiles. Can you work hard at your job without being consumed by it? Do you have the self-discipline to know when to stay late and when not to? Can you bring the atmosphere of the kingdom to your department at the company? Perhaps God's Presence in your business might even affect the bottom line. Would God do something like that? Does the Most High God care about your business being done in a way that honors him? Could you actually have an intelligent conversation with God about how to better your company's performance? While we must avoid idolizing our financial statement, it is an important consideration in doing good work.

Next, look at the way you treat people. Figure out ways to express love appropriate to the people around you at work. Learn to treat all of your co-workers and especially your boss as you would if they were Jesus himself. Of course, they don't deserve to be treated this way... but why let their behavior determine yours? How could you show respect to your manager or fellow employees? How can you make your boss succeed? How can you improve the performance of your co-workers? Maybe you need to spend your commute to work or your first five minutes there in tenacious prayer for those you will work with that day.

If you work in "customer service", learn to serve each customer as you would serve Christ. Look deeply into their eyes-- see Christ looking back at you. Determine to wash the feet of Christ through each exchange with both customers and co-workers. Go above and beyond for every person, especially the most difficult and troublesome ones, "the least of these". Bring joy into the lives of those you touch! Serve them with Christ-like enthusiasm and energy.

Perhaps your job is essentially creative—this is a great opportunity to work in tandem with the Creator! Every time you work on something, pray that God would create through you... then pay attention to what God's Spirit may do or say. Don't make entertainment, create art. Make meaning that will communicate something of value and beauty to those who enjoy it. If you have a more task-oriented, routine job, then make your cubicle into a prayer chapel, a place of worship. Learn to sing hymns, recite Scripture or breathe prayers in rhythm with your work. Pray for the person who will take the results of your labor. Even the most boring of jobs can become illumined with the glow of eternity.

If you have a management job, you must think even more deeply about the influence you wield and use it in a way that would honor God. How can you treat each employee as a person of incalculable value, a masterpiece of God's own hand? How can you show respect for your staff while still showing respect for your superiors who expect specific results out of you and them? How can you equip your employees to excel? How can you help your business to excel? How can you reflect God's order and goodness?

Are you unemployed? That is fine as long as it is not an excuse for laziness! There are too many good works to be done to dawdle around in idle pursuits! You can still make a difference in the world. There are no useless people in God's kingdom. Whether you are retired, disabled, between jobs, dirt poor or filthy rich, be sure to spend the hours of your day doing something good and useful. Find a worthwhile vocation. Perhaps you can volunteer your time serving the less fortunate, encouraging the downtrodden, or supporting your spiritual community in some way or another. Even if you cannot leave your bed, you can take up a full-time vocation of prayer and intercession. The toilsome work of prayer can turn even the feeblest saint into the stoutest warrior. Perhaps you can call or email people with words of encouragement. Every soul has something of significance to contribute to God's kingdom.

1. **Meditation Exercise:** Slowly read through **Ephesians 5:21-6:9**.

2. Spend a few minutes watching yourself in your imagination going through your average work day... Now imagine what would happen if Jesus came in as your replacement... What would he do differently? Watch him go about his day, working in your job...

3. Make a list of 5 of the most significant things you could at your job to be more like Jesus... Pick one that you will begin to practice, starting today...

100. On Education
Your Opportunity for Intellectual Formation

very disciple is a learner. Disciples of Christ should be constantly open to being taught—our Teacher is ever present. Part of spiritual formation is *intellectual formation.* It is our moral obligation to seek truth and wisdom. Truth is liberating! It is an indispensible tool for the renewing of our minds and the transforming of our lives. Pick up that oddest of human habits: the habit of thinking. God's purposes are never served by sloppy thinking. For God's sake, commit your life to sniffing out wisdom wherever it may be found. God uses many diverse teaching methods. He is not limited to church gatherings or academic schools. In the words of Augustine, *"all truth is God's truth."* It doesn't matter who speaks it. Become a student of life. Learn through every avenue: sermons, professors, books, observing, listening, experiments, and little children, just to name a few. Cast the dead weight of ignorance from your mind! The ordinary human mind has extraordinary potential for expansion. You don't have to become a scholar, but you should keep your mind sharp. Use it often.

If you have been given the opportunity to attend school right now, fall to your knees in thanks to your Maker for such a time as this! You've been bestowed with one of the greatest privileges on our planet. Please don't waste it or take it for granted! For as long as it lasts, treat this as your God-ordained vocation. Your education is a holy responsibility, to be undertaken with the utmost seriousness. Throw yourself into your studies with religious fervor, for this is a reasonable act of worship. Ask God to accompany you to every class you take. In the midst of each class, ask God what he wants to teach you here. Discern how this learning intersects with the truths of God's kingdom. But do guard yourself against the learned arrogance of the educated which runs rampant across college campuses and private prep schools around the world. The virus of vainglory is an epidemic among academics. Many scholars develop a snobbish self-importance, fancying themselves superior people with their newfound knowledge. Make sure your learning never imperils your humility. Remember that the very highest wisdom is accessible to the simplest of simpletons and often eludes the smartest of scholars.

One unfortunate fallacy perpetuated by both universities and churches is the alleged antagonism between *faith* and *reason*. They are allies, not enemies! Many great examples of tremendous faith were also examples of towering intellect. Survey the works of such saints as Paul, Augustine, Aquinas, Calvin, Kierkegaard and Pascal to see the subtle symbiosis of spirituality and intelligence. The world-architecture described by Christ is ruthlessly logical. It only appears unreasonable to those who refuse to reconsider their conjectures. Every system of logic starts with a few basic, unproven beliefs. All reasoning is circular in principle. If you begin with the *a priori* assumption that *God cannot possibly exist*, no amount of logic can convince you otherwise! Many serious disciplines have unfortunately smuggled this hypothesis into their curriculum. And since almost everything else flows from this one ruling opinion, their conclusions often unwittingly "prove" their presuppositions.

Always keep your "truth-detector" on. Ask yourself, "Do I believe this is true?" When you find a morsel of truth lying on the ground, take it, cherish it, and integrate it with the rest of your knowledge. However, we cannot just swallow everything thrown to us just because it was spoken by a man with a white beard, a lanky lab coat, and important-sounding letters after his name. All learning at every level is an act of faith. We place our trust in the "experts." But remember: *"experts" also are human— fallible, broken, and biased just as you are* (something to keep in mind when others call *you* an expert!). When authorities disagree, it is worth asking why. You also may disagree... but you should have a reason for it. You cannot just reject what you don't like. Make it a habit to hear both sides of every argument. Learn to spot the unspoken assumptions behind every assertion of "truth". See if you can guess the "world view" of your teachers—their ultimate beliefs about God, themselves and the universe. Many "facts" conceal an implicit agenda.

It does not have to be a "religious" subject to be useful, good or right. *Mathematics is the language of natural reality.* It enables you to think logically, to make reasonable assumptions about the world of particulars. It also lets you see differently, drawing patterns and pictures out of overwhelming quantities of seemingly "meaningless" data. The natural sciences such as biology, chemistry, physics, and geology are exciting explorations of God's creative methodology. Glimpse the mind of God as you study the structure of the atom or the biological processes of digestion as it converts matter into energy! This is your Father's world—study, examine and wonder! But also expect tediousness and repetition in any learning environment. Most subjects require the disciplined  integration of ideas that do not by themselves seem very valuable. Don't get bored, always grumbling, "When will I ever need to know this?" Just as learning the alphabet is the key to unlock the vast storehouse of reading, you will need many skills and tools to unlock the treasure chests of learning in each discipline.

The arts and humanities are the language of spiritual reality. When a person creates, they reveal something of their inner universe. We see in literature, music, poetry, and art, the soul stripped bare. We see the nature of the human spirit in all of its beauty and brokenness. Philosophy, history, psychology, religion, sociology, anthropology, and many business and leadership classes are fascinating forays into the mysteries of human belief and behavior. We study the making of meaning in life and society. We learn to communicate our own interior world to others.

If you are a teacher of any sort, you wield the power of life and death. Don't just teach lessons, form souls! Everything you are speaks. Encourage as well as educate. Call out sleeping potential in the hesitant and timid. Challenge the heart and the mind. Many people remember for decades one or two teachers who inspired and impacted them for a lifetime. What was it about them? If you teach young people, see if you can *be that teacher* for as many young lives as possible. Beware: ideas are the most dangerous weapons in the world, for better or for worse. The ideas currently tossed around by eccentric professors in the halls of academia, are often the raw material of popular culture for the next 100 years. The university and the classroom is where much of tomorrow's world is shaped. Although ideas exist only in the minds of rational beings, they yet drive all of creation. If you want to be a part of determining the future, you would do well to learn all you can.

In all of our learning, we must remain humble enough to recognize that not every mystery will bend to our intellect. There are infinite depths that no human eye will ever fully penetrate. We must have the wisdom to know what we do not know. God alone knows all things. Wisdom is the knowledge of foundational causes. And in all things, God is *the* most foundational Cause. As we look toward the horizon of human knowledge, we know only that there is One who knows all! And perhaps as we extend the shores of our intellect, we will be more convinced of how much lies beyond our comprehension. Lactantius writes, *"Where, then, is wisdom? It consists in thinking neither that you know all things, which is the property of God; nor that you are ignorant of all things, which is the way of a beast. Man's place is, rather, somewhere in the middle."*

1. **Meditation Exercise:** Slowly and meditatively read **Proverbs 4**.

2. If you are in school right now, go through your class schedule in prayer. Ask God what he wants to teach you through each class...

3. For each class, discover where this field of study intersects with God's work. Does the Bible give foundational guidance to it?

101. On Singleness
Your Calling to Single-minded Focus

I f you are single right now, then *singleness is presently your calling*. Embrace it! Enjoy the simple life for all it's worth... for as long as it lasts. Don't spend these spacious days of unattached freedom and flexibility pining for the day when you are finally bound in marriage! Live in the sacred present, not in some imagined future. Spend your youth and strength on God's glory! Make the most of all this free time and disposable income you enjoy... starting a family will require all of it! Until you say, "I do", live a robustly single life. Learn to be content now. Godly fulfillment must be found in whatever circumstance you find yourself. If you cannot find contentment in God alone, I guarantee you will not find contentment in marriage. Two empty, dissatisfied singles will inevitably produce a horribly dissatisfying marriage. Two divinely-satisfied singles will form a deeply satisfying marriage.

Just because you are single doesn't mean you have to live alone. If you are unwed, I recommend living in community with other singles of the same gender and spiritual bent. Rent a house together where brothers or sisters can dwell together in unity. For men, the experience of living in fraternity with a band of brothers will probably provide many of the greatest memories of your life as you forge friendships that last a lifetime. For women, it will fashion a sisterhood you can laugh and cry with, and share all the joys and sorrows  of life together. Don't get me wrong—it will be trying and difficult. But in this "monastic" environment, honesty is inevitable. You are forced to love one another... not as a theoretical platitude but as a daily practice. Yes, it will cost much: your privacy, preferences, and selfish comforts... but the spiritual benefits are immeasurable.

Not all singles are called to seek marriage. Lifelong celibacy has a long and storied tradition of producing an army of devoted and God-enraptured souls whose lives were focused like a laser beam on God's greater glory. The calling to lifelong singleness is an ideal place to follow Christ! Don't forget that our Lord himself was celibate throughout his earthly life. It removes all of the huge complications, considerations and confusions of matrimony. Remaining unmarried will keep your energy for God simple and undistracted. Do not give in to social pressures and family expectations to settle down, get married and start a family if that is not what God wants for you.

There is also nothing wrong with actively seeking marriage, if that is God's calling for you. If you are looking for a husband or wife, then make it your aim to conduct this search under the guidance of God's Spirit. This is not a side project outside of your spiritual life—it is central to your relationship with God. Please *do not* leave your loving Lord and Master out of this life-altering decision! Take some time to surrender the desire for a husband or wife to God and ask for his leading. Are you confident that your heavenly Father wants to bless you in this search? Does "trusting Jesus" apply even to your love life? You know God wants the best for you, don't you? Or are you convinced he will sentence you to a miserable, loveless marriage if you are gullible enough to follow his leading? Unfortunately, those who can't wait for God's best often find themselves in nightmarish marriages where long-term joy eludes them.

If you are dating, do you know why? Are you going somewhere or just wandering aimlessly? The purpose of dating is to find a future marriage partner, not to escape loneliness. Whether you call it "dating", "courting", or "going out", your aim is to decide whether you can make a lifelong commitment to them. It is a trial period to see if you would make it in a real marriage. If you discover that it won't work, get out of the relationship as soon as possible! Don't dishonor them by stringing them along until a better prospect comes along. If you are convinced that you have found your future spouse, then begin to plan for your upcoming marriage as soon as appropriate. Break-ups always hurt, but they are manageable if both partners have been honestly communicating where they are in this relationship. One way to completely ruin the natural progression of dating leading to marriage is to start sleeping with each other before sealing the sacred covenant. Don't let this happen! A lasting marriage is not built on "sexual compatibility" but on trust, friendship, and real commitment. Add sex only after you have these in spades.

A follower of Christ should not date "just for fun." A human heart is not a toy to play with! This is not a game! Recreational dating is using another human being for your own selfish benefit-- seeking the benefits of marriage without the commitment, a throwaway lover. We just want someone attractive on our arm or in our bed. Don't get romantically involved without a clear direction. *Without the pursuit of permanence, the nature of the relationship will always be self-centered.* That is not love—it is only lust. It will be driven by what you can *get* out of this person, not how you can *give* of yourself to them. Do not dare toss around the word "love" with someone you will not commit to! *"I love you"* does *not* mean *"I'm strongly attracted to you"!* It means *"I value you enough to restructure my life around you! I commit myself to bringing what's best into your life."* Otherwise is it only a disposable relationship: you are the consumer and they are the product (or are they the consumer?). Whether or not sex is involved, you are only using them cheaply, collecting a dirty laundry list of "future ex-girlfriends" or "future ex-boyfriends". Sexual temptation is almost unbearable when the relationship is not progressing toward something which could legitimately become splendidly sexual (i.e., marriage). If you are burning with desire for this person, then let that intense passion drive you down the road toward the altar. If they are not someone you could commit your life to, what are you doing with them?!?

How do we safeguard our sexual integrity while dating? First, admit your weakness and vulnerability to temptation. Avoid situations that might possibly undermine your best intentions. Don't let your sexual attraction drive you further than is reasonable to go.

423

The more physically intimate you become, the harder it will be to put the brakes on and the more painful breaking up will be. We stir our hormones into a frenzy and then we wonder why it all blows up. Until you are walking down the aisle, it's best to keep your sexual desires in check. Practically, this probably means keeping your kisses short and sweet (or save your first kiss until after you've lifted the veil). It may mean keeping your hands from anything you wouldn't want their last boyfriend or girlfriend to have touched. Perhaps, the best advice is simply to recognize that *Christ is with you*—so don't do anything you would want to hide from him (or from your spiritual director!).

If you are still waiting for the right person to come along, learn to enjoy the wait. Your "love life" is a great place to practice your patience muscle. Many single men and women seem convinced that eternal joy lies at the end of the romance rainbow. And we can't seem to understand why God is taking so long to bring this blessing. It is during the waiting period that we are tested and prepared to make the most of the blessing. Do not expect a perfect partner, but do hold out for a partner God is perfecting. Your time is better spent not trying to *find* the right person, but learning to *be* the right person.

1. **Meditation Exercise:** Slowly read through **I Corinthians 7:25-40**.

2. If you are single, do you see yourself getting married in the future or staying single? Talk to God about his will for you in this area...

3. If you are planning on getting married, decide what you are looking for in a partner. Make a *very short* list of the non-negotiable qualities you would like... What is really essential? Is it important to you that they love Jesus as deeply as you do? Is Christ-like character important? Or are you more concerned about outward things like looks, money, and popularity?

102. On Marriage
Your Discipline of Practical One-ness

othing tests and forms the quality of your spiritual life quite like marriage. Some dimensions of spiritual maturity you can only learn in this *"school of character"*, as Martin Luther called the institution of marriage. Gary Thomas rightly asks, *"what if marriage is not to make you happy, but to make you holy?"* I cannot help but think you will be disappointed if you think marriage is merely a practical means to your own pleasure. Perhaps happiness is more a fringe benefit of marriage rather than its goal. Surely the experience of being a husband or wife should be a help to knowing God and not a hindrance. Holy matrimony is a sacramental lesson in relationships like none other— a "crash course", perhaps even a "collision course", in day-to-day oneness with another human being.

Marriage will teach you what true love is. If your "love" does not survive the test of wedlock, it was only a pseudo-love. The kind of sacrificing *agape* love that God requires is the same kind of love marriage requires. Even the pagan, the atheist, or the doubter may experience a taste of the committed, courageous love of Christ if they are willing to abide by God's marital law: *"til death do us part."* This entails a strong and forceful species of love that preserves union with the beloved, regardless of the cost to one's self. It is a fierce love that finds a way to reconcile any conflict and suffers any discomfort for the sake of the marriage relationship. It is strengthened through testing, forging a bond that is stronger than death.

Marriage reveals you as nothing else. Your spouse becomes a mirror of your flaws and weaknesses; these must be dealt with or they will ruin your lives. There is no place to hide your true self in the gridlock of wedlock. If anything irritates you, you will find your spouse always seems to do exactly this. All of the deepest areas of life are involved: money, sex, family, self-image, work, future,

425

dreams, and anything else important to you. It is the perfect self-diagnostic tool, if you are honest with it. Your areas of brokenness and hurt are forced to the surface. Your ability to trust is tested through such vulnerability. Home decorating, budgeting and sexual intimacy requires sacrifice and unselfishness from both partners. The marriage bed can be a place of deep expressions of healing love or of hurtful self-centeredness. A happy marriage requires you to learn to communicate lovingly, openly and honestly.

All our issues surface in marriage because it is the most intimate human-to-human spiritual union possible. It is the closest approximation of our oneness with God—two individuals voluntarily united to one another in unbreakable bond. How do two souls become intertwined so tightly that they may be spoken of as one? A healthy marriage plays out the drama of God's love on the stage of human life. This is truly holy ground. Marriage forces you to love as God loves—unconditionally, unrelentingly, unendingly. It calls forth the same perseverance, sacrifice and passion that Christ displayed on the cross.

Male and female are fearfully and wonderfully different. Men are supposed to act like men; women should radiate a womanly splendor. The beauty of a woman and the strength of a man—what a glorious union! Our gender differences are what spark both the attraction and the animosity between lovers. This explosive potential can result in a delightful cooperation of friends or a disastrous competition between foes. A good marriage requires an understanding of each other's strengths, perspectives, gifts, and abilities. Disregarding your spouse's opinions will destroy any hopes for a joy-filled home. Are you humble enough to compromise and work with someone who thinks, acts, and lives differently?

Men, your woman needs to feel loved. Show her she is valued, desired, and cherished. Listen to her like you care more about her than anyone else in the world! Protect and provide for her. Spoil her with so much tenderness and affection that she wishes you didn't have to leave each morning. *Women, your man needs to feel respected.* Show him you appreciate and admire him. Treat him with such honor and esteem that he looks forward to coming home to you every night. When a man is emasculated and disdained at home, he usually checks out on the marriage, even if physically present. These dynamics are explored in Emerson Eggerich's excellent book, *Love and Respect.* Don't buy into twisted caricatures of oppressive macho stereotypes or radical militant feminism. Instead, explore how God uniquely created you and live out of the depths of your core masculinity or femininity.

Husbands and wives are *equal in value* but *different in roles*— essential equality with functional differences. The controversial concept of male authority in the home produces a divinely-ordered partnership and keeps the marriage from degenerating into a power play. Having a "head of the house" does *not* imply that men are somehow better than women! Many cannot grasp how this is possible. We automatically assume greater authority means greater self-worth! Why do we base our worth upon our roles? We still suspect that the CEO is somehow more valuable than the VP. This false correlation must be corrected if humans are ever to work together non-competitively! Men must learn to assume loving leadership in their homes; women must learn the lost art of submission. After having seen so many misuses and abuses by small and selfish men, we may assume all male authority is domineering and destructive. True leadership never devalues or squashes someone's spirit. A man who always insists on his own way and cannot listen to his wife is not exercising leadership—he is only exposing his own shortcomings. And a wife who refuses to submit is not displaying her independence, but parading her own insecurity.

Many marriages die from neglect. It takes time and hard work to keep the fire alive. Keep your finger on the pulse of your marriage-- it must remain full of passion and life. Do you have a lively conversational relationship and an engaging sexual relationship? Intimacy is cultivated through talk and touch. Date like teenagers! "Waste time" together doing something fun, anything that you both enjoy. Build a close friendship by spending time just talking about stuff (and actually listening to each other!). Plan a *weekly date night* to give undivided attention to your sole partner. Think ahead: How could I really bless my spouse? Gary Chapman's helpful book, *The Five Love Languages*, describes five primary ways we give and receive love: *words of affirmation, meaningful touch, acts of service, giving gifts, and quality time*. The key is to know your own love language and to discern your partner's primary expression of love. Then regularly express your love in their dialect!

Resolve conflicts respectfully. Arguments are a normal and inevitable part of marriage. Don't let disagreements turn you against one another. Work on your differences as allies, not as enemies. Stop trying to figure out who is right or wrong (usually both of you have something to learn). Instead, work on understanding their point of view before you try to express your own (i.e., listen before you talk!). Once each of you sees the other's perspective, you can work out a solution you can both live with. *Never* express disdain for one another, threaten one another, attack one another, or otherwise try to force the other person into surrendering to you. If you ever find yourself taking revenge or punishing your spouse (in subtle or not-so-subtle ways), go apologize at once for such selfishness and spite!

1. **Meditation Exercise:** Meditatively read **I Corinthians 7:1-24**.

2. **Communication Exercise:** Ask your spouse the following questions. Write down *their* answers and discuss them honestly and openly (without getting defensive!):
a. What makes you feel loved and appreciated?
    What makes you feel close to me?
    What makes you feel unloved and unappreciated?
    What makes you feel distant from me?
b. In our marriage, what makes you feel happy? Sad? Secure?
    Afraid? Excited? Angry? Comfortable? Uncomfortable?

c. What do you like most about yourself?

   What do you hate most about yourself?

d. What do we have a hard time talking about? Why is it so difficult?

e. What is one thing I could do to improve our marriage for you?

After you discuss it with them, ask if they want to hear *your* answers to these same questions...

3. What are your biggest areas of conflict? What do your typical arguments sound like? What is your spouse trying to get you to understand? What are you wishing your spouse could understand? Ask God for help in these "problem areas"...

4. Think of five things you could do to bless your spouse. Choose one to do this week.

103. On Parenting
Your Assignment of Soul-Shaping

Parenting might be the greatest privilege on earth: "disciple-making" at its finest. Your family is your lasting legacy, your most critical mission, your first responsibility. Even if you were to fail at work, at ministry, and everything else, you would still be a raging success in the eyes of God if you established a loving, Christ-filled home. No amount of success abroad can justify the neglect of your own household. This does not mean we must coddle, spoil or pander to our children's every want and whim! A Christ-centered home may require risk-taking, discipline, sacrifice, and self-denial even on the part of the children, yet it is ultimately the ideal place for a child to grow up. If you are a single parent, this job will be especially tough— lean on your spiritual community for as much support as you need.

Parents are held responsible for the nurture of these wonder-filled souls. Schools and churches may assist in this process, but fathers and mothers are the ones who ultimately answer to God for how their children were raised. *Parents should be the primary spiritual authorities in a child's life.* There is *no excuse* for neglecting their spiritual formation. Many parents run themselves ragged to get their child into a good school to further their educational goals while utterly ignoring their spiritual instruction! Some parents go to great lengths to keep their kids physically healthy and do absolutely nothing for their spiritual well-being! *Children must be taught right from wrong!* They must be trained up in the fear of the LORD. They must be introduced to Jesus Christ who alone can guide them into their full potential in this universe. Do all you can to direct your child in the way they should go... then give them back to God. Even the best of parents may have children who stray. We cannot live their lives for them. We cannot force anyone into a relationship with God. But we can, *we must* show them the Way.

Shaping a child's soul is far more difficult than programming a computer. All our formulaic methodology we employ to control things no longer work with a flesh-and-blood person. The perfect cause-and-effect pattern of the material world does not apply to this brand new spiritual being, beautiful, imaginative, willful and free. Whenever you bring a child into the world, a miracle has taken place. The unseen Breath of God infuses a clump of biological matter with a unique, eternal soul! And as the physical body grows from a tiny cell of recombinant DNA into a fully-formed human life, the spiritual potential also waits to be unlocked.

Raising a child teaches us to love like God. (All this little creature does is scream at us and soil us with disgusting bodily fluids—and we absolutely love them! Could our Father in heaven love us that much?) We quickly gain "sympathy" for our heavenly Father: the simple joys of having our child love us, though they do nothing impressive or useful! We see how difficult it is to help a disobedient child without seeming mean or uncaring. We understand how wrongdoing could never make us hate our child, yet we hate that they do it. We discover the delicate balance between blessing and spoiling-- and how our child probably won't know the difference. We experience the heartache when our child is on a chosen path of self-destruction, knowing how little we can do without their trust. We find our hearts crying in resonance with the words God spoke to his children even as he disciplined them severely: *"I know the plans I have for you, plans to prosper you and not to harm you, plans to give you a hope and a future!"*

Every parent must learn the difficult *dynamics of discipline.* Without some form of fairly-strict discipline, your children will live scattered, aimless lives. Don't be afraid to say "no" regularly and rigorously! John Rosemond, in his many excellent books on parenting, tells us that children need rules, boundaries, directions, and leadership in order to thrive. They need to know their parents are in control. *Require obedience of your children... and be willing to enforce it.* Children do not naturally do what is best for them— is this

431

news to you? That is what parents are for: to make them do what they do not yet realize they should be doing themselves. Don't feel bad about using your authority to impose goodness upon them. You are allowed to punish your children— but do it for their good, not to satisfy your anger. If you correct them fairly for their own benefit, they will eventually love and trust you for it. If you retaliate out of your own woundedness, you will harm their little souls. Whether you use time-outs, spankings, or removal of privileges, make it painfully clear: *bad decisions lead to bad consequences!*

With kids, actions speak louder than words so save your breath. Instead of yelling and screaming, state the consequences clearly and enforce them calmly. No bargaining, no persuading, no drama, no drawn-out explanations. You may explain *after* they have obeyed, not *before*. But always *temper discipline with tenderness*. Do not let bitterness take root in their hearts from excessive harshness... this provokes rebellion. Cultivate a flexible inflexibility... there are times for lenience, but too much laxity erodes your foundation of discipline. After every correction, show compassion and comfort as soon as they can receive it. Establish a daily habit of expressing affection and lavishing love upon them. Hug them, kiss them, laugh and play with them, read them stories. And every night, pray with your children and bless them as you tuck them into bed.

And as you discharge this sacred responsibility, don't forget to have some fun along the way. Fill their childhood years with joyful memories and laughter. Few things are more spiritually healthy for a child than to see their parents smile. If they watch you love your spouse and enjoy life, they will probably learn to do the same. Form some meaningful and fun family traditions that they will remember with fondness. *Set aside at least one night a week for family fun night.* Spend hours enjoying life together! Don't waste all your time together watching TV!

Life is hard work! Do your kids know this? From the time they are born till the time they leave the house, each child should make the journey from being completely controlled by their parents to being completely self-controlled. Your job is to work yourself out of the job of caring for this child. Hand that task over to them. *Children need chores to grow up!* Progressively give more and more responsibilities, rights, and decisions to them as they get older. Teens are adults-in-training. Have you assigned enough household chores that they will be capable of running a household themselves? Are they almost ready to be self-sufficient? They will eventually have to make their own mistakes. So be there for them when that happens. Fill their minds with conversations about what's important in life!

Ultimately, *your example is your most convincing form of teaching*. Your life will speak much louder than your words, for better or for worse. Rarely will a child do as you say and not as you do. Many parents attempt to atone for their own sins through their children. We control our children since we cannot control ourselves. Such obvious hypocrisy is doomed for failure. Are you prepared to see your own sins reproduced in the next generation? The best way to teach your child to love is simply to love. Their wide eyes will ever be watching how you treat your spouse and how you treat God. They will know in living experience how you loved your children and how you loved your neighbor... and you will not be able to contradict the substance of your life with hollow words. So the very best thing you can do for your children is... to love God and to love people. Through a living spirituality, teach them to obey, to trust, to listen, to love, and to be loved.

As a parent, you will make many mistakes. But never allow guilt over past mistakes resign you to make more mistakes. Don't succumb to the pressure of having to be a perfect parent! Guilt-driven parenting will leave your children feeling driven by this same guilt. Instead, fill your own life with God's grace and it will also abound to your children. Before they were your children, they were God's children. He loves them even more than you do. And even though he has entrusted you with their care, he is still watching over them.

1. **Meditation Exercise:** Read slowly through **Psalm 127 and 128.**

2. Write out a one-page parenting *"crib sheet" for each child* you have been entrusted with: How is this child unique? What are they good at? What do they enjoy doing? What motivates them?
How do they receive love and encouragement?
What are their weaknesses? Their strengths? Their fears?
Their hopes? Their dreams? How do they learn best?
How should we discipline them?
What character qualities, interpersonal skills, concrete abilities, and basic chores should they be learning right now to prepare them for adulthood? How could you help them to learn this?
What do they need to learn about God, money, sex, friendships, etc.?
What is your "discipleship plan" for this child?(It doesn't have to be rigid or complicated, but it should be intentional.)
Could you read them Bible stories? Memorize a few short Bible verses with them? Sing praise songs with them?
Discuss theology questions with them? ("What is God like? What does God do? What does God want for you? Who is Jesus?")
Or just meet at a restaurant once a week to talk about life...
Once you have finished your parenting "crib sheet" for each of your children, share it with your spouse and see if they have any other ideas or insights to include.

3. Ask your spouse to help you to put together a **Household Rule** (in Appendix).

104. On Citizenship
Your Responsibility to Social Justice

ongratulations! You have been selected to serve the global good! "God so love the world"...but do you? You've been ordained with the Herculean ordeal of cleansing our filthy world. But do not just go haphazardly chopping off heads... this does more harm than good. Instead, combine *submission* and *subversion* into a defining lifestyle: become both an upstanding citizen and a rebel against society! Seek to undermine injustice, oppression, corruption, and all the structural evils of society, but do so with a dove-like innocence and serpentine shrewdness. At any point where the world aligns with basic goodness and godliness, we are to be models of civility, actively supporting that-which-is-good. But let the powers that be cross the line into that-which-is-bad and we must square our shoulders against the social order. Whether the issue is human trafficking, racism, systemic poverty, pollution, genocide, exploitation, prostitution, abortion, or sexism, you no longer have the option of sitting on your couch and watching your world fall apart.

God loves justice... and hates injustice. Each act of hate and oppression cuts him to the core. He hears the cries of every soul that has ever suffered unfairly. He hears the desperate sobs of the twelve-year-old girl forced into prostitution, raped day after day after day, in an endless, senseless nightmare. He sees the tear-streaked cheeks of the single mother whose husband left her to raise three small children alone. He knows every scar on the back of the refugee, forced from his homeland in a brutal tribal war. He feels the knot in the stomach of the seven-year-old boy, whose classmates mercilessly mock him in his disability. Do you also hear their cries? Sometimes the world needs, not an all-powerful God, but an all-suffering God. Take comfort in knowing Christ was not only the victor but also the victim— he enters willingly into our pain, and even when he delays to alleviate it, he feels it. Has he placed part of his heartache in you? Which wounds of the world do you feel most deeply? What needs and pains do you feel driven to address?

The King of Kings has scattered his beloved sons and daughters to the nations as agents of compassion and change. He has given us this charge: *Go! Do justice to the world.* Defend human rights and serve human needs. Stand in solidarity with hurting humanity... and, if possible, stop the wheels of the machine that grinds them into the dirt. As Christ's disciple, you are a member of this underground resistance force. You are called to resist evil wherever it appears— not with the weapons of violence, political manipulations, or double-talk, but with the slow and steady work of selfless love, unadorned truth, and our living  example of righteousness. Defend the helpless, the oppressed, the diseased, the poor, and the exploited. Care for the fatherless and the widow. Give a voice to those who have no voice. Be a peacemaker wherever strife reigns. Touch the leper. Cure the sick. Reconcile enemies. Dedicate your life to the upheaval of structures that enslave. And even when you cannot stop the pain, perhaps you can sit beside the sufferer in silence so they know they are not alone.

Creation itself groans. God entrusted us with *the care of our environment.* God made Adam responsible for the entire ecosystem: *"rule over the fish of the sea and the birds of the air, over the livestock, over all the earth, and over all the creatures that move along the ground."* This mandatory mandate has not been rescinded. Humankind stands accountable for the condition of our polluted planet. Have we been symbiotic stewards of our natural resources, using them wisely and sustainably? Or have we been parasites on our planet: greedy, careless, and messy? What have we done to his oceans, skies, forests, and mountains?

You are first and foremost a citizen of God's kingdom. All other allegiances are binding only as far as they fit into this final purpose. Your loyalty to nations, political parties, citizen groups, even religious groups extends only as far as their alignment with eternity. What is truly good is always of God. Whenever we pray, *"Thy kingdom come, Thy will be done on earth as it is in heaven,"* we are inviting the force of God's goodness to sweep across the face of the earth like a tidal wave. This includes the concentric circles of your nation, your state, your city, your neighborhood, your church, your workplace, your family, and your own soul.

Jesus Christ was a threat to everyone in power: those on the right and the left, in the religious establishment and the political establishment. Why? He had an unflagging dedication towards that-which-is-good and an untiring opposition towards that-which-is-bad. Don't just parrot political slogans, blaming everything on those greedy conservatives or those bleeding-heart liberals. We could learn a lot by listening to the opposition instead of vilifying them. Jesus never played political favorites: He refused to approve of wrongdoing no matter if it was the Romans, the Pharisees, the Sadducees, or even his own disciples. This contrary agenda will be seen as high treason against the Caesars of the world. But if standing with Christ is a crime, then only the criminal is free. If following God's law puts you in opposition to the law of the land, then like Daniel in the den of lions, smilingly accept your punishment, relying upon God to guide and secure your fate.

The place to start is with your feet in the mud, not with your head in the clouds. There are too many people who want to get their hands into the political process and too few willing to roll up their sleeves and get their hands dirty by actually working on the problem itself. If you want to help the homeless, don't just pick up the phone and lobby the lawmakers to spend more money on homeless shelters. Instead, go meet some homeless people: touch them, feed them, love them and bring them hope. If you want to stop abortions, don't spend all your time pushing for anti-abortion laws. Instead, go volunteer your time to help a handful of teenage mothers-to-be deal realistically with this tragic and difficult decision: care for them, love them, and help them financially. Unless you're prepared to put your money where your mouth is, keep it shut. If you want to protect the environment, start by helping to clean up a stream or pick up trash in your own neighborhood. Once your hands are calloused and cracked from working on the problem, perhaps you have the right to tell the government how they can assist you in solving it.

Can we eliminate systemic poverty? Can we stop nations from going to war? Can we end criminal behavior? Such noble aims are often complicated by a complex mess of assumptions. Many well-intentioned crusaders never consider the unintended side-effects of their short-sighted solutions. We are obligated to think through carefully the implications of each decision. Poverty is an inexact label, often stretched to the point of pointlessness. Every dollar the government spends on one person is taken from another. Sometimes this is justified; often it is not. Each dollar given becomes an incentive to get more of it. *Money will always be scarce in our fallen world*— if this is unclear to you, read up on economics before you hurt someone! You are free to generously redistribute your wealth and reap the blessing. But think twice before reaching into other peoples' pockets to force them into coerced generosity. Changing laws does not change human hearts. And beware of the hypocrisy that asks the government to do what we will not do ourselves. Pray for your political leaders. Require honesty, responsibility and justice from those in power. But do not expect the state to solve all our problems. When we begin expecting perfection from our president, we have set up a golden calf that will not save us.

1. **Meditation Exercise:** Slowly and meditatively read **Psalm 146**.

2. Who does your heart break for? Is there an area of societal brokenness that really burdens your heart? Find one issue and begin to research it... Then decide what you may be able to do about it...

105. Afterword
The Beginning of the Journey

his is only the start of your spiritual life. If you are right now overwhelmed by the amount of "stuff" you have to do, I want you to breathe a sigh of relief. We are washed in *grace* every new morning! God's gratuitous grace is available for every slip-up, shortcoming, and sin we commit. Don't worry about doing every spiritual discipline you have learned in this book. Let God's Spirit lead you each day. I must emphasize once again that the spiritual life is initiated by God and we only respond to his daily leading. This is not a self-improvement project that you can accomplish with heroic effort. I have only sketched out for you many parts of the path you may expect to come across on your spiritual journey. Walking with Christ is not as orderly, nor as strict or structured as this seems to make it. It is really a messy business that doesn't always fit neatly into the categories I have described for you. And it really doesn't require that you practice every exercise written in this book. I will emphasize once again that the disciplines in this training manual are like tools in a toolbox that you can use as needed and customize to your own style. You will probably eventually become disillusioned with some of the particular construction materials in this book. And may God be praised for this! Let illusions fall away until all you are left with is pure reality!

Jesus Christ is so much greater than I have been able to show here in these pages. Just as a boot camp prepares you for the rigors of army life but is not itself army life, this guidebook has been only an introduction. It would be well to lay it aside for a while. Then come back to it from time to time just to brush up on some of the basics. But I do hope and pray that you will "outgrow" this curriculum. Use it as a launching pad to get you off the ground and into the bright blue sky. And the further you get, the more you will realize, you are still only a beginner... in an eternal kind of life that is only just beginning.

Also, let me warn you: *as you walk in this new life, you will fall.* It is not a matter of "if" but "when". You may fail miserably and often. And when you do, your loving Father will always be there to pick you back up. Don't be discouraged or disheartened that you find yourself still stumbling into sin. It is probably more obvious now than when you began your spiritual life! But be assured... the only way you can lose the race is by giving up. You may be knocked down, but as long as you keep your courage, and get up again, you cannot be conquered. You will find that you cannot live the life you intend... yet your weakness keeps you close to God. As you continue on life's voyage, you may sometimes notice yourself drifting off course. When you begin to feel your heart growing cold, one of the surest remedies is to lock yourself in a room with Jesus Christ for a few days. Re-acquaint yourself with the Master of Life, allowing him to revive your heart and restore your soul. Practice the habit of re-turning to your first love.

After all of Jesus' training and commissioning, he left his disciples with one final assurance: *"And surely I am with you always, to the very end of the age."* No matter how well or how poorly we do, we know that *he will never leave us nor forsake us!* We may stumble every single step we take. We may fall a hundred times a day. We may fail in our mission... with flying colors! And yet God's undying devotion to us will never end. Hear St. Paul's resounding reassurances: *"If we are faithless, he will remain faithful, for he cannot deny himself." "For I am convinced that neither death nor life, neither angels nor demons, neither the present nor the future, nor any powers, height nor depth, nor anything else in all creation will be able to separate us from the love of God that is in Christ Jesus our Lord.!"*

Meditation Exercise

Preparation: Close your eyes, quiet your mind and invite God to speak to you.

Scripture: Slowly and meditatively read through **John 21.**

1. The disciples had just watched their conquering Lord struck down and killed—and then resurrected... What emotions must they have felt over the last week? They had deserted and betrayed their beloved Master, watched him die, and then saw him come back from the dead! How would this have affected them?
Listen as Simon Peter says to his companions, *"I'm going out to fish."* Why does he decide to go fishing right now? Is he overwhelmed? Disillusioned? Frustrated? Disappointed? Is he feeling unworthy to be a disciple? Is he unsure of what to do next? Spend some time trying to figure out what was going through Peter's mind...

2. While they are fishing, it becomes apparent that Jesus is the mysterious stranger watching from the seashore. How does Peter feel when he realizes this? Why does Peter impulsively jump into the water to swim ashore?

3. Now listen as Jesus questions Peter... Why does Jesus ask him three times, *"Do you love me?"* And why the same basic reply, *"Feed my sheep"*? How do you think Peter is feeling during this conversation? What is Jesus trying to say?

4. Hear Peter's question, *"What about him?"* We all have our "What about _____?" questions. What are some of your unanswered questions? Write them down in your journal...
Now hear Christ issue the final challenge: *"What is that to you? You must follow me."* How is this "follow me" different from the first time, years earlier, when Jesus asked Peter to follow him? How has

Peter changed during this time? How have you changed since you started following him? How has your perspective changed?

5. Finally, watch Jesus dusty feet making their way across the rocky coastline... Are you sure you still want to follow him? After all you have been through, do you still think it's worth it? Now that you know what it will cost you, will you follow him even if it leads to your death? Will you follow him even if he requires things of you that he doesn't require of others? If so, get up... and follow him...

6. At this point, I encourage you to sign the **Holiness Covenant** (in Appendix). This is an annoyingly specific commitment to follow Christ in overall lifestyle. Look it over. Could you sign this covenant? Does it encapsulate your heart? This is not a guarantee that you will not falter. It is only a statement of intent: what you want to do, not what you will do. If and when you fall, confess it, pick yourself back up, and continue on your journey.

Kyrie Eleison ...
(The Lord have mercy upon you)

CHRIST-CENTERED

SPIRITUALITY

A HANDBOOK OF *CATECHESIS*
for
the training of novices
in
THE WAY OF CHRIST

APPENDIX

Monthly Budget

Net Income $_____

Monthly salary/avg. wages, investment interest, dividends, child support, welfare, etc.

Giving $_____

Tithe, offerings, charitable donations, sponsoring a child, giving to the needy, etc.

Housing $_____

Rent/mortgage, utilities, telephone, long distance, cell phone, electricity, gas, water, sewage, homeowner's insurance, real estate tax, home improvements/ maintenance, etc.

Transportation $_____

Auto loan/savings, gas, insurance, registration, maintenance/repair, bus/taxi, etc.

Medical $_____

Health insurance, life insurance, doctor/dentist fees, medication, contacts, supplements, etc.

Groceries/ Household Items $_____

Food, toiletries, laundry, cleaning, light bulbs, etc.

Children $_____

Diapers, wipes, school, books, toys, allowance, lunch, childcare, tuition, college fund, savings, etc.

Clothing/Cosmetics $_____

Clothes, haircuts, make-up, beauty products, jewelry, etc.

Entertainment $_____

Eating out, coffee, cable TV, internet, music, movies, books, magazine subscriptions, hobbies, sports, recreational equipment, gym fees, vacations, etc.

Gifts $_____

Christmas gifts, birthday gifts, weddings, friends and family, etc.

Savings / Debt Reduction $_____

Credit cards, loans, equity line of credit, savings accounts, investments, retirement, 401k, etc.

Miscellaneous $_____

Income taxes, business expenses, miscellaneous fees, special needs, etc.

Total Expenses $_____

Make sure your total expenses are less than or equal to your net income.

Weekly Schedule

	Monday	Tuesday	Wednesday	Thursday	Friday	Saturday	Sunday
6:00 am							
7:00 am							
8:00 am							
9:00 am							
10:00 am							
11:00 am							
12:00 pm							
1:00 pm							
2:00 pm							
3:00 pm							
4:00 pm							
5:00 pm							
6:00 pm							
7:00 pm							
8:00 pm							
9:00 pm							
Goals							

Rule of Life

Life Vision:

Priorities:

I. Love the Lord your God with all your heart, with all your soul, with all your mind and with all your strength.

1. Spiritual Discipline (with all your heart)
Daily Spiritual Exercises (Everyday!)

Weekly Spiritual Exercises

2. Moral Discipline (with all your soul)
Cultivating Virtue/Christ-like Character –

Removing Vice/Sins –

3. Intellectual Discipline (with all your mind)

4. Physical Discipline (with all your strength)

II. Love your Neighbor as Yourself

1. Your Household/Family

2. Your Spiritual Community

3. Your Neighborhood

447

Questions for Sharing your Faith

Having the right questions is more useful than having the right answers!
There is no pressure to correct errors, tell them what to believe, or "close the sale"!
Just ask questions and listen!

Underline the questions you think will be most natural or useful for you:
Some Opening Questions: (Start wherever they are at!)
Do you ever think about God or spirituality? Are you a spiritual person?
What is your religious background? What do you believe in?
Do you think there is a God? What do you think God is like?
If you could ask God one question, what would it be?
Where are you at with God right now? Do you feel close to him right now?
Do you ever talk to God? Do you think God hears you when you pray?
Is God good? Do you think it's possible for God to be evil or imperfect?
Do you think God thinks, feels, chooses, talks or loves? Can God do miracles?
Does God change to fit our beliefs? Can every statement about God be true?
Do you think there is a right and wrong? Or is everything right?
Who or what ultimately decides what is right and what is wrong?
What do you think happens to us after we die? Do our lives today affect eternity?
Do you think there is a heaven or hell or something else?
Who or what determines what happens to us in the afterlife?
Do you think your life has a purpose? What do you think it is?
Is there any transcendent meaning to existence? Do our lives ultimately matter?
What are you looking for in life? What kind of person do you hope to be?
Where do you think the universe came from? Why does anything exist at all?
What do you think about Christians or church?

Some Clarifying Questions: (Get beyond their "surface" answers!)
What does that look like? Tell me more about that... What do you mean by that?
Why do you believe that? How did you come to believe that?
How do you know this? Is there any guarantee that you're right about this?

Some Christ- Centered Questions: (Eventually, you want to zero in on Christ!)
Have you ever considered Jesus?
What do you think of Jesus? Who do you find more convincing than Jesus?
What do you think of the Bible? What do you find more convincing than it?
Do you think Jesus was really God in the flesh?
Do you think Jesus really rose from the dead? Is that too hard for God to do?
Are you a follower of Jesus? Do you want to follow Jesus?

Household Rule

Turn your household into a spiritual community structured around the goal of glorifying God! If your home, like a Benedictine monastery, was "a school for the Lord's service", how would it need to be ordered?

Household Vision:

Sleep: What are the bedtimes for each family member (so that everyone gets a full night sleep as often as possible)? What time does each family member need to wake up? What routines need to happen before bedtime? After waking up?

Meals: How often will our family eat together? Which meals? Will we face one another at the dinner table or ignore one another and watch TV? Who will do the chores associated with preparation and clean-up?

Chores: What weekly tasks is each household member responsible for?

Spiritual Instruction: What discipleship does each family member need?

Media: How many hours a week will family members be allowed to watch TV? Play video games? Surf the internet? (Add these up: is anyone sitting spellbound before a screen for more than 15 hours a week? If so, find ways to cut it down!) How do we protect family members from internet sin?

Recreation: When is family fun night? When is date night?

Holiness Covenant

Because I love Jesus and have surrendered my life to his purposes,
I today make this covenant, by the grace of God, to live according to the following:

1. I will remain celibate from all sexual relations outside the sacred bonds of marriage. (Lust)

2. I will give away at least 10 % of my income to the work of God. I will not steal, cheat or take any money unjustly. (Greed)

3. I will submit myself to the oversight of a spiritual director...unless asked to do something directly contrary to God's will. (Pride)

4. I will not gossip, slander, or tear down others behind their backs with my words. (Envy)

5. I will not get drunk with alcohol or use any drug illegally. (Gluttony)

6. I will not strike another person out of anger. (Anger)

7. I will spend my days doing good works, with appropriate times of rest. (Laziness)

8. I will seek God regularly through appropriate spiritual disciplines. (Exercises)

9. I will participate regularly in the gatherings of a community of faith. (Community)

10. I will love and serve the poor, the hurting, the lost, and the outcasts of society. (Mission)

If I falter in any of the above areas, I will immediately confess it to God and another disciple, receiving God's abundant grace, and taking any appropriate steps to remedy the situation.

_____   _____
Signature   Date

Lectio Divina

Preparation: Quiet your heart. Ask God to speak.

1. Read the passage slowly with your understanding. (*Lectio*)

2. Reflect on the passage with your imagination. (*Meditatio*)

3. Respond to what you have read in prayer. (*Oratio*)

4. Rest in God's presence with an open heart. (*Contemplatio*)

Lectio Divina

Preparation: Quiet your heart. Ask God to speak.

1. Read the passage slowly with your understanding. (*Lectio*)

2. Reflect on the passage with your imagination. (*Meditatio*)

3. Respond to what you have read in prayer. (*Oratio*)

4. Rest in God's presence with an open heart. (*Contemplatio*)

Lectio Divina

Preparation: Quiet your heart. Ask God to speak.

1. Read the passage slowly with your understanding. (*Lectio*)

2. Reflect on the passage with your imagination. (*Meditatio*)

3. Respond to what you have read in prayer. (*Oratio*)

4. Rest in God's presence with an open heart. (*Contemplatio*)

Lectio Divina

Preparation: Quiet your heart. Ask God to speak.

1. Read the passage slowly with your understanding. (*Lectio*)

2. Reflect on the passage with your imagination. (*Meditatio*)

3. Respond to what you have read in prayer. (*Oratio*)

4. Rest in God's presence with an open heart. (*Contemplatio*)

NT Scripture Plan

— Mark
— John
— Ephesians
— Philippians
— Colossians
— James
— I, II, III John
— Luke
— Acts
— Galatians
— Romans
— Hebrews
— I, II Corinthians
— Titus
— Philemon
— I, II Timothy
— Matthew
— I, II Peter
— I, II Thessalonians
— Jude
— Revelation

OT Scripture Plan
(Part I)

The Histories

— Genesis
— Exodus 1-20, 24, 31-34
— Numbers 9-17, 20-25
— Deuteronomy 1-6, 30-34
— Joshua
— Judges
— Ruth
— I, II Samuel
— I, II Kings
— Daniel
— Ezra
— Nehemiah
— Esther
— I, II Chronicles

The Wisdom Books

— Psalms
— Proverbs
— Ecclesiastes
— Song of Songs
— Job

NT Scripture Plan

— Mark
— John
— Ephesians
— Philippians
— Colossians
— James
— I, II, III John
— Luke
— Acts
— Galatians
— Romans
— Hebrews
— I, II Corinthians
— Titus
— Philemon
— I, II Timothy
— Matthew
— I, II Peter
— I, II Thessalonians
— Jude
— Revelation

OT Scripture Plan
(Part II)

The Law

— Genesis
— Exodus
— Leviticus
— Numbers
— Deuteronomy

The Prophets

— Isaiah
— Jeremiah
— Lamentations
— Ezekiel
— Hosea
— Joel
— Amos
— Obadiah
— Jonah
— Micah
— Nahum
— Habakkuk
— Zephaniah
— Haggai
— Zechariah
— Malachi

The Novitiation

The Novitiation is a pattern for implementing *Christ-Centered Spirituality* as a curriculum for Christ-likeness in your spiritual community. In the tradition of the ancient *catechesis* practiced in the catacombs by the early church, the body of Christ can receive new members with a crash course in a new way of life. If you are a spiritual director, small group leader, pastor, or just a disciple wanting to make disciples, you may use this as a discipleship training class, membership class, baptism class, small group program, or leadership training class. Please go through the curriculum yourself before leading others through it.

It takes one year to complete in three 14-week semesters, each concluding with a weekend mini-retreat. The first semester, *The Mysteries of the Universe,* could go from August to December. The second semester, *Disciplines for Christ-likeness,* can go from January to April (perhaps concluding with an Easter Baptism?). The third semester, *A Life Consecrated to Mission,* can go from May through July. Classes can meet whenever novices are available: Sundays after church, Tuesday nights, Saturday mornings, etc. Each class meets two hours a week, covering three lessons (one is homework). Classes should be less than 20 novices each.

While novices should not be graded, they should be required to attend class and do the homework assignments. The teacher should take attendance at each class and note if they did their homework. If a novice gets in a pattern of missing classes or homework, talk with them privately and encourage them to catch up. If it continues, tell them they may need to wait till the next class is offered. Highly-motivated novices may do it independently with coaching, but most need a group format.

The format given here is only a suggestion. You are free to modify any part as you feel is appropriate! You may skip any lesson that clashes with your particular denominational stance. You may also clarify any disagreements you have with the viewpoints expressed.

Novitiation Class Format

0. Open with Prayer

1. Homework Check-up: (20 min.)
>   Did you all do your homework assignment?
>   What did you learn from it?
>   Do you have any questions about it?

2. First Lesson: (40 min.)

5 min.   Intro/Summary from Teacher
>   Share any important points/ highlights about that topic
>   or just have novices take 5 minutes to read it silently

20 min.   Practice Exercises
>   Read each line of instruction to them
>   Use appropriate periods of silence
>   Invite them to close their eyes, when necessary
>   Have someone read each Scripture passage aloud slowly
>   As you go, pause for reflection, as needed
>   Don't rush!

15 min.   Discussion
>   Ask what insights they learned and what questions they have
>   Explore what they experienced during the meditation exercises

3. Break: (10 min.) Snacks

4. Second Lesson: (40 min.)   Same as above

5. Close with Prayer

Novitiation Semester I

The Mysteries of the Universe (Christ/God/The Soul)
(14 weeks + 2-day retreat – each week covers 2 lessons and 1 for homework)

Semester Schedule:
Week 1: Lessons 1-2
  __ write a half-page description of Jesus: "Who is Christ?"
  __ assign lesson 3
Week 2: Lessons 3-5
  __ do you have a Bible? do you have a journal?
  __ assign lesson 6
Week 3: Lessons 6-8
  __ assign lesson 9
Week 4: Lessons 9-11
  __ assign lesson 12
  __ check-up: have you been doing the journal entries for assignments?
Week 5: Lessons 12-14
  __ assign lesson 15
Week 6: Lessons 15-17
  __ assign lesson 18
Week 7: Lessons 18-20
  __ assign lesson 21
Week 8: Lessons 21-23
  __ write a half-page description of God: "Who is God?"
  __ assign lesson 24
Week 9: Lessons 24-26
  __ assign lesson 27
Week 10: Lessons 27-29   end each week reciting the Apostles' Creed
  __ assign lesson 30
Week 11: Lessons 30-32
  __ assign lesson 33
Week 12: Lessons 33-35
  __ write a half-page description: "What is the meaning of life?"
  __ assign lesson 36
Week 13: Lessons 36-38
  __ assign lesson 39
Week 14: Lessons 39-41
  __ assign lesson 42

Semester 1 Retreat: (Friday night to Saturday night)

Goal: Bring all novices to a place of life-long commitment to a radical vision
of following Jesus (i.e., repentance/faith/commitment)

Friday Night Sharing Time (7 pm to 9 pm)

What are the most significant lessons you've learned this semester?

__ Cover Lessons 42-43 together

Ask them to look over the Resolution and pray about whether they will be ready
to sign it tomorrow night.

Saturday Morning Sharing Time (9 am to 12 noon)

Life stories/ Testimonies: "Tell us about your journey with Christ so far..."

Ask them to tell about their childhood/family, spiritual journey, hopes
and dreams, struggles and challenges, and places of greatest pain.

Ask them what God has been teaching them through all of it.

The group should respond by listening carefully, gently probing into their lives,
asking questions, offering encouragement and understanding-- NOT trying to fix
their problems. Try to help them identify the movement of God in their lives

Saturday Afternoon Fun Time (1 pm to 5 pm)

Play games, go hiking, go swimming, watch movies, have fun!

Saturday Evening Sharing Time (6 pm to 8 pm)

Do you feel a desperate need for God in your life?

Do you think getting right with him is the most important thing in the world?

Do you really trust Jesus? With your life?

Do you honestly feel accepted by God? Like you are his child?

Do you feel that you belong to him? Even in your brokenness and sin?

Are you ready to commit your life to following Christ?

__ Each novice who is ready signs resolution to follow Christ

__ End with unified prayer of commitment/Read Resolution in Unison

__ Each novice kneels and receives the sign of the cross on their forehead
and a prayer of blessing

__ Give framed certificate and cross for home

Novitiation Semester II
Disciplines for Christ-likeness
(14 weeks + 2-day retreat – each week covers 2 lessons and 1 for homework)

Semester Schedule:

Week 1: Lessons 44-45

___ assign lesson 46

Week 2: Field Trip: Practice Silence at a Beach or Park

___ meet at beach/park for 90 minutes of silence

___ gather at the end to sing and share

Week 3: Lessons 46-48

___ what is your daily time, place and posture of prayer?

___ practice breathing (check that they know how to breathe properly)

___ assign lesson 49

Week 4: Lessons 49-51   end each week reciting the Lord's Prayer together

___ assign lesson 52

Week 5: Lessons 52-54

___ assign lesson 55

Week 6: Lessons 55-57

___ assign lesson 58

Week 7: Lessons 58-60

___ assign lesson 61

Week 8: Lessons 61-63

___ give Brother Lawrence's book, *The Practice of the Presence of God*

___ assign lesson 64

Week 9: Lessons 64-66

___ are you currently part of a life group?

(join one or form one from current novices.)

___ who is your spiritual director?

(if they don't have one, help them find one! teacher may volunteer.)

___ are you currently participating regularly in communal worship?

___ have you been baptized? would you like to get baptized?

___ assign lesson 67

Week 10: Lessons 67-69

___ write a half-page description of a "Christ-like you."

___ assign lesson 70

Week 11: Lessons 70-72

___ assign lesson 73

___ memorize Jeremiah 29:11

457

Week 12: Lessons 73-75
    __ assign lesson 76
Week 13: Lessons 76-78
    __ assign lesson 79
Week 14: Lesson 79
    __ prepare monthly budget (bring to retreat)
    __ prepare weekly schedule (bring to retreat)
    __ prepare rule of life (bring to retreat)

Semester 2 Retreat: (Friday night to Saturday night)

Goal: Help each novice realign their lives by preparing and committing to a Rule of Life, a Weekly Schedule and Monthly Budget that reflects a Christ-like lifestyle.

Friday Night Sharing Time (7 pm to 9 pm)
What are the most significant lessons you've learned this semester?
Share "weekly schedule", "rule of life" and "monthly budget" with one another.
Which spiritual disciplines do you have the toughest time with?
What do you need to prioritize? How can you best seek God's Presence?

Saturday Morning Sharing Time (9 am to 11 am)
Gender Specific Groups
    What are the biggest obstacles to Christ-likeness in your life?
    What do you most need to work on?
    Do you need accountability? Freedom from something?
    Pray for one another

Saturday Afternoon Solitude Time (11 am to 5 pm)
Fasting, Silence and Solitude
    (May include a 15 min. appointment with Spiritual Director?)
Share meal at 5 pm

Saturday Evening Sharing Time (6 pm to 8 pm):
Hot Seat Edification Exercise:
    Everyone shares: "How do you see Christ in this person?"

___ Create Rule of Life with Daily Disciplines
___ Create Weekly Schedule
___ Create Monthly Budget
___ Each student should get baptized, if not already baptized.
    Schedule a community baptism soon, if needed. (Easter morning?)

Novitiation III
Semester 3 – A Life Consecrated to Mission
(14 weeks + 2-day retreat – each week covers 2 lessons and 1 for homework)

Semester Schedule:

Week 1: Lessons 80-81
   __ assign lesson 82
Week 2: Lessons 82-83
   __ who do you need to forgive?
   __ who do you need to seek forgiveness from?
   __ assign lesson 84
Week 3: Lesson 84-85
Week 4: Lessons 86-87
   __ ask if anyone needs exercise partners
   __ assign lesson 88
   __ write a half-page description of a "sin-free you"
Week 5: Lesson 88
   __ identify focal sin to work on
   __ break into gender-specific groups and confess this sin area
   __ share patterns and plans for victory, ask for prayer
   __ assign lesson 89
Week 6: Lessons 89-91   end each week reciting St. Francis' Prayer
   __ assign lesson 92
   __ lay hands on each student and simply invite the Holy Spirit to fill them
   (this should not turn into drawn-out Pentecostal pressure tactics!)
Week 7: Lessons 92-94
   __ homework: look for opportunity to pray with someone for healing
   __ assign lesson 95
Week 8: Lessons 95-97
   __ assign lesson 98
   __ choose which questions for sharing the faith you feel comfortable with
   __ homework: look for opportunity to ask someone these questions
Week 9: Outreach Field Trip: Pray with Prostitutes Downtown
   __ in groups of two or three, talk with some prostitutes; try to bless them
Week 10: Outreach Field Trip: Homeless for a Night
   __ fast that evening, take a blanket or sleeping bag
   __ sleep in a city park or on a sidewalk in groups of at least two
   (take all necessary safety precautions! no women ever left alone, etc.)

459

Week 11: Outreach Field Trip: Prophetic Prayer with a Stranger
__ meet at a mall, park or public place; walk and pray, two by two
(ask God to lead you to someone; approach them respectfully;
ask if you can pray for them; listen: is God saying anything specific?)
Week 12: Lessons 98-100
__ assign lesson 101
Week 13: Lessons 101-103
__ assign lesson 104
Week 14: Lessons 104-105
__ do you know your calling?
__ have you identified your mission field/gifts? what are you good at?
__ homework: look over the holiness covenant to decide if you are willing
to sign it at the retreat.

Semester 3 Retreat: (Friday night to Saturday night)
Goal: Get all novices filled with the Spirit and deployed on their mission

Friday Night Sharing Time (7 pm to 9 pm):
What are the most significant lessons you've learned this past year?
Where do your gifts and passions collide? When have you felt God's anointing?
Help one another identify their calling. Brainstorm opportunities to serve.
Group answers: How do you see this person impacting the world?
What has God created them to do? What ministry would fit them?
Let's get you set up for it!

Saturday Morning Sharing Time (9 am to 12 noon)
Hot Seat Prayer: Pray blessings, calling, etc. for each person
Prophetic Prayer (what is God saying to them or about them?)
Laying of hands for the filling of the Holy Spirit

Saturday Afternoon Solitude Time (1 pm to 4 pm)
Pray over Holiness Covenant

Saturday Night Sharing Time (6 pm to 8 pm)
Graduation Ceremony
__Sign Holiness Covenant
__ Anoint with Oil
__ Final Gifts: St Francis Prayer Wall Plaque and Bible Dictionary

(These are all suggestions. Modify them according to your own situation!)

461

JOEL ELIES is a spiritual director, teacher, and pastor at Hope968, a small, experimental community of Jesus' disciples: broken people who are learning to live like Christ. His main interest is in spiritual formation throughout church history and across every Christian tradition. He also loves drinking coffee at Honolulu Coffee Company, listening to music of almost every sort, and studying various world philosophies and religions.

He has helped to organize various community renewal ventures in the Honolulu area, working with the homeless, and cleaning up trash and graffiti. He has also been involved in ministry to high school students, college students, and adults. And he is the former bass player for the alternative rock band, Frolic like a Heifer.

Joel lives in Honolulu, Hawaii with his wife, Amy, and their three boys, Jordan, Evan, and Jonathan. They love hiking together, walking together, reading together and movie nights together.

For additional information, please visit www.sanctusbooks.org.
For information about Hope968, visit www.hope968.com.

Made in the USA
Lexington, KY
21 April 2011